A GENEALOGY

OF THE DESCENDANTS OF

RICHARD PORTER,

WHO SETTLED AT WEYMOUTH, MASS., 1635,

AND ALLIED FAMILIES:

ALSO,

SOME ACCOUNT OF THE DESCENDANTS OF

JOHN PORTER,

WHO SETTLED AT HINGHAM, MASS., 1635,
AND SALEM, (DANVERS) MASS., 1644.

BY

JOSEPH W. PORTER,

OF BURLINGTON, MAINE,

MEMBER OF THE NEW ENGLAND HISTORIC GENEALOGICAL SOCIETY;
OF THE MAINE GENEALOGICAL AND BIOGRAPHICAL SOCIETY;
AND OF THE MAINE HISTORICAL SOCIETY.

BANGOR:
Burr & Robinson, Printers.
1878.

PORTER FAMILIES.

Nearly all the families bearing the name of Porter, in the United States, can trace their origin to a very few imigrant ancestors.

RICHARD PORTER,

Settled in Weymouth, Mass., in 1635. He was my ancestor; and a few years since, although not especially fitted for such a work by education or occupation, I began a Genealogy of his descendants. It has been a work demanding patience and persistence; but it has been a pleasure. The very many pleasant letters received from members of the family, in nearly every state and territory in the union, containing information and encouragement, I would here gratefully remember. I give in this little book the result, not that it is perfect or complete, but it is what I have.

JOHN PORTER.

Of Hingham, and Salem, was at Hingham in 1635—not more than three miles distant from Richard Porter, at Weymouth. I believe they were brothers, but have no positive proof of the fact.

In the course of my researches, I have accumulated much information relating to the earlier generations of this highly respectable family; with some accounts of later generations. I have concluded to print what I have, hoping that it may be of some benefit, by the way of assistance towards a more complete Genealogy of this family, and of interest until that is accomplished.

JOHN PORTER, of Windsor, Conn., settled there, 1638, and said to have been previously at Dorchester, Mass. Hon. Samuel W. Porter, of Rochester, New York, Henry Porter Andrews, of New York City, and Rev. Edward C. Porter, of Racine, Wis., have given much time and research to a Genealogy of this family, the last named gentleman having prosecuted his work in England.

ROBERT and THOMAS PORTER, brothers, were of the eighty-four proprietors of Farmington, Conn., in 1640. The first named was ancestor of President Noah Porter, of Yale College.

DANIEL PORTER, surgeon, of Farmington, Conn., before 1653, said by one authority to have been a brother of Robert and Thomas, of that town.

ABEL PORTER, of Boston, Mass., admitted to the church there Jan. 23, 1641.

JOHN PORTER, of Roxbury, freeman, Nov., 5, 1633, removed to Boston, where in March, 1636, he was appointed by court a referee in a case John Burr vs. Mr. Dummer. He was a follower of Rev. John Wheelwright and Ann Hutchinson, in their "seditious doctrines," and (with others,) was warned before the 30th of November, 1637, to deliver up his guns, pistols, powder, shot and match, at Mr. Cane's house in Boston, there to be kept till further orders by the court. "March 12, 1638, John Porter and others * * * having license to depart, summons is to go out for them to appear (if they are not gone before,) at the next court, the third month, to answer such things as shall be objected." Judge Savage, in his Genealogical Dictionary of New England, says that "he removed to Rhode Island, signed their compact in 1638; was an assistant in 1641, and after for some years. Lived in Portsmouth, R. I., in 1655, and at Wickford, R. I., 1674. Hazard II, 612." It has been by some thought that this man was the same as John, of Hingham and Salem, but I do not see how such can be the case. There are some other families who have come into the country since 1800, from England, Ireland, and the British Provinces.

JOSEPH W. PORTER.

Burlington, Maine, 1878.

NOTE—Where no state is named in connection with towns, Massachusetts is the state, except in cases of well known cities.

GENEALOGY.

RICHARD PORTER,

Settled in Weymouth, Mass., in 1635. In the New England Historical and Genealogical Register, Vol. 25, page 13, is a "list of passengers at Weymouth, England, March 30, 1635, bound for New England," in which is the name of Richard Porter. In this list, also, are the names of other men, who settled at Weymouth, some of whose descendants of the same names continue there until this day. Rev. Joseph Hull, minister; Massachiel Barnard, of Badcomb, in the county of Somerset; John Whitmarsh, William Reed, of Badcomb; Zechary Bicknell, Henry Kingman, Thomas Holbrook, Robert Lovell and others.

"July 8, 1635, the General Court granted leave to Mr. Hull, a minister, and twenty-one families, to sit down at Wessaguscus."

September 2d, 1835, the General Court changed the name of Wessaguscus to Weymouth, so named, no doubt, for Weymouth, England. During the late war, the selectmen had occasion to look up the incorporation of the town, and found no other authority to act as a town, than this.

For two hundred and forty-three years, Weymouth has been the only ancient town in Massachusetts, with possibly one exception, which has preserved its original boundaries. Nothing has been added, nothing taken away. Long may the old town continue before it is cut up into insignificance.

The town records of Weymouth, prior to 1648, are very meagre. In that year and in 1654, 1661, 1663, and 1668, grants of land were made to Richard Porter. For many years he was continually in office as selectman, constable, and upon committees; he was a member of the original church, and the name of "brother Richard Porter" often occurs on the old records. He lived not far from where the meeting house of the North Parish, in Weymouth, now stands; probably between there and the old burial ground. In 1651 a road was laid out between Richard Porter's meadow and Stephen French's land. In 1663 the town voted "that the flats upon the back river shall be let out for town's use for the ensuing year, for the thatching of houses, and this to be done by the selectmen. By flats we understand all these flats on this side of river, begining at Snooke's Marsh until you come to the upper end of Richard Porter's marsh." In 1673 Abiah Whitman and Thomas Hunt, were appointed fence viewers for "middle of the town so far as the brook that runs by Richard Porter's house." In 1661 brother Richard Porter, John Rane, John Bicknell, Stephen French, and John Porter, chosen committee to repair meeting house. "Bro. Bicknell, for making the meeting house tite, 3 pounds." The name of his wife was probably Ruth, and he was probably married after arriving in this country. On Boston records is the following birth: "Ruth, daughter of Richard Porter, born at Weymouth, Oct. 3, 1639." He died between Dec. 25, 1688, the date of his will, and March 6, 1689, the date of the inventory of his estate. I give a copy of his will which I found in the Suffolk Probate office, unrecorded.

I, Richard Porter, of Weymouth, in New England, being apprehensive of my near approaching departure out of this world, and being through the mercy of God of a short memory and disposing mind; trusting in the mercy of God through ye Lord Jesus Christ for Etternall Life: Do make this my last will and testament as folowth:

Item: I do give and bequeath unto my grandchild, Thomas Porter, the only sone of my sone Thomas Porter, deceased, my now dwelling house and barn and orchard, the swampy meadow, and ye land adjoining ffrom ye swampy land of James Lovelll, and Joseph Dyer, downward along by ye country highway, so far as the gate by which wee did turne out of the highway into ye feild comonly called ye middle gate, and from that gate crose ye feild upon a streight line into ye land now in ye ocupation of John Blanchett (Blanchard.)

Also, I give unto my said grandchild the one full halfe of my lott of land being in the second devision of common lott, the divission to be made when ye said Thomas shall come to ye age of twenty years; always provided, and it is my will, that if ye said Thomas shall dye before he come to ye age of twenty years, that then the foresaid estate shall be and remaine so, to my grandchild Ruth Richards, and the heirs borne of her body, if any be then living, if not then to return to my sone John, to him and his heirs: my will is that ye said Thomas Porter shall have the income of his part of ye estate immediately after my decease. I give and bequath unto my Grandchild, Samuel Bayley, that my two Acres of Land on King Oak Hill. Also I give and bequath unto my daughter, Mary Bicknell, ten pounds of my estate to be paid by my Executors after my decease. All the rest of my estate not before given by this my will, I give and bequeath to my sone, John Porter, whom I do make, constitute, and appoint my sole executor to this my last will and testament, and I do desire and appoint my loving ffriends, James Lovell, sen'r, and Thomas Reed, as overseers to this my last will and testament, in all respects that it may be fulfiled; and I do hereby make void and null all other former wills by me made and declared, and do declare and publish this to be my last will and testament. In witness thereof I have hereunto sett my hand and seal, the five & twentieth day of December, in ye year of ye Lord one thousand six hundred eighty and eight, in ye fourth year of his Majesty's reign James the Second, by ye grace of God, King of England, and defender of ye faith.

RICHARD ⋈ PORTER,

Signed, sealed and published in presence of Abiah Whitman, Zechariah Bicknell, Stephen Ffrench, sen'r.

Weymouth, March 6, 1689.

An Inventory of ye estate of Richard Porter, late of Weymouth, deceased, appraised by ye subscribers.

To his purse and wearing apparell	03.00.00
To 1 ffeather bed and bedding	04.10.00
To 1 Chest and 5 Chaires	00.06.00
To a dwelling house, barn and orchard, and about ten acres of land adjoining	40.00.00
To 2 Acres of land in King Oak Hill	04.00.00
To 9 Acres of pasture land	18.00.00
To 1 piece of salt meadow upon ye Back river	08.00.00
To 1 lott of land in ye second devision	02.00.00
To 1 broad ax and adds	00.04.00
Sumar.	80.00.00

Signed, John Porter, Stephen French, Joseph Green.

The names of his children, of whom I have no dates of birth, except Ruth, were:

2. i. John,[2] m. Deliverance Byrum, 9th Feb., 1660.
3. ii. Ruth,[2] b. Oct. 3, 1639, m. Thomas Bailey Jr., 19th Sept., 1660.
4. iii. Thomas,[2] m. Sarah Vining.
5. iv. Mary,[2] m. John Bicknell, Jan. 2, 1659.

SECOND GENERATION.

Sergeant John[2] Porter of Richard[1] Porter. Lived in Weymouth, with the possible exception of a few years in Bridgewater, of which I am doubtful. He was one of the most enterprising men of his time. He had many land grants in Weymouth. He was also a large purchaser of lands in ancient Bridgewater, in 1686, 1687, 1693, 1694, 1696 and in 1699. In Bridgewater, Feb. 13, 1686, at a meeting of purchasers of Bridgewater lands, "they did agree to give to Rev. Mr. Keith, so many as were willing, out of their thirty acre wood lots as followeth, two acres each;" this agreement was signed by John Porter. About the same time he with others agreed to give land for a common in Bridgewater "for good of all." In 1693 he built the first saw mill in what is now South Abington at "Little Comfort." In 1696 he sold half of this mill to Joseph Josselyn. In 1680 he and John Holbrook of Weymouth took a mortgage of a brewery in Boston, of Robert Cox, which stood not far from the site of the present postoffice. In 1705 he and his wife sold Grape Island, in Weymouth; he was a useful, honored citizen, holding all the various town offices at different times; committee to run town lines several times. One remarkable fact about him is, that I cannot find that he was ever made a freeman by the General Court—without which in those times, no man could hold public office, it was said. He married Deliverance, daughter of Nicholas, and Martha (Shaw) Byram, Feb. 9, 1660. He died in Weymouth, Aug. 7, 1717; his widow died Sept. 30, 1720.

I give a copy of his will from Suffolk Probate Records:

In the Name of God, Amen: This Eight day of Febuary, Annoqe Domini One thousand Seven hundred and * * Fifteen or Sixteen, I, John Porter, of Weymouth, in the County of Suffolk, in New England, Yeoman, being aged but of perfect memory and Disposing mind, Do make this my last Will and Testament in manner and form following:—First and Principally I commit my Soul to God that gave it, hopeing for Salvation through the alone merits of Jesus Christ my Redeemer, and my Body to the Earth to be burried in such desent manner as to my Executrix hereafter named shall be thought meet. And as touching my worldly Estate, my mind and Will is the same shall be Imployed and bestowed as in and by this my Will is Expressed. Imprimis, I Will that my just Debts and Funeral charges shall be well and truly paid in Convenient time after my Decease by my Executrix hereafter named.

Item.—I give to my well beloved wife Deliverance Porter, the Easterly end of my Dwelling house, with all the Rooms belonging to it, and one-half of the back Rooms of North side of the West end of the House and all my Orchard and convenient Ground for a Garden, and also all my moveable Estate in the Dwelling House, of what kind whatsoever, and two Cowes such as she shall make choice of. Also my Mind and Will is that my Two sons, namely, Thomas Porter and Ebenezer Porter, shall annually, during the terms of my said Wifes naturall Life, at their own proper Cost and Charge, provide Summer meat and Winter meat for two cows for the use of my said Wife; Also two fat Hoggs, ten Bufshells Indian Corn, four Bufshells of wheat, and Two Bufshells of Rie, and forty Shillings in money during the terme of her natural life as above said, and also sutable Firewood during the terme aforesaid.

Item.—I give my son, John Porter, all my Salt meadow near the Steping Stone Bridge in Weymouth, also all my Right in the Lot called Parker's Lott in the Township of Abington, on the Easterly side of the Saw Mill; also all the remainder of a Lot in the Second Division of Common Lotts first granted to my Father, Richard Porter, a part whereof being sold to Jacob Turner, and also two acres in the Swamp called the Pine swamp, all which I give to my said son, to him his Heirs or afsigns forever.

Item.—I give, devise and bequeath to my Son, Samuel Porter, to him his Heirs or afsigns forever, the one-half of my part of a Lot of Land lying in the Township of Abington, called Torrey's Lot.

Item.—I give, devise and bequeath to my Son, Nicholas Porter, to him, his Heirs or afsigns forever, the House where he now dwells, also all my part of that Lot where his house now stands, being in the Township of Abington; also all my part in the Mill and Mill Lot in the Township of Abington; also all the one-half part of my right in that Lot called Torrey's Lot; also all my Meadow Land at Broad Cove, in Bridgewater; also Six acres of Land lying near the Saw Mill in Abington.

ITEM.—I give, devise and bequeath to my Son, Thomas Porter, to him his Heirs and afsigns forever, all the Housing and Lands that I bought of David Carver, where my said Son now Dwelleth; also the one-half part of all my Lands and fresh Meadows adjoining to my Dwelling House in Weymouth, excepting the Orchard; also all that my Lot which I bought of the Lincolns, lying in the fourth Division in the Township of Abington; also one-half of my Salt Marsh, with one-half of the flatts and banks belonging thereunto, lying at the Back River in Weymouth; also one-half of my meadow lying near Rod's Hill in Weymouth; also the one-half of a Lot of land lying near Lieutenant Nash's Mill in Abington; also one-half of a Lot of Land in Abington aforesaid, lying Westerly of William Turrell's Mill, and also the one-half of my part of the Saw Mill in Weymouth.

ITEM.—I give, devise and bequeath to my Son Ebenezer Porter, to him his heirs or afsigns forever, all my Dwelling House, Out housing and Barn—that is to say, one-half at my decease and the other half at my Wifes decease; also one-half of the Land and Meadow adjoining to the said House, excepting the Orchard, which shall be his at my wife's decease; also the one-half of my Meadow Flatts and Bank at the back River, in Weymouth aforesaid, and also one-half of my Meadow at Rhod's Hill in Weymouth; also one-half of my Lot of Land lying in the Township of Abington, lying near Lieutenant Nash's Mill; also a lot of land lying in the fourth division of Abington, upland that I bought of Bealles; also one-half part of a Lot of Land lying in the Township of Abington, lying West from Turrill's Saw Mill; also four acres of Land in the Township of Abington, lying Southerly from the House of Philip Reads, deceased; also one-half part of my part of the Saw Mill in Weymouth, all which I give to him, his heirs and afsigns forever.

ITEM.—My mind and Will is that my son, John Porter, shall pay to my Daughter Mary Pitty, fourteen pounds in Goods at money's price. My Son Samuel Porter, shall pay to my daughter, Ruth Willis, fourteen pounds in Goods at money's price. My Son, Ebenezer Porter, shall pay my daughter Susannah Pratt, fourteen pounds in Goods at money's price, and my Son, Thomas Porter, shall pay to my Daughter Sarah Dingly, fourteen pounds in Goods at money's price. All which my abovesaid four Sons shall pay to my said daughters, within one year after my decease.

ITEM.—I give to my said Wife, to her and her heirs and assigns forever, the one-half of the Twenty three acres called the House Lot, and all that my Lot called Byrom's Lot.

ITEM.—I give to my son, Nicholas Porter, to him his heirs or afsigns forever, the other half of the Twenty three acres called the House Lot.

ITEM.—As for the residue and remainder of my Estate, both Real and Personal, not heretofore in this my will disposed of, after Debts and Funerall Charges are paid, it shall be equally divided among my four Sons, namely:—John, Samuel, Thomas and Ebenezer Porter.

ITEM.—I do hereby nominate, constitute and appoint my well beloved Wife, sole Executrix of this my last Will and Testament.

In Witness whereof I have hereunto set my hand and seal, the day and year first above written.

JOHN PORTER's mark and a Seal.

Signed, Sealed and Published by the said John Porter, to be his last will and testament, in presence of us witnesses.

THOMAS ANDREWES,
EBENEZER WHITMARSH,
SAMUEL THAXTER.

Children all born in Weymouth.

6. i. Mary,[3] b. Oct. 12, 1663; m. Wm. Pittee.
7. ii. Susanna,[3] b. June 2, 1665; m. Matthew Pratt.
8. iii. John,[3] b. July 2, 1667; m. Mary.
9. iv. Samuel,[3] m. Mary Nash.
10. v. Nicholas,[3] m. Bathseba Reed.
11. vi. Ruth,[3] b. Sept. 18, 1676; m. Nath. Willis of Bridgwater,
12. vii. Thomas,[3] m. Susanna Pratt.
13. viii. Ebenezer,[3] m. Sarah Humphrey.
14. ix. Sarah,[3] m. John Dingley of Marshfield.

3

Ruth[2] Porter of Richard[1] Porter, b. Oct. 3, 1639, m. Thomas Bailey, Jr., of Weymouth, Sept. 19th, 1660. Children:

15. i. Christian,[3] b. Oct. 26th, 1662, m. Ebenezer [2] Whitmarsh, he son of John [1] Whitmarsh, b. May 14, 1658. Died in Abington, April 8, 1718. Had children, Ebenezer,[4] 1683; Richard,[4] 1685; Thomas,[4] 1702; Ruth,[4] 1691, m. Hezekiah Ford; Mary,[4] m. John Reed; Ebenezer,[4] again, 1688.

16. ii. Samuel,[3] b. Feb. 21, 1666; d. before his father.
17. iii. Mary,[3] b. Feb. 10, 1670.
18. iv. Sarah,[3] b. Sept. 29, 1674; prob. m. Joseph White, 1704.
19. v. Thomas,[3] living at death of his father, 1691.
20. vi. Ruth, [3] m. Henry Ward of Hingham, before 1691. Had children, Elizabeth,[4], Henry,[4] Ruth,[4] Mary,[4] Rachel,[4] Lydia,[4].
21. vii. Martha,[3] living at death of her father.
22. viii. Sarah,[3] was a minor in 1691. Mrs. Ruth Bailey died, and he married 2d the widow Hannah (Rogers) Pratt, by whom he had one child. Thomas, born April 24, 1687. Thomas, sen'r, died about 1691; his estate was divided by Ephraim[3] Hunt, Stephen[2] French, John Porter, sen'r, and Edward[2] Bates, between widow Hannah, the only surviving son Thomas Christian Whitmarsh, Ruth Ward, Sarah and Martha. His widow died May 29, 1721, æt. 77.

4

Thomas[2] Porter, of Richard[1] Porter, lived in Weymouth, died in 167½. Married Sarah, sister of John Vining. In 1672, his widow and Richard Porter, petitioned the Court that she and her brother John Vining, should settle the estate, which request was granted.

The estate was appraised at twenty-seven pounds and thirteen shillings. There was one child:

23. i. Thomas,[3] posthumous, Feb. 3, 1672.

5

Mary[2] Porter, of Richard[1] Porter, m. John Bicknell, son of Zachary and Agnes Bicknell, Dec. 2, 1658. (He had 1st wife Mary, who died Mar. 25, 1658, by whom he had children. John[3] b. 1654, d. Aug. 4, 1737; Mary,[3] m. John Dyer; Naomi[3] b. June 21, 1657.) He was an important and useful man in the town, selectman many years; representative to General Court in 1677, for which he received from the town three shillings per day, for 33 days. His will dated Nov. 6, 1678, probated Jan. 20, 1679, names wife Mary, son John, executor, and John Dyer's three children. Children by 2d wife:

23\. i. Ruth,[3] b. Oct. 26, 1660, m. James[2] Richards, son of William[1] Richards. She was mentioned in her grandfather Porter's will. He died Mar. 8, 1711; she died Feb. 12, 1728. Children were Benjamin,[4] b. Aug. 4, 1684, died Dec. 20, 1733; Ruth,[4] m. Joseph Lovell, and died June 2, 1766; Mary[4], b. April 9, 1697.

24\. ii. Joanna,[3] born Mar. 2, 1663.

25\. iii. Experience,[3] b. Oct. 20, 1665.

26\. iv. Zechary,[3] b. Feb. 7, 1668--Lived in Weymouth, removed to Swanzey now Barrington, R. I., about 1705, where he died; m. Hannah Smith, Nov. 24, 1692. Children were Zecheriah,[4] b. in W., Jan. 9, 1695, of Ashford, Conn.; Hannah,[4] b. do., Mar. 16, 1698; James,[4] do., b. May 18, 1702; Mary,[4] Aug. 21, 1703. Peter,[4] and Joshua,[4] b. in Barrington.

27\. v. Thomas,[3] b. Aug. 12, 1670, m. Ann Turner, at Hingham, by Rev. J. Norton, Feb. 16, 1696, removed to Middleborough, where he died Feb. 17, 1718.

28\. vi. Elizabeth,[3] b. April 29, 1673.

29\. vii. Hannah,[3] b. Nov. 15, 1675.

30\. viii. Mary,[3] b. March 15, 1678, m. Maurice Truphant; he died May 13, 1740; she died Oct. 13, 1764, of Weymouth. Their children were David,[4] b. April 11, 1705; Jonathan,[4] b. June 28, 1709; Joseph,[4] b. May 5, 1701; Joshua,[4] b. Dec. 28, 1712.

THIRD GENERATION.

6

Mary [3] Porter of John [2] Porter, b. Oct. 12, 1663, m. William [2] Pittee, Jr., of Weymouth. He born, May 12, 1661, died June 6, 1728. His widow died Dec. 24, 1746. Children:

31\. i. James,[4] b. Nov. 16, 1686, m. Hannah, dau. of Thomas Reed, Jan. 8. 1729; he died Jan. 28, 1764, aged 78. She died April 5, 1779. Gen. Solomon Lovell, administered on his estate. Their children were, Hannah[5] b. Dec. 8, 1730, m. Gen. Solomon Lovell, 1762; his 2d wife, she died July 8, 1795; James,[5] b. Jan. 1st, 1733, died 1744; James,[5] b. March 27, 1748, died 1749.

32\. ii. Nathaniel,[4] m. Mary, daughter of James Richards, Aug. 4, 1743.

33. iii. Mary,[4] m. David Holbrook, pub. June 2, 1716. Removed to Braintree, 1720, where she died 1756. Their children were David,[5] b. June 26, 1717, m. Mary Hayden; Ichabod,[5] b. Mar. 12, 1719, m. Hannah Hayden; Nehemiah,[5] b. May 16, 1722, m. Christian Thayer; Mary,[5] b. Nov., 1726, d. soon; Mary,[5] b. Nov., 1727, m. Ziba Howard; Ruth,[5] b. 1730, m. Tower.

34. iv. Thomas,[4] drowned Nov. 9, 1716.

35. v. Ruth,[4] m. Dea. Abiah Whitman, pub. Oct. 28, 1715; she died Sept. 15, 1738; he died Jan. 30, 1770. He was for many years Dea. of the So. Parish church in Weymouth.

36. vi. John,[4] drowned Sept. 4, 1716.

37. vii. Deliverance,[4] b. 1706, m. Jonathan Proctor, Jan, 1, 1729. He died Feb. 28, 1732; no children. She m. 2d, John Bates, Nov. 19, 1733; John Bates died 1765, and his widow died 1803, aged 97 years. Children were Thomas,[5] b. Aug. 22, 1734; Remember,[5] dau., b. Mar. 9, 1739; Mary,[5] b. July 17, 1741; Robert,[5] b. Feb. 4, 1744; Eunice,[5] b. 1749; Jonathan,[5] b. Apr. 29, 1750; Experience,[5] b. Sept. 29, 1736, m. James Trufant; Dilly,[5] b. June 30, 1748.

7

Susanna[3] Porter, of John[2] Porter, b. June 2d, 1665, married Matthew Pratt, of Weymouth; he probably removed to Abington. One child:

38. i. Mary,[4] b. Nov. 27, 1699; m. Rev. Samuel Brown, first minister of Abington, Feb. 11, 1719. They had four children who all died young. This was his second marriage. He was born at Newbury, Mass., Sept. 5, 1687. Graduated at Harvard Col., 1705; went to Abington to preach 1711; ordained Pastor of the church Nov. 14, 1714. Died Sept. 19, 1749 at the age of sixty-two. His widow married Josiah Torrey, of Abington.

8

Seargent John[3] Porter, of John[2] Porter, born July 2, 1667. Lived in Weymouth; was selectman, and held other town offices. Married 1st, Mary, who died Mar. 8, 1709. Married 2d, "In Marshfield, June 16, 1709, John Porter to Margaret, dau. of Dea. William Ford, and wife Sarah Dingley." He died May 22, 1723; his widow died June 11,

1734. His wife and son Joseph administered on the estate. Peter and Margaret chose George Humphrey of Hingham, to be their guardian. Children:

39. i. Mercy,[4] b. Sept. 28, 1694.
40. ii. John,[4] b. Nov. 19, 1695; died early.
41. iii. Joseph,[4] b. Feb. 6, 1697; m. Mary Randall.
42. iv. Mary,[4] b. Jan. 11, 1700.
43. v. John,[4] b. Aug. 23, 1702; m. Sarah Nash, 1728.
44. vi. Richard,[4] b. Jan. 8, 1705; m. Ruth Whitman, 1730.
45. vii. Deliverance,[4] b. 1707; m. John Beal, of Hingham, 1727.
46. viii. Peter,[4] b. Feb. 15, 1709-10; m. Mercy Vickery Dec. 5, 1732.
47. ix. William,[4] b. Sept. 12, 1712; died Aug., 1713.
48. x. Sarah,[4] b. Sep. 27, 1713; m. Seward Waters, of Boston, 1731.
49. xi. Margaret,[4] b. July 26, 1714; m. Phillip Torry, 1729.

9

Samuel[3] Porter, of John[2] Porter. Town officer in Weymouth, 1705. Probably removed to Abington about that time; shoemaker and schoolmaster. Jan. 30, 1712, he "bought of Daniel Axtell, tanner, his farm in Abington, consisting of a dwelling house and half of the Grant to the Briggs". Assessor of Abington 1716, selectman 1714, and three years after. In 1724 selectmen employed him to keep school; March, 1727, they were directed to "draw six pounds out of the treasury, and pay Mr. Samuel Porter, deceased, his keeping school." He was one of the original members of the church in Abington. He married Mary, daughter of Jacob[2] and Abigail (Dyer) Nash, of Weymouth, about 1698. He died in Abington, Aug. 31, 1725.

I give below a copy of his will from Plymouth Co. Records.

"In the Name of God Amen.—I, Samuel Porter, of Abington in ye County of Plymouth in New England, Sen'r, being in perfect mind & memory (Blessed be God,) do on this twenty-fourth day of August Anno Domni one thousand seven hundred twenty & five, and in ye twelfth year of ye Reign of our sovereign Lord George, King of England, &c., make & ordain this my last Will and Testament, and after having committed my soul to God who gave it & my body to ye dust to be decently buried at ye discretion of my Executors hereafter herein mentioned, in a full and certain hope of a future ressurrection.

And as for my worldly estate I dispose of in manner & form as followeth (viz.)

First, I give to my beloved wife Mary Porter, all my household goods & ye income of my third part of all my Real Estate during her life.

ITEM.—I give to my son Samuel Porter, two acres of land where his house stands, beginning at ye Road six rods northerly from his house and running South-west & then turning a corner South East & running to the place first mentioned and so encompassing to him his heirs & assign forever.

ITEM.—I give to my son Samuel Porter & my son Jacob Porter all ye rest of my home living or farm on both sides of ye Road with my house & barn & all my right in ye undivided land in Bridgewater & that tract of land which was laid out to me in Bridgewater by a Committee in ye year one thousand seven hundred & twenty four, & my right in ye Saw mill in Abington with all my stock of Cattle & Horses, sheep & swine & all my personal Estate not yet disposed of. I will give all these to them their heirs & assigns forever; and it is to be equally divided between two.

ITEM 4.—My will further is that my cow & ye half of a Bull & 4 swine which I determined to kill shall be for the support of my family, with the corn which I raise this year both English and Indian.

ITEM 5.—I give to my son David & my son John my hundred acres of Land in ye old Men's shares which I had of my father in law Lieut. Jacob Nash, to be equally divided between them their heirs & assigns forever.

ITEM 6.—My will further is that my son Samuel Porter & my Son Jacob Porter pay to my daughter Mary Porter fifty Pounds in money or Bills of Credit within three months after my decease, and also that my two sons Samuel & Jacob shall pay to my daughter Hannah fifty Pounds in money or Bills of Credit when she shall arrive to the age of Eighteen years; this is to my two daughters their heirs & assigns forever.

ITEM 7.—My will is that my son David Porter & John Porter shall pay fifty Pounds money or Bills of Credit to my daughter Abigail when she shall arrive to ye age of Eighteen years to her heirs & assigns forever. And I nominate and appoint my son Samuel Porter & my son Jacob Porter to be my Executors on my Estate to prove my will and settle my Estate & to pay my funeral charges & all my just debts & receive all my just dues, and I do hereby exclude all other wills & declare this to be my last will & Testament, and I have hereunto set my hand & Seal ye day & year above mentioned.

SAMUEL PORTER. Seal.

Signed sealed & delivered in presence of

NICHOLAS PORTER.
SAMUEL POOLL.
SAMUEL NOYCE.

Children:

50. i. Samuel,[4] b. in Weymouth, May 14, 1699.
51. ii. Mary,[4] b. in Weymouth, Oct. 5, 1701.
52. iii. David,[4] b. in Weymouth, 1702.
53. iv. Jacob,[4] b. in Weymouth, Aug. 10, 1704.
54. v. Hannah,[4] b. in Abington, Dec. 16, 1712.
55. vi. John,[4] b. in Abington, Feb. 2, 1716.
56. vii. Abigail,[4] b. in Abington, June 23, 1719.

10

Nicholas[3] Porter, of John[2] Porter, b. April 11, 1672, removed from Weymouth to Abington, about 1705. In 1709, appraised Caleb Chard's estate. Surveyor of highways in Abington, in 1713, 1714. He married 1st, Bashua, daughter of William[2] and Esther (Thompson) Reed, of Weymouth; 2d, the widow Sarah Noyes, 1725. He removed to Bridgewater, where he died in 1773. "Aged one hundred years, lacking three months." Children:

57. i. Nicholas,[4] b. in Weymouth, Oct. 26, 1700; m. Ruth Rogers, Sept. 24, 1722.
58. ii. William,[4] b. in Weymouth, Aug. 19, 1702.
59. iii. Bathsheba,[4] b. Sept. 17, 1707; m. David French, April 17, 1729; his second marriage.
60. iv. Daniel,[4] b. in Abington, June 15, 1708.
61. v. Susannah,[4] b. in Abington, Mar. 20, 1710; m. Abner Bradford of Kingston, 1735.
62. vi. Job,[4] b. in Abington, June 26, 1714; married.
63. vii. Esther,[4] b. in Abington, June 20, 1716; m. Joshua Fobes, March 29, 1740.
64. viii. Abner,[4] b. Abington, Nov. 27, 1718; m. Jane Cheesman, 1744.
65. ix. Sarah,[4] b. in Abington, April 3, 1722.

11

Ruth[3] Porter, of John[2] Porter, b. Sept. 18, 1676, m. Nathaniel Willis, of Bridgewater. She made her will in 1739, giving her estate to her niece, Esther Porter, daughter of Nicholas. Children:

66. i. Ruth,[4] b. 1708.
67. ii. Nathaniel,[4] b. 1709.
68. iii. Azariah,[4] b. 1712.

12

Thomas³ Porter, of John² Porter, born and lived in Weymouth, m. Susanna, daughter of Matthew and Sarah (Hunt) Pratt, about 1706—she born Sept., 1684. Children:

69. i. Nathaniel,⁴ b. Nov. 23, 1707; died Apr. 1, 1724.
70. ii. Thomas,⁴ b. Apr. 27, 1713; m. Mercy Bates, Jan. 24, 1740.
71. iii. Jonathan,⁴ b. Mar. 6, 1715; died young.
72. iv. Jonathan,⁴ b. Jan. 22, 1718.
73. v. Josiah,⁴ b. Mar. 6, 1720; died young.
74. vi. Ezra,⁴ b. Apr. 6, 1722; died young.
75. vii. Matthew,⁴ b. Sept. 8, 1725; m. Sarah Pratt, 1750.
76. viii. Ezra,⁴ b. Sept. 8, 1725; m. Hannah Lovell, 1751.
77. ix. Susannah,⁴ b. July 12, 1728.

13

Lieutenant Ebenezer³ Porter, of John² Porter, born and lived in Weymouth. In 1725, deeded land in Abington; married 1st, Sarah of Nathaniel and Elizabeth Humphrey, Dec. 3, 1707, born Jan. 28, 1690. She died March 1, 1749 —the mother of his children. Married 2d, widow Jael Wheaton, of Christopher, pub. Jan. 9, 1750. She died Feb. 10, 1754. He died, 1763. Children:

78. i. Sarah,⁴ b. 1708; died young.
79. ii. Ebenezer,⁴ b. Nov. 9, 1708; died young.
80. iii. Ebenezer,⁴ m. Mary Lovell, July 29, 1730.
81. iv. Sarah,⁴ m. Joseph Truphant, 1729.
82. v. Tabitha,⁴ b. March 22, 1719; m. Daniel Burrell, 1741.

14

Sarah³ Porter, of John² Porter, married John³ Dingley, of Marshfield, Jan. 27, 1703. He was son of Jacob² and Elizabeth (Newton) Dingley, and grandson of John¹ and Sarah Dingley, of Lynn, Sandwich and Marshfield. Mrs. Sarah Dingley, died March 3, 1741, aged 61. John³ Dingley, died Dec. 12, 1763, aged 94. The old homestead in Marshfield, is now in possession of his descendants, never having been sold out of the family. Children:

83. i. Jacob,⁴ b. Oct. 31, 1703; m. Mary Holmes of Kingston, daughter of Joseph; their son Joseph, b. 1729, was the first settler of Richmond, Maine. Jacob died Dec. 4, 1772; his widow Aug. 13, 1797, aged 97.

84. ii. John,[4] b. Aug. 13, 1706; m. Keziah, daughter of Dea. Israel Thomas, Nov. 17, 1730. He resided on the ancestral farm.

85. iii. Sarah,[4] b. Feb. 22, 1709; m. Joseph Hewett, of Marshfield, Dec. 10, 1728; children, Tabitha, b. Mar. 11, 1734; Hannah, b. Dec. 24, 1736; Joseph, b. June 7, 1739.

86. iv. Martha,[4] b. Feb. 22, 1713.

87. v. Ann,[4] b. Dec. 12, 1716; m. Jacob Pillsbury, of Abington. Their daughter Elizabeth, m. Col. Aaron Hobart, of Abington, Nov. 5, 1753.

88. vi. Elizabeth,[4] b. June 11, 1723; m. John Sherman, of Marshfield, Aug. 21, 1746, by the Rev. Mr. Hill.

23

Thomas[3] Porter, of Thomas[2] Porter, b. Feb. 3, 167½. He was a cordwainer. Removed from Weymouth to Taunton, about 1701. July 5, 1701, John Briggs and wife, of Taunton, sold Thomas Porter of Weymouth, forty acres of land with dwelling in Taunton, for seventy pounds. Aug. 17, 1723, Samuel Andrews of Dighton, sold land to Thomas Porter of Taunton, for 135 pounds. In 1743, Thomas Porter of Taunton, sold land in Taunton to James Codding, for thirty pounds. April 16, 1744, Thomas Porter, of Taunton, sold forty acres of land and dwelling house and barn to son Joseph Porter, for 1000 pounds. In 1744, Thomas Porter, gave land to Ebenezer, Joshua, Samuel, John, Jacob, and Mary, children of his son Ebenezer, late of Taunton, deceased. This land was divided in 1753. (Bristol Co. Records.)

He married Abigail, daughter of Capt. John and Abigail (Pierce of Capt. Michael,) Holbrook. She was born, 1675.

He died about 1754, as his estate was divided in that year. Children:

89. i. Thomas,[4] b. in Weymouth, May 26, 1696; witnessed a deed in Taunton, 1743.

90. ii. Abigail,[4] b. do., Jan. 19, 1700.

91. iii. Ebenezer,[4] b. Dec. 1701; died Mar. 26, 1741, 40th year.

92. iv. Joseph.[4]

FOURTH GENERATION.

41

Joseph[4] Porter, of John[3] Porter, b. Feb. 6, 1697; lived in Weymouth. Married 1st, Mercy daughter of John Randall, pub. Dec. 18, 1723; she b. Nov. 16, 1704. Married 2d, Sarah White, pub. Feb. 1, 1766.

He died 1768; estate settled that year, "wife Sarah;" children baptised South Parish.

93. i. John,[5] June 23, 1725; m. Martha Bates, 1754.
94. ii. Nehemiah,[5] b. July 2, 1728; m. Sarah Waters, 1752.
95. iii. Joseph,[5] b. Aug. 17, 1732; m. Hannah Ripley, 1753.
96. iv. Abner,[5] b. Jan. 22, 1737; died Feb. 17, 1737.

42

Mary[4] Porter, of John[3] Porter, b. Jan. 11, 1700; m. Thomas[3] Standish, in Marshfield, Jan. 29, 1717. He, son of Alexander[2] and Desire Standish, b. in Marshfield, May 5, 1689. Removed to Pembroke, where his name first appears in 1718. Children:

97. i. David,[5] b. Marshfield; m. Hannah Magoun, 1746; died 1793, leaving David, Jr., Lemuel who went to Bath, Me., and other children.
98. ii. Amos,[5] prob. b. Marshfield—"Amos Standish, an adult baptised, Marshfield, 1742," or 1746.
99. iii. Thomas,[5] b. Pembroke, 1725; died there 1780. He m. Martha Bisbee, 1748.
100. iv. Mary,[5] b. do. 1733.
101. v. William,[5] b. do. 1737; m. Abigail, dau. of John Stetson, Pembroke, Dec. 8, 1763.
102. vi. Betty,[5] b. do. 1739.

43

John[4] Porter, of John[3] Porter, b. Aug. 23, 1702, of Weymouth; m. Sarah Nash, Dec. 12, 1728, by Rev. James Bayley. He died Sept. 23, 1767. Children baptised South Parish.

103. i. John,[5] b. Sept. 8, 1729; m. Temperance Shaw, 1753.
104. ii. Richard,[5] bap. July 16, 1731.
105. iii. William,[5] b. June 7, 1731; married.

106. iv. Sarah,[5] b. June 8, 1733.
107. v. Isaac,[5] b. Nov. 15, 1736; m. Eunice Pratt.
108. vi. Abner,[5] b. June 6, 1739.
109. vii. Mercy,[5] b. Mar. 22, 1742.
110. viii. Peter,[5] b. June 8, 1744; died in Weymouth, 1831.
111. ix. Mary,[5] b. Apr. 15, 1747.

44

Richard[4] Porter, of John[3] Porter, b. Jan. 8, 1705, lived in Weymouth; m. Ruth, daughter of Dea. Samuel and Mary (Richards,) Whitman, by Rev. James Bayley, Jan. 29, 1729. She b. March 27, 1710, died Sep. 13, 1759; he died 1759. Children:

112. i. Samuel,[5], b. Mar. 9, 1731; died Mar. 28.
113. ii. Samuel,[5] b. May 8, 1733; m. Esther Beal, Feb. 18, 1753.
114. iii. Mary,[5] b. Sept. 25, 1734; m. Ben. Beal, Feb. 18, 1753.
115. iv. Lydia,[5] b. Jan. 31, 1738; died Feb. 17, 1738.
116. v. Josiah,[5] b. Aug. 27, 1739; m. Deborah Higgins, 1761.
117. vi. Micah,[5] b. Dec. 21, 1742; m. Mary—
118. vii. Sarah,[5] b. Aug. 22, 1746; m. Eb. Shaw, Jr.
119. viii. Lydia,[5] b. Feb. 9, 1751; died March 2, 1752.
120. ix. Noah,[5] b. May 20, 1753; died June 27, 1753.

45

Deliverance[4] Porter, of John[3] Porter, b. 1707; m. John Beal, Jr., of Cohasset, Dec. 28, 1727, by Rev. James Bayley. He died Mar. 23, 1776, aged 71. Children—baptisms from Cohasset church records.

121. i. Lydia,[5] baptised Nov. 10, 1728; died June 20, 1736.
122. ii. John,[5] " Oct. 18, 1730.
123. iii. Mercy,[5] " Oct. 29, 1732.
124. iv. Jacob,[5] " July 9, 1735.
125. v. Lydia,[5] " Feb. 20, 1737.
126. vi. Mary,[5] " Aug. 12, 1739.
127. vii Deborah,[5] " Jan. 10, 1742.
128. viii. Sarah,[5] " April 15, 1744.
129. ix. Hannah,[5] " Oct. 12, 1746.

46

Peter[4] Porter, of John[3] Porter, b. July 26, 1714; m. Mercy Vickery, of Hingham, Dec. 5, 1732, by Rev. Mr. Gay. Children:

130. i. Elizabeth,[5] b. Hingham, Sept. 9, 1733; baptised Oct. 7, 1733, by Rev. Mr. Gay—m. Andrew Burrill, 1756; she died Feb. 2, 1785, aged 51.
131. ii. Peter,[5] b. Weymouth, Feb. 12, 1737.

49

Margaret[4] Porter, of John[3] Porter, b. July 26, 1714; m. Phillip Torrey, Jr., of Weymouth, Nov. 30, 1740, by the Rev. Wm. Smith. He died 1785, aged 71 years; his wife died of small pox in 1761. Children:

132. i. Mary,[5] b. Aug. 30, 1741.
133. ii. Margaret,[5] b. Dec. 23, 1744.
134. iii. Phillip,[5] b. Feb. 20, 1747; m. Mary Bicknell, pub. Sept. 21, 1771. Their children were Elizabeth,[6] b. Nov. 19, 1772; Mary,[6] b. 1776; died 1778; Margaret,[6] b. Aug. 18, 1777; Margaret,[6] again, Aug. 27, 1779; Sarah,[6] June 3, 1785.

50

Samuel[4] Porter of Samuel[3] Porter, b. May 14, 1699. He lived in Abington and Bridgewater; m. 1st, Sarah, daughter of Joseph and Sarah (Ford) Josselyn, of Abington, July 2, 1722. He m. 2d, widow Ruth Reed, in Bridgewater, May 31, 1764. He and wife Sarah, deeded house and sixty acres of land in Abington to his brother Jacob, Dec. 1, 1742. He probably removed to Bridgewater soon after. A way was laid out by his house there, 1745–6. Children:

135. i. Sarah,[5] b. May 26, 1723; (died June 25, 1798, aged 76.)
136. ii. Mary,[5] b. Feb. 9, 1725; died Mar. 1, 1725.
137. iii. Samuel,[5] b. Oct. 12, 1727; m. Hannah Green, 1758.
138. iv. Joseph,[5] b. Feb. 27, 1730; m. Elizabeth Burrill, 1753.
139. v. Ebenezer,[5] b. Sept. 15, 1731; m. Lydia Loring, 1754.
140. vi. Mary,[5] b. Aug. 3, 1733.
141. vii. Adam,[5] b. Feb. 24, 1735.
142. viii. Hannah,[5] b. Feb. 18, 1736; m. Judah Wood, 1757.
143. ix. Betterus,[5] b. Sept. 23, 1737; unmarried—lived and died with her sister Hannah, in Halifax, Mar., 1814, aged 77.

144. x. Noah,[5] b. May 13, 1740.
145. xi. Jonathan,[5] b. Aug. 27, 1741; m. Mary Chipman, 1763.
146. xii. Deliverance,[5] b. July 19, 1742.
147. xiii. Abigail,[5] b. July 7, 1743.
148. xiv. Tabitha,[5] b. 1744; m. Samuel Brown, Jr., 1780.
148A. xv. Sarah,[5] m. Noah Tinkham, 1757.

52

David[4] Porter, of Samuel[3] Porter, b. in Weymouth, 1702; lived in Abington—unmarried—farmer. Some of the French neutrals lived with him in 1755; died Sept., 1778. In his will he mentions his brother John's children, and children of his brothers, Samuel and Jacob deceased, also his sisters, Hannah Thompson and Abigail Packard.

53

Jacob[4] Porter, of Samuel[3] Porter, b. Aug. 10, 1704. Lived in Abington, was a prominent and influential citizen there; a Rep. to General Court in the years 1753-54-56-57; selectman three years from 1736; built the first mill on Beaver Brook, 1739. He married Esther, daughter of Ensign Andrew and Mercy (Whitmarsh) Ford, Jan. 6, 1732; she born 1714, and died Nov. 20, 1789. He died Oct. 26, 1778, aged 74. Children:

149. i. Jacob,[5] } b. Oct. 6, 1732; both died early.
150. ii. Esther,[5] }
151. iii. Esther,[5] b. Mar. 19, 1733; m. Abel Packard, 1757.
152. iv. Mary,[5] b. Aug. 27, 1735; m. Sam. Norton, 1760.
153. v. Jacob,[5] b. July 23, 1737; m. Rachel Reed, 1763.
154. vi. John,[5] b. Apr. 24, 1740.
155. vii. Adam,[5] b. Nov. 6, 1742.
156. viii. Noah,[5] b. Aug. 16, 1744.
157. ix. Abigail,[5] b. Mar. 15, 1747; unmarried, died 1809, aged 62.
158. x. Hannah,[5] b. Oct. 17, 1748; m. Isaac Tirrell, Jr., 1770.
159. xi. Seth,[5] b. Nov. 24, 1752.
160. xii. Abner,[5] b. 1757.

54

Hannah,[4] of Samuel[3], b. Dec. 16, 1712; m. Dea. Barnabas Thompson, of Halifax, Mar. 13, 1740; he died 1798, aged 94. His wife died May 2, 1787, in the 75th year of her age. Children:

161. i. Abigail,[5] b. 1741; died, 1747.
162. ii. Barnabas,[5] b. 1742; died 1742.
163. iii. Jacob,[5] b. 1743; died young.
164. iv. Samuel,[5] b. 1743; died in 1747.
165. v. Jabez,[5] b. 1744; died 1744.
166. vi. Asa,[5] b. 1745; died 1747.
167. vii. Noah,[5] b. 1747; m. Priscilla Holmes.
168. viii. Hannah,[5] b. 1748; m. Elisha Mitchell; she died 1839.
169. ix. Isaac,[5] b. 1749; m. Huldah Sturtevant; she died 1839.
170. x. David,[5] b. 1750; died 1750.
171. xi. Olive,[5] b. 1752; died 1776.
172. xii. Alice,[5] b. 1752; died 1754.
173. xiii. Adam,[5] b. 1754; m. Molly Thompson; he died 1821.
174. xiv. Ichabod,[5] b. 1756; m. Lydia Hall; he died 1821.

55

Rev. John[4] Porter, of Samuel[3] Porter, b. Abington, Feb. 2, 1716. Grad. Har. College, 1736; ordained minister at North Bridgewater, (now Brockton) Mass., Oct. 15, 1740. He was a man of more than average ability, of good education and acquirements, and as a preacher and writer had a good reputation. He was much engaged in controversy—not that he loved it, but he thought it a necessity of the times. He preached the doctrines of the gospel from his standpoint with ability and success. His reputation for prudence, integrity and wisdom was great, causing him to be much sought for to heal difficulties and promote harmony in neighboring churches. He possessed the affection and respect of his own people to a remarkable degree. The periodical visits of himself and wife to his parishioners were days of pleasure and rejoicing to young and old. Several of his sermons were printed, among them one, "a sermon preached at Freetown, Dec. 2, 1747, at the ordination of the Reverend Mr. Silas Brett," a copy of which I have—and in these enlightened days it will be considered a remarkable sermon. Mr. Porter continued to preach until Sept. 1, 1800, when warned by increasing age and infirmities, he asked for a colleague. Rev. Thomas Crafts, his son-in-law, preached for a while, and soon after Rev. Asa Meech, from Conn., was invited to become colleague pastor, which call he accepted, and was ordained Oct. 15, 1800. Mr. Porter continued to perform pastoral labor, preaching occasionally, till his decease."

The following, copied from Moses Carey's Genealogy of Families in North Bridgewater, will be of interest:

"In the year 1769, when the disputes between England and America had begun, and the importation of foreign goods was stopped, it became customary for people to manufacture their own clothing, and in many places the young ladies had spinning matches, at their minister's, for the benefit ot their families.

On the 15th of August, 1769; at two o'clock P. M., ninety-seven young ladies met at the house of their pastor, the Rev. John Porter, and generously gave his lady, for the use of her family, three thousand three hundred and twenty-two knots of linen, tow, cotton and woolen yarn, which they had spun for that purpose! At three o'clock, something of American produce only was set before them for their refreshment, which was more agreeable to them than any foreign dainties, considering the situation of the country at that time. At four o'clock the ladies walked in procession to the meeting-house, where a discourse was delivered by their pastor, from Acts ix. 36;—"This woman was full of good works"; in which piety, industry, frugality, and benev - lence, were recommended and encouraged. The closing prayer being made, the following lines, composed by their pastor, were sung:

Ye rubies bright, ye orient pearls,—
How coveted by men!—
And yet, the virtuous woman's price
Excells the precious gem.

How kind and generous her heart!—
How diligent her hand!
How frugal in economy,
To save her sinking land!

Foreign productions she rejects,
With nobleness of mind,
For home commodities; to which
She's prudently inclined.

She works, she lends, she gives away,
  The labors of her hand;
The priest, the poor, the people all
  Do find in her their friend.

She clothes herself and family,
  And all the sons of need;—
Were all thus virtuous soon we'd find
  Our land from slavery freed."

He married 1st, Olive Johnson of Canterbury, Ct.; she died Feb. 25, 1749, aged 23 years. He married 2d, Mary, daughter of Dea. Samuel Huntington, Leabanon, Ct. She died Nov. 22, 1801. "She was a woman of very exemplary habits, and a devoted mother in Israel." He died March 12, 1802, in the 87th year of his age, and the 62d year of his ministry. Children:

175. i. Olive,[5] b. Feb. 14, 1749; died same year.
176. ii. John,[5] b. Feb. 27, 1752.
177. iii. Olive,[5] b. May 23, 1753; m. John Crafts, 1790.
178. iv. Huntington,[5] b. March, 27, 1755.
179. v. Jonathan,[5] } b. July 5, 1756.
180. vi. David,[5] } " " died May, 1767.
181. vii. Eliphalet,[5] b. June 11, 1758.
182. viii. Mary,[5] b. Nov. 16, 1762; m. Rev. Thomas Crafts, 1786.
183. ix. Sibyl,[5] b. May 1766; died unmarried, at Princeton.

56

Abigail[4] Porter, of Samuel[3] Porter, b. June 23, 1719; m. Capt. Isaac Packard, of Bridgewater, Mar. 28, 1745. He was the son of David and Hannah (Ames) Packard, b. June 2, 1720; died 1792, aged 72. Children:

184. i. Alice,[5] b. Apr. 12, 1746; died Mar. 14, 1747.
185. ii. Isaac,[5] b. Feb. 3, 1750; m. Mary Atwood, of Eastham, Mass., 1776. Their child, Isaac,[6] b. Mar. 16, 1778; m. Cobb, of Boston, and moved to New York. The father died June 17, 1778; his widow married Daniel Cooley, Esq., of Amherst, Mass., Jan. 18, 1796.

186. iii. Abigail,[5] b. Oct. 25, 1754; m. Hon. Daniel Howard, Dec. 22, 1776. Their children were, Betsey,[6] b. 1777; m. Dr. Moses Baker, 1803; afterward John Crafts. Francis,[6] b. 1778; grad. B. U., 1797; lived in Boston; died young. Abigail,[6] b. 1779. Susannah,[6] b. 1781. Daniel,[6] b. 1783; died 1814. Mary,[6] b. 1784. Ellen,[6] b. 1787. Sybil Porter,[6] b. 1789. Lucy,[6] and Lois,[6] b. 1791; Lois died unmarried, 1798. John E,[6] b. 1793; grad. B. U., 1815; m. Harriet Pratt, 1821. Jona,[6] b. 1795. Judge Howard died 1832, aged 83; his wife died 1818.

57

Nicholas[4] Porter, of Nicholas[3] Porter, b. in Weymouth, Oct. 26, 1700. Lived in Abington and Marshfield; married Ruth Rogers, of Marshfield, Dec. 19, or Sept. 24, 1722. "Nicholas Porter and wife owned the covenant May 1, 1726, and had their son Nicholas baptised"—Abington church records. Wife probably died Aug. 31, 1775. Children:

187. i. Nicholas,[5] b. Jan. 11, 1724; died March 31, 1724.
188. ii. Job.[5]
189. iii. Daniel.[5]
190. iv. Nicholas,[5] baptised May 1, 1726.
191. v. Lucy.[5]
192. vi. Ruth,[5] baptised May 12, 1728; m. Samuel Eames, of Marshfield, May 16, 1750.

60

Daniel[4] Porter, of Nicholas[3] Porter, b. in Abington, June 15, 1708. Cyrus Nash, in his manuscript History of Abington, says he went west, and came back to Abington on a visit in 1775.

62

Job[4] Porter, of Nicholas[3] Porter, b. June 26, 1714. Lived in Marshfield, and married there, and had children.

63

Esther[4] Porter, of Nicholas[3] Porter, b. June 20, 1716; married Joshua Fobes, of Bridgewater, Mar. 29, 1740. He was the son of Joshua and Abigail (Dunbar) Fobes, b. 1715. Children:

193. i. Azariah,[5] b. 1741.
194. ii. Daniel,[5] b. 1742; m. Hannah Standish, 1769.

195. iii. Ruth,[5] b. 1744; m. Ebenezer Alden, of Middleborough, 1763.
196. iv. Abigail,[5] b. 1747; m. Joseph Cowan, 1772.
197. v. Joshua,[5] b. 1749.
198. vi. Caleb,[5] b. 1750; m.; went to Lyme, Conn.
199. vii. Robert,[5] b. 1753.
200. viii. Solomon,[5] b. 1756; married.

64

Abner[4] Porter, of Nicholas[3] Porter, b. Nov. 27, 1718. Lived in Abington, married Jane Cheesman of Braintree, 1744. He died Feb. 20, 1793, aged 76; his widow died Mar. 13, 1814, aged 93. Children:

201. i. Ruth,[5] b. April 21, 1745; died unmarried, 1780.
202. ii. Bershabe,[5] b. June 28, 1746; died unmarried, 1780.
203. iii. Edward,[5] b. June 11, 1748.
204. iv. William,[5] b. Sept. 27, 1750; married.
205. v. David,[5] b. April 2, 1753.
206. vi. Matthew,[5] b. May 20, 1755; married.
207. vii. Abner,[5] b. Aug. 8, 1757.
208. viii. Jane,[5] b. April 15, 1759; unmarried.
209. ix. Clifford,[5] b. April 6, 1762; married.
210. x. Abijah,[5] b. Nov. 18, 1764; married.

70

Thomas[4] Porter, of Thomas[3] Porter, b. Weymouth, April 27, 1713. Lived in Weymouth; died 1758; married Mercy Pratt, Jan. 24, 1740, by Rev. James Bayley. Children:

211. i. Mercy,[5] b. Mar. 24, 1741; m. Lemuel Barber, 1761.
212. ii. Hannah,[5] b. Feb. 24, 1744; died 1756.
213. iii. Jonathan,[5] b. Sep. 18, 1746.
214. iv. Emma,[5] m. Peter Pratt, 1772.
215. v. Thomas,[5] bap. N. P., Mar. 31, 1751.
216. vi. Josiah,[5] bap. N. P., Mar. 31, 1751.

75

Matthew[4] Porter, of Thomas[3] Porter, b. Sept. 8, 1725. Lived in Weymouth; m. Sarah, daughter of Samuel and

Hannah Pratt, pub. Jan. 9, 1750. She born Sept. 12, 1729. (Widow m. David Lincoln, of Hingham, pub. Jan. 18, 1770, m. Feb. 8, 1770.) Children:

217. i. Nabby,[5] b. April 7, 1753; m. Stephen Hollis, Dec. 18, 1783.
218. ii. Thomas,[5] b. June 21, 1755; died Sept. 29, 1776, aged 22.
219. iii. Hannah,[5] b. April 25, 1759; m. Wm. Loud, Jr., April 28, 1785.
220. iv. Sarah,[5] b. Oct. 8, 1762.
221. v. Susanna,[5] b. Feb. 10, 1765; m. Jos. Vining, Jr., 1787.
222. vi. Elesabeth,[5] b. Aug. 15, 1769.
223. vii. Lydia,[5] b. May 6, 1774.

76

Ezra[4] Porter, of Thomas[3] Porter, b. Sept. 8, 1725. Lived in Weymouth; m. 1st, Hannah, daughter of Joseph and Ruth (Richards) Lovell; pub. April 13, 1751; she born Dec. 17, 1723. Married 2d, Patience, daughter of Solomon and Temperance (Hathaway) Barber; pub. Aug. 17, 1762; she born Oct. 21, 1741. Children:

224. i. Josiah,[5] bap. N. P., Dec. 22, 1751.
225. ii. Molly,[5] b. Jan. 26, 1753; m. Samuel Pratt, 1770.
226. iii. Lucy,[5] bap. N. P., Oct. 1769.
227. iv. Ezra,[5] b. Aug. 23, 1763.

80

Ebenezer[4] Porter, of Ebenezer[3] Porter, b. 1708; lived in Weymouth; held numerous town offices. Married 1st, Mary, dau. of Joseph and Ruth (Richards) Lovell, Dec. 17, 1730, by Rev. James Bayley. She born Oct. 21, 1712; died Nov. 6, 1749. Married 2d, widow Melea (of Elisha) Lincoln; pub. Dec. 24, 1749. He died 1763. Children:

228. i. Ebenezer,[5] } b. April 13, 1732; died April 17.
229. ii. Joseph,[5] }
230. iii. Ebenezer,[5] b. Dec. 7, 1733.
231. iv. Mary,[5] b. Dec. 15, 1739.
232. v. Ruth,[5] b. Nov. 22, 1743.

81

Sarah[4] Porter, of Ebenezer[3] Porter, b. Jan. 12, 1711; m. Joseph Trufant, of Weymouth, May 15, 1729; he son of Maurice and Mary Trufant, b. May 5, 1701. She died Oct. 8, 1778, aged 67. Children:

233. i. James,[5] b. Mar. 8, 1730; m. Experience, dau. of John[3] Bates, Dec. 26, 1754; he died Aug. 6, 1771.

234. ii. Joseph,[5] b. Sept. 28, 1732; died Mar. 13, 1734.

235. iii. Sarah,[5] b. July 9, 1735.

236. iv. Joseph,[5] b. Mar. 8, 1738; m. Deborah Colson, May 14, 1761, by Rev. James Bayley. Children: Deborah,[6] b. Feb. 5, 1770. James,[6] b. Aug. 26, 1773. John,[6] b. Dec. 10, 1779. Christopher,[6] b. June 15, 1782.

237. v. Job,[5] b. Dec. 21, 1743; m. Chloe White, pub. Dec. 17, 1763. Children: Sarah,[6] b. Feb. 16, 1765. Stephen,[6] b. July 29, 1766. A Job Trufant in Bowdoinham, Me., 1784.

82

Tabitha[4] Porter, of Ebenezer[3] Porter, b. Mar. 22, 1719; m. Daniel Burrill, of Weymouth, Jan. 22, 1741; he son of Ephraim and Mary (Pratt) Burrill, born Mar. 22, 1720. Children:

238. i. Daniel,[5] b. Jan. 9, 1745.

239. ii. Tabitha,[5] b. June 12, 1747.

240. iii. Sarah,[5] b. Aug. 28, 1751.

241. iv. Mary,[5] b. April 17, 1755.

91

Ebenezer[4] Porter, of Thomas[3] Porter, b. Dec., 1701; lived in Taunton. In 1744, "Thomas[3] Porter, of Taunton, gave land to children of his son Ebenezer, late of Taunton, deceased—Ebenezer, Joshua, Samuel, John, Jacob, and Mary." In 1753, a guardian was appointed for Jacob, John, Mary and Samuel. Married 1st, Mary—; married 2d, probably Phebe Hoskins. He died in Taunton, Mar. 26, 1741, aged 39. Children:

242. i. Ebenezer,[5] b. July 24, 1728; died Feb. 5, 1792.

243. ii. Joshua,[5] b. Feb. 16, 1730.

244. iii. Samuel,[5] b. June 4, 1733; m. Esther Lincoln.

245. iv. Thomas,[5] b. Feb. 17, 1735; died Feb. 2, 1775.

246. v. John,[5] b. Aug. 8, 1736.

247. vi. Jacob,[5] b. May 30, 1738.

248. vii. Mercy,[5] b. Sept. 7, 1741; m. Ebenezer Cobb, of Taunton.

249. viii. Phebe,[5]; prob. m. Andros.

ix. Joseph[5]

92

Joseph[4] Porter, of Thomas[3] Porter, b. Taunton; lived there. Married Sarah,[2] daughter of James[1] Pinneo, of Bristol, R. I., and Lebanon, Conn.—she born Dec. 19, 1712. In 1735, Joseph Porter and wife Sarah, daughter of James Pinneo, lately of Lebanon, Conn., deceased, quit-claim to her brother, James Pinneo, all right in her father's estate. (Lebanon Town Records, vol. 5, page 319.) In 1744, "Thomas Porter of Taunton sold son Joseph Porter forty acres of land and a dwelling house for 1,000 pounds." July 7, 1746 "James Codding and Thomas Liscomb appointed guardian of Joseph Porter, non-compos." Sept. 11, 1750, widow Sarah Porter appointed administrator of estate of Joseph Porter. Nov. 18, 1754, Sarah Sullard, late widow of Joseph Porter, now of Lebanon, Conn., closes settlement of estate; she had in mean time married Sullard. Children:

250. i. Jonathan,[5] b. Sept., 1732.
251. ii. Joseph.[5]
252. iii. Peter,[5] guardian ap., 1754.
253. iv. James,[5] of Taunton; administration of his estate, 1757.
254. v. Ann.[5]
255. vi. Abigail.[5]
256. vii. Sarah.[5]

FIFTH GENERATION.

93

John[5] Porter, of Joseph[4] Porter, b. June 23, 1725. Lived in Weymouth. Married 1st, Martha Bates, Mar. 20, 1754; she daughter of Joshua[4] and Martha (Orcutt) Bates, born Sept. 26, 1724. Married 2d, Francis Burrill, pub. May 22, 1762; she daughter of Ephraim[4] Burrill, born April 20, 1730. Child:

257. i. Martha,[6] b. July 31, 1755; m. Timothy Nash, 1777.

94

Nehemiah[5] Porter, of Joseph[4] Porter, b. in Weymouth, July 2, 1728. Married his cousin Sarah Waters, dau. of Seward and Sarah (Porter) Waters, of Boston, June 11, 1752, by Rev. James Bayley. He lived in Weymouth; removed to Scituate, about 1757; returned to Weymouth, before 1770, as he was a town officer there that year. In Mr. Ezra Stearns' History of Rindge, N. H., page 644, I find that "Nehemiah Porter, from Weymouth, came to Rindge near the close of the year 1771; was several months in the army; was in Capt. Phillip Thomas' Company in 1775. He had with him their children, Nehemiah, Joseph, Benjamin, Silvanus, Sarah, Lydia, Ebenezer and Mary. He removed or died between 1780 and 1793." Children:

258. i. Seward,[6] b. in Weymouth, Aug. 5, 1753.
259. ii. Joseph,[6] b. in Weymouth, Nov. 6, 1754.
260. iii. Sylvanus,[6] b. in Weymouth, 1756.
261. iv. Jacob,[6] b. in Weymouth, July 18, 1757.
262. v. Nehemiah,[6] b. Scituate, Dec. 14, 1758.
263. vi. Benjamin,[6] b. Scituate.
264. vii. Sarah,[6] b. Scituate; unmarried; died in North Yarmouth Me., 1839.
265. viii. Lydia,[6] b. Scituate; m. Mitchell, N. Yarmouth.
266. ix. Molly,[6] b. Scituate, 1766: m. William Barbour, of Gray, Me.; removed to Portland.

95

Joseph[5] Porter, of Joseph[4] Porter, b. Aug. 17, 1732; lived in Weymouth; married 1st, Hannah, daughter of Josiah[4] and Mary Ripley; 2d, widow Deborah Porter, Nov. 16, 1783; he died 1821, aged 92, and his widow Deborah died 1822, aged 76. Children:

267. i. Hannah,[6] b. Aug. 28, 1755.
268. ii. Jacob,[6] b. July 18, 1757.
269. iii. David,[6] b. Dec. 29, 1759.
270. iv. Mercy,[6] b. Mar. 6, 1762.
271. v. Betty,[6] b. Apr. 25, 1764.
272. vi. Sarah,[6] b. June 18, 1766.
273. vii. Joseph,[6] b. June 19, 1768.
274. viii. John,[6] b. Apr. 10, 1770.
275. ix. Josiah,[6] b. Oct. 8, 1773.

103

John[5] Porter, of John[4] Porter, b. Sept. 8, 1729; lived in Weymouth; married 1st, Maria Lincoln, of Hingham, Feb. 21st, 1751; she died Feb. 3, 1752. Married 2d, Temperance Shaw, Sept. 20, 1753. He died Jan. 15, 1769. Children:

276. i. Mary,[6] b. Jan. 21, 1754; m. Samuel Badlam, Jr., 1773.
277. ii. Mercy,[6] b. Aug. 14, 1755.
278. iii. Child,[6] bap., 1758.

105

William[5] Porter, of John[4] Porter, b. June 7, 1731; resided in Weymouth; died there in 1812; married Tabitha Orcutt, probably; pub. July 17, 1773; his will proved in 1812; wife Tabitha and cousin Lifee Holbrook administered. Widow Tabitha will probated October 10, 1840; Asa Hunt, executor. No children alive; estate went to Abi, wife of Samuel Newcomb, and George Thayer, of Randolph.

106

Sarah[5] Porter, of John[4] Porter, b. June 8, 1733; married Josiah, of Abiezer and Ruth (Vinson) Holbrook; pub. May 22, 1762; he born Sept. 27, 1727; died Weymouth, 1805, aged 78; his wife died 1804, aged 71. Children:

279. i. Sarah,[6] b. Dec. 14, 1762.
280. ii. Hannah,[6] b. Feb. 19, 1765.
281. iii. Lifee,[6] b. Feb. 15, 1768.
282. iv. John,[6] b. June 6, 1772.
283. v. Molly,[6] b. Sept. 13, 1776.

107

Isaac[5] Porter, of John[4] Porter, b. Nov. 15, 1736; lived in Weymouth, on Queen Ann's Turnpike, near house of the late Hon. Abner Holbrook, Pleasant street, west of Lovells' corner. He married Eunice, daughter of Capt. Thomas and Mary (Vinson) Pratt, Aug. 18, 1763; she born April 6, 1746; died 1820, aged 74. He died June 15, 1800; his estate administered upon in 1800. Children named in the will, Sarah, Jane, Mary White, and Lois White. Children:

284. i. Mary,[6] b. Nov. 4, 1764; m. Capt. Asa White, May 24, 1784; she died 1809, aged 45.

285\. ii. John,[6] b. Apr. 8, 1767; died 1767.

286\. iii. Lois,[6] b. April 6, 1769; m. Thomas White, "Skeeter Plain," April 9, 1801.

287\. iv. Sarah,[6] b Oct. 25, 1774; unmarried; died, 1843.

288\. v. Jane,[6] b. Aug. 21, 1780; unmarried; died, 1807.

108

Abner[5] Porter, of John[4] Porter, b. June 6, 1739; lived in Weymouth; probably died 1822. An Abner Porter married widow Miriam Tirrell, in Weymouth, 1785. Abners' wife died 1819.

113

Samuel[5] Porter, of Richard[4] Porter, b. May 8, 1733; lived in Weymouth; was in Capt. Ward's company, in 1758; married Esther, of William and Hannah (Smith) Beal, Nov. 22, 1753. She born Apr. 14, 1733. His widow probably married Thomas Kingman, in 1760.

114

Mary[5] Porter, of Richard[4] Porter, b. Sept. 25, 1734; married Benjamin Beal, of Abington, Feb. 18, 1753; he was son of Jeremiah and Mary (Colson) Beal, b. in Weymouth, Dec. 9, 1731, but removed with his father to Abington. He died, 1805. His wife died, 1806. Children:

289\. i. Chloe,[6] b. Dec. 3, 1753; died young.

290\. ii. Mary,[6] b. Oct. 11, 1755; m. Ebenezer K. Hunt, Nov. 5, 1778. Their children, b. in Abington, Ebenezer,[7] b. Aug. 3, 1779. Sarah[7], b. July 5, 1781; m. David Townsend, Nov. 10, 1800; and died in Maine. Mary Beals,[7] b. Oct. 21, 1783; m. Isaac Pool, of Weymouth, Mar. 1, 1804; died April 1, 1806. Ruth,[7] b. Mar. 4, 1786; m. David Blanchard, Jr., Sept. 19, 1803; died Mar. 20, 1833. John,[7] b. June 1, 1788; m. Patience Pratt, Sept. 20, 1814; died July 12, 1854. Betsey,[7] b. Sept. 10, 1789; died Aug. 2, 1831. Twins, died May 30, 1792. Hannah,[7] b. Dec. 13, 1795; m. Samuel Colson, Jan. 14, 1836; Mrs. Hunt died Feb. 14, 1835.

291. iii. Benjamin,[6] b. Oct. 30, 1757; m. Mary Noyes, June 21, 1787, and moved to Turner, Me. Their children were, Zenas[7], a physician. Ira.[7] Betsey,[7] m. Bird. Sophia,[7] m. Phillip True. Axa,[7] m. Matthew Packard. Polly,[7] m. Ara Holmes. Samuel.[7] Benjamin.[7] Celesta.[7]

292. iv. Chloe,[6] b. Oct. 8, 1759; unmarried; died Jan. 1, 1848.

293. v. Samuel,[6] b. Oct. 8, 1761; bap. S. P., Weymouth, Oct, 11; m. Cobb, Mar. 6, 1782. She died May 4, 1784. He then removed to Winchendon, Mass. He left a numerous posterity;—some in Abington, some in Boston, some in Winchendon, and some in California, and elsewhere.

294. vi. Ruth,[6] b. Sept. 14, 1763; m. Noah Hersey, of Abington, 1787, and moved to the town of Minot, Maine. Children: Noah,[7] m. Phebe Howard. Benjamin,[7] m. Sally Bradbury; went to Foxcroft, Me. Polly,[7] m. Marcus Conant, and died in Bath. Betsey,[7] m. Whiting. Sally,[7] m. Hueston, of Charleston, Me. Ira,[7] b. 1801. Hiram,[7] and Lewis.[7]

295. vii. Priscilla,[6] b. Feb. 14, 1766; unmarried; bap. S. P., Weymouth, May 25.

296. viii. Zelotes,[6] b. Feb. 23, 1768; m. Sarah Burrill, Mar. 2, 1797.

297. ix. Lydia,[6] b. Feb. 13, 1770; m. David Trufant, of Weymouth, Dec. 6, 1792.

298. x. Sarah,[6] b. Nov. 11, 1772; m. Nath. Tirrell, Jan. 4. 1795.

299. xi. Nathaniel,[6] b. Feb. 11, 1775; m. Tamar, dau. of Elijah Hobart, Jan., 1807; resided in Abington; had several children, and died there, Feb., 1820.

300. xii. Mehetable,[6] b. May, 1777; m. Abner Holbrook, of Weymouth, Mar. 1st, 1796; his son, Hon. Abner,[7] (among other children) b. 1811, in Weymouth; died there 1875; was a man much respected, a merchant, and often in public office.

116

Josiah[5] Porter, of Richard[4] Porter, b. Aug. 27, 1739; lived in Weymouth. Married Deborah Higgins, Sept. 23, 1761, by Rev. James Bayley. He died intestate, 1783; widow administered; Micah, Jonathan, and Samuel Porter, were her bondsmen. Widow married Joseph Porter, Nov. 16, 1783. She died 1822, aged 76. Children:

301. i. Samuel,[6] b. Feb. 2, 1764; m.

302. ii. Deborah,[6] } Twins, b. Dec. 8, 1865; prob. d. 1853, aged 88.
303. iii. Mary,[6] }

304. iv. Eunice,[6] b. Mar. 4, 1768; died in Boston.
305. v. Nancy,[6] b. Oct. 8, 1770; m. Jacob Reed, of Abington, Nov. 18, 1799.
306. vi. Ruth,[6] bap. S. P., 1773; m. Haynes, of Canaan, N. H.
306A. vii. Richard,[6] bap. Feb. 5, 1775; died 1783.
307. viii. Sarah,[6] bap. May 28, 1775.
307A. ix. Sarah,[6] bap. 1777; m. John Withington, of Dorchester.
308. x. Naomi,[6] m. Atherton, and went west.

117

Micah[5] Porter, of Richard[4] Porter, b. Dec. 21, 1742; lived in South Parish, Weymouth; married Mary Stockbridge, Oct. 18, 1764. Children:

309. i. Hannah,[6] b. May 12, 1767; m. Jacob Turner, Mar. 27, 1788.
310. ii. Elias,[6] b. Jan. 14, 1769; m. Sarah Bates, 1792.
311. iii. Micah,[6] b. May 12, 1772.
312. iv. Noah,[6] b. May 13, 1774.
313. v. Abby,[6] b. } May 25, 1776.
314. vi. Ellen,[6] b. } " "
315. vii. Betsey,[6] bap. June 30, 1776; m. Brackly Shaw, Nov. 24, 1796.
316. viii. John,[6] b. Feb. 24, 1779.
317. ix. Nehemiah,[6] bap. May 20, 1781.
318. x. William,[6] bap. May 20, 1781.
319. xi. William,[6] b. June 11, 1782.
320. xii. David,[6] b. 1787.
321. xiii. Samuel,[6] b. 1787.
322. xiv. Reuben,[6] b. 1790.

118

Sarah[5] Porter, of Richard[4] Porter, b. Aug. 22, 1746; married in Weymouth, Ebenzer Shaw, Jr., of Abington, 1765; pub. Weymouth, and also in Abington, Aug. 10, 1765. Had large family of children.

137

Samuel[5] Porter, of Samuel[4] Porter, b. Abington, Oct. 12, 1727; lived in East Bridgewater; surveyor 1758; hogreave 1769; constable 1773; married widow Hannah (Jackson) Green, Sept. 28, 1758; she widow of Samuel Green, and grand-daughter of Edward Jackson, born Aug. 7, 1727; died July 7, 1786, aged 59. He died Oct. 5, 1811, aged 84. Children, the four first of whom are recorded in Bridgewater records:

332. i. Samuel,[6] b. May, 24, 1759; died Aug. 22, 1775, aged 16.
333. ii. Betterus,[6] b. Oct. 19, 1761; m. Abner Gardner, 1782.
334. iii. Abigail,[6] b. Dec. 18, 1763; m. Sam. Pool, Jr., 1786, Minot, Me.
335. iv. Ruth,[6] b. Feb. 1st, 1766; m. James Reed, 1784.
v. Jerusha,[6] b. Aug. 28, 1768; died Dec. 7, 1789, aged 13.
vi. Oliver,[6] b. Apr. 27, 1770; died Jan., 1772, aged 20 months.

138

Lieut. Joseph[5] Porter, of Samuel[4] Porter, b. Abington, June 10, 1730; lived in Bridgewater and Stoughton; April 9, 1765, he bought house and lot of his uncle, Isaac Packard, in what is now West Bridgewater, where Pardon Keith now lives. (1878.) In 1777, April 20, he sold the same to Nathan Keith, and removed about that time into Stoughton, near North Bridgewater line. He and wife both admitted to North Bridgewater church, in 1780, of which his uncle John Porter, was the minister. He was a Lieutenant in the militia in the time of the Revolutionary war. He married Elisabeth, daughter of Samuel and Content (Whitcomb) Burrill, of Weymouth, Jan. 25, 1753; she was born July 4, 1733; she went to Abington to teach school, and was there married. She was a woman of remarkable personal beauty, as were her daughters also. He died Jan. 15, 1803, in the 75th year of his age. His widow died Mar. 26, 1822, aged 89. His will, of which subjoined is a copy:

In the Name of God, Amen.—I, Joseph Porter, of Stoughton, in the county of Norfolk and Commonwealth of Massachusetts, Gentlemen, being advanced in age, but of sane mind and memory, do this sixteenth day of February, one thousand eight hundred and two, make and publish this my last will and testament.

Imprimis—I give to my beloved wife, Elizabeth, the easterly end or half of my new dwelling house, and so much of the cellar as is necessary for her use, also one-half of the buttery, in the other part of the house, and the privilege of the oven, well, dooryard, &c., during her natural life; also the improvement of one good cow which is to be kept on my farm for her use during natural life; also one good yearling hog, well fatted yearly, and nine bushels of Indian corn and three bushels of rye, six pounds of goods sheep's wool, twelve pounds of good flax (well dressed) yearly, and a sufficiency of cider, apples and sauce, and a sufficiency of wood to keep one fire, cut up fit for the hearth, and at the door, during her natural life, and ten dollars in cash, yearly, so long as she lives; also all my indoor movables and household furniture (except my wearing apparel, barrels, casks, &c.) during her natural life.

Item.—I give to my son Joseph Porter, all my new dwelling house and land it stands on, well, dooryard, &c., forever, reserving to his mother the improvement of so much of the same as is above expressed, during her natural life; also my horse for the purpose of helping his mother to meeting on the Lord's days as often as she is able and inclined.

Item.—I give to my son Robert Porter my old dwelling house which he now lives in (and not the land it stands on.)

Item.—I give to my son Isaac Porter one hundred and forty dollars and thirty-three cents, to be paid by my executors after named, in two years after my decease.

Item.—I give to my son Lebbeus Porter, one hundred and forty dollars and thirty three cents, to be paid by my executors in two years after my decease.

Item.—I give to my daughter Elizabeth, the wife of Samuel Linfield, twenty dollars,to be paid by my executors in two years after my decease; also one equal share with her three sisters of the indoor moveables and household furniture which is given to her mother (after her decease.)

Item.—I give to my daughter Hannah, the wife of Jonathan Battles, twenty dollars, to be paid by my executors in two years after my decease; also an equal share with her three sisters of the indoor moveables and household furniture which is given to her mother, (after her decease.)

Item.—I give to my daughter Content, the wife of Benjamin Gill, twenty dollars, to be paid by my executors in two days after my decease; also an equal share with her three sisters of the indoor moveables and household furniture which is given to her mother, (after her decease.)

Item.—I give to my daughter Mehitable, the wife of Daniel Brown, twenty dollars, to be paid by my executors in two years after my decease; also an equal share with her three sisters of the indoor movables and household furniture which is given to her mother (after her decease.)

Item.—I give to my five sons, Joseph, Robert, Isaac, Lebbeus and Cyrus, all my wearing apparel, to be equally divided among them.

Item.—After my just debts and funeral charges and the aforesaid legacies are paid, all the remainder of my estate, real or personal, of whatever name or nature, or wherever the same may be found, I give to my three sons, Joseph Porter, Robert Porter, and Cyrus Porter, their heirs and assigns, to be equally divided among them, they paying as above expressed in this Instrument.

Lastly—I do constitute and ordain my three sons last mentioned, viz: Joseph, Robert, and Cyrus, sole executors of this my last will and testament. In witness whereof, I do hereunto set my hand and seal this day and year as above written.

(Seal) JOSEPH PORTER.

Signed, sealed, and published and pronounced and declared, by the said Joseph Porter, as and for his last will and testament, in the presence of us, who, at his request and in his presence, hereunto set our names as witnesses to the same.

SAMUEL TALBOT.
EBEN'R CRANE.
JONAH FULLER.

Children, of whom the first seven are recorded in Bridgewater records:

336. i. Elisabeth,[6] b. Nov. 8, 1753; m. Samuel Linfield.
337. ii. Joseph,[6] b. June 10, 1754; m. Milly Capen.
338. iii. Hannah,[6] b. July 21, 1758; m. Jona Battles.
339. iv. Robert,[6] b. Mar. 30, 1762; m. Elis. Gay.
340. v. Isaac,[6] b. Feb. 23, 1765; m. Susanna Packard.
341. vi. Content,[6] b. Feb. 5, 1767; m. Wm. Glover.
342. vii. Mehetable,[6] b. April 15, 1769; m. Daniel Brown.
343. viii. Lebbeus,[6] b. April 22, 1771; m. Polly Brastow.
344. ix. Cyrus,[6] b. 1774; m. Rebecca French.

139

Ebenezer[5] Porter, of Samuel[4] Porter, b. Abington, Sept. 15, 1731; he lived in Abington and Bridgewater. Married 1st, Lydia Loring, 1754; she died 1771, aged 36 years. M. 2d, widow Bathheba Richmond, 1772. His death on Abington town records Jan. 19, 1801, aged 70. His widow probably died in Halifax, 1831. Children: the first six of whom born in Bridgewater, according to town records:

345. i. Sarah,[6] b. Jan. 13, 1756; m. Capt. Abijah Snow, 1775; removed to Plainfield, Mass.
346. ii. Lydia,[6] b. 1758; m. Dea. Joseph Beal, of Plainfield, 1774.
347. iii. Polly,[6] b. Oct. 8, 1760; m. Capt. Joseph Joy.
348. iv. Olive,[6] b. Jan. 23, 1763; m. Ben. Pool, May 17, 1786.
349. v. Susannah,[6] b. July 1, 1765; m. Andrew Richmond, of Halifax, pub. July 6, 1788.
350. vi. Ebenezer,[6] b. May 8, 1769; m. Betty Reed, Jan. 12, 1792.
351. vii. Samuel,[6] by 2d wife, m. Mehetable Reed, 1801.
352. viii. Nancy,[6] b. in Abington, April 9, 1784; m. Thos. Wilkes, June 10, 1801; lived in East Windsor, Mass.
353. ix. Roxanda,[6] m. Daniel Nash, May 17, 1792; and 2d, Phillip Torrey.
353A. x. Loring,[6] died young.

142

Hannah[5] Porter, of Samuel[4] Porter, b. Feb. 18, 1736; married Judah Wood, of Halifax, Dec. 15, 1757. Children:

Timothy,[6] m. Salvina Soule, of Plympton.
Judah,[6] m. Tabatha Holmes, of Halifax.
Samuel,[6] unmar.
Hannah,[6] unmar.
Ebenezer,[6] m. Cynthia Soule, of Plympton.

145

Jonathan[5] Porter, of Samuel[4] Porter, b. Aug. 27, 1741; lived in Halifax, Mass. Married Mary Chipman, Feb. 16, 1763. She died Sept. 6, 1784. He died 1818. Children:

363. i. Jonathan,[6] b. Oct. 28, 1764; m. Betsey Wood.
364. ii. Bethiah,[6] b. Aug. 7, 1766; m. Dr. Eastman, and died soon.
365. iii. Oliver,[6] Aug. 2, 1774.

148

Tabitha[5] Porter, of Samuel[4] Porter, b. 1744; married Samuel Brown, Jr., 1780. Children:

Robert.[6]
Noah,[6]; lived in Vermont, and had a son[7] in Randolph, Mass., a printer.
Alice[6], m. Zadoc Fuller, and went west.

148A

Sarah[5] Porter, of Samuel[4] Porter; married Noah Tinkham, of Halifax, 1757. Children:

Moses,[6] died in infancy.
Noah,[6] died at age of 21.
Sarah,[6] died at age of 75.
Mary,[6] died March, 1814, aged 57.
Joseph,[6] m. 1st, Lucy Lucas; and 2d, Priscilla Weston, of Middleborough. He died Dec. 18, 1841, aged 77. No children living of this family. Mr. Chipman Porter, now owns and lives on the Noah Tinkham farm.

151

Esther[5] Porter, of Jacob[4] Porter, b. Mar. 19, 1733; married Abel Packard, of North Bridgewater, Jan. 24, 1751. He removed to Cummington, Mass., June, 1774. He became blind at the age of 40 years; was an Ensign, and kept a public house. He was the son of John and Lydia (Thompson) Packard, born Bridgewater, Sept. 8, 1729; died Cummington, Mar. 4, 1804, aged 75. Widow died there May 30, 1812, aged 79. Children, all born in N. Bridgewater, except the last:

366. i. Abel,[6] b. April 16, 1754; m. Mary Bisbee, Sept. 20, 1783; she died Sept. 1, 1807, aged 48; m. 2d, Rachel Porter, of Jacob Porter, Jr., Oct., 1808; she died Aug. 31, 1851, aged 86; he died in Cummington, April 30, 1832, aged 78. His children were, Eliphalet,[7] b. Sept. 2, 1784; m. three times; died June 3, 1868, at Crystal Lake, Wis., aged 83. Chester,[7] b. June 6, 1788; living in Dayton, Wis., in 1871. Betsey,[7] b. Mar. 9, 1791; m. Nehemiah Richards, April 3, 1810; living near Washington, D. C., 1871. Theophilus,[7] b. Nov. 30, 1793; died Granville, Ohio, Mar. 8, 1867.

367. ii. Esther,[6] b. June 21, 1756; m. Ephraim Williams, Esq., of Ashfield, Mass., Nov. 21, 1793—his 2d wife; she died May 31, 1826, aged 70. He died Mar. 9, 1839, aged 92.

368. iii. Adam,[6] b. Feb. 11, 1758; resided in Cummington; m. Abigail Porter, of Jacob Porter, Jr., Nov. 11, 1790.

369. iv. Lydia,[6] b. July 4, 1760; died unmarried, Dec. 23, 1836, aged 76.

370. v. Mary,[6] b. Sept. 29, 1764; m. Col. Lebbeus Bates, of Cummington, Mar. 20, 1778; he was son of Abraham,[4] and Sarah (Tower) Bates, of Weymouth, Mass., b. Jan. 16, 1760. He was uncle to Joshua Bates, banker, of London; was youngest of four brothers, who were in the Revolutionary war, in different parts of the field, and who returned home in safety at the close of the war, not having seen each other during the whole time. He was at the capture of Burgoyne, near Saratoga, in Oct., 1777. His first wife died Aug. 27, 1804, aged 40. He died Sept. 6, 1844, aged 84. Children were, Sibyl,[7] b. July 23, 1789; m. Joseph Phillips, of Windsor, Apr. 19, 1826. Quincy,[7] b. Mar., 7, 1791; living in Goshen, Mass., 1871. Galen,[7] b. May 4, 1794; died Nov. 8. Polly,[7] b. Sept. 23, 1798; m. Almon Allen, Sept. 1, 1819; living in Mansfield, Penn., 1871.

371. vi. Olive,[6] b. Feb. 3, 1767; m. Capt. Joseph Narramore, of Goshen, Dec., 1785. He born Aug. 13, 1760; died Oct. 2, 1834, aged 74. She died Sept. 7, 1835, aged 68. Children: Deborah,[7] b. April 1, 1787; died Dec. Clarissa,[7] b. Feb. 4, 1789; m. Adam G. Porter, Feb. 22, 1784. Olive,[7] b. June 11, 1791; m. Solomon Hawks, Dec. 2, 1819; she died Walnut Grove, Knox Co., Ill., Jan. 3, 1866. Samuel,[7] b. Aug. 30, 1793; d. Goshen, Oct. 4, 1829. Deborah,[7] b. Oct. 24, 1795; m. Robert Dawes, Nov. 22, 1821; living in Salem, Ill., 1871. Abigail,[7] b. Dec. 31, 1798; m. Dea. James W. Briggs, of Cummington, Aug. 8, 1826. Electa,[7] b. Apr. 5, 1800; m. Ebenezer Parsons, Nov., 1823; she died Sept. 23, 1824. Esther,[7] b. Jan. 7, 1803; m. John W. Norton, of Cummington, Jan. 12, 1830. Joseph,[7] b. Feb. 5, 1805; died Aug. 26, 1810. Abel,[7] b. Oct. 28, 1807; d. Aug. 29, 1810.

372. vii. Theophilus,[6] b. Mar. 4, 1769; grad. D. C., 1796; studied theology with Rev. Dr. Asa Burton, of Thetford, Vt.; ordained minister, Shelburne, Mass., Feb.20,1799, where he continued until Feb. 20, 1842. From 1846 to 1854, he lived with a daughter, in South Deerfield, but spent the last year or two of his life at Shelburne. He was a Trustee of Williams College, from 1810 to 1825; on the Board of Overseers of Amherst College, from 1821 to 1854; had degree of D.D. from Dartmouth College, 1824; representative to Gen.Court from Shelburne, 1829-30-39. He m. Mary, dau. of Dea. Isaac Tirrell, Jr., of Abington,

Feb. 9, 1800. She b. Nov. 17, 1775; died Dec. 4, 1865, aged 90. He died Sept. 17, 1855, aged 86. Children: Rev. Theophilus,[7] Jr., born Feb. 1, 1802; grad. Amherst Col., 1823; ordained colleague Pastor, Shelburne, May 12, 1828; dismissed at his own request, Dec. 6, 1853; has since preached and lived at Lyme, Ohio; Mt. Pleasant, Iowa; Manteno, Ill.; South Deerfield, Mass.; Greenfield; Chicago, Ill., 1869, and 1870, to Manteno, Ill., where he now resides; m. May 21, 1839, Elisabeth P., dau. of Rev. Samuel Ware, of Ware. (Their children: Theophilus,[8] Isaac Ware[8]; Samuel[8]; Elisabeth Ware[8]; Geo. Hastings[8]; and Arthur Dwight.[8]) Isaac Tirrell,[7] b. June 27, 1804; d. Sept. 17, 1820, aged 16. Louisa,[7] b. May 15, 1806; died Mar. 10, 1841. Marian,[7] b. Dec. 5, 1809; m. Harry Severance, May 28, 1846. Esther Porter,[7] b. Oct. 25, 1811; m. Caleb A. Cooley, Apr. 11, 1839; died Mar. 15, 1858. Sibyl Tirrel,[7] b. Jan. 29, 1814; m. Abijah H. Dole, Feb. 23, 1843, of Manteno, Ill., (1878.) Laura Emily,[7] b. Oct. 8, 1815; died June 9, 1838. Lucy Jane,[7] b. Aug. 17, 1817; m. Col. Geo. Hastings, Sept. 25, 1844; d. Sept. 17, 1856.

viii. Jacob,[6] b. Jan. 22, 1771; died same day.

ix. Noah,[6] b. April, 10, 1774; died same day.

x. Abigail,[6] b. June 21, 1779; died Dec. 26, 1781.

152

Samuel Norton, son of Capt. John and Elisabeth (Thaxter) Norton, of Hingham, born Oct. 22, 1721; went to Abington about 1749; important man in town; selectman from 1756 to 1764, eight years. Married 1st, Mary, dau. of James Nash, Jan. 31, 1750; she died May 24, 1759; m. 2d, Mary,[5] dau. of Jacob[4] Porter, May 29, 1860. Children:

i. Mary, b. Mar. 7, 1752.

ii. Sarah, b. June 14, 1754; m. John Gurney.

iii. Elisabeth, b. Feb. 8, 1759.

iv. Benjamin,[6] b. Aug. 31, 1761; soldier in war of 1812; died in Abington, 1849, aged 88.

v. Samuel,[6] b. Aug. 31, 1761; twin with Benjamin; resided in Abington; selectman from 1798, 12 years; town clerk and treasurer from 1815, to 1820; Hobart's History of Abington, says he "was a conspicuous man in town;" he married Silence Hersey—"cried Oct. 1,

1786." He died May 29, 1826, aged 65. I have of their children: Samuel,[7] only son, b. Jan. 18, 1790; m. Mehetable Porter, Sept. 2, 1824. Mary Porter,[7] b. Dec. 6, 1793. Elisabeth,[7] m. Deane Reed, July 28, 1812.

vi. Jacob,[6] b. Sept. 26, 1762; died Dec. 13, 1763.

vii. Jacob,[6] b. Feb. 12, 1764. "Grad. Harvard College, 1786, with distinction, and at the time of his death, was the oldest surviving graduate of the College. He was ordained over the First Parish church, in Weymouth, Oct. 10, 1787, where he continued until 1824, when he resigned, and a few years afterward removed to Billerica, where he resided the remainder of his long life. He retained his mental and physical powers, to a remarkable degree, until past the age of 90; for the last year or two, he spent most of the time during the day reading, and without glasses, which he never used with exception of a short time, and then laid them aside as useless." (Boston Daily Advertiser.) He died in Billerica, Sunday morning, Jan. 17, 1858, aged 93 years 11 months 5 days. He married Elisabeth Cranch, Feb. 11, 1789. She was dau. of Richard and Mary (Smith) Cranch; died Jan. 25, 1811, aged 47. She was the grand-daughter of Rev. William Smith, of Weymouth, and niece of the wife of President John Adams. I find in Weymouth town records, the following: "Rev. Jacob Norton, of Weymouth, and Miss Hannah Bowers, or Barrows, intend marriage, Feb. 20, 1813." His children were: Richard Cranch,[7] bap. Mar. 14, 1790; graduated Harvard College, 1808; died 1821; he was room-mate and class-mate, with Dr. Ebenezer Alden, of Randolph. William Smith,[7] bap. Jan. 1, 1792; graduated Harvard College, 1812; died, 1827. Edward,[7] bap. Oct. 25, 1795; "1814, Sept. 29, died, my son Edward, age 19, of lung fever, in Dartmore Prison, England." Jacob Porter,[7] bap. Dec. 22, 1793. "1818, Oct. 4, Jacob P. Norton, (my son) married to Harriet Holbrook, both of Boston." Thomas Boylston Adams,[7] bap. Feb. 17, 1799. Elisabeth,[7] bap. May 30, 1802. Mary Cranch,[7] bap. May 20, 1804. Lucy Ann,[7] bap. May 18, 1806. I copy from First Parish records of Weymouth, the following: "The Rev. Jacob Norton, became a Unitarian, which was the chief cause of his dismission. For the last three years, he has professed to be a Universalist * * *

Weymouth, Feb. 24, 1843." It is due to him to say, that the neighboring Orthodox clergymen "thought highly of him as a man, while deploring his change of belief."

viii. Bela,[6] b. July 21, 1765.

ix. Hannah,[6] b. Feb. 13, 1767; m. Woodbridge Brown, son of Samuel and Deborah (Perry) Brown, born Feb. 1, 1763; resided in Abington. Children: Nancy,[7] b. Oct. 6, 1786. Walston,[7] b. Aug. 20, 1788; m. Betsey Wales. Elisabeth T.,[7] b. Aug. 3, 1790. Samuel N.,[7] b. Jan. 9, 1794; m. Priscilla S. Beal. Austin,[7] b. April 4, 1798; m. Abigail Noyes. Bela,[7] b. Sept. 23, 1803; m. Ruth Whiting.

x. Noah,[6] b. Mar. 7, 1775; m. Sarah Noyes, in Bridgwater, 1803; had daughter Maria,[7] who married Rev. Matthew Kingman, Sept. 8, 1835; she died Feb. 18, 1851. Noah Norton died. His widow m. 2d, Seth Snow.

xi. Mary,[6] b. Oct. 22, 1777.

153

Jacob[5] Porter, of Jacob[4] Porter, b. July 23, 1737; lived in Abington and Worthington; married Rachel, dau. of Daniel and Ruth (White) Reed, Jan. 6, 1763; she born Dec. 20, 1740; died 1818. He died 1820, aged 84. Children, the first seven of whom were born in Abington, the others in Worthington:

373. i. Jacob,[6] b. Oct. 28, 1764; killed by a fall from a tree, when a boy.

374. ii. Rachel,[6] b. Mar. 17, 1765; m. Dea. Abel Packard, Jr., of Cummington, Oct., 1808; where she died Aug. 31, 1851; no children.

375. iii. Abigail,[6] b. April 3, 1768; m. Adam Packard, Nov. 11, 1790.

376. iv. Asa,[6] b. Jan. 25, 1771; m. Betsey Huntington, Mar. 23, 1797.

377. v. Hannah,[6] b. Jan. 18, 1775; m. Sackett.

378. vi. Daniel,[6] b. April 20, 1775; m. Bates.

379. vii. Mary,[6] b. June 4, 1777; m. Sigourney.

380. viii. Ruth,[6] b. April 3, 1780; unmarried; died Oct., 1829.

381. ix. Jacob,[6] b. Oct. 15, 1782; m. Hannah Burr.

382. x. Olive,6 b. Oct. 3, 1786; m. Moses Fiske, 1820.

154

John[5] Porter, of Jacob[4] Porter, b. April 24, 1740; lived in Abington; married Deborah, daughter of Lieut. Nicholas Shaw, Jan. 17, 1765. She died 1828, aged 88. He died Dec. 13, 1823, aged 84. Children:

383. i. Deborah,[6] b. Dec. 6, 1765; m. Jonathan Reed.
384. ii. John,[6] b. July 26, 1767; m. Susanna Groves, 1790.
385. iii. James,[6] b. Oct. 11, 1768; removed to New York state.
386. iv. Elias,[6] b. June 26, 1770; do.
387. v. David,[6] b. Jan. 22, 1773; m. Polly Ford.
388. vi. Noah,[6] b. Jan. 11, 1775.
389. vii. Mary,[6] b. Sept. 24, 1780; m. Adam Reed, Jr., Feb. 25, 1819; and had one child, Mary Porter, b. Sept. 16, 1823.

155

Adam[5] Porter, of Jacob[4] Porter, b. Nov. 6, 1742; grad. at Harvard College, 1761; no profession. Removed to Cummington, Mass., May 25, 1773; married 1st, Deborah Gannett, of Bridgewater, Oct. 3, 1776, by Rev. Samuel Angier; she was the daughter of Capt. Joseph and Betty (Latham) Gannett, born 1755; died Sept. 3, 1805, aged 51. Married 2d, widow Sarah Hunt, Sept. 9, 1806, by the Rev. Asa Meech, at North Bridgewater; he died Apr. 24, 1820; she died in Abington, Nov. 12, 1838, aged 84. Children:

390. i. Betty,[6] b. Thursday, July, 30, 1778, about 2 o'clock in the morning; died Nov. 9, 1785, about 9, A. M., aged 7 years, 3 mos. and 10 days.

391. ii. Deborah Gannett,[6] b. Saturday, July 15, 1780, about 3 o'clock P. M.; died Dec., 1822.

392. iii. Nabby,[6] b. Friday, May 7, 1782, about 3 o'clock P. M.; m. Dea. Byram Green, of Sodus, N. Y., she died July 19, 1815.

393. iv. Adam Gannett,[6] b. Sunday, Feb. 22, 1784, about 7 o'clock A. M.

394. v. Jacob,[6] b. Thursday, Feb. 23, 1786, about 1 o'clock P. M.; died about 9 A. M., aged about 1 day.

(See pages 49 and 199.)

Noah[5] Porter, of Jacob[4] Porter, born at Abington, Aug. 16, 1744; removed to Cummington, about 1773, and died there about 1776, as his son William was four years old at the time. He was said to have been the first person who died in that town from Abington. His farm, upon which he was buried, was the estate of the late William C. Bryant. He married Mary, daughter of William Norton, in Abington, Feb. 2, 1766. She married 2d, Lieut. Stephen Warner, and died in Westmoreland, N. Y., 1826. Children, all born in Abington:

i. Noah,[6] born April 17, 1767.

ii. Mary,[6] born May 18, 1769; died in Burlington, Vt., Oct. 2, 1846; married at Abington, (Town Records,) Jan. 19, 1789, Dr. John Pomroy, son of Francis, Jr., and Sarah (Nye) Pomroy, of Middleborough; born May 9, 1764; removed to Burlington, Vt., where he died Feb. 19, 1844. Children, all born in Burlington: Cassius Francis,[7] was a promising physician and surgeon, died unmarried, March 23, 1813. Rosamond Porter,[7] married 1816; died without surviving children, Feb. 9 1819. John Norton,[7] resides in Burlington, Vt., 88 years old; m. March 25, 1819, Lucia Loomis; she died Dec. 29, 1877, aged 78.

iii. Norton,[6] born 1771.

iv. William,[6] born Aug., 1773; baptised at Abington, Oct. 4. (Church Records.)

Noah[6] Porter, Jr., of Noah[5] Porter, born Abington, April 17, 1767; settled in Palmyra, N. Y., about 1790, where he died in 1814, leaving a name which is to-day spoken of in all that region with honor and respect. He married in Palmyra, 1793-4, Ruth Rogers, dau. of William and Ruth Hayward Rogers, of Rhode Island; she died 1821. Children, all born in Palmyra:

i. Cynthia,[7] b. Mar. 27, 1795; she died in Lewiston, Niagara Co., N. Y., Feb. 15, 1870; she married, Oct. 18, 1812, Dr.

Seymour Scovell; he born Lemster, N. H., July 25, 1785; died in Lewiston, N. Y., Feb. 12, 1852. Children: Thos. Porter,[8] born Palmyra, N. Y., Nov. 22, 1814; grad. Yale College, 1836; unmarried. Leander K.,[8] born Palmyra, Mar. 5, 1817; married Emeline Alice Ways, Jan. 17, 1839. Children, all born in Lewiston: Joseph Evans,[9] born Jan. 25, 1840; died May 31, 1841. Mary Evans,[9] b. Sept. 4, 1842; married at Lewiston, Sept. 6, 1865, Dr. Geo. P. Eddy, Jr. (Children, Catharine A.,[10] born Sept. 2, 1866. Seymour S.,[10] born Mar. 12, 1868. Leander K.,[10] born Jan. 13, 1872.) Leander Ways,[9] born Aug. 17, 1846; died Aug. 17, 1872. Cynthia R.,[8] born Oct. 22, 1821; married 1st, Phillip C. H. Brotherson, in Lewiston, Sept. 18, 1838; he died in Manchester, Mich., Sept. 18, 1852. One child Peter Porter,[9] born Aug. 18, 1839, in Lewiston; married in Galveston, Texas, Feb. 7, 1861, Caroline H. Kauffman; died in Galveston, June 22, 1874. (Children, all born there: Elisabeth C.,[10] born Jan. 21, 1862. John K.,[10] born June 17, 1864. Phillip Charles Hamilton,[10] born July 29, 1866. Peter Porter Seymour,[10] born Sept. 6, 1868. Andrew F.,[10] born Aug. 26, 1873; (died July 26, 1874;) married 2nd, W. W. Anstey, of London, Eng., Dec. 18, 1854. (Children, all born in Province of Ontario, Canada: Maria Theresa,[10] born Oct. 7, 1855. William C.,[10] born March 1, 1857. Isabella B.,[10] born May 30, 1859.) Maria R.,[8] born Feb. 8, 1824; married Henry F. Hotchkiss, April 18, 1843; he died Jan. 9, 1872; no children. Edwin,[8] twin of Maria R.,[8] died Aug. 13, 1824; and two other children,[8] who died in infancy unnamed.

ii. Norton,[7] born Aug. 15, 1797, in Palmyra; died in Youngstown, Niagara Co., N. Y., May 9, 1854; married Bathshua Sheffield, in Palmyra, 1826; she born June 8, 1796; died Jan. 25, 1873, in Youngstown. Children: Ruth,[8] born June 17, 1827; married Thomas Taylor, Feb. 14, 1850; no children; resides at Ontario Centre, Wayne Co., N. Y. Cynthia,[8] b. Dec. 2, 1828; died Feb. 23, 1854. Norton,[8] born June 25, 1830. Bathshua B.,[8] born May 7, 1833; married in Youngstown, Oct. 15, 1873, Wm. McCormick; she died Jan. 31, 1875. Mary Maria,[8] born June 26, 1838.

iii. William Rogers,[7] born Palmyra, N. Y., April 21, 1799; died in Adrian, Mich., Dec. 11, 1872; married Marina White, Nov. 26, 1823; she died March 28, 1877;

emigrated to Adrian, in 1834. Children: Cullen,[8] born Nov. 26, 1824; married Cynthia Hutchinson, Jan. 1, 1855. (Three children, Orson,[9] born Sept. 30, 1855; died Oct. 19, 1855. Lucius,[9]A born Jan. 6, 1857. Duane,[9] born Jan. 29, 1859.) Seymour,[8] born Dec. 11, 1826; married Mary Henica, July, 1851. (Children, Hattie,[9] born 1856; died 1870. Minnie,[9] born 1861.) Cynthia,[8] born Feb. 4. 1829; died Sept. 19, 1873; married Allen Warren, Dec. 12, 1849. (Children: Seymour,[9] born Feb. 24, 1851; married Mary Scott, Dec. 31, 1874. One child, Alvah,[10] born Sept. 9, 1877. Alice,[9] born May 30, 1852; married Albert Rood, Dec. 7, 1871. Children: Archie,[10] born April 30, 1874. Mabel,[10] born June 16, 1876.) Halsey,[8] born Jan. 4, 1839.

iv. Noah,[7] born June 12, 1801; married Amanda Lyndon, Oct. 1, 1834; removed to Michigan in 1835; wife died in 1865. Children: Noah,[8] born Aug. 1, 1835, in Lima, Washtenau County, Mich.; married Carrie Hewlett, May 10, 1865. (Children, all born in Leroy, Mich.: Alma,[9] born Aug. 30, 1866. Verner L.,[9] born Mar. 19, 1868. Robert N.,[9] born Aug. 4, 1869. Jesse R.,[9] born July 2, 1871. Clayton J.,[9] born Nov. 16, 1873.) Susan Amanda,[8] born Sept. 14, 1837, at Lima; married Charles E. Root, in Kalamazoo, Mich., March 29, 1864. (Children: Hattie C.,[10] born Feb. 24, 1865; died in Winfield, Henry Co., Iowa, Aug. 10, 1866.) Roby,[8] born Mar. 18, 1839, in Lima; married William B. McGowan, in Lansing, Mich., May 29, 1865, by Rev. H. B. Burgess. Rosamond,[8] born in Lima, Jan. 10, 1841; married A. B. Brown, in Lansing, April 23, 1866. Marina C.,[8] April 14, 1844, in Madison, Mich.; married George C. Champlain, in Lerpy, Mich., May 3, 1863. (Children: Alta E.,[10] (?) born May 9, 1864, in Leroy. Seymour P.,[10] born Sept. 29, 1866, in Leroy. Edith R.,[10] born July 12, 1873, in Crystal, Mich.; died Nov. 23, 1874.) Caroline E.,[8] born Nov. 23, 1845; died April 23, 1858, at Canton, Mich.

v. John[7] Pomroy, born Sept. 14, 1807; married Elisabeth Celestia Weston, Mar. 21, 1839, in Youngstown, Niagara Co., N. Y., by Rev. John Elliot; she daughter of William Andrews and Clarinda (Hathaway) Weston, born Pembroke, N. Y., Jan. 21, 1821. He went to Youngstown, in 1830, having been appointed Deputy Collector of Customs at that port, which office he held for nineteen years. Removed to Lewiston, N. Y.,1853; from 1864 to 1873, engaged in busines in the oil regions in Penn.; returned to Lewiston in 1873. One child, Cynthia Celestia,[8] born Oct. 16, 1842, in Youngstown, N. Y.

Norton[6] Porter, of Noah[5] Porter, born at Abington, 1771. (Page 82.)

William[6] Porter, of Noah[5] Porter, born Abington, Aug., 1773; baptised there Oct. 4, 1773. (Church Record.) Married Lydia Claghorn, in Palmyra, N. Y., 1797; she born Jan., 1780, in Williamsburg, Mass.; died in Macedon, N. Y., 1867; he died in Palmyra, N. Y., now Macedon, March, 1819. Children, all born in Palmyra, N. Y.:

i. Mary,[7] born Feb. 22, 1798; married Wm. Plunkett Richardson, Dec., 1815; she is now a widow, living in Lyons, N. Y., has six children, among whom is David P.,[8] b. May 28, 1833, a member of Congress.

ii. Salome,[7] born June 9, 1800; married John Lapham, Jan. 8, 1817; nine children. She is now a widow, living in Macedon, N. Y.

iii. Elisabeth C.,[7] b. July 4, 1802; married Joseph Noble, April 6, 1826; one child. She is now a widow, living in Brockport, N. Y.

iv. Joseph B.,[7] born Nov. 10, 1805; died 1815.

v. William C.,[7] born April 1, 1807; married —— Rapalje, 1830; he died in Albion, N. Y., Nov., 1867. Children: Abraham,[8] born 1830; died in infancy. Lydia,[8] born Macedon, 1834. Maria,[8] born 1837. Jerome,[8] born 1840; married in 1873, in Mankato, Minn., where he resides. William,[8] born Carlton, N. Y., 1842; married ——Getz, of Buffalo, N. Y., 1871; resides Detroit, Mich.

vi. Nancy F.,[7] born Jan. 26, 1810; married Abraham Lapham, April, 1826; eleven children. Resides in Pike, N. Y.

vii. Stephen W.,[7] born Aug. 12, 1812; married in 1838; died 1845. One child, Philetus,[8] born Carlton, N. Y., 1839; married 1876; resides in —— Ontario Co., N. Y.

viii. Lydia M.,[7] born Nov. 18, 1814; married Albert H. White, Nov. 21, 1832; had one child: Haller Porter,[8] born 1833; died 1834. Resides New York city.

ix. Rosamond W.,[7] born Jan. 16, 1817; married Edward L. Clark, 1837; she had five children, and died in Fentonville, Michigan, Feb., 1873.

156

Noah[5] Porter, of Jacob[4] Porter, b. Aug. 16, 1744; m. Mary Norton, in Abington, Feb. 2, 1766; she prob. daughter of Noah Norton; (?) the family removed to Cummington. The children of Noah Porter were:

394A. i. Noah,[6] b. Abington, Apr. 17, 1767.

394B. ii. Norton,[6] b. do., 1771.

iii. Mary,[6] "married, in Abington, Mass., 1789, Mary Porter, of Cummington, formerly of Abington, to Dr. John Pomroy;" he was afterward of Burlington, Vermont. After the death of Noah[5] Porter, his widow married— Warner, and by him had Stephen[7]; Nancy,[7] who m. Fobes; Lois[7] m. Frisbie; and a daughter who m. Dr. Baldwin. William Cullen Bryant owned the homestead of Noah Porter, and occupied it for his summer residence.

158

Hannah[5] Porter, of Jacob[4] Porter, b. Oct. 17, 1748; m. Isaac Tirrell, Jr., of Abington, Oct. 25, 1770. He was deacon of the church before the town was cut up into insignificance. They both died in Sherburne, Mass., on a visit to their daughter, Mrs. Wells—the father, Sept. 18, 1823, aged 78; the mother, Feb. 26, 1826, aged 77 years; and were both buried in the Tirrell family tomb, in Abington. Their children, all born in Abington, were:

i. Oakes,[6] b. Apr. 26, 1772; died Nov. 23, 1862, at Burlington, Mass. Lived in Boston from 1825 to 1858; m. Hannah Snell, of North Bridgewater, Sept. 15, 1805. She daughter of Issachar and Sarah (Hayward) Snell, born Jan. 1, 1781; died Nov. 27, 1861. Their children, all born in Abington: Mehetable,[7] b. June 13, 1806; died March 12, 1832. Charlotte,[7] b. Apr. 12, 1808; m. John Reed, of Roxbury, Mass., May 12, 1837; died Brooklyn, N. Y., July 2, 1874. Eliza A.,[7] b. Nov. 15, 1809. Jacob Porter,[7] b. Oct. 19, 1811; m. Feb., 18—; died in St. Louis, Mo., June 15, 1873. Hannah Snell,[7] b. July 3, 1815; m. Waitstill Hastings, of Brooklyn, N. Y., April 23, 1851; has two children—son and daughter. Willard,[7] b. June 9, 1817; died Boston,

7

July 5, 1854. Oakes,[7] b. May 31, 1820; resides Brooklyn, N. Y.; m. Augusta Maxwell, of N. Y., May 31, 1856; has one son. Henry,[7] b. July 2, 1823; m. Aug. 6, 1857, Louisa Klinefelter, of Pittsburg, Penn.; died in Bunker Hill, Ill., April 13, 1877, leaving four sons and two daughters.

ii. Mehetable,[6] b. March 1, 1774; m. Daniel Brown, of Plainfield, Dec. 1, 1791; she died Aug. 27, 1796, aged 23. She had two children—Charlotte,[7] b. Aug. 21, 1796, and Oakes Porter,[7] b. Aug. 21, 1796. After her decease; Mr. Brown m. second, Mahetable, daughter of Joseph Porter, of Stoughton, Mass. (See No. 342.)

iii. Mary,[6] b. Nov. 17, 1775; d. South Deerfield, Dec. 4, 1865, aged 90; m. Rev. Theophilus Packard, D. D., Feb. 9, 1800, in Abington. (See No. 372.)

iv. Hannah,[6] died July 28, 1780, aged 1 year 4 1-2 months.

v. Abigail,[6] b. April 26, 1780; m. Capt. Walter Wells, of Shelburne, Mass., June 6, 1807; she died April 12, 1859, aged 79; he died Nov. 30, 1853, aged 83. Children: Mary,[7] b. Apr. 3, 1800; unmarried. Abigail,[7] b. June 6, 1810; m. Ormond Newhall, of Conway, Mass. Eunice,[7] b. Jan. 21, 1813; unmarried; died Brattleboro, Vt., Mar. 1, 1869. Charles,[7] b. Feb. 8, 1815; died Oct. 8. Charles,[7] (again) b. Dec. 3, 1816; resides Shelburne, Mass.; m. Mary Smead. Jane,[7] b. Sept. 11, 1821; m. Joseph A. Stevens, of Brattleboro, Vt.

vi. Isaac,[6] b. May 23, 1782; resided in Boston; Aug. 17, 1849, probably m. Mary Keen, of Duxbury, Mass. Had sons George A., of Boston; and Isaac, Jr.; and dau. Sybil.

vii. Hannah,[6] b. Mar. 2, 1784; died Shelburne, Mass., May 11, 1867, aged 82; m. Dea. Ebenezer Fisk, of Shelburne; he died Dec. 25, 1846. Children: Clarissa Tirrill,[7] b. Feb. 18, 1811; m. Frank Mather. Francis Alvarez,[7] b. July 8, 1813; m. Ophelia Bardwell. Ebenezer,[7] b. Aug. 28, 1815; m. Elisabeth Smead. Pliny,[7] b. July 30, 1817; grad. Amherst College, 1840; taught school in Greenfield, Mass., and Bernardston, twenty years; then bought a farm in Shelburne, where he died, 1872. Daniel Taggart,[7] born Mar. 29, 1819; grad. Amherst Col., 1842; principal of Amherst Academy one year; grad. Andover Seminary, 1846; ordained minister of Belleville Congregational Church, Newburyport, Mass., Aug. 18, 1847, of which he is now pastor; Doctor of Divinity; married 1st, Eliza P. Dutton; 2d,

Rev. John[5] Porter, of Rev. John[4] Porter. Relating to him—a correspondent of the Brockton (Mass.) Gazette, of Dec. 26, 1878, probably Ellis Ames, Esquire, of Canton, gives the following:

"John Porter, Jr., after graduating at Yale, studied for the ministry, and used to preach occasionally and to teach school; the late Joseph Sylvester, Esq., stating to the writer many years since that he was one of his pupils. He was residing in the North Parish in 1779, when a call was made by the Continental Congress upon the state of Massachusetts to fill up their quota of fifteen battalions in the Continental army. Young Porter, then twenty-seven years of age, responded to the call, and procuring the necessary authority to recruit a company, undertook the work of enlistment in the four parishes of Bridgewater and in Easton. His efforts were successful, and at the election of officers he was chosen captain, and himself and company were mustered into the regular army. He was soon after appointed chaplain of the regiment, but at the same time retained command of his company. The writer has several times talked with one of the privates who enlisted in Capt. Porter's company in 1779, and with another soldier who was in the same regiment, both of whom spoke of him as a brave man and an efficient and enthusiastic officer. He was soon after promoted to the rank of Major, and in 1780, in the absence of the Colonel and Lieut. Colonel, he was for some time in command of the regiment.

One extremely hot day in August of this year, the army was on a forced march through New Jersey, and the soldiers suffered much from heat, dust and thirst; nevertheless as orders were pressing, the officers continued to push them forward as fast as possible. About one o'clock in the afternoon Major Porter's regiment came along to a place in the road where there were some shade trees; the men were covered with sweat and dust, and in their weariness they could not resist the temptation to cast themselves down in the cooling shade and take a few minutes' rest. Shortly after, Gen. Poor, of Exeter, N. H., who was in command of the brigade, rode up and ordered Major Porter to call up his men and proceed on their march. The latter, though sympathizing deeply with his soldiers, and knowing with them that a brief halt would furnish them with all the more strength for the remainder of the march, had no alternative but to issue the order given him, but not a man started in response. But a few minutes elapsed before Gen. Poor again rode up and thundered out to the regiment to fall in and move forward, at the same time bestowing upon their commander a variety of epithets and offensive comments becoming neither an officer nor a gentleman. The Major was not a man to take these insults unmoved, and addressing Gen. Poor said to him that if he were of equal grade and rank he should "hold him responsible" for the language he had used. Gen. Poor instantly replied that he would waive his rights and privileges as his superior officer, and the result was that he shortly after received from Porter a challenge to mortal combat which he promptly accepted, and the duel was fought at break of day the next morning. The seconds arranged that each should stand back to back, against the other, with loaded pistol in hand, each should advance five paces, fire over their shoulders at each other when the word should be given, then advance upon one another and finish the contest with swords. At the fire Gen. Poor fell, wounded in the back by the ball of his adversary. Major Porter, not wounded, instantly turned, drew his sword and advanced upon his foe, when the seconds interfered and stopped all further proceedings. Gen. Poor's wound proved fatal, and he died on the 8th of September following. The affair was hushed up as much as possible, but Major Porter was not long after relieved of his command in consequence. Rev. John Porter and all the family were greatly distressed by this conduct of one so near to them, and rarely made allusion to it. Indeed, it is not supposed that it was generally known among the people of the time.

Major Porter's accomplishments as an officer were widely known, and a few years after he was designated as aide-de-camp of Gen. Layfayette, and on the return of the latter to France at the conclusion of the Revolutionary War, accompanied him thither. On his return home, Major Porter used to narrate to his friends here, his introduction by Gen. Lafayette to Louis XVI, king of France, and to his queen, Maria Antoinette. He subsequently moved to the small island of Curacoa, in the West Indies, where he engaged in mercantile pursuits and where he probably died, though the time and circumstances of his decease were never known to his friends."

Carrie W. Drummond. Charlotte,[7] b. April 6, 1822; m. Francis Slater (?) Isaac Tirrill,[7] b. July 27, 1824; m. Hannah Parsons; and 2d, Rose Crosby. Henry Martyn,[7] b. July 21, 1827; m. Ellen Gale; died April, 1875. Levi Parsons,[7] b. Mar. 29. 1829; d. May 24, 1860.

viii. Sybil[6], b. Jan. 14, 1785; unmarried; died Nov. 5, 1815.

ix. Clarissa[6], b. Jan. 20, 1793; m. Zera Hawks, of Shelburne, Mass., 1827; she died July 5, 1871, aged 79 years; he died July 7, 1861; had one child, Isabel,[7] who married David O. Fiske, of Shelburne, Mass., and has a large family of children.

159

Seth[5] Porter, of Jacob[4] Porter, b. Nov. 24, 1752; removed from Abington to Cummington. Married 1st, Mary, dau. of Capt. Edward Cobb, Mar. 6, 1783; she born Aug. 1758; died April 2d, 1786, aged 29. Married 2d, Lois, dau. of Nicholas Shaw, May 7, 1789; she died May 23, 1819, aged 59. Married 3d, Elisabeth Leonard, May 22, 1821; she died July 23, 1831, aged 74. He died Nov. 25, 1834. Children:

395. i. Jacob,[6] b. Abington, Dec. 30, 1783; died Nov. 15, 1846.

396. ii. Seth,[6] b. do., Jan. 27, 1785; m. Polly Mitchell, June 22, 1819.

176

John[5] Porter, of the Rev. John[4] Porter, b. Feb. 27, 1752; fitted for college at Lebanon, Conn.; grad. Yale College, 1770; studied divinity, and preached a short time; when the Revolutionary war broke out, he received a Captain's commission, and went into the army; he was a good officer, and was soon promoted to rank of Major. He left the army a short time before peace was declared, went to the West Indies, and there died.

177

Olive[5] Porter, of Rev. John[4] Porter, b. May 23, 1753; m. John S. Crafts, Sept. 9, 1790; he son of Dr. John Staples Crafts; lived in North Bridgewater; he died July 14, 1849, aged 82; had one son.

397. i. Jonathan[6] Porter, b. Sept. 8, 1792; grad. Brown Univer., 1817; studied medicine; died 1822, aged 30 years.

178

Rev. Huntington[5] Porter, of Rev. John[4] Porter, b. March 27, 1755; grad. Harvard College, 1777; ordained minister at Rye, N. H., Dec. 29, 1784. He continued to preach there for upwards of fifty years. After he preached there forty-three years, Rev. Bezaleel Smith, a graduate of D. C., was ordained as colleague with him. He printed many of his occasional sermons. He married first, Susanna, daughter of Hon. Nathaniel P. Sargent, of Haverhill, some time Chief Justice of Mass. She died Feb., 1794, aged 30. He married, second, at North Hampton, N. H., March 30, 1797, Sarah, daughter of Gen. Jonathan Moulton, of Hampton, N. H., by Rev. Benjamin Thurston, who after the death of her father had married her mother, the widow of Gen. Moulton. She was baptised and married as Sally. She was born in Hampton, June 13, 1779, and died there Jan. 2, 1835. He died March 7, 1844. Children:

398. i. Samuel Huntington,[6] b. July 11, 1787.
399. ii. Nathaniel Sargent,[6] b. May 29, 1789.
400. iii. John,[6] b. Sept. 6, 1791.
401. iv. Caroline,[6] b. Oct. 23, 1793; died unmarried, at Roxbury, at age of 75.
402. v. Maria,[6] b. Feb. 12, 1798.
403. vi. Eliphalet,[6] b. Apr. 25, 1800.
404. vii. Oliver,[6] b. Mar. 3, 1802.
405. viii. Louisa,[6] b. May 18, 1803.
406. ix. Martha Ruggles,[6] b. June 11, 1805.
407. x. Susan Sargent,[6] b. April 12, 1807.
408. xi. Sarah Emery,[6] b. June 2, 1809.
409. xii. Olivia,[6] b. Feb. 15, 1811.
410. xiii. Huntington,[6] b. Dec. 4, 1812.
411. xiv. Emery Moulton,[6] b. April 1, 1815.
412. xv. Charles Henry,[6] b. Aug. 7, 1816; died same year.
413. xvi. Charles Henry,[6] } b. Sept. 19, 1817.
414. xvii. William Henry,[6] } b. Sept. 19, 1817.
415. xviii. Elvira,[6] b. Jan. 11, 1820.

179

Jonathan[5] Porter, of Rev. John[4] Porter, b. July 5, 1756; grad. Harvard College, 1777; studied medicine, and was a successful practitioner in Boston for a short time, and in the time of the Revolutionary war, (being single) was persuaded to go out as Surgeon of a twenty-gun ship, under Capt. Coffin, of Newburyport, and was never heard from afterward.

181

Rev. Eliphalet[5] Porter, D. D., of Rev. John[4] Porter, b. June 11, 1758; grad. Harvard College, 1777, with his brothers John and Huntington. Neither of the three were fined or censured for any delinquency during their college life. He was settled in the ministry at Roxbury, Mass., Oct. 2, 1782, and continued in the ministry there a little more than fifty-one years. He printed many of his sermons and occasional discourses. He was long connected with Harvard College, as one of the corporation and overseers. An honorable testimonial was given him after his decease, by the faculty. He was a sound and faithful minister. He married Martha, daughter of Major Nathaniel Ruggles, of Roxbury, Oct., 1801. They had no children. She died Dec., 1814; he died Dec. 7, 1833. His funeral was Dec. 11—Rev. Dr. Lowell, Rev. Dr. George Putnam, and Rev. John Peirce, D. D., officiating.

182

Mary[5] Porter, of Rev. John[4] Porter, b. Nov. 16, 1762; married Rev. Thomas[6] Crafts, Dec. 28, 1786; he son of Dr. John[5] S. Crafts, b. 1759; he son of Lieut. Moses[4] (son of Samuel,[3] of Samuel,[2] of Griffin[1].) Thomas[6], grad. Harvard College, 1783; settled as minister at Princeton, 1786, and at Middleborough, 1791. He died Feb. 27, 1819, aged 60; his widow died Jan. 4, 1843, aged 80. Children:

416. i. Mary Sybil,[6] b. Jan. 5, 1788; died unmarried.

417. ii. Thomas Prince,[6] b. July 8, 1789; master mariner; died unmarried, at Darien, Ga., 1817.

418. iii. Betsey,[6] b. June 13, 1791; m. Hon. Jesse Perkins, of N. Bridgewater, Nov. 9, 1815; she died 1870; he died May 7, 1857, aged 66. Children: Caroline B.,[7] b. Oct. 6, 1816. Thomas C.,[7] b. July 28, 1819. Mary P.,[7] b. Oct. 2, 1821. Frederic,[7] b. Nov. 5, 1823. Elisabeth,[7] b. Aug. 31, 1825.

419. iv. Sophia,[6] b. Nov. 21, 1793; m. Harvey Hartshorn, of Southbridge, Mass., Oct. 30, 1823.

420. v. Frederic,[6] b. June 5, 1797; grad. B. U., 1815; m. Hannah, dau. of Alfred Williams, of Taunton, Mass., Jan. 4, 1832; she b. Jan. 26, 1812; he died Apr. 20, 1874; they had six children.

421. vi. Eliphalet Porter,[6] b. Nov. 23, 1800; grad. Brown University, 1821; studied theology at Cambridge; minister East Bridgewater, 1828 to 1835; then at Sandwich, 15 years; afterward at Eastport, Me., from 1866 to 1876, when he resigned and removed to Brighton, Mass. He m. Augusta, daughter of John and Mary (Kendall) Porter, of Sterling, Mass., June 13, 1832. She born July 31, 1809; died at Eastport, Me., Jan. 8, 1876. Children: Emelia C.,[7] b. April 14, 1833. Charlotte A.,[7] b. Sept. 8, 1835. Ellen Isadore,[7] b. June 25, 1846; m. Rev. Edward J. Galvin, of Brighton, Mass., April 29, 1874, and died June 25, 1876. Anna Isabella,[7] b. June 25, 1846; m. Charles Fiske, Mar. 11, 1868.

188

Job[5] Porter, of Nicholas[4] Porter, Jr. Nash, in his manuscript history, says he "married in Marshfield, and had three children, and went away to sea and died."

190

Nicholas[5] Porter, of Nicholas[4] Porter, baptised, Abington, May 1, 1726; lived in Marshfield; marriéd Sarah Decrow, Dec. 27, 1749; may have had wife before her. (His widow married Ephraim Little, of Marshfield, Oct. 1, 1795.) Children: probably not in order.

424. i. Oliver,[6] m. Lucy Keene, Aug. 11, 1773.
425. ii. Charles,[6] married; lived Boston.
426. iii. William,[6] m. Margaret James.
427. iv. Isaac,[6] m. Sarah B. Hall, Oct., 1785.
428. v. James,6 m. Nabby Whitman.
429. vi. Amasa,[6] m. Margaret Hoag.
430. vii. Calvin,[6] died young, West Indies.
431. viii. Ruth,[6] m. Berry Eames, Oct. 28, 1773.
432. ix. Sarah,[6] m. Daniel Wright, May 9, 1777.

433. x. Lydia,[6] m. Jere Hatch, Nov. 22, 1778; moved Maine.
434. xi. Nabby,[6] m. Edward Jarvis, Feb. 3, 1793.
435. xii. Lucy,[6] m. Joshua Taylor, of Pembroke, Mar. 13, 1798.
436. xiii. John,[6] m. Ruth Stevens, Dec. 2, 1784.
437. xiv. Abigail[6].

191

Lucy[5] Porter, of Nicholas[4] Porter, b. Abington; probably married Ephraim Pratt, Jr., of Weymouth; pub. Jan. 12, 1760. Children:

Joseph,[6] b. Dec. 8, 1760.
Asa,[6] b. Dec. 5, 1766
Ephraim,[6] b. July 13, 1769.
Lydia,[6] b. Mar. 9, 1772.
Lucy,[6] b. Dec. 12, 1778.
Elisabeth,[6] b. Oct. 29, 1785.

203

Edward[5] Porter, of Abner[4] Porter, b. Abington, June 11, 1748. Cyrus Nash, in manuscript history of Abington, says he "went west."

204

William[5] Porter, of Abner[4] Porter, b. Sept. 27, 1750; lived in Abington, Mass. Married his cousin, Mary Cheesman, of Braintree, 1775; he died Feb. 15, 1824; his widow died 1836, aged 85. Child:

438. i. William,[6] b. 1779; died June 3d, 1803, aged 23.

205

David[5] Porter, of Abner[4] Porter, b. Abington, April 2, 1753; removed to Quincy. Married first, Lydia Harmon, of Braintree, June 21, 1777; married second, widow Hannah Trask. He died in Quincy, 1827; his will proved Feb. 13, 1827. Gave his wife Hannah use of homestead for life, and all indoor movables; after her death to go to her son, William Trask, and his heirs forever; and all personal except that, given to his mother; wife to be executrix. She gave bond for $10,000. Inventory shows real estate, $1,420; personal, $1,548. Widow died Nov., 1862; her will proved Feb. 28, 1863. Charles Hardwick, administrator. Her children named "Mary Hardwick, wife to Charles Hardwick; Jane J. Trask, deceased; Theodore Trask, of Quincy; John Trask, of Lynn; William H. Trask, grandson, of Quincy; Margaret King, of Boston, wife to Carmi E. King; also children of O. T. Rogers, deceased. Grand-children of deceased: Octavius A., Mary J., Frederick, Elisabeth, Henrietta, and Arthur, all of Milton."

206

Matthew[5] Porter, of Abner[4] Porter, b. Abington, May 20, 1755; lived in Abington; Plympton; Plymouth, N. H.; Cornish, Vt.; Leverett, Mass.; then to New York; probably Buffalo, where he died. He was at Abington, Mass., on a visit, in 1831, being then 76 years old, and weighing 289 pounds. Married 1st, Lucy Bryant, of Plympton, Mass.; married 2d, in Randolph, Mass. Children:

439. i. Matthew,[6] m. Caroline Merryfield, of Cornish, Vt. He removed to Buffalo, N. Y., where he died.
440. ii. David,[6] m. Jane Butler, of Farmington, Me.; removed to Cornish, Vt.
441. iii. Isaac,[6] b. Plymouth, N. H., Dec. 8, 1789; married.
442. iv. Ruth,[6] m. Dr. (William) Taylor, of Cornish, Vt.
443. v. Sarah,[6] m. Moses Emerson, of Hopkinton, Mass.; at one time lived in Cornish, Vt.
444. vi. Son,[6] died early.
445. vii. Son,[6] died early.

207

Abner[5] Porter, of Abner[4] Porter, b. Aug. 8, 1757; of Abington. Died of wounds received in the Revolutionary war.

209

Clifford[5] Porter, of Abner[4] Porter, b. April 6, 1762; married Mary; he died East Bridgewater, 1788. Had one child:

446. Bathsheba,[6] b. May 29, 1786.

210

Abijah[5] Porter, of Abner[4] Porter, b. Nov. 18, 1764; lived in Abington and Randolph; married, first, Elisabeth H. Paine, 1795; she died 1796, aged 29. Married second, Sally Woods, 1797. Married third, Betsey, of Israel Beals, Oct. 29, 1812. Children:

447. i. Child,[6] died 1796.
448. ii. Samuel,[6] by 2d wife.
449. iii. Sally,[6] by 2d wife, m. Clapp, of Scituate.
450. iv. Stillman,[6] by 3d wife—died Randolph, 1845, aged 25.
451. v. Betsey,[6] by 3d wife.

211

Mercy[5] Porter, of Thomas[4] Porter, b. March 24, 1741; married Lemuel Barber, of Weymouth; he was a soldier in the French War, 1758; probably removed to Chesterfield. "Lemuel Barber, of Chesterfield, married Mrs. Abigail Turner, in Weymouth, Feb. 25, 1790." Children born in Weymouth:

452. i. Hannah,[6] b. Nov. 15, 1762.
453. ii. Zacheus,[6] b. April 2, 1764.
454. iii. Thomas,[6] b. Mar. 27, 1768; m. Silence Whitmarsh, in Weymouth, Feb. 25, 1790.

213

Jonathan[5] Porter, of Thomas[4] Porter, b. Sept. 28, 1746; lived in Weymouth; married Hannah Burrill; pub. Apr. 17, 1773. Wife died 1825, aged 79 years; he died 1829. Children:

455. i. Mercy,[6] b. Mar. 28, 1774; died unmarried, 1849, aged 75.
456. ii. Hannah,[6] b. April 12, 1776; m. Isaac Williams, 1811.
457. iii. Lucy,[6] b. Aug. 31, 1777; died unmarried, 1852, aged 73.
458. iv. Molly,[6] b. Aug. 8, 1781; died unmarried, 1866, aged 84.
459. v. Thomas,[6] b. Oct. 5, 1783; died 1829, aged 45.
460. vi. Laban,[6] b. 1786; m. Deborah Thompson, 1806.

214

Emma[5] Porter, of Thomas[4] Porter, b. Weymouth; married Peter Pratt; pub. Dec. 26, 1772. Children:

Samuel,[6] b. Dec. 8, 1774.
Samuel,[6] b. Dec. 7, 1775.
Becca,[6] b. May 12, 1777.
Molly,[6] b. Sept. 22, 1779.
Jenny,[6] b. Nov. 2, 1782.

225

Molly[5] Porter, of Ezra[4] Porter, b. Jan. 26, 1753; married Samuel Pratt, of Weymouth, S. P., Dec. 3, 1770. Children:

Daniel,[6] b. Sept. 20, 1771.
Ezra,[6] b. Dec. 8, 1772.
Hannah,[6] b. Aug. 6, 1774.
Ezra,[6] b. Oct. 8, 1776.
Mary,[6] b. Sept. 29, 1777.
A child,[6] b. Sept., 1778.
Gideon,[6] b. Apr. 20, 1780.
David,[6] b. Mar. 6, 1782.
Caleb,[6] b. May 13, 1784.
Hannah,[6] b. May 6, 1785.

230

Ebenezer[5] Porter, of Ebenezer[4] Porter, b. Dec. 7, 1733; lived in Weymouth; married Tabitha Pratt; pub. April 7, 1754. She daughter of Ebenezer and Tabitha (Crane) Pratt, b. April 18, 1732. He died 1763: his will proved Oct. 7, 1763, names wife, Tabitha; children, Ebenezer, Ezekiel, Ruth, Jael, Tabitha, and Mary. (Widow married Dea. Jonathan Collier, from Hull, who came to live with her, by whom she had children born in Weymouth: Gershom, b. Jan. 13, 1765, who went to Farmington, Maine, with his half brother, Ezekiel, in 1790; Ruth, b. Nov. 17, 1766; Jonathan and Hannah, twins, b. July 13, 1769.) Children:

497. i. Jael,[6] b. Mar. 8, 1755.
498. ii. Tabitha,[6] b. Feb. 1, 1757.
499. iii. Mary,[6] b. Dec. 17, 1758.
500. iv. Ebenezer,[6] b. Nov. 25, 1760; soldier in the Revolutionary war, in which he died.
501. v. Ezekiel,[6] b. Nov. 10, 1762.
502. vi. Ruth.[6]

Of the daughters, one married Russell, and died in Farmington, Me.; one married Ezekiel Peirce, of Chesterfield, N. H.; and one married Johnson, of Putney, Vermont, and died there.

231

Mary[5] Porter, of Ebenezer[4] Porter, b. Dec. 15, 1739; married Abner Pratt, of Weymouth; pub. June 19, 1756; he son of Ebenezer, Jr. and Tabitha (Crane) Pratt, b. Jan. 11, 1736. Children:

503. i. Laban,[6] b. May 9, 1758; m. his cousin Lucy, daughter of Matthew Pratt, April 14, 1785, and had Lucy,[7] b. Aug. 16, 1785, and Norton[7].

Mary,[5] wife of Abner Pratt, died; and he married 2d, Margaret Humphrey, Dec. 19, 1758, and had children:

232

Ruth[5] Porter, of Ebenezer[4] Porter, b. Nov. 22, 1743; married Noah Tirrell, of Weymouth, Feb. 15, 1759; he son of John and Deborah (Whitmarsh) Tirrell, b. March 18, 1837. Children:

504. i. Noah,[6] b. Nov. 18, 1759; m. Lucy Bicknell, June 8, 1782. Children: Noah,[7] m. Susan Holbrook. Ezra,[7] m. Susan French; Lucy,[7] m. Isaac P. Sampson. Mary,[7] m. Caleb Joy. Ruth,[7] m. Jos. H. Whitehouse. Nathan,[7] died young.

505. ii. James,[6] b. Aug. 8, 1762; died unmarried.

506. iii. Levi,[6] b. June, 1772; m. 1st, Betsey Nash, daughter of Zadoc. Children, Ebenezer,[7] b. 1795; died soon. Jenny,[7] b. 1801, died 1802. Betsey,[7] m. Alexander Shaw. Ruth,[7] m. Reuben Tirrell, of Greenbush, N. Y. Bitha,[7] m. Lieut. Daniel Loud, his 2d wife. Elbridge,[7] m. Sophia Porter. Jane,[7] m. Theophilus Dame. M. 2d, widow Hannah Bates, and had by her, Levi,[7] and Rachel.[7]

507. iv. Ruth,[6] b. May 9, 1779.

242

Ebenezer[5] Porter, of Ebenezer[4] Porter, b. Taunton, July 24, 1728; resided in Taunton, Mass.; married Bethiah Codding, (or Crossman) Dec. 20, 1763. He died Feb. 5, 1792.

244

Samuel[5] Porter, of Ebenezer[4] Porter, b. June 4, 1733; resided in Taunton; married Esther, daughter of Thomas Lincoln, of Taunton; she b. Oct. 23, 1738; said to have been "sister of Abraham Lincoln, great-grandfather of President Abraham Lincoln." He died in Taunton, Jan. 10, 1800; his estate divided 1802. Children:

508. i. Bethiah,[6] b. Oct. 9, 1765; unmarried; died May 9, 1845.
509. ii. Samuel,[6] died 1839. Married.
510. iii. Lincoln,[6] m. Selah Lincoln; died 1828.
511. iv. Edmund,[6] b. May 27, 1774; died April 1, 1833.
512. v. Esther,[6] died young.

246

John[5] Porter, of Ebenezer[4] Porter, b. Taunton, Aug. 8, 1736; lived in Taunton. "John Porter, of Taunton, in Capt. Job Winslow's company, in French war, 1758; sheriff and tavern-keeper." "John Porter, Murrenite Episcopalian, in Taunton, 1787." Married Lydia ——; she born April 14, 1742; died Aug. 15, 1811; he died Oct. 8, 1817. Children, all born in Taunton:

514. i. Betsey,[6] b. Dec. 19, 1759; died Dec. 9, 1805.
515. ii. Jacob,[6] b. Mar. 26, 1762; died Aug. 12, 1796.
516. iii. Mercy,[6] b. Sept. 2, 1764; died Sept. 26, 1829.
517. iv. John,[6] b. Sept. 10, 1766; died July 6, 1807.
518. v. Lydia,[6] b. Sept. 26, 1768; died 1859.
519. vi. Leonard,[6] b. June 8, 1771; died Feb. 21, 1802.
519A. vii. William,[6] b. April 15, 1773.
519B. viii. James,[6] b. April 11, 1775; died April 26, 1777.
519C. ix. Mary,[6] b. Oct. 21, 1777.
519D. x. James,[6] b. Nov. 11, 1779; died Sept. 10, 1817.
519E. xi. Sarah,[6] b. July 9, 1783; died July, 1845.

247

Jacob[5] Porter, of Ebenezer[4] Porter, b. May 30, 1738; of Taunton; married Mary; he died about 1761. Estate settled next year, by brother Samuel. One child:

520. i. Jacob.[6]

250

Jonathan[5] Porter, of Joseph[4] Porter, b. Taunton, Sept., 1732; lived in Middleboro; married Mercy, daughter of William Redding, of Middleborough, May 12, 1761. He was in Capt. Henry Peirce's company, in Col. Cotton's regiment in the Revolutionary war. He died June 11, 1791, intestate, aged 58 years, 9 months; his widow born 1740; died July 22, 1833, aged 93. Their graves are on "the green," near the meeting house of First Church, in Middleborough. Children:

521. i. Peter,[6] b. Sept. 22, 1766; settled in New York state. Mar.
522. ii Zecheriah,[6] b. June 9, 1769; m. Priscilla Miller.
523. iii. Sarah,[6] b. Sept. 29, 1771; m. Dr. Friend Sturtevant, Apr. 25, 1793.
524. iv. Bathsheba,[6] b. Sept. 29, 1773; m. Edward Sparrow, Jr.
525. v. Deborah,[6] } b. Nov. 13,1778; m. Jona. Strong, New York.
526. vi. Sylvanus,[6] } married.
527. vii. Jonathan,[6] b. Jan. 21, 1785; unmarried; died West Indies, 1810.
528. viii. William,[6] b. Feb. 1, 1763.
529. ix. James,[6] m.
530. x. Mercy,[6] b. Mar. 8, 1762; m. Jacob Bennett.

251

Joseph[5] Porter, of Joseph[4] Porter, b. at Taunton; married Martha Rider, Mar. 11, 1760, of Middleborough. Children, born in Middleborough:

531. i. James,[6] b. June 5, 1760; died July 3, 1763.
532. ii. Martha,[6] b. Mar. 9, 1763.
533. iii. Joseph,[6] b. Mar. 6, 1765.

SIXTH GENERATION.

257

Martha[6] Porter, of John[5] Porter, b. Weymouth, July 31, 1755; married Lieut. Timothy Nash; pub. June 16, 1777; he was son of Job and Abigail (Haynes) Nash, of Weymouth, b. Oct. 9, 1759. Children, in part:

543. i. Timothy,[7] b. Nov. 13, 1777; prob. died Mar. 27, 1840, or Jan. 7, 1852.
544. ii. Silence,[7] b. Dec. 13, 1780.
545. iii. Sukey,[7] b. Jan. 2, 1783.
546. iv. Eliza,[7] bap. North Parish, Weymouth, June 29, 1800.

547. v. John Porter,[7] bap. North Parish, June 29; m. and settled at Weymouth Landing; he was a most worthy and exemplary citizen; deacon of the Union Congregational church, of Weymouth and Braintree, from Jan. 3, 1833, up to the time of his death, March 18, 1860. His son, Stephen W. Nash, one of the largest boot manufacturers in Weymouth, was elected deacon of the same church, Feb. 28, 1861.

258

Seward[6] Porter, of Nehemiah[5] Porter, b. Weymouth, Aug. 5, 1753; went with his father to Rindge, N. H.; thence to Falmouth, and afterwards settled at Freeport, Maine, at what is now Porter's Landing; he bought land of William Coolidge, of Waltham, Mass., in Falmouth, 1777. He married Eleanor, dau. of Elias Merrill, of Falmouth, Me., now Portland; she born May 14, 1759; died Nov. 22, 1833. He died in Freeport, Dec. 12, 1800. Children:

548. i. Joseph,[7] b. Falmouth, April 8, 1778.
549. ii. Samuel,[7] b. Falmouth, April 10, 1779.
550. iii. Joshua,[7] b. Falmouth, Nov. 1, 1781.
551. iv. Sarah,[7] b. Freeport, July 19, 1782.
552. v. Seward,[7] b. Freeport, July 24, 1784.
553. vi. Mary,[7] b. Freeport, April 5, 1786.
554. vii. Elias,[7] b. Freeport, June 17, 1789.
555. viii. William,[7] b. Freeport, Sept. 17, 1788.
556. ix. Ebenezer,[7] b. Freeport, May 19, 1790; unmarried; lost at sea in the "Dash," privateer.
557. x. John,[7] b. Freeport, Nov. 27, 1792.
558. xi. Charles,[7] b. Freeport, June 17, 1794.
559. xii. Jeremiah,[7] b. Freeport, Feb. 14, 1796; unmarried; lost at sea in the "Dash," privateer.
560. xiii. George,[7] b. Freeport, July 2, 1797.

262

Nehemiah[6] Porter, of Nehemiah[5] Porter, b. Scituate, Dec. 14, 1758; lived in North Yarmouth, Me., married Joanna Barber, of Gray, Me.; she born Mar. 25, 1764; died Mar. 31, 1854. He died Feb. 20, 1846. Children, all born in North Yarmouth:

580. i. Sylvanus,[7] b. Oct. 11, 1783; m. Sylvia Bartlett, 1809.

Susanna,[7] b. Aug. 24, 1785; m. John Hamilton, 1804.
. Lucy,[7] b. Sept. 21, 1787; m. Timothy Chase, 1805.
iv. Lydia,[7] b. May 30, 1789; m. Benj. Herrick, of N. Yarmouth, 1805.
584. v. Stephen,[7] b. June 16, 1791; m. Rebecca Cobb, Jan., 1816.
585. vi. John,[7] b. Oct. 7, 1793; m. Eunice Hicks, 1816.
586. vii. Charles,[7] b. June 10, 1794; m. Rachel Hamilton, 1816.
587. viii. Benjamin,[7] b. Dec. 10, 1796; m. Zeruiah Ring.
588. ix. Joanna,[7] b. Aug. 6, 1798; m. Wm. Stearns, Jr., 1817.
589. x. Mary,[7] b. Feb. 10, 1800; m. Benj. Cole, 1823.
590. xi. Seward W.,[7] b. June 3, 1805; m. Eliza Daniels, 1830.
591. xii. William Barbour,[7] b. Mar. 31, 1807; died unmarried, May 20, 1838.
592. xiii. Rufus,[7] b. April 25, 1810; m. Mary Favor, of North Yarmouth, Feb. 20, 1831.

263

Benjamin[6] Porter, of Nehemiah[5] Porter, b. in Scituate; lived in Freeport, Me.; married Hannah Sylvester, 1789—she in 18th year, he in his 26th; he died May 31, 1825; his widow died Jan. 13, 1850. Children:

593. i. Mahala,[7] b. July 15, 1790; died Oct. 26, 1850.
594. ii. Rebecca,[7] b. Mar. 15, 1792; m. Eleazer Pinkham; died Nov. 18, 1839.
595. iii. Hannah,[7] b. July 21, 1794; died 1860.
596. iv. Cyrene,[7] b. Mar. 8, 1796; died Aug. 24, 1858.
597. v. Patience,[7] b. 1798; died same year.
598. vi. Joseph,[7] b. Mar. 18, 1799; m. Eliza Houston, 1823.
599. vii. Sarah Morse,[7] b. Nov. 1, 1801; died June 3, 1852; m. John Hayes.
600. viii. Mary,[7] b. Nov. 1, 1803; m. Dea. Edward R. Titcomb, 1830.
601. ix. Eleanor,[7] b. Apr. 4, 1805; m. Sam. Fogg; died May, 1877.
602. x. Eliza,[7] b. Feb. 2, 1807; m. Enoch Pratt.
603. xi. Patience Sylvester,[7] b. Aug. 16, 1809; m. Theophilus Herrick.

266

Molly[6] Porter, of Nehemiah[5] Porter, b. in Scituate, Mass.; married Wm. Barbour, of Gray, Maine, and removed to Portland. Probably had Children:

John,[7] and Charles,[7] died unmarried.
William,[7] married Buck.
Mary,[7] married 1st, Leavitt; and 2d, Doctor Allen.

271

Betty[6] Porter, of Joseph[5] Porter, b. Apr. 25, 1764, in Weymouth; married John Ward Bates, Jan. 20, 1782; he was the son of Samuel and Hannah (Burrill) Bates, b. Apr. 4, 1759; resided in Weymouth. Children:

Ira,[7] Porter.[7]

272

Sarah[6] Porter, probably of Joseph[5] Porter, b. June 15, 1766; married David Dunbar, of Hingham, Oct. 15, 1797, by Rev. Daniel Shute; she died April 16, 1801. Children:

i. David,[7] } b. June 13, 1798; died March 13, 1799.
ii. Joshua,[7] } b. June 13, 1798; twin to David; removed to New Bedford, where he married and had a family.

David Dunbar m. 2d, widow Hannah Lane. He died Hingham, June 14, 1826, aged 57.

273

Joseph[6] Porter, of Joseph[5] Porter, b. June 19, 1768; of Weymouth; married; wife died 1805, aged 37 years. A son b. May 8, 1796; and a daughter b. Oct. 23, 1799; child died Aug. 25, 1800; births taken from record of Dr. Shute, of Hingham, Mass.

276

Mary[6] Porter, of John[5] Porter, b. Jan. 21, 1754; married Samuel Badlam, Jr., of Weymouth; pub. Oct. 1, 1773; he son of Samuel and Unity (Morse) Badlam, b. Oct. 20, 1749. Children:

John Porter,[7] b. June 11, 1775.
Mary,[7] b. Aug. 25, 1777.
Stephen,[7] b. April 4, 1779.

301

Samuel[6] Porter, of Josiah[5] Porter, b. Weymouth, Oct. 2, 1764; married Mehitable Vining, July 6, 1783. One child:

i. Lydia,[7] bap. S. Parish, 1785.

302

Deborah[6] Porter, of Josiah[5] Porter, b. Dec. 8, 1765; died 1853, aged 88. Estate administered upon by Noah Torrey, Mar. 11, 1854. Next of kin, Nancy Reed, Ruth Haines, Sarah Withington, Naomi Atherton, Richard Porter, Samuel Porter.

304

Eunice[6] Porter, of Josiah[5] Porter, b. Mar. 4, 1768; unmarried; resided in Boston last part of her life, and died there. In her will she left a sum of money in trust with the Bromfield Street Methodist Church, of Boston, "for the building of a Methodist church in South Weymouth, whenever there was sufficient encouragement for the undertaking."

305

Nancy[6] Porter, of Josiah[5] Porter, b. Weymouth, Oct. 3, 1770; married Jacob Reed, of Abington, Nov. 18, 1799; he son of Daniel and Mary (Turner) Reed, b. Sept. 12, 1762; he died Jan. 21, 1839. Children:

i. Bela,[7] b. Dec. 2, 1803; m. Joanna S. Lane. Children: Jacob,[8] b. April 5, 1827. Nancy,[8] b. Jan. 31, 1832; died young. Elisabeth Richmond,[8] b. Oct. 8, 1835.

ii. Ezekiel,[7] b. Oct. 14, 1810; m. Cephiza Studley, of Hanover; pub. Dec. 18, 1831; resides Abington; Children: Emily C.,[8] b. April 29,1832; died young. George T.,[8] b. May 31, 1834. Mary Turner,[8] b. July 29, 1838; died young. Mary A.,[8] b. Jan. 6, 1843; died young. Charles,[8] b. July 19, 1847.

iii. Jacob,[7] b. Mar. 7, 1801; died Aug. 1, 1819.

307A

Sarah[6] Porter, of Josiah[5] Porter, bap. South Weymouth, 1777; died Sept. 29, 1865, aged 95 years 3 mos. 6 days; married John Withington, of Dorchester. Children:

Josiah,[7] married, and had a daughter, who m. Luther H. Felton, of Newton and South Boston. John.[7] Sallie.[7] Eunice,[7] m. John Keyes, of Dorchester, Mass. Caroline,[7] m. Cheever. William,[7] unmarried.

310

Elias[6] Porter, of Micah[5] Porter, b. Jan. 14, 1769; lived in Weymouth; married Sarah Bates, 1792. Children:

626. i. Micah,[7] bap. S. P., Nov. 10, 1793.
627. ii. Daniel,[7] b. Sep. 6, 1796.
628. iii. Alfred,[7] b. Oct. 8, 1797.

319

William[6] Porter, of Micah[5] Porter, b. June 11, 1782; married Sally Jones, 1803-4; she dau. of Moses and Abigail (Tirrell) Jones. This family removed west; wife's sister, Charlotte Jones, went with them.

333

Betterus[6] Porter, of Samuel[5] Porter, b. East Bridgewater, Oct. 19, 1761; married Abner Gardner; pub. May 11, 1782, in Abington. Child:

Mehetable,[7] m. Jacob Reed, 1811. Children: Samuel P.,[8] m. Lemira D. Hurd, 1840. Timothy,[8] went west. Mehetable,[8] m. Alvan Porter, 1844. (See No. 1611.)

335

Ruth[6] Porter, of Samuel[5] Porter, b. in East Bridgewater, Feb. 1, 1766; married James Reed, of Abington, 1784; son of William and Silence (Nash) Reed; born Oct. 6, 1764. He died Oct. 30, 1855, aged 90 years, respected and beloved by all who knew him. Children:

638. i. Mehetable,[7] b. 1784; m. Samuel Porter. Children: Mehetable,[8] b. May 6, 1804. Ruth,[8] b. Dec. 24, 1810. (See 351.)
639. ii. Hannah,[7] b. March 12, 1786; m. Jacob Fullerton, of Abington. Children: Hannah,[8] b. Nov. 27, 1808. Betsey Jane,[8] James Reed,[8] Jacob,[8] and Timothy.[8]
640. iii. James,[7] b. Aug. 13, 1788; m. Mehetable Dyer, April 19, 1810; died Dec. 23, 1810.
641. iv. Jane,[7] b. June 10, 1791; m. Daniel Bates, Jan. 10, 1811. Children: Jane Gurney,[8] b. March 19, 1812. Emily,[8] b. Aug. 15, 1814. Daniel,[8] b. May 10, 1818. Mary Brown,[8] b. April 27, 1820. Eliza Ann,[8] b. June 16, 1822. Mr. Bates d. June 10, 1826.

642. v. Samuel,[7] Porter, b. May 4, 1793; died Sept. 9, 1815.

643. vi. Timothy,[7] b. March 22, 1796; died Oct. 17, 1815.

644. vii. Marcus,[7] b. Aug. 23, 1798. Known as Major Reed, a much respected and valued citizen of Abington (South), often in town office, and a most intelligent gentleman. Married Mehetable Jenkins, May 17, 1821. Children: Marcus,[8] b. Nov. 19, 1823; m. Jennette S. Sprout. James,[8] b. Feb. 26, 1831; m. Peddy W. Howland, Sept. 7, 1851. Timothy,[8] b. Sept. 25, 1826; m. Lydia Ann Bourne.

645. viii. Cyrus,[7] b. July 23, 1800; m. Mary Noyes, Nov. 12, 1829. Children: Cyrus,[8] b. Dec. 16, 1834. Samuel W.,[8] b. Dec. 15, 1837; m. Ada Norton.

336

Elisabeth[6] Porter, of Joseph[5] Porter, b. March 8, 1753; married Capt. Samuel Linfield, of Randolph, 1776; he was son of David and Hannah (Vinton) Linfield, b. April 28, 1755; died Feb. 23, 1827; his wife died Dec. 1, 1818, aged 64. Children:

646. i. John,[7] b. June 12, 1788; m. Mary Richards, April, 1801, she born June 24, 1782; died Dec. 28, 1871; he died Feb. 7, 1856. Children: Isaac,[8] b. Mar. 29, 1802; m. Harriet Webb, of Maine, Aug. 19, 1825; she born Aug. 10, 1805; died Mar. 10, 1875; no children. Maria,[8] b. Jan. 22, 1804; died May 4, 1805. Arad Thompson,[8] b. Mar. 25, 1806; m. Sallie (Burrill) Pratt, of So. Weymouth, Dec. 31, 1839; she born Dec. 18, 1817; they had four children. He died Dec. 7, 1866. John Porter,[8] b. Mar. 26, 1810; m. Louisa Fisher, of Walpole, Sept. 18, 1844; she born Mar. 19, 1823; had four children; died Jan. 29, 1871. He married 2d, Anna W. Richardson, of Boston, Jan. 1, 1872. Mary Richards,[8] b. May 18, 1818; m. John Mason, of Keene, N. H., Dec. 12, 1839; he born Mar. 19, 1814; one child.

647. ii. Betsey,[7] b. Aug. 29, 1781; m. Benjamin Richards, of Stoughton; he born May 2, 1779; died Nov. 24, 1853. She died Aug. 11, 1851. They had one son, Joseph Linfield,[8] b. Jan. 26, 1806; died Sept. 20, 1809.

648. iii. Hannah,[7] b. Jan. 23, 1785; m. Charles,[7] Bicknell, of Quincy, Feb. 16, 1809, his 2d wife; he son of Peter and Mary Bicknell, b. Feb. 24, 1783, in Weymouth; died July 17, 1813; she died Oct. 18, 1865. They had one

child, Joseph Palmer,[8] b. Dec. 17, 1810; m. Lois S. Dickerman, of Stoughton, May 7, 1835; she born Dec. 28, 1815; he died April 27, 1876; they had one child, Joseph Linfield,[9] b. 1842.

649. iv. Samuel,[7] b. Dec. 18, 1786; m. Lois Howard, Nov., 1812; she b. North Bridgewater, Mar. 23, 1789; died Dec. 26, 1846; he m. 2d, Elisabeth A. Phelan, Mar. 3, 1859; she born June 24, 1816; he died Mar. 18, 1865. Children by 1st wife: Charles Bicknell,[8] b. Mar. 9, 1815; m. Julia Ann French, of Stoughton, Nov. 24, 1836; she born Feb. 10, 1819; died Mar. 10, 1870—had nine children (one of whom is Elmer C.,[9] Linfield of Randolph.) Emeline,[8] born July 4, 1817; m. John Bennett, of Boston, Jan. 1, 1839; he born July 13, 1818.

650. v. Joseph Porter,[7] b. Sept. 17, 1794; died Nov. 5, 1818.

337

Joseph[6] Porter, of Joseph[5] Porter, b. June 10, 1754; lived in Stoughton. Married Milly Capen, Feb. 7, 1790; she dau. of Jonathan, Jr., and Jerusha (Talbot) Capen, born Sept. 10, 1757. He died May 21, 1832; had one child, died young.

338

Hannah[6] Porter, of Joseph[5] Porter, b. July 21, 1758; married Jonathan Battles, Sept. 4, 1783. He was son of John and Hannah (Curtis) Battles, b. East Stoughton, March 27, 1755; died there, Dec. 31, 1830. Mrs. Battles was a woman remarkable for her gentle disposition and handsome person. Her children had for her the most unbounded love and admiration. She died Nov. 10, 1827. Children:

652. i. Jonathan,[7] b. July 17, 1786; m. Mariah Dickerman, Apr. 4, 1811. She was daughter of Peter and Rebecca (Tilden) Dickerman, b. June 27, 1789; died June 10, 1867. He died Oct. 3, 1871. Children: Jonathan,[8] b. Sept. 7, 1812; resides Harrison Square, Boston; m. Lucy Pope, Aug. 25, 1840. Edwin,[8] b. May 22, 1814; resides Nashua, N. H.; m. Josephine Curtis, Sept. 14, 1843. Mariah Dickerman,[8] b. March 25, 1816; m. Richard Stevens, of Randolph, Nov. 25, 1852. Winslow,[8] b. Sept. 30, 1818; resides Randolph—a gentleman much respected by his acquaintances; has been a member of the General Court, and held other important offices. Mary,[8] b. March 11, 1821; m. Abram

Mead, of Braintree, Mass., Sept. 10, 1845. Amory,[8] b. June 1, 1823; grad. Harvard College, 1850; is the well known Universalist clergyman, of Bangor, Me.; m. Pamelia A. Barker, May 25, 1854.

653. ii. Hannah,[7] b. May, 1788; m. Hosea Osgood, of Stoughton; had son Hosea[8]; she died Jan. 24, 1867.

654. iii. Joseph,[7] b. July 27, 1790; m. Judith Baxter, daughter of Ahaz and Judith (Baxter) French, of Braintree. He lived from 1811 to 1832, in Dorchester; from 1832 to 1841, in Lowell; afterward in Andover, and Derry, N. H., where he died Aug. 17, 1846. He and his brothers Benj. and Cyrus, were cotton manufacturers for more than 30 years; his wife b. Feb. 20, 1797; died July 5, 1840. Children: Charles French,[8] b. Dorchester, Apr. 5, 1818; m. Elisabeth O. Blake, of Epping, N. H.; had charge of the Atlantic Cotton Mills, of Lowell, many years; he died Nov. 16, 1870. Frank Fobes,[8] b. Dorchester, Feb. 12, 1820; m. Emily G. Shattuck, of Springfield; resides in Lowell, where he has been connected with the Massachusetts Cotton Mills, for more than 30 years. Joseph Porter,[8] b. Dorchester, April 23, 1822; m. Sarah, dau. of Gen. Henry K. Oliver, of Salem; resides in Lawrence, and has charge of the Atlantic Cotton Mills. Emeline A.,[8] b. Dorchester, Oct. 4, 1825; m. David Nichols, a native of Bath, Eng., May 24, 1855; resides Lowell. Frederic B.,[8] b. Dorchester, Dec. 16, 1828; resides Lowell. Marietta J.,[8] b. in Lowell, July 5, 1840.

652A. iv. Benjamin,[7] b. July 27, 1790; twin with Joseph; lived many years in New Market, N. H.; afterwards, Lowell and Chelmsford, Mass., where he died, Feb. 17, 1858; he m. Charlotte Smith, who was living in Lowell, 1876, in her 83d year; they had four sons and three daughters.

653A. v. Betsey,[7] b. July 11, 1792; died Oct. 1, 1795.

654A. vi. Frank,[7] b. May 14, 1794; died Milledgeville, Ga., July 12, 1819.

655. vii. Cyrus,[7] b. Aug. 20, 1796; m. Eliza Morton; resided New Market, N. H., in Lowell, Tewksbury, and Easton, Mass., where he died April 12, 1872; his widow died Jan. 2, 1873.

656. viii. Elisabeth,[7] b. Aug. 20, 1799; m. Lemuel Drake, of Stoughton, Nov. 20, 1820. Children: Frank Battles,[8] b. Nov. 23, 1823; died Aug. 24, 1825. Hannah Porter,[8]

b. Nov. 17, 1825; M. Augustus Gill, of Canton, Sept. 29, 1840, (see number 676.) Martha Ann,[8] b. Jan. 3, 1828; died Feb. 11, 1828 Louisa,[8] b. Mar. 23, 1829; m. Jonathan S. Drake, June 16, 1841. Cyrus Battles,[8] b. Aug. 24, 1831; died Mar. 5, 1832. Susan Harlow,[8] b. July 18, 1833. Lemuel Francis,[8] b. Sept. 13, 1835. Mr. Lemuel Drake, died July 19, 1870; Mrs. Drake is still living, (1878.)

339

Capt. Robert[6] Porter, of Joseph[5] Porter, b. Bridgewater, March 30, 1762; farmer; resided Stoughton, Mass.; captain of militia; married Elisabeth Gay, June 5, 1794; he died Aug. 18, 1835; his will proved Sept., 1835, names wife Elisabeth, sons Robert, John, Joseph, daughters Sally and Fanny; his widow died 1852; her will, proved Jan. 24, 1852, names daughters Sarah Clark and Fanny Tower, and sons Robert and John. Children:

657. i. Robert,[7] b. Feb. 25, 1795; d. July, 1797.
658. ii. Robert,[7] b. Dec. 19, 1798; m. Fanny Capen.
659. iii. John,[7] b. Dec. 25, 1800; m. Mehetable B. Kingman.
660. iv. Joseph,[7] b. May 11, 1805; m. Martha Edson.
661. v. Betsey,[7] b. Feb. 25, 1797; unmarried; d. Jan. 6, 1827, aged 30.
662. vi. Sally,[7] b. Dec. 16, 1806; m. Franklin Clark.
663. vii. Fanny,[7] b. Oct. 2d, 1808; m. Joseph Tower.

340

Isaac[6] Porter, of Joseph[5] Porter, b. Bridgewater, Feb. 23, 1765; admitted N. Bridgewater Church, in 1780; resided in Middleborough and Bridgewater; surveyor highways in Bridgewater, 1797. He married Susanna, daughter of Reuben and Anna (Perkins) Packard, of Bridgewater; she was a woman of remarkable energy and perseverance of character, and succeeded in bringing up her large family in a most respectable manner, and the children were worthy of such a mother. She was b. Dec., 1763; died Oct. 29, 1841, aged 77. Her death is recorded in Middleborough town records. Their children, of whom probably the first five were born in Middleborough, and the last five in Bridgewater:

664. i. Susanna,[7] b. April 17, 1788; m. Galen Thompson, in Middleborough, Jan. 1, 1807; died Jan. 16, 1808.
665. ii. Isaac,[7] b. Apr. 20, 1790; died Aug. 9, 1815.
666. iii. Sybil,[7] b. Apr. 13, 1792; m. Ichabod Noyes, 1820; she admitted first church, Middleborough, April 3, 1808, as "dau. of Isaac Porter, of Halifax," and dismissed to Plainfield, 1838, where she died 1841, without children.
667. iv. Rhodolphus,[7] b. Jan. 25. 1794; m. Sarah F. French, 1820.
668. v. Reuben,[7] b. Mar. 23, 1798; m. Rhoda Curtis, 1822.
669. vi. Martin,[7] b. July 21, 1800; m. Rebecca A. Reed, 1823.
670. vii. Samuel,[7] b. May 12, 1796; m. Sally Gill, 1817.
671. viii. Ira,[7] b. April 5, 1803; m. Eulatia Belcher, 1829.
672. ix. Galen Thompson,[7] b. Nov. 5, 1807; m. Mary E. Fletcher, 1829.
673. x. Anna,[7] b. Apr. 20, 1805; m. Wm. W. Cushing, 1827.

341

Content[6] Porter, of Joseph[5] Porter, b. Feb. 5, 1767; married 1st, William Glover, of Canton, July 1, 1780 (?) he born Stoughton, July 17, 1759; died Mar. 23, 1788, aged 29. They had one son:

674. i. William Glover,[7] Jr., born 1787, who died Aug. 28, 1807, aged 29.

She married 2d, Benjamin Gill, of Canton, about 1790; she died April 26, 1816, aged 50. Children by Mr. Gill:

675. ii. Benjamin,[7] b. May, 1693; m. and went to Iowa, and died there in Jan., 1866.
676. iii. James,[7] b. Apr. 10, 1795; m. Miriam French, and had one son Augustus Gill,[8] Esq., of Canton; m. Hannah P. Drake, of Stoughton, Sept. 29, 1840. (See No. 656.)
677. iv. Sally,[7] b. July 5, 1797; m. her cousin Samuel Porter, Sept. 1, 1817; went to Canton, Ill.; she died in St. Louis, Mo., Oct. 18, 1851. (See No. 670.)
678. v. William Glover,[7] b. Nov. 9, 1806; m. Susan Field, of Dorchester; m. 2d time; died 1814.

342

Mehitable[6] Porter, of Joseph[5] Porter, b. Apr. 5, 1769; married Daniel Brown, of Abington, 1797; he son of Samuel and Deborah (Torrey) Brown, born Dec. 31, 1769—(his second wife; his first, Mehitable Tirrell. Children: Charlotte, b. Apr. 2, 1793; Oakes P., b. Aug. 21, 1796.) Children of Daniel and Mehitable (Porter) Brown, were:

679. i. Daniel Emery,[7] b. Apr. 25, 1798.

680. ii. Joseph Porter,[7] b. Dec. 23, 1801; m. Mary Porter. Child: Charlotte A.,[8] b. Mar. 3, 1830, who m. William Noyes.

681. iii. Mehetable,[7] m. Cyrus Brown.

682. iv. Samuel W.[7]

683. v. Cyrus Livingston,[7] b. Sept. 5, 1812; married.

343

Lebbeus[6] Porter, of Joseph[5] Porter, b. in Stoughton, Apr. 22, 1771; resided in Stoughton and Wrentham. An honest, upright christian husband, father and citizen. Married 1st, Polly, daughter of Thomas and Susannah (Fisher) Brastow, of Wrentham, Mass., Dec. 4, 1794; she was b. Sept. 5, 1773; died June 2, 1810. Married 2d, Nancy Hall, Apr. 23, 1812; died Feb. 27, 1815. Married 3d, Nancy King, daughter of Samuel King, Aug. 19, 1816; she died Dec. 31, 1822. Married 4th, Mrs. Roxa Day, Nov. 28, 1839; she died Jan. 8, 1852. He died April 17, 1848, aged 77 years. Children:

684. i. Polly,[7] b. in Stoughton, Sept. 20, 1797; unmarried; died 1838.

685. ii. Martha B.,[7] b. in Stoughton, Sept. 28, 1795; unmarried.

686. iii. Whitcomb,[7] b. in Stoughton, Mar. 10, 1799; m. Susan B. Hunt.

687. iv. Joseph,[7] b. Wrentham, Dec., 19, 1800; m. Mary Stetson.

688. v. William Glover,[7] b. Wrentham, Sept. 24, 1802; m. Hannah Torrey.

689. vi. Elisabeth Burrill,[7] b. Wrentham, June 24, 1804; m. Ellis Pond.

690. vii. Caroline,[7] b. Wrentham, May 7, 1806; m. Rev. William Harlow.

691. viii. Thomas Brastow,[7] b. Wrentham, Jan. 17, 1808; m. Emily Vining.

692. ix. Susannah Fisher,[7] b. Wrentham, April 22, 1810; m. Isaac B. Warren.

693. x. John Hall,[7] b. Wrentham, Feb. 16, 1815; m. Mehetable H. Parker.

694. xi. Nancy King,[7] b. Wrentham, July 18, 1817; m. Dr. L. W. Sherman.

695. xii. Harriet Everett,[7] b. Wrentham, Oct. 21, 1821; unmarried.

696. xiii. Samuel King,[7] b. Wrentham, Dec. 14, 1822; m. Sarah Ann Gilman.

344

Col. Cyrus[6] Porter, of Joseph[5] Porter, b. 1774; resided Stoughton; farmer; was colonel of the regiment; much in public affairs, and highly respected. He m. 1st, Rebecca, daughter of Capt. William and Mary (Perkins) French, 1800. M. 2d, Sept. 8, 1835, widow Martha Alden, of Calvin Alden, and daughter of Ebenezer Hayden, of Stoughton. He died May 29, 1855, aged 80 years; his estate settled Oct. 6, 1855; children named in the settlement—Alvira, Cyrus, Luther, William, Mehitable, Rebecca, and Eliza Ann. Children:

697. i. Olive,[7] b. Oct. 16, 1800; m. Caleb Copeland, Jr., 1821.
698. ii. Ahira,[7] b. Nov. 9, 1801; m. Rachel D. Swan, 1826.
699. iii. Rebecca,[7] b. Nov. 11, 1803; died May 25, 1804.
700. iv. Cyrus,[7] b. June 12, 1807; m. Eliza J. Dunbar, Apr. 30, 1837.
701. v. Luther,[7] b. Dec. 18, 1814; m. Lucy Talbot, 1836.
702. vi. Mehitable,[7] b. Dec.3,1808, m. Ezra Churchill, of Stoughton.
703. vii. Eliza Ann,[7] b. Apr. 5, 1829; m. Wm. Hall, of North Bridgewater.
704. viii. William French,[7] b. Jan. 23, 1823; m. Harriet Sears, 1847.
705. ix. Rebecca,[7] b. 1805; m. Marcus Copeland, June 6, 1826.

346

Lydia[6] Porter, of Ebenezer[5] Porter, b. in Abington, 1758; married Joseph Beal, of East Bridgewater, Oct. 29, 1774; he was a son of Jonathan and Abigail (Harlow) Beal, b. 1752; he removed to Plainfield, Mass., in 1779, where he is known as the "Mountain Miller." Many years ago, Rev. William A. Hallock wrote a tract for the American Tract Society, (No. 254) giving an account of his life, under the name of the "Mountain Miller," which has had an immense circulation. I am indebted to it for much information relating to Mr. Beal. Pecuniary embarrassments induced Mr. Beal, in 1779, to provide for himself and family a new home, and he accordingly removed to Plainfield, where his axe soon laid open a spot sufficient to build thereon a house. In 1789, a year of great scarcity of provisions, in the absence of himself and wife, his house was burned, and nearly all his store of provisions he had laid in,—thus losing the fruits of nearly ten years of toil and labor. This great loss induced him to seek the consolations of religion, and he was about that time converted, and in 1791, publicly consecrated himself to the cause of Christ, by uniting with the Congregational Church, which had been formed in the district where he lived. His was a beautiful, christian, manly life; he was especially active and useful in visiting the sick and afflicted. In all the circumstances of his life, his christian course was remarkably uniform; no calamity on the one hand, however severe, depressed his spirits; nor on the other, did any scene through which he passed, greatly elate them. He died suddenly July 20, 1813, aged 61, with no opportunity to add anything to that best evidence of his good estate, "a life of devoted piety." His wife died on the second day after his decease, July 22, 1813. At one time previous to 1800, Mrs. Beal came from Plainfield to Abington with a horse and carriage, and carried her father and mother home with her on a visit. Children:

Samuel,[7] b. Sept. 26, 1775; died June 30, 1851. Joseph,[7] b. July 3, 1778. Robert,[7] b. Dec. 7, 1780; died July 2, 1844. Lydia Loraine,[7] b. May 19, 1787; died Dec. 4, 1804. Polly,[7] b. April 13, 1789; died July 30, 1810. Louisa,[7] b. Jan. 4, 1799.

347

Polly[6] Porter, of Ebenezer[5] Porter, b. Bridgewater, Oct. 8, 1760; married Capt. Joseph Joy, of Abington, and Plainfield; she died 1826. Children:

713. i. Clarrissa,[7] b. Feb. 21, 1788; died Sept. 26, 1856.
714. ii. Leonard,[7] b. Mar. 14, 1790.
715. iii. James,[7] b. Sept. 1, 1793; m. Mary Whiting, dau. of Dan- Whiting; he died June 22, 1826.
716. iv Polly,[7] b. May 10, 1796.
717. v. Merilla,[7] b. Oct. 8, 1798; died Dec. 19, 1799.
718. vi. Merilla,[7] b. Aug. 20, 1800.
719. vii. Electa,[7] b. Feb. 11, 1803.

348

Olive[6] Porter, of Ebenezer[5] Porter, b. Bridgewater, Jan. 23, 1763; married Benj. Pool, of Abington, May 17, 1786; he born Feb. 6, 1765; died 1821. Children:

Molly,[7] b. Feb. 1, 1787. Benjamin,[7] b. July 7, 1789. Lydia,[7] b. April 20, 1791. Olive,[7] b. July 24, 1795. Watson,[7] b. Sept. 4, 1798.

350

Ebenezer[6] Porter, of Ebenezer[5] Porter, b. Abington, May 8, 1769, and lived there; married Betsey Reed, Jan. 12, 1792; she dau. of William and Silence (Nash) Reed, born Feb. 23, 1760. He died 1860, aged 92. Children:

725. i. Betsey,[7] b. Oct. 17, 1792; m. Christopher Dyer, Jan. 10, 1810.
726. ii. Lydia,[7] b. Feb. 16, 1800; m. Edward Vinton, Feb. 16, 1820.
727. iii. Sarah,[7] b. Feb. 16, 1803; m. Spencer Vining, Oct. 14, 1824.

351

Samuel[6] Porter, of Ebenezer[5] Porter, resided Abington. (See 638.) Married Mehitable, dau. James and Ruth Reed, May 10, 1801. He died Oct. 28, 1864, aged 84 years 9 mos. 24 days; she died Sept. 8, 1846, aged 62 years 5 months. Children:

728. i. Mehetable R.[7] b. May 6, 1804; m. Sam. Norton, Sept. 2, 1824.
729. ii. Ruth,[7] b, Dec. 24, 1810; unmarried.

353

Roxanda[6] Porter, of Ebenezer[5] Porter, b. Abington. Married 1st, Daniel Nash, of Abington, May 17, 1792; he son of James and Tamar (Bates) Nash, b. 1767; died Nov. 13, 1804. Married 2d, Phillip Torrey, 1817, of Abington. Children by Nash:

Harriet,[7] m. Havelin Torry. Loring.[7] Mehetable,[7] b. 1799; died Oct. 29, 1805, aged 6. Clarissa,[7] m. Cyrus Gurney. And three others who died in infancy.

363

Jonathan[6] Porter, of Jonathan[5] Porter, b. Halifax, Oct. 28, 1764; resided in Halifax; married Betty Wood. Children:

741. i. Mary,[7] b. 1791; m. Josiah Sears, of Halifax, 1817.
742. ii. Betty,[7] b. 1793; m. Johnson.
743. iii. Rebecca W.,[7] m. Chas. Lincoln, of N. Bridgewater, Oct. 13, 1816.
744. iv. Millicent,[7] m. John Battles, of N. Bridgewater.

745. v. Bethiah,[7] m. Appollos Howard, of N. Bridgewater.
746. vi. Lucy.[7]
747. vii. Serena,[7] m. Kinsley.
748. viii. Dulcena,[7] m. Wheeler.

365

Oliver[6] Porter, of Jonathan[5] Porter, b. Halifax, Aug. 2, 1774; resided in Providence, R. I., and Stoughton, Mass. Married 1st, Phebe Barrows, of Carver, 1796; died Jan., 1801. Married 2d, Ruth Raymond, of Plymouth, 1802. Married 3d, Sarah Orcutt, of Middleborough, 1810. He died 1818. Children:

749. i. Chipman,[7] b. Jan. 7, 1797; m. Ruth Hathaway, Jan. 1, 1826.
750. ii. Sarah,[7] b. March 14, 1799; m. Seabury C. Hathaway, 1813.
751. iii. Cynthia,[7] b. Oct. 2, 1803; m. Isaac Fuller, 1824.
752. iv. Nathaniel,[7] b. June 3, 1805.
753. v. Louisa,[7] b. 1811; m. John Barnicoat, of Lynn; widow living there 1877.

374

Rachel[6] Porter, of Jacob[5] Porter, b. Nov. 17, 1765; married Dea. Abel Packard, Jr., of Cummington, Mass., Oct., 1808—his second wife. She died Aug. 31, 1851; he died April 30, 1832, aged 78.

375

Abigail[6] Porter, of Jacob[5] Porter, b. April 3, 1768; married Adam Packard, Esq., of Cummington, Mass., Nov. 11, 1790—her cousin; he son of Abel and Esther (Porter) Packard, b. North Bridgewater, Feb. 11, 1758; died in Cummington, July 20, 1810, aged 52; widow died there July 13, 1829, aged 61. Children, all born in Cummington:

754. i. William,[7] b. Oct. 25, 1791; justice of the peace; treasurer of the parish 30 years, and of the town of Cummington, more than 40 years. In 1869, removed to Worthington, where he died, Nov. 2, 1870. Married Oct. 25, 1824, Sarah Stoddard of Plainfield.
755. ii. Olive,[7] b. Oct. 9, 1793; m. Dec. 29, 1814, Jacob Whitmarsh, b. Cummington, Jan. 1, 1789; they had seven children. She died July 25, 1870, aged 76.
756. iii. Philo,[7] b. Oct. 7, 1795: died Aug. 8, 1797.

757. iv. Philo,[7] b. Jan. 11, 1798; married three times; died Aug. 5, 1870, aged 72.

758. v. Ruby,[7] b. Oct. 21, 1799; died July 25, 1837.

759. vi. Abel,[7] b. Sept. 18, 1802; grad. Amherst Col., 1824; studied medicine, New Haven; practised in Walcott Conn., and Cummington, where he died Dec. 12, 1830; m. Maria, of Dea. James Briggs, Oct. 30, 1825. Children: Francis E.,[8] and Calvin E.[8] Widow m. Doct. J. L. Field, of Waterbury, Conn., Oct. 30, 1831.

760. vii. Polly Porter,[7] b. May 9, 1806; died Nov. 14, 1815.

761. viii. Abigail,[7] b. Jan. 3, 1811; m. Asa H. Porter, Feb. 7, 1802; she died Feb. 24, 1835, aged 24; one dau. Sarah.[8]

376

Asa[6] Porter, of Jacob[5] Porter, b. Abington, Jan. 25, 1771; lived in Cummington; m. Betsey Huntington, Nov. 23, 1797; she was youngest daughter of Rev. Mr. Huntington, first minister of Worthington, Mass. He died April 10, 1855; wife died before him. Children:

762. i. Enos,[7] b. Feb. 2, 1798; m. Caroline Priestly, 1827.

763. ii. Jonathan,[7] b. Mar. 13, 1800; married twice.

764. iii. Asa Huntington,[7] b. Feb. 7, 1802; m. Abigail Packard.

765. iv. Nahum,[7] b. Jan. 7, 1804; m. Hannah C. Henshaw, 1837.

766. v. Milton,[7] b. July 26, 1806; m. Lodiska Hume, 1837.

767. vi. Jacob R.,[7] b. Aug. 29, 1808; died Nov. 1, 1808.

768. vii. Betsey E.,[7] b. Oct. 1, 1809; died July, 1854.

769. viii. Polly,[7] b. Dec. 8, 1811; m. Charles Wilbur, of Brooklyn, N. Y., 1840.

770. ix. Sarah,[7] b. Apr. 27, 1815; died Sept. 4, 1829.

771. x. Ruth,[7] b. April 24, 1817; m. Montague, and resided in town of Montague, Mass.; died there, leaving one son.

772. xi. Ellen,[7] b. Mar. 22, 1819; died April 10, 1819.

378.

Daniel K.[6] Porter, of Jacob[5] Porter, b. Abington, April 20, 1775, of Oberlin Ohio, where he died, 1812; m. Sallie Bates. Children: (No grandchildren.)

773. i. James Norton,[7] unmarried; died, aged 67.

774. ii. Daniel,[7] b. 1811; unmarried.

775. iii. Wealthy,[7] m. Henry Bellinger.

776. iv. Amanda,[7] b. 1802; unmarried; resides Oberlin, Ohio.

777. v. Mary,[7] unmarried; died, aged 26.

381

Jacob[6] Porter, of Jacob[5] Porter, b. Oct. 15, 1782; lived in Worthington, Mass.; married 1st, Hannah Burr; 2d, Sallie Packard. One child died in infancy, by each wife. Children:

778. i. Daniel R.,[7] b. 1821.
779. ii. Phebe,[7] died Oct., 1851.
780. iii. Jacob Clark,[7] b. 1829; died Aug., 1854.

383

Deborah[6] Porter, of Jacob[5] Porter, b. Dec. 6, 1765; married Jonathan Reed, of East Bridgewater; pub. April 13, 1788; he son of Jonathan and Mary (Tirrell) Reed, b. Feb. 2, 1767. Children:

781. i. Mary,[7] b. 1788.
782. ii. Jonathan Loring,[7] b. 1791; m. 1st, Charlotte Brown, Dec. 18, 1816. M. 2d, Lucy Champney, of Brighton, Mass.; pub. Feb. 25, 1827.
783. iii. John Porter,[7] b. 1793; m. Polly Ramsdell, 1816. Children: Mary Loring,[8] b. August 26, 1817; m. Edwin Brown, of E. Bridgewater, Nov. 30, 1837. John Porter,[8] b. July 19, 1819; m. Adaline Brown. Lloyd Watson,[8] b. Jan. 7, 1822; m. Lucy Bryant; lives South Abington. Mehetable,[8] b. Sept. 15, 1824; m. David Gurney, Nov. 19, 1843. Thomas Baldwin,[8] b. July 29, 1827, of South Abington.
784. iv. Deborah,[7] b. 1795; m. Jona R. Gurney, 1816.
785. v. Elisabeth,[7] b. 1797.
786. vi. Ebenezer,[7] b. 1801; m. Patience Penniman. Children: Ebenezer,[8] b. Nov. 23, 1829. George A.,[8] b. Oct. 3, 1831. William H.,[8] b. Apr. 12, 1833. Elisabeth Thaxter,[8] b. Dec. 4, 1834. Emeline F.,[8] b. Sept. 29, 1837. Maria F.,[8] b. Aug. 25, 1840.
787. vii. Clarissa,[7] b. 1805.
788. viii. Almira,[7] b. 1806.
789. ix. David Porter,[7] b. 1808.
790. x. Thaxter,[7] b. 1809; m. Mehetable Brown; pub. Feb. 4, 1827. Children: Mehetable,[8] b. May 8, 1830; Heman Thaxter,[8] b. Aug. 5, 1833; m. Sophronia Barker, of Hanson, 1857.

384

John[6] Porter, of John[5] Porter, b. Abington, July 26, 1767; he was one of original members of First Church, South Abington, in 1807; probably lived in East Bridgewater, near Abington line. John Porter, surveyor, Bridgewater, 1812-1814. Married 1st, Susanna, daughter of Ephraim and Susanna (Bowditch) Groves, 1790. Married 2d, Elinor Doten, of Plymouth; pub. 1801. He died Dec. 6, 1861, aged 94 years 4 mos. 10 days. Children: (Bridgewater Records.)

791. i. Allen Marshall,[7] b. Nov. 26, 1791; died Oct. 21, 1874; field driver, 1820; hog reeve, 1817; m. Betsey Beals, of Hanson, 1816. Son, F. W.,[8] Porter, resides East Bridgewater.

792. ii. Deborah,[7] b. Feb. 27, 1796.

386

Elias[6] Porter, of John[5] Porter, b. in Abington, June 26, 1770; removed to Whitesboro, N. Y., where he died.

His son Samuel,[7] was a Presbyterian clergyman; at one time settled in Lodi, Ohio.

385

James[6] Porter, of John[5] Porter, b. Abington, Mass., Oct. 11, 1768; removed from Abington to Skaneateles, N. Y., about 1790. In 1825, removed to Ohio, and died at Chagrin Falls, 1855, aged 87. Married Mary Bullard, of Abington, Mass. Children:

800. i. Seth John,[7] b. in Skaneateles, N. Y., Jan. 2, 1803.

801. ii. Mary,[7] b. 1801; m. Cornelius Northrop, 1820, at Skaneateles, N. Y.; in 1844 to Chagrin Falls, Ohio; and in 1850 removed to Menasha, Wis.; both died there, at the age of 74 years—she in 1875. Children: Corydon Porter,[8] b. 1822. Caroline,[8] b. 1825. Ann Eliza,[8] b. 1840. Fannie,[8] b. 1845. All living, except Fannie, and residents of Menasha, Wis.

387

Daniel[6] Porter, of John[5] Porter, b. in Abington, Jan. 22, 1773, and lived there; married Polly Ford, Jan. 29, 1801; she dau. of Jacob Ford. He died July 13, 1808, aged 35. Children:

810. i. Mary,[7] b. Jan. 21, 1802; died June 20, 1807.
811. ii. Noah,[7] b. Dec. 29, 1803; died April 4, 1826.
812. iii. Sally,[7] b. Sept. 27, 1806.
813. iv. Mary,[7] b. Jan. 17, 1809—"of Widow Mary Porter."

388

Noah[6] Porter, of John[5] Porter, b. Abington, Jan. 11, 1775; removed to New Hartford, N. Y., about four miles from Utica, when he died. He was a Puritan of the strictest kind; married Williams; had sons Francis[7], and William[7], and oldest daughter Julia Ann[7], who married Bigelow, of Waterville, Oneida Co., N. Y.

389

Mary[6] Porter, of John[5] Porter, b. Sept. 24, 1780; married Adam Reed, Jr., Feb. 25, 1819. One child:

Mary,[7] b. Sept. 16, 1823; probably m. Edwin Reed, of South Abington.

391

Deborah Gannett[6] Porter, of Adam[5] Porter, b. July 15, 1780; married Ebenezer Snell, Jr., of Cummington; he son of Ebenezer and Sarah (Packard) Snell, of Cummington. (They were also parents of Prof. Snell, of Amherst College; of Rev. Thomas Snell, D. D., of North Brookfield; and of the mother of William Cullen Bryant.) She died Dec., 1822, aged 42. Mr. Snell married 2d, Lydia R. Richards. The children of Ebenezer and Deborah Snell, were:

814. i. Samuel,[7] m. Vesta Beals, of Plainfield. They had two daughters. Sarah,[8] married, and died. Martha,[8] m. Thaddeus Rowe; lives in South Haven, Mich.
815. ii. Betsey,[7] b. Sept. 30, 1803; m. Leavitt Hallock, of Plainfield, Sept. 1, 1829; he was son of Rev. Moses Hallock, born Jan. 21, 1798; died Oct. 16, 1875; widow died

Dec. 9, 1877. Children: Fannie,[8] b. May 12, 1830; m. Rev. Henry M. Hazeltine, Oct. 7, 1857. Eliza,[8] b. twin with Fannie; m. Rev. Thomas H. Rouse, Sept. 17, 1851. William Allen,[8] b. Aug. 27, 1832; m. Sept. 19, 1860. Sarah,[8] born May, 11, (3) 1835; died Feb. 6, 1837. Mary Snell,[8] b. July 10, (3) 1837; died Sept. 3, 1846. Moses Gerard,[8] b. Nov. 24, 1840, (39); d. Sept. 3, 1846, (1847.) Leavitt Homan,[8] b. Aug. 15, 1842; minister at West Winsted, Conn.; m. June 11, 1867; wife died Oct. 2, 1873, Ellen Elisabeth,[8] b. March 16, (18) 1845; died, aged 6 months.

816. iii. Mary,[7] m. Dr. John Smith, and went with him as a foreign missionary. Children: Thomas,[8] missionary in Ceylon. Eunice,[8] died Aug. 14, 1872, aged 24. Laura,[8] died at sea, June 8, 1872, aged 26. William H.,[8] now in Theo. Seminary, Hartford, Conn. Henry.[8] Mary.[8]

817. iv. Ebenezer,[7] m. Rachael Bardwell, of Goshen, Mass.; now physician in California.

393

Adam Gannett[6] Porter, of Adam[5] Porter, b. Cummington, Feb. 22, 1784; lived there; married Clarissa, daughter of Capt. Joseph Narramore, of Goshen, Mass., Feb. 22, 1809; she b. Feb. 4, 1789; died Nov. 19, 1851; he died May 19, 1852, aged 62 years. Children:

820. i. Deborah Gannett,[7] b. Mar. 13, 1810.

821. ii. Clarissa,[7] b. Oct. 21, 1811; died Dec. 21, 1811.

822. iii. Clarissa N.,[7] b. Dec. 22, 1812; died Dec. 9, 1843.

823. iv. Joseph Narramore,[7] b. Oct. 24, 1814; unmarried; died Sept. 16, 1859.

824. v. Horatio E.,[7] b. Mar. 24, 1817.

825. vi. Sophia L.,[7] b. Oct. 19, 1819.

395

Jacob[6] Porter, of Seth[5] Porter, b. in Abington, Dec. 30, 1783; graduated at Yale College; resided in Plainfield, Mass.; physician; married 1st, Betsey Mayhew; published Jan. 10, 1813; she died July 3, 1813. Married 2d, Sally Reed, Nov. 18, 1819. He died Nov. 15, 1846; left his papers to Yale College. His widow was living in 1876, with her daughter in Wisconsin. Children:

826. i. Juliet,[7] b. Apr. 5, 1821; died Aug. 22, 1841.
827. ii. Clarissa,[7] b. Oct. 30, 1825; died Oct. 23, 1838.
828. iii. Elisabeth,[7] b. May 24, 1829; m. Lorenzo Mitchell; resides Wisconsin.

395B

Norton[6] Porter, of Noah[5] Porter, b. Abington, Mass., 1771; removed to Cummington, Mass., with his father; physician; settled in Westmoreland, Oneida Co., N. Y., 1791; removed to Whitestown, same County, N. Y., 1831, where he died Nov. 18, 1852. Married Sarah Cobb, of Cummington, Mass., 1796—she daughter of Amos and Sally (Orcutt) Cobb. Children:

i. Delia,[7] b. May 22, 1797; died Aug. 12, 1807.
ii. Franklin,[7] b. July 25, 1799; died Aug. 13, 1837.
iii. Julia Ann,[7] b. Oct., 1801; m. Rev. Rufus R. Deming, Feb., 1824; she died 1872. Children: Henry F.,[8] b. Dec. 25, 1825; m. lived in Minnesota; farmer; member of Legislature 1875; has 4 children. Julius R.,[8] b. May 17, 1827; m; lives in Mass. Philander,[8] b. Feb. 6, 1829; A. M.; A. B.; Vermont University; counsellor at law; contributor to Atlantic Monthly; resides, Albany, N. Y. Helen E.[8] b. Nov. 5, 1831; died Aug. 12, 1833. Ann Eliza,[8] b. Mar. 16, 1834. Edwin P.,[8] b. Jan. 17, 1836. Delia M.,[8] b. Feb. 11, 1838. Lucius,[8] b. Aug. 20, 1840. Albert N.,[8] b. Apr. 15, 1843; died March, 1844.
iv. Sarah,[7] b. Oct. 14, 1803.
v. Mariah,[7] b. Aug. 18, 1805; died 1807.
vi. Charlotte,[7] b. Dec. 12, 1808; died March 1, 1810.
vii. Henry,[7] b. Sept. 11, 1811; died Feb. 20, 1812.
viii. Delia Ann,[7] b. July 24, 1813; died Oct., 1813.
ix. Henry N.,[7] b. Nov. 5, 1816; grad. (M. D.) Geneva College, N. Y., 1841; practiced medicine in Lee, N. York, from 1841 to 1862; then removed to New York Mills, Oneida Co., N. Y., where he now lives. M., Jan. 25, 1842, Helen F. Polson, b. in Scotland, Sept. 20, 1818. Children: Sarah E.,[8] b. Nov. 21, 1842; m. David M. Davis, of Washington, D. C., and has four children—Frances E.,[8] b. Oct. 13, 1845; Henry R.,[8] b. Feb. 13,

1848; grad. (M. D.) Georgetown, D. C., Medical College, March, 1872; appointed House Surgeon Columbia Hospital; Acting Assistant Surgeon U. S. Army, 1873; served under General Crook as Camp Surgeon, in Apache war, in Arizona; also under General Custer, in Sioux war, and was the only surviving surgeon in the Custer expedition of June, 1874; m. Miss Lottie Viets, of Oberlin, Ohio, 1877, and is now practising medicine in Bismarck, Dakota Territory.

The subject of the following sketch from the Utica (N. Y.) Herald, was a graduate of the Medical Department of Georgetown University, and subsequently was resident physician at the Washington Hospital:

Our readers are, at least partially, familiar with the brave part taken by Dr. H. R. Porter, (son of Dr. Porter, of New York Mills,) in the expedition under Major Reno against the Indians, in 1876, and how narrowly he escaped from the disasters of the day on the Little Big Horn. But there is much in the thrilling reminiscences of the events in which he took part furnished by a Bismarck correspondent of the Minneapolis Pioneer-Press of a recent date, which will be read with interest by the many friends of Dr. Porter in central New York. The writer speaks of him as "one of the heroes who was not remembered in the official reports," and after speaking of the eagerness of Dr. Porter to accompany the command, and describing the scattering of Reno's forces, says:

"Porter was by the side of a dying soldier. His orderly and supplies were gone, and the command was off several hundred yards. He was alone. Bullets were pruning the trees, and a terrific yell was sounding the alarm of universal death. Porter left his last patient, and led his horse to the embankment that protected the woods. He was startled by Indians dashing by him within ten feet. They were rushing along the foot of the little bluff. Their aim was so direct in the line of the flying battalion that Porter's presence was unnoticed. He was unarmed, and his powerful black horse reared and plunged as if he was mad. Porter saw the fate that was in the immediate future if that horse escaped before he was on his back. He held on with superhuman strength; he could hold him, but that was all. To gain the saddle seemed a forlorn hope. Leap after leap with the horse quicker than he. It was a brief ordeal, but in the face of death it was a terrible one. One supreme effort, and half in the saddle the dusky charger bore away his master like the wind. He gained the full seat, and lying close upon his savior's neck was running a gauntlet where the chances of death was a thousand to one. The Indians were quick to see the lone rider, and a storm of leadened hail fell around him. He had no control of his horse. It was only a half mile dash, but it was a wild one. The horse was frenzied; he reached the river in a minute, and rushed up the bluff where Reno had gone and was then recovering himself. The horse and rider were safe. It was destiny. Porter's first remark to the officers: 'Pretty badly demoralized.' 'No,' answered Reno. 'It was a charge.' Porter took the hint, but it was a charge different from any he had ever seen or read of. * * * Porter's associate was killed, and he was alone. The afternoon of the 25th, all night, throughout the 26th, the night of that date until the forenoon of the 27th, Porter worked as few men are ever called upon to work. He had no idea that he would get out alive, and believed every man around him was doomed. Still he was the same cool and skillful surgeon that he is to-day. He had a duty to perform that seldom falls to a man of twenty-six, and yet he performed it nobly. He was surrounded by the dead, dying and wounded. Men were crying for water, for help, for relief, for life. The sun was blazing hot, the dead horses were sickening, the air heavy with a hundred smells, the bullets thick, the men falling, and the bluffs for miles black with the jubilant savages. The work of the others was not like Porter's. He must know no fear, no trembling, and no rest. He had every agonizing sight before his eyes. The afternoon of the 26th, when the Indians ceased their firing and begun to move off, there were around Porter on the ground fifty dead and fifty wounded. One in every three was either killed or maimed. I know little of hospital history, but I doubt if there is much that overshadows Porter's experience upon the bluffs overlooking the Little Big Horn. If I had the genius of Buchanan Reid, I would weave it into a song more heroic than Sheridan's Ride.

Of the doctor's service during the passage of the steamer Far West down the river with wounded, the writer says: 'There were wounds of every character, and men more dead than alive. The suffering was not terminated with the removal from the field to the boiler deck. It continued and ended in death more than once before Fort Lincoln was hailed. Here again the son of New York Mills, of the empire state, was tested. Porter watched for fifty-four hours. He stood the test.'

396

Seth[6] Porter, of Seth[5] Porter, b. Abington, June 27, 1785; resided in Cummington; married Polly Mitchell, June 22, 1819; he died Dec. 8, 1834, aged 49. She died Oct. 27, 1856. Children:

829. i. Edward C.,[7] b. Sept. 10, 1820.
830. ii. Mary,[7] b. July 7, 1822.
831. iii. Henry,[7] died young.
832. iv. Henry,[7] b. Jan. 27, 1827.
833. v. Elisabeth,[7] b. 1836.

398

Samuel H.[6] Porter, of Huntington[5] Porter, b. in Rye, N. H., May 29, 1789; received a good common school education; learned the printing trade with Manning & Loring, of Boston, and at twenty was co-editor of a juvenile newspaper, called "The Fly." Next year he commenced to travel through the states for the purpose of visiting the most celebrated printing establishments; he was taken sick and died at Charleston, S. C., Sept. 7, 1807, highly respected for his enterprise, genius, and correct moral character.

399

Nathaniel S.[6] Porter, of Rev. Huntington[5] Porter, b. Rye, N. H., May 29, 1789; received a good common school education, and removed to Richmond, Kentucky; taught school there, and became a merchant; married Elizabeth Comstock, of Lexington, Ky., Jan. 8, 1811; he died Aug. 30, 1827. His widow died Feb. 19, 1877, aged 85 years. Children:

834. i. Samuel Huntington,[7] b. Oct. 13, 1812; died Feb. 19, 1876.
835. ii. Oliver Fuller,[7] b. Sept. 14, 1814; died April 17, 1815.
836. iii. Emily Comstock,[7] b. May 15, 1816.
837. iv. Caroline,[7] b. Oct. 22, 1818.
838. v. Sarah Anne,[7] b. April 17, 1821.
839. vi. Eliza,[7] b. July 26, 1823.
840. vii. John Sargent.[7]

400

John[6] Porter, of Rev. Huntington[5] Porter, b. Rye, N. H., Sept. 6, 1791; prepared for college at Phillips Academy, Exeter, N. H.; grad. Harvard College, 1819; studied divinity there; preached occasionally in several places; officiated sometime as assistant librarian in the college; was distinguished for his musical talent and proficiency in botany; died of consumption at his uncle's house, in Roxbury, March 28, 1825, aged 37 years.

402

Maria[6] Porter, of Huntington[5] Porter, b. Rye, N. H., Feb. 12, 1798; married Asa Robinson, of Brentwood, N. H. Children:

841. i. **Dudly Huntington,**[7] b. 1823; m. 1st, Mary A. Thing; she died in 1854. M. 2d, Melissa Ann Kimball. He was a soldier in the late war, and died 1863. Children: Frank Herbert,[8] died in infancy. Charles Dudly.[8] Annie Maria.[8] Mabel Huntington.[8]

842. ii. **Eliphalet Porter,**[7] b. 1825.

843. iii. **Charles Asa,**[7] b. 1827; died the same year.

844. iv. **Asa Augustus,**[7] b. 1828; died in 1837.

845. v. **Charles,**[7] b. 1829; died the same year.

846. vi. **Maria Louisa,**[7] b. 1839; m. Thomas J. Farmer, of Brentwood, N. H.; she died 1873; had four children—Nellie Huntington.[8] Herbert Robinson.[8] Howard Porter.[8] Everett Wellington.[8]

403

Eliphalet[6] Porter, of Rev. Huntington[5] Porter, b. Rye, N. H., Apr. 25, 1800; he was a merchant in Portsmouth, N. H.; in a tour to New Orleans, was cast away near the Bahama Islands, and was lost with all on board, excepting one, at the age of 24 years.

404

Oliver[6] Porter, of Rev. Huntington[5] Porter, b. Mar. 3, 1802; had two terms of academical education at Hampton, and Exeter, N. H., with view of a college course, but health failing, gave it up and went into a store as clerk, at Portsmouth, N. H., with his brother, 1820 and 1821; then clerk for D. & D. Brewer, Portland, Me., about four years; then went in business at Atkinson, Maine, under the firm name of Porter & Grant; in about three years bought out Grant, and continued about two and a half years longer; then went into Register of Deeds office in 1832 and 1833; then after getting married, started in business in Levant, Me., remaining about two years; then removed to Lynn, Mass., built a house and store and remained there about fourteen years, when he sold out and removed to Waterford, Maine, in the fall of 1848, where he now resides, and is Postmaster. He has been 58 years behind the counter, 52 of them in business for himself; his credit never having been doubted—is in good circumstances—out of debt, but not rich. In 1829, he gave up liquor selling, believing it to be wrong; was the second merchant in the state who did so, there having been one in York County, Me., before him. Married 1st, Aurora Freeman Stimson, Sept. 2, 1832, at Palmyra, Me.; she was the daughter of Rev. Daniel Stimson, (most the time an itinerant Methodist minister in Penobscot and Piscataquis counties, in Maine, who was a very good man, born in York county, whose wife was an Eastman, born in Strong, Me.,) born Mar. 16, 1815; died in Waterford, Me., Jan. 22, 1849; she was in all respects a splendid specimen of womankind. Mar. 2d, Mary Jane Seal, dau. of Capt. Thomas Seal, of Westbrook, Me., Dec. 10, 1849; she born Mar. 24, 1811; and died Mar. 5, 1861. Mar. 3d, Mrs. Betsey (Griffin) Hammond, widow of Ezra Hammond, of Paris, Me., April 6, 1864; she died Jan. 26, 1875, aged 70. Children:

847. i. Laura Stimson,[7] b. at Levant, Me., June 22, 1834.

847½. ii. Helen Maria,[7] b. at Lynn, Mass., Jan. 13, 1837; she taught school at Brooklyn, N. Y., a few years, and died there, much beloved for her amiability and goodness, Oct. 7, 1857.

848. iii. Huntington,[7] b. Lynn, April 29, 1839.

849. iv. Eliphalet,[7] b. Lynn, May 2, 1844.

850. v. Horace,[7] b. Waterford, Me., April 11, 1851; unmarried; resides in Waterford, Me.

405

Louisa[6] Porter, of Rev. Huntington[5] Porter, b. Rye, N. H., May 18, 1803; taught school several years in Dover and Greenland, N. H. Married William Weeks, of Greenland, N. H.; farmer. (Son of Wm. Weeks, of Hopkinton, N. H., who graduated at Harvard Coll., 1775.) Children:

Ann Louisa,[7] b. March 22, 1836. Ellen Maria,[7] b. Jan. 23, 1838. Sarah Porter,[7] b. Oct. 27, 1839. George William,[7] b. Sept. 8, 1841. John Porter,[7] b. Jan. 24, 1844; mar. Nellie Hatch, only daughter of Hon. Charles W. Hatch, April 26, 1870; she died June 16, 1874, and he married 2d, Laura A., daughter of Nathan R. Foss, Esq., Sept. 14, 1876.

406

Martha Ruggles[6] Porter, of Rev. Huntington[5] Porter, b. Rye, N. H., June 11, 1805; she lived some years with her uncle, Eliphalet Porter, D. D., of Roxbury; m. Chas. Knapp Dilloway, Esq., of Boston, Aug. 27, 1838. He was a graduate of Harvard, 1825. Children:

856. i. Caroline Porter,[7] b. May 11, 1836; died April 8, 1839.
857. ii. Mary Emma,[7] b. March 22, 1838; m. Hayward Lee, June 7, 1866. They had one son—Douglas.[8] The mother died Sept. 16, 1872.
858. iii. Charles Porter,[7] b. April 9, 1840.
859. iv. Francis Henry,[7] b. May 8, 1843; died Oct. 4, 1844.
860. v. George Wales,[7] b. Oct. 18, 1845; lawyer; resides in New York city.

407

Susan Sargent[6] Porter, of Rev. Huntington[5] Porter, b. Rye, N. H., Apr. 12, 1807; m. Maj. John H. Moulton, of Centre Harbor, N. H., merchant, May 23, 1832. Children:

861. i. Susan Huntington,[7] b. 1835; m. Smith F. Emery, 1860.
862. ii. Franklin Hall,[7] b. 1838; died 1840.
863. iii. Oliver Porter,[7] b. 1840; died the same year.

408

Sarah Emery[6] Porter, of Rev. Huntington[5] Porter, b. Rye, N. H., June 2, 1809. She was for some time preceptress of Taunton Academy. Mar. Charles Adams, D. D., July 29, 1833; he b. Stratham, N. H., Jan. 24, 1808; he graduated at Bowdoin Coll., 183—; he was for some years principal of Newbury Academy, Vt.; afterward pastor 1st. M. E. Church, Lynn, Mass.; and Prof. in Jacksonville (Ill.) Coll. She died Aug. 6, 1858. Children:

864. i. Sarah Porter,[7] b. Rye, N. H., Aug. 24, 1834; m. William H. Barnes, of Cincinnati, Ohio, July 29, 1857; editor and author; now resides 226 Indiana Avenue, Washington, D. C.
865. ii. Charles Henry,[7] b. Newbury, Vt., April 24, 1836; m. Elmira C. Hamilton, of Illinois, June 30, 1861. He was in the army as Major and Lieut. Colonel of the First Illinois Artillery, and lives now in Chicago, Ill. Their children are Albert,[8] Caroline Porter,[8] Howard Hamilton.[8]
866. iii. Charlotte,[7] b. Newbury, Vt., Sept. 15, 1837; m. Jacob Haynes, of Jacksonville, Ill.; now of Bell Brooks, Ohio.

867. iv. Mary Elizabeth,[7] b. Lynn, Mass., Dec. 7, 1840.

868. v. Edward Adams,[7] b. Wilbraham, Mass., Dec. 21, 1842; killed in battle at Jackson, Miss., June 10, 1863; Second Lieut. in First Artillery, of Illinois.

869. vi. George Huntington,[7] b. Boston, Jan. 14, 1846; graduated at Harvard College, 1870; lawyer, No. 35 Pine street, New York city; he was Captain in the 4th U. S. Col. Artillery, and Brevet Major in the late war; married E. Augusta Holmes, April 26, 1877.

870. vii. Frank,[7] b. Lowell, Mass., Sept. 25, 1849; died 1864, in Omaha.

409

Olivia[6] Porter, of Rev. Huntington[5] Porter, b. Feb. 15, 1811; m. Luther Hall, of East Boston, Aug. 16, 1837; he b. in Concord, N. H., Oct. 8, 1804; died Dec. 21, 1869. Mrs. Olivia Hall resides with her son, Luther A.,[7] at East Boston.

i. Olivia P.,[7] b. June 8, 1838; died.

ii. Caroline P.,[7] b. June 18, 1840; died.

871. iii. Luther Abbot,[7] b. Jan. 30, 1843; m. Alice Durrell.

872. iv. Frank Parker,[7] b. Jan. 30, 1852; died in childhood.

410

Huntington[6] Porter, of Rev. Huntington[5] Porter, b. at Rye, N. H., Dec. 4, 1812; fitted for college, at Exeter Academy, N. H.; graduated at Harvard Coll., 1833; taught school in Pittsburgh, Penn.; then entered on the study of medicine at Lexington, Ky.; took the small pox on his way home on a visit, and died on Rainsford Island, Boston harbor, June 21, 1836, aged 24.

411

Rev. Emery Moulton[6] Porter, of Rev. Huntington[5] Porter, b. Rye, N. H., Apr. 1, 1815; fitted for college at Andover; entered Dartmouth College; remained one year, and then admitted sophomore at Harvard College, and graduated there 1838; student of theology one year at Andover; the second year at Yale College, and again at Andover Theological Seminary; now an Episcopal clergyman at Lonsdale, R. I. Married 1st, Charlotte A. Buxton, of Newbury, Vt., Sept. 1,

1842; she died Aug. 31, 1844. Married 2d, Betsey M. Arnold, of Smithfield, R. I., May 26, 1846; she died July 4, 1853. Married 3d, Louisa A. Arnold, of Smithfield, R. I., Sept. 18, 1855. Children:

873. i. Emery Huntington,[7] b. April 22, 1844.
874. ii. George Whipple,[7] b. April 10, 1847.
875. iii. Mary Huntington,[7] b. July 7, 1849.
876. iv. Louisa Arnold,[7] b. June 6, 1853; died in infancy.

412

Charles Henry[6] Porter, of Rev. Huntington[5] Porter, b. Rye, N. H., Sept. 19, 1817; fitted for college at Andover, and entered Yale College; at the close of second year, was taken sick of a fever, and died Sept. 4, 1839, aged 21.

414

William H.[6] Porter, of Rev. Huntington[5] Porter, b. Rye, N. H., Sept. 19, 1817; twin with Charles H.; fitted for college at Andover; graduated Yale College; married Mary Frances, daughter of Paul Wentworth, of Sandwich, N. H., May 19, 1844; she also sister of Hon. John Wentworth, of Chicago. He died May 26, 1861. Children:

877. i. Mary Frances Wentworth,[7] b. March 8, 1845; died Sept. 24, 1850.
878. ii. William Henry Huntington,[7] b. July 21, 1846; died 1865.
879. iii. John Wentworth,[7] b. June 21, 1855; resides in Rochester, Minn.; his mother also.

415

Elvira[6] Porter, of Rev. Huntington[5] Porter, b. Jan. 11, 1820; married Charles M. Weeks, physician. Graduated Dart. Col., 1830; settled in Elliot, Me.; now at Golden Spring, Jamaica, West Indies. Wife died May 6, 1868. Children:

Albert Huntington,[7] b. 1841; m. Naomi Brooks; resides Woodville, Ga. Edgar S.,[7] b. 1844; died 1864. Caroline Porter,[7] b. Sept. 22, 1847; m. Joseph A. Holmes, of Greenland, N. H., Sept. 12, 1874.

424

Oliver[6] Porter, of Nicholas[5] Porter, b. Marshfield; prob. lived in Marshfield; master mariner, and merchant; married Lucy Keene, Aug. 11, 1773. Children:

883. i. Oliver,[7] married.
884. ii. Lemuel,[7] b. Dec. 15, 1777.
885. iii. Lucy,[7] m. Joshua Taylor, 1798.
886. iv. Patience.[7]
887. v. George.[7]
888. vi. Charles,[7] b. Oct. 25, 1790.

425

Charles[6] Porter, of Nicholas[5] Porter, b. Marshfield; lived in Boston. Married 1st, Betsey Rice. Married 2d, Sarah Wilkinson. A Charles Porter estate settled in Boston, 1808; wife, Elizabeth. Children: Sally, Charles, Calvin, Betsey, minors over 14.

426

William[6] Porter, of Nicholas[5] Porter, b. Marshfield; lived there; master mariner. Married Margaret Jarvis, of Boston. He died 1800; his estate settled that year, and the three children put under guardianship. His widow married 2d, Joseph Ewell, of Marshfield, and had by him seven children. Children:

892. i. Peggy,[7] b. May 6, 1788; m. John Holmes, of Pembroke, 1809; she died 1866.
893. ii. William,[7] b. Sept. 14, 1790; master mariner; died Providence, R. I., 1820.
894. iii. Edward Jarvis,[7] b. March 5, 1793.

427

Capt. Isaac[6] Porter, of Nicholas[5] Porter, b. Marshfield; removed to Mount Vernon, Maine, with his family, 1805. He married Sarah B. Hall, of Scituate, 1785; he died Apr. 29, 1830, aged 69; his widow died Feb. 5, 1839, aged 74. His will, Apr. 29, 1830, proved June 29, 1830, names wife, Sarah. Children: Isaac, Amasa, Clarissa Currier, Harvey, Calvin,

Betsey Pishon, and Sarah Gill;—Nathan, executor. Children, all b. Marshfield, Mass.:

895. i. Isaac,[7] b. Nov. 1, 1786.
896. ii. Amasa,[7] b. May 23, 1790.
897. iii. Clarissa,[7] b. June 12, 1788.
898. iv. Harvey,[7] b. Nov. 25, 1792.
899. v. Calvin,[7] b. Nov. 10, 1794.
900. vi. Betsey,[7] b. June 2, 1798; m. Frederick Pishon.
901. vii. Nathan,[7] b. Oct. 28, 1801; m. Harriet A. Gove.
902. viii. Sarah,[7] b. Dec. 14, 1803; m. Joseph Gill.

428

Capt. James[6] Porter, of Nicholas[5] Porter, b. in Marshfield; resided in Abington, Plainfield, and North Bridgewater. Married Mary, daughter of Eleazer and Abigail (Alden) Whitman, of East Bridgewater, Aug. 1, 1777; she b. 1751. He died at North Bridgewater, 1802. Administrator appointed of James Porter's estate, of Bridgewater, 1803. In 1806, the estate divided between Mary Fullerton, Abigail Keith, Hannah and Sallie Porter. His wife died about 1841, aged ninety years. Children:

903. i. Polly,[7] b. Abington, Feb. 25, 1778.
904. ii. Abigail,[7] b. Abington, Dec. 28, 1779.
905. iii. Hannah,[7] b. Plainfield, Nov. 3, 1781.
906. iv. James,[7] b. Plainfield, June 25, 1788.
907. v. Sarah,[7] b. Abington, July 8, 1792.

429

Amasa[6] Porter, of Nicholas[5] Porter, b. in Marshfield, 1765; lived in Boston, Newton, and Charlestown; married Margaret Hoag, of Newton, 1791. She was b. 1773; died 1841. He died in Charlestown, May, 1842. Children:

908. i. Amasa,[7] Jr., b. Newton, 1793.
909. ii. Margaret,[7] b. Newton, 1795.
910. iii. Pamelia,[7] b. July 4, 1797.
911. iv. Elizabeth,[7] b. Aug. 1, 1799.
912. v. William N.,[7] b. 1804.
913. vi. James A.,[7] b. 1806.
914. vii. Sarah,[7] b. Charlestown, 1811.
915. viii. Alfred H.,[7] b. July 9, 1814.

Some years since, the children were all weighed,—total 1,745 pounds,—average, 218⅛ pounds.

431

Ruth[6] Porter, of Nicholas[5] Porter, b. Marshfield. Married Capt. Benj. Eames, of Marshfield, Oct. 28, 1773; he b. Dec. 12, 1745; died April 24, 1824, aged 78. She died May 10, 1842, aged 88. Children:

Benjamin.[7] Joseph,[7] lost at sea. Abner.[7] Thomas,[7] a Baptist clergyman. Ruth,[7] m. John Taylor. Sarah,[7] m. John Chandler. William.[7] Jesse,[7] b. Dec., 1797; died April 27, 1861, aged 64. Nabby,[7] married Albert Ames.

432

Sarah[6] Porter, of Nicholas[5] Porter, b. Marshfield. Married Daniel Wright, of Marshfield, 1775. Children:

Sally,[7] m. Joseph Prior, of Duxbury. Polly,[7] m. Seth Winslow. Charles Porter,[7] b. 1782; died July 13, 1854, aged 72. Betsey,[7] b. 1789; died Aug. 23, 1857, aged 68.

436

Capt. John[6] Porter, of Nicholas[5] Porter, b. about 1762; lived in Marshfield. Married Ruth Stevens, Dec. 2, 1784. He died Aug. 9, 1843, aged 81; his widow died Dec. 17, 1851, aged 90. Children:

929. i. John,[7] b. Dec. 13, 1785; married; master mariner, of Marshfield; no children.
930. ii. Nathaniel,[7] b. Dec. 12, 1787; unmarried; died young.
931. iii. Ruth,[7] b. March 11, 1789.
932. iv. Bethiah,[7] b. Sept. 8, 1791; m. Prince Lapham.
933. v. Sarah,[7] b. Nov. 7, 1792; m.
934. vi. Lydia,[7] b. May 13, 1794; unmarried; died young.
935. vii. Avery,[7] } b. Aug. 17, 1796; unmarried; died young.
936. viii. Alvin,[7] }
937. ix. Eliza,[7] b. May 25, 1799.
938. x. Nicholas,[7] b. Jan. 18, 1801.

441

Isaac[6] Porter, of Matthew[5] Porter, b. Plymouth, N. H., Dec. 8, 1789. Married Elmira Stoddard, May, 1817. He or wife died July, 1857. Children all born in Farmington, Me.:

939. i. Jeremiah,[7] b. Dec. 31, 1818.
940. ii. William B.,[7] b. June 26, 1821.

941. iii. Selina E.,[7] b. Oct. 8, 1824.

942. iv. Mary,[7] b. July 21, 1835; m. James Dodge, at Salem, Me., Nov., 1852. She died Oct., 1861. One daughter, Clara P.,[8] born Jan. 4, 1856; m. Rufus Beedy, of Madrid, Me.

448

Samuel[6] Porter, of Abijah[5] Porter, b. Abington; lived in Randolph. Married 1st, Hannah Stetson. M. 2d, Crane, and had several children.

460

Laban[6] Porter, of Jonathan[5] Porter, b. Weymouth, 1787; lived there; married Deborah Thompson, 1786. Children:

i. Daughter,[7] b. Feb. 22, 1808. Dr. Shute's record.

ii. Daughter,[7] b. Feb. 27, 1811. Dr. Shute's record.

943. iii. Hiram.[7] Lived in Stoughton.

501

Col. Ezekiel[6] Porter, of Ebenezer[5] Porter, b. Weymouth, Mass., Nov. 10, 1762. Was a Revolutionery soldier; said to have resided in Groton, Mass. (?) of Hallowell, Me., where he was a merchant, and captain of the militia, 1787. Failing in business, in 1790, he and his half brother, Gershom Collier, from Weymouth, removed and settled in Farmington, on what was afterward known as Porter Hill,—they being the first settlers there. Col. Porter carried on farming on a larger scale than was ever before in that region. In 1803, he went into trade again, and traded largely for a few years. First representative from the town of Farmington to General Court of Mass., in 1799; and again in 1805. The town was originally "Sandy River Plantation," but Col. Porter had it named Farmington. He was noted for his enterprise, intelligence and wit. In Rev. Paul Coffin's "Journal of a Missionary in Maine, in 1800," in Maine Historical Society Collections, vol. 4, page 394, he says: "Sept. 15, Farmington, preached; lodged on my return at Col. Ezekiel Porter's. Porter has 50 acres corn; 50 black cattle; a large house; three barns; he lives on the hill,—a sightly place." In the probate record for Kennebec County, Maine, is the following record: "Feb. 12, 1816. Petition from widow Betsey Porter, and son, Jeremy Porter, of Ezekiel Porter, of Farmington, stating that Ezekiel Porter left his home Feb. 10, 1813, to go to Boston and Weymouth, on a visit, and had not been heard from for two years and eleven months, and asking for letters of administration on his estate." Petition was granted, and the widow administered upon the estate, which was large. He married Betsey, dau. of Asahel and Rebecca Wyman, of Groton, Mass., 1784. The children, as per Farmington, Me., records:

950. i. Sukey,[7] b. Groton, Mass., May 4, 1785.
951. ii. Alexander,[7] b. Hallowell, Me., Oct. 10, 1787.
952. iii. Thirza,[7] b. Hallowell, Me., June 1, 1789.
953. iv. Ezekiel,[7] b. Farmington, July 4, 1791.
954. v. Jeremy W.,[7] b. Farmington, Oct. 13, 1792.
955. vi. Polly,[7] b. Farmington, July 26, 1794.
956. vii. Zerviah,[7] b. Farmington, March 14, 1797.
957. viii. Ebenezer,[7] b. Farmington, Feb. 25, 1800; died at age of 7 or 8 years.
958. ix. Ashael,[7] b. Farmington, May 5, 1802.
958A. x. Eliphaz,[7] died in Farmington, Me., at age of one year.
958½. xi. Eliza,[7] b. 1807; m. Zebediah Sweet, of Strong, Me., 1836; farmer and miller. Widow resides New Vineyard, Me. Children: Andrew J.[8] Susan A.[8] Zebediah.[8] Prob. Alexander P.[8]

510

Lincoln[6] Porter, of Samuel[5] Porter, b. Taunton; lived there. Married 1st, Celia Lincoln. Married 2d, Lydia Brown. One Child:

Celia,[7] b. Jan. 26, 1800; now living in Taunton. Two children by 2d wife, who died young.

511

Edmund[6] Porter, of Samuel[5] Porter, b. Taunton, May 27, 1774, lived in Taunton. Married Polly Lincoln, 1800; she b. Apr. 24, 1777; died Feb. 3, 1860. He died April, 1833. Children:

960. i. William W.,[7] b. Jan. 11, 1803.

961. ii. Sally,[7] b. July 9, 1804; m. Ambrose Byington, of Camden, N. Y., 1839.

962. iii. Benjamin,[7] b. Sept. 25, 1806; died 1872.

963. iv. Mary,[7] b. June 7, 1800.

515

Jacob[6] Porter, of John[5] Porter, b. Taunton, Mar. 26, 1762, and lived there. Married Mary, dau. of Thomas and Ruth (Carver) Cushman, of Taunton, 1786; b. March, 1762, and died Feb., 1851. He died August 12, 1796. Estate settled, 1799. Children, (per Cushman Genealogy, page 207-208.)

964. i. Anne,[7] b. Aug. 4, 1786; died unmarried.

965. ii. Charles,[7] b. Mar. 17, 1788; died Taunton, 1855.

966. iii. Christopher,[7] b. Oct. 18, 1789; died Taunton, 1824.

967. iv. Caleb B.,[7] b. Aug. 4, 1791; died unmarried.

968. v. John,[7] b. Jan. 27, 1793; died Mar. 21, 1839.

969. vi. Mary,[7] b. Mar. 22, 1795; married John Howard, of Taunton; died 1840. Had child, dau., who married Henry Wicks, of Deer Park, L. I.; she died 1874, leaving one son and three daughters.

522

Zecheriah[6] Porter, of Jonathan[5] Porter, b. June 9, 1769; lived Middleborough. Married Priscilla, daughter of John and Zilpah Miller, Dec. 3, 1794. She b. April 16, 1773; died Mar. 3, 1865. He died July 31, 1853. Children:

970. i. Sarah,[7] b. Mar. 10, 1796; m. Dr. Brown.

971. ii. Zecheriah,[7] b. Nov. 7, 1797; married.

972. iii. Priscilla,[7] b. Aug. 7, 1799.

973. iv. Jefferson Burr,[7] b. July 25, 1801; married.

974. v. Lydia Wood,[7] b. May 3, 1804; unmarried.

975. vi. Deborah Strong,[7] b. Dec. 9, 1807; unmarried.

976. vii. Jonathan O.,[7] b. Aug. 27, 1811; married.

977. viii. Henry Clinton,[7] b. June 26, 1812; unmarried.

978. ix. George,[7] b. Feb. 7, 1819; unmarried.

523

Sarah[6] Porter, of Jonathan[5] Porter, b. Sept. 29, 1771. Married Dr. Friend Sturtevant, April 25, 1793; he was son of Dr. Josiah and Lois (Foster) Sturtevant, b. in Halifax, Feb. 19, 1767; died in Hartland, Vt., Aug. 26, 1830. His widow died June 20, 1864. Dr. Josiah Sturtevant was a loyalist, and during the Revolutionary war, he fled to Boston, and was given a position in the British army as surgeon, which he held till his death, which occurred soon after, from disease contracted by exposure. He was buried under the Old South Church. In the family record is this entry made by his widow: ("Aug. 18, 1776, my dear husband departed this life,—he was in his fifty-fifth year,—at Boston, whither he was driven by a mad and deluded mob, for no other offense than his loyalty to his sovereign. God forgive them, and grant that his death may be sanctified to me and all the children for our souls' everlasting good.") Friend Sturtevant studied medicine at Middleboro, with an older brother, Dr. Thomas Sturtevant; after his marriage, went to New York state; thence to Pittsfield, Mass.; thence, in 1804, to Woodstock, Vt.; and in 1807, to Hartland, Vermont, where he was the only educated physician for some years, and had an extensive pratice. During the war of 1812, he enlisted in the U. S. Army, as surgeon; was quartered at Plattsburgh, but was taken sick and returned home before the close of the war, and continued the practice of his profession until his death. Children:

979. i. Cullen Friend,[7] b. April 21, 1795, in Pittsfield, Mass.; m. Harriet Morey, of Strafford, Vt., Nov. 27, 1833; she died June 20, 1874. Children: Everline,[8] b. Aug. 29, 1834; m. William J. Sumner; resides in Holyoke, Mass. Amelia Morey,[8] b. Sept. 15, 1835; died May 19, 1854. Caroline,[8] b. Mar. 23, 1837; m. Frederic Bates, Aug. 18, 1859, and removed to Macon, Ga.; now reside in Titusville, Penn.; (Have children: Carroll Lund.[9] Frederick.[9] Harriet.[9] Crayton Sturtevant.[9]) Francis Crayton,[8] b. Dec. 13, 1838; m. Harriet Ellis; Hartford, Conn.; 4 children. Albert Audobon,[8] b. Sept. 22, 1840; m. Louise Marsh, of Woodstock, Vt.; reside Hartford, Conn.; have 2 children. Ann,[8] born Sept. 13, 1842; m. George H. Hebard, of Hartford, Conn. Wilbur R.,[8] b. Nov. 22, 1844, to whom I am indebted for this account of the family, resides Hartland, Vermont; he married Lenora Robinson, of Chelsea, Oct. 18, 1871; has three children.

980. ii. Thomas Foster,[7] b. May 12, 1798; died Dec. 4, 1874; m. Rosalind T. Taylor, Dec. 10, 1823. Children: Susan Waters,[8] b. Oct. 13, 1824; m. William Webster, of Windsor, Vt.; resides in Red Wing, Minnesota; have one son. Edwin,[8] b. Sept. 24, 1826; m. Sarah Ann Gilson, of Hartland; reside in Bethel, Vt. Mary Taylor,[8] b. Apr. 10, 1829; m. Theodore B. Sheldon; reside in Red Wing, Minn.; have one son. Robert Bruce,[8] m. Irene Hamilton, of Hartford, Conn.; she died, and he mar. 2d, Gabrielle Lyman; have two children; reside Hartford. Sarah Porter,[8] b. Apr. 11, 1837; m. E. H. Blodgett, of Windsor, Vt.; reside Red Wing, Minn. Thomas Foster,[8] b. Aug. 18, 1845.

981. iii. Edwin,[7] b. Feb. 8, 1801; died Nov. 27, 1804.

982. iv. George Fitz Edward,[7] b. Nov. 21, 1804; died Jan. 8, 1836; m. Mellissa Daniels, of Hartland, Vt. Children: Charles D.,[8] m. Alice Taylor; live in New Orleans. Samuel F.,[8] m. Julia Alexander; reside in Hamilton, Ont. Mary,[8] m. Nathaniel W. Weed; reside in Hamilton, Ont. Foster E.,[8] reside Milford, Mass. Geo. P.[8]

982A. v. Edwin,[7] b. May 19, 1806; educated at a military school, Middletown, Conn; class-mate of Gen. Magruder, for whom he composed "Magruder's Waltz"; teacher of music, in which he was highly successful: died at Charleston, S. C., 1836.

982B. vi. Eveline,[7] b. Nov. 30, 1808; m. Marshall Clark; he died, and widow resides in Illinois.

982C. vii. Sarah Ann,[7] b. June 21, 1811; m. Curtis Cady, of Hartland; resides Windsor, Vt. Children: William Porter,[8] and Hermon,[8] of Chicago, Ill. Elbert,[8] and Ella,[8] of Windsor, Vt.

524

Bathsheba[6] Porter, of Jonathan[5] Porter, b. Middleborough, Sept. 29, 1773. Married Edward Sparrow, Jr., Feb. 8, 1798; he son of Col. Edward and Rhoda (Bumpus) Sparrow, of Eastham; b. Jan. 10, 1768; died in Middleborough, Nov. 18, 1863; his wife died March 27, 1853. Children:

983. i. Bathsheba[7] Porter, b. Aug. 23, 1800; m. Martin Keith, Jr., Sept. 22, 1824; he son of Martin and Hope (Sturtevant) Keith, b. in Middleborough, Mass., June 27, 1799; died in Baltimore, Md., June 26, 1858. Children: Helen B.,[8] b. Jan. 26, 1827; died Sept. 11. Julia S.,[8] b. Dec. 13, 1827. Edward M.,[8] b. July 28,

1829; m. Maria Maynard, of Waltham, Mass., Jan. 24, 1861. Georgianna,[8] b. March 7, 1833; died April 15, 1857. John A.,[8] b. Aug. 31, 1835; died June 14, 1852. William H.,[8] b. Baltimore, Dec. 23, 1841; m. Clemence T. Hyde, of Baltimore, Oct. 23, 1866. Mabel Ida,[9] daughter of Wm. H.[8] and Clemence T. Keith, b. Baltimore, July 17, 1877.

984. ii. Clarinda,[7] b. March 8, 1802; m. Darius Miller, of Middleborough, Nov. 13, 1823; he son of Seth and Hannah (Alden) Miller; b. in Wareham, Nov. 13, 1796; died there, Feb. 20, 1874. Children: Clarinda S.,[8] b. Dec. 4, 1824; m. Samuel E. Turner, of Baltimore, son of William and Judith (Holyoke) Turner, of Salem, Mass.; b. Dec. 2, 1809. Darius E.,[8] b. April 27, 1830; m. Lydia F. Crowell, dau. of Obed and Hannah (Besse) Crowell; he died 1860; and his wife died April 29, 1863.

985. iii. Nancy,[7] b. Jan. 21, 1807; unmarried.

986. iv. Julia Ann,[7] b. Jan. 30, 1809; m. Abisha Miller, of Middleborough, Dec. 4, 1838; he son of John and Susanna (Sparrow) Miller, of Middleborough. Mrs. Miller died Oct. 29, 1840. Mr. Miller has resided in Boston, but now resides in Middleborough; is a man of great respectability of character, and influence. Mr. and Mrs. Miller had one child—Julia Henrietta,[8] b. Boston, Mar. 31, 1840.

987. v. Edward H.,[7] b. Middleborough, Sept. 4, 1812; of Wareham; m. Cordelia Bartlett, dau. of Lewis and Keziah (Leach) Bartlett, of Wareham, Oct. 17, 1839; she b. June 8, 1819; died Sept. 6, 1854. Children: Edward B.,[8] b. Oct. 16, 1841; m. Mary Ann Gammell, of Palmer, Oct. 11, 1863; he died in Palmer, Feb. 10, 1865. Cordelia C.,[8] b. Aug. 17, 1844; died Boston, April 27, 1847. Ella C. Porter,[8] b. Boston, March 23, 1848; m. Alex. Jameson, of Milford, Conn., June 8, 1874. Their daughter, Annie May,[9] b. Bridgeport, Conn., Nov. 24, 1876.

525

Deborah[6] Porter, of Jonathan[5] Porter, b. Nov. 13, 1775; married Jonathan Strong, of Rome, N. Y. Children: Porter.[7] Parthenia,[7] m. Andrews. Harriet,[7] died unmarried.

526

Sylvanus[6] Porter, of Jonathan[5] Porter, b. Nov. 13, 1778; resided Middleborough. Married Nancy McClinch, of Boston, August or September, 1804; she b. June 13, 1776; died in Boston, Jan. 12, 1827. He died in Middleborough, May 11, 1821. Children:

991. i. Nancy,[7] b. July 12, 1805; died Boston, Dec. 16, 1806.
992. ii. George Sylvanus,[7] b. Jan. 29, 1807; married.
993. iii. John Kirkland,[7] b. Dec. 25, 1808; married.
994. iv. Frances Elizabeth,[7] b. Sept. 8, 1811; married.
995. v. Ann Withington Emery,[7] b. Nov. 14, 1812.

527

Jonathan[6] Porter, of Jonathan[5] Porter, b. Jan. 21, 1785; went supercargo of a vessel to West Indies, and died there of yellow fever, in 1810.

528

William[6] Porter, of Jonathan[5] Porter, b. Feb. 1, 1763; lived in Middleborough; blacksmith; married Rebecca Wood, Dec. 13, 1792; she b. March 31, 1772; died July 4, 1855. He died Dec. 28, 1840. Children:

996. i. Peter,[7] b. Sept. 21, 1793; unmarried, died New Orleans, Sept. 27, 1822.
997. ii. Andrew Wood,[7] b. March 2, 1795; married.
998. iii. Minerva Wood,[7] b. Dec. 21, 1796; married.
999. iv. Mercy,[7] b. Feb. 5, 1799; married.
1000. v. William,[7] b. Feb. 20, 1801; married.
1001. vi. Edwin,[7] b. April 26, 1803; married.
1002. vii. James,[7] b. March 21, 1808; married.
1003. viii. Rebecca Wood,[7] b. March 2, 1810; married.

529

James[6] Porter, of Jonathan[5] Porter, b. 1792; removed from Middleborough, Mass., to Pittsford, Vermont; thence to Keene, Essex county, N. Y. Married Zilpah Miller; he died Dec. 5, 1820; she died Aug. 13, 1825, at Dart Settlement, Tioga county, Penn. Children:

1004. i. James,[7] b. Middleborough, June 30, 1792; unmarried; died Feb. 11, 1828.
1005. ii. Leonard,[7] b. Middleborough, Aug. 17, 1794; unmarried; died in Detroit, Mich., 1858.

1006\. iii. John Miller,[7] b. Pittsford, Rutland Co., Vt., Mar. 9, 1797.

1007\. iv. Zilpah Miller,[7] b. Hindsburg, Chittenden Co., Vt., June 18, 1799; married.

1008\. v. Royal Augustus,[7] b. Hindsburg, Chittenden Co., Vt., May 13, 1802; unmarried; died New Orleans, Aug. 2, 1873.

1009\. vi. Sophronia L.,[7] b. Keen, Essex Co., N. Y., Feb. 16, 1809.

1010\. vii. Sarah Rowena,[7] b. Keen, Essex Co., N. Y., Mar. 7, 1811; married.

530

Mercy[6] Porter, of Jonathan[5] Porter, b. March 8, 1762; married Jacob Bennett, Esq., of Middleborough, Oct., 1780; he son of Jacob and Hope (Nelson) Bennett, b. August 7, 1756; died Feb. 14, 1832. Mrs. Bennett died July 6, 1847. Children:

1011\. i. Patience,[7] b. July 14, 1781; m. Nathan Bennett, Sept. 5, 1802. Children: Harriett,[8] b. July 14, 1803; died Dec. 13, 1806. Hepsibah N.,[8] b. Aug. 21, 1806; died Feb. 20, 1838. Sarah H.,[8] b. Sept. 14, 1812; married Samuel Gifford, Oct. 22, 1837. (Children: Lucy Ann,[9] b. Sept. 11, 1839; died Jan. 4, 1841. Andrew Porter,[9] b. Sept. 5, 1843; died Feb. 2, 1845. Elvira Morton,[9] b. Feb. 22, 1845; m. Charles A. Tuell, Sept. 9, 1873. Corneilus Grinnell,[9] b. Mar. 27, 1847; died Feb. 5, 1849. Mary Jane,[9] b. Jan. 31, 1849; died Dec. 13, 1850.)

1012\. ii. Jacob,[7] b. Sept. 3, 1784; died Feb. 18, 1795.

1013\. iii. Mercy,[7] b. Oct. 10, 1787; married John Shaw, Jr., of Carver, 1819. Children: Jacob Bennett,[8] b. June 24, 1820; m. Ann M. A. Shaw, June 5, 1848; she dau. of Elhanah, b. July 27, 1828. (Children: Eva M.,[9] b. Sept. 26, 1851. Mary L.,[9] b. Nov. 20, 1855.) John,[8] b. Dec. 3, 1822; m. Hannah F., dau. of Andrew and Luanda (Seward) Nye, Apr. 15, 1833. (Children: John,[9] b. Nov., 1855; died June 11, 1870. Helen,[9] b. Feb. 18, 1859. Lizzie L.,[9] b. Mar. 5, 1864.) George,[8] b. Dec. 3, 1822; m. Polly, dau. of William Atwood, Dec. 30, 1847. One child, George.[9]

1014\. iv. Theodate,[7] b. Mar. 27, 1794; m. Ransom T. Wood, June 16, 1836. No children.

1015\. v. Hope,[7] b. Feb. 11, 1798; m. Zacheus Pickens, April, 1834. No children.

SEVENTH GENERATION.

548

Joseph[7] Porter, of Seward[6] Porter, b. Falmouth, Maine, April 8, 1778; resided Freeport, Me.; when quite young began to go to sea; continued in that business many years; captain of a ship; "never struck a sailor, in all his going to sea." During the war of 1812, he was in Russia, and had to remain there with his ship for some time, until peace was declared; after that went to Turks Island, in ship America; lost his ship on his return home. After that went into trade at Porter's Landing, Freeport. Married Deborah Nye; he died Oct. 18, (1849,) aged 76. His widow died June 14, 1854. Children:

1016. i. Elizabeth Nye,[8] b. Freeport, Sept. 2, 1817.
1017. ii. Joseph Nye,[8] b. Oct. 31, 1818; died 1818.
1018. iii. Mary Ann Wood,[8] b. April 9, 1819; died Feb. 26, 1827.
1019. iv. Mary Ann Greer,[8] b. Jan. 22, 1831; died 1838.
1020. v. Joseph Nye,[8] b. Portland, Oct. 31, 1833.

549

Samuel[7] Porter, of Seward[6] Porter, b. Falmouth, Me., April 10, 1779; lived in Portland and Freeport, Me. He and his brothers Seward and William, carried on ship building at Porter's Landing, in Freeport; they built the privateers America and Dash, during the war of 1812. Jeremiah (Captain,) John and Ebenezer were lost in the Dash, and never heard from. Samuel[7] Porter, married Nancy or Anne Storer; he died in Portland, 1847. Children:

1021. i. Delia Ann,[8] b. Dec. 18, 1803; m. Joseph Dennison.
1022. ii. Jane,[8] b. Oct. 9, 1805; died.
1023. iii. Eliza,[8] b. Aug. 31, 1808; died.
1024. iv. Mary,[8] b. April 13, 1811.
1025. v. Caroline,[8] b. Aug. 3, 1814.
1026. vi. Charles H.,[8] b. Dec. 6, 1816; died in New Orleans, 1841.

550

Joshua[7] Porter, of Seward[6] Porter, b. Falmouth, Me., Nov. 1, 1781; master mariner; lived and died in Westbrook, Me. Married 1st, Mary A. Wood; married 2d, Sarah Gray. Children by 2d wife:

1027. i. George,[8] lives Suisun City, Cal.
1028. ii. John,[8] lives Suisun City, Cal.

551

Sarah[7] Porter, of Seward[6] Porter, b. Freeport, Me, July 19, 1782. Married 1st, Leonard Morse, lawyer, of Freeport, Feb. 20, 1803. Children:

Susanna,[8] b. Aug. 2, 1803; m. John Marston. Seward.[8] John.[8] Eleanor,[8] married Hosmer, of Camden, Me. Mary.[8] Frederick.[8] Elizabeth.[8]

She married 2d, James Simonton, of Camden, Me; he son of James and Susan (Grose) Simonton, b. Dec. 19, 1797. She died 1855. Her children by second marriage:

Dorcas,[8] b. Freeport, 1822; m. H. H. Cleveland, of Camden, Me. George W.,[8] b. 1824; chief clerk in California Navy Yard. Joshua P.,[8] b. 1826, of Camden; farmer and teacher.

552

Seward[7] Porter, of Seward[6] Porter, b. Freeport, Me., July 21, 1784; merchant, of Portland, Me.; representative to General Court, from Portland, 1813,-'14-'15. Owned the first steamboat in Maine.

"In July, 1823, a great event happened in Portland; nothing less than the arrival in the harbor of the first steamboat ever brought into Maine. This was the Patent, a vessel of about one hundred tons burthen, owned by Capt. Seward Porter, of Portland, who had bought her in New York to run as a passenger boat between Portland and Boston. Capt. Porter had in 1822 placed an old engine in a flat bottomed boat, which he run to North Yarmouth, and the islands in Casco bay. This he named the Kennebec, but the people called it the Horned Hog. (Varney's History of Maine, page

245.) Married Betsey Tukey, of Portland, Me.; she b. there Aug. 2, 1784; died in New Orleans, Dec. 28, 1864. He died in Augusta, Me., March 29, 1838. Children, all b. in Portland:

1039. i. Seward,[8] b. Aug. 23, 1813; unmarried; died in Lavaca, Texas, Nov. 1, 1862.

1040. ii. George F.,[8] b. Aug. 27, 1819; of New Orleans.

1041. iii. Elizabeth Otis,[8] b. Dec. 1, 1821; of New Orleans.

553

Mary[7] Porter, of Seward[6] Porter, b. Freeport, Me., April 5, 1786; married Joel Hall, of Portland, June 12, 1808; he son of Jedediah Hall, b. Falmouth, Me., and died in Portland, May 27, 1851, aged 75 years 5 months and 23 days. His widow died Dec. 6, 1874. Children:

1042. i. Eleanor,[8] b. Jan. 22, 1809; m. John Neal, Jr., her cousin; he was son of John Neal, b. in Portland, Aug. 25, 1793, and died there June 20, 1876. His widow died Dec. 24, 1877. Mr. Neal was one of the most original and voluminous of early American authors; shop boy at age of 12; in 1813, teacher of drawing; next, clerk in Boston; afterwards went into partnership with Joseph L. Lord and John Pierpont, (poet and preacher) going with their business to Baltimore, in 1815, where they failed. He then studied law, and wrote novels which brought money and fame. In 1825 he went to England, where he was successful as an author. In 1827 he returned to the United States, and took up his residence in Portland, Me., where he continued to live during his life. He practiced law, edited newspapers, and accumulated property by various speculations. He was honest, generous, warm hearted and passionate, despised shams and humbugs; a warm friend, and an open square enemy, who despised subterfuge, and never hit in the dark. He had the respect and confidence of the community in which he lived. (Condensed from the Maine Genealogist and Biographer for Sept., 1876, from a notice written by Edward H. Elwell, Esq., of Portland.)

1043. ii. Margaret Ann,[8] b. Dec. 5, 1810; m. Robert Southgate Boyd, March 14, 1832; he was son of Joseph and Isabella (Southgate) Boyd, of Portland. He died Dec. 1, 1877, aged 73 years. Children: Joel Hall,[9] b. Dec. 9,

1836; m. Mary Caroline Whitmore, Feb. 13, 1862. Samuel Stillman,[9] b. May 16, 1838; m. Harriet Eliza Churchill, Oct. 6, 1864, and has six children ; is a lawyer and resides in St. Louis, Mo. Robert Southgate,[9] b. Dec. 11, 1842; m. Elizabeth S. Wilson, of Cambridge, Mass., Sept. 29, 1869. William Edward,[9] b. June 4, 1844; died June 1, 1845.

1043½. iii. William Edward,[8] b. Feb. 1, 1824; m. Jane L. Gertz, Sept. 20, 1855, she died Dec. 13, 1859, aged 24; he died Jan. 29, 1865, aged 40 years. They had two children: Margaret Boyd,[9] b. Sept. 22, 1856; died. Eleanor Neal,[9] b. Oct. 17, 1859; died Dec. 15, 1868, aged 9.

555

William[7] Porter, of Seward[6] Porter, b. Freeport, Me., Sept. 17, 1788; U. S. Consul at Tripoli; he died 1868. Married 1st, Ann Field, of Boston, Nov., 1815. They had one child, who died in infancy. Married 2d, Miss O'Riely, in 1864. His widow now resides in France.

556

John[7] Porter, of Seward[6] Porter, b. Nov. 27, 1792; lived in Freeport, Me.; lost in the Dash privateer, (in war of 1812;) married Lois Cushing, of Portland. (Widow married John Dunlap.) Child:

1044. i. John,[8] died in Portland some years since.

557

Charles[7] Porter, of Seward[6] Porter, b. Falmouth, Me., Jan. 17, 1794; lived in New York city; died Nov. 29, 1841; married Mary Leek Brown, in New York, May 17, 1817; she b. in New York, Aug. 13, 1801; died there Sept. 22, 1847. Children:

1045. i. Mary Brown,[8] b. April 2, 1818.
1046. ii. Noah Brown,[8] b. Nov. 21, 1819; m.; died Apr. 23, 1855.
1047. iii. Julia Ann,[8] b. Aug. 30, 1822; died July 11, 1823.
1048. iv. William Bartlett,[8] b. Jan. 29, 1824; died March 9, 1851.
1049. v. Anna,[8] b. Jan. 17, 1826.
1050. vi. Eleanor Ruth,[8] b. Feb. 10, 1828; died Feb. 22, 1852.
1051. vii. George Sumner,[8] b. June 3, 1831.

1052. viii. Emma Fields,[8] b. March 24, 1833; died July 6, 1833.
1053. ix. Henry,[8] b. Apr. 8, 1834; died same day.
1054. x. Rebecca Comstock,[8] b. Mar. 13, 1836.

580

Sylvanus[7] Porter, of Nehemiah[6] Porter, b. Oct. 11, 1783; lived in North Yarmouth, Me.; died there Oct. 22, 1815. Married Sylvia Bartlett, of Bethel, Maine, June 7, 1809. (Widow married 2d, David Trickey, (?) had one child:)

1055. i. Barbour B.,[8] b. Aug. 4, 1810; married.

581

Susanna[7] Porter, of Nehemiah[6] Porter, b. Aug. 24, 1785; married John Hamilton, of North Yarmouth, Me., 1804; she died Nov. 11, 1828, or Nov. 17, 1823. Her children:

1056. i. Charles,[8] b. 1808; m. Barbour; sea captain; died in Portland, 1843.
1057. ii. Jacob,[8] b. 1810; m. 1st, Johnson, of Gray, Me.; m. 2d, Mrs. Fisk; resides East Dover, Me.
1058. iii. Nehemiah,[8] b. 1812; died at sea.
1059. iv. Ezekiel,[8] b. 1814; lives in Ohio.
1059A. v. Sylvanus,[8] b. 1816; died in Cuba.

582

Lucy[7] Porter, of Nehemiah[6] Porter, b. Sept. 21, 1787; married Timothy Chase, of Paris, Me., 1805; she died Feb. 15, 1838. Children:

1059B. i. Mary Ann,[8] m. Marshall Stearns, of Paris, Me.; died March, 1870.
1059C. ii. Lowell,[8] lived Portland; died June, 1874.
1059D. iii. Susan,[8] m. Lewis Sturdivant, of Portland, Me.
1059E. iv. Hannah,[8] m. Alfred Staples, of Portland, Me.
1059F. v. Edward P.,[8] resides Portland; State Liquor Commissioner.
1059G. vi. William,[8] of Paris; died March, 1876.
1059H. vii. Ann,[8] m. Blake, of Chelsea, Mass.
1059I. viii. Granville,[8] of Portland; died Dec., 1873.

584

Stephen[7] Porter, of Nehemiah[6] Porter, b. June 16, 1791; resided North Yarmouth, Me.; farmer; captain in the war of

1812; married Rebecca Cobb, of Gray, Jan., 1816. He died Dec. 3, 1869, aged 78; wife died Aug. 6, 1855, aged 68. Children:

1060. i. Abigail,[8] b. Oct. 20, 1816.
1061. ii. Matilda,[8] b. July 25, 1818.
1062. iii. Jedediah Cobb,[8] b. Nov. 12, 1820; died April 24, 1842.
1063. iv. William R.,[8] b. May 20, 1825; married.
1064. v. Martha,[8] unmarried; died 1835, aged 11.
1065. vi. Clarissa,[8] unmarried; died 1830.
1066. vii. Ann Maria,[8] m. Alexander Buchanan, of Camden, Me.

585

John[7] Porter, of Nehemiah[6] Porter, b. Oct. 7, 1793; resided West Paris, Maine; married Eunice Hicks, Jan. 22, 1816; b. Sept. 27, 1790. He died Oct. 12, 1855. Children:

1067. i. Sylvanus,[8] b. March 31, 1817.
1068. ii. Ezekiel L.,[8] b. Oct. 3, 1819; died Jan. 14, 1869.
1069. iii. John Barbour,[8] b. Aug. 12, 1821.
1070. iv. Harriet,[8] b. Aug. 20, 1823; m. Solomon J. Millet, of Norway, Me., Feb. 22, 1857.
1070A. v. Joseph Hicks,[8] b. March 4, 1826; m. Sarah Holmes, Dec. 31, 1854.
1070B. vi. Franklin,[8] b. Oct. 18, 1829.

586

Charles[7] Porter, of Nehemiah[6] Porter, b. June 19, 1794; lived Paris, Me.; married Rachel Hamilton, Jan. 21, 1816; she was daughter of William and Rachel (Lufkin) Hamilton, of North Yarmouth, b. July 19, 1794. He died Apr. 3, 1861; she died Jan. 1, 1877. Children:

1071. i. Mary Ann,[8] b. Aug. 21, 1817.
1072. ii. Lucy Hamilton,[8] b. April 21, 1820; m. 1st, Hiram Knight, of Paris; m. 2d, Wm. Allen, of Poland.
1073. iii. William Henry,[8] b. May 8, 1822.
1074. iv. Rachel Lufkin,[8] b. Feb. 11, 1824.
1075. v. Samuel Newell,[8] b. May 14, 1826; died 1827.
1076. vi. Charles Newell,[8] b. April 7, 1828.
1077. vii. Alvan H.,[8] b. July 2, 1831; died 1833.
1078. viii. Granville,[8] b. June 11, 1833; died 1856.

587

Benjamin[7] Porter, of Nehemiah[6] Porter, b. Dec. 10, 1796; married Zeruiah Ring, of North Yarmouth, Me.; went to Paris, Me., where they had one child, Olive.[8] The wife and mother both died, and he removed to Deerfield, Vermont, between 1835 and 1840, and there married a Miss Bean, by whom he had one son, William,[8] who went into the army a short time before his father's death, in 1863.

588

Joanna[7] Porter, of Nehemiah[6] Porter, b. Aug. 6, 1798; married William Stearns, Jr., of Paris, Me, June 30, 1817; he and his father born Waltham, Mass. He died Mar. 20, 1877; widow still living. Children:

1080. i. William Porter,[8] b. Aug. 28, 1819; m. Ellen B. Hamlin, of Wiscasset, Me., Dec. 11, 1843; resides Portland, Me. Children: Isadore E.,[9] George W.,[9] and William A.[9]

1081. ii. Charles H.,[8] b. Oct. 28, 1820; m. Henrietta C. Cowdrey, of Wakefield, Mass., May 30, 1844, where he resides. Children: Etta May,[9] Myra A.,[9] Clinton Harris.[9]

1082. iii. James,[8] b. Aug. 9, 1823; m. A. Augusta Pond, Sept. 10, 1850; resides Cambridge, Mass. Has two children: Fred H.,[9] and Annie Pond.[9]

1083. iv. George Francis,[8] b. Sept. 26, 1825; m. Ellen Hutchinson, of Hartford, Me., June, 1839; resides Richmond, Ind. Has children: Mary Blake,[9] Edward Hutchinson,[9] George,[9] and Harry.[9]

1084. v. Lucy Ann,[8] b. April 12, 1828; m. Jacob Woodman, of Dorchester, Mass., June, 1852; he b. Durham, N. H. Children: Edwin L.,[9] George Francis,[9] William,[9] Stearns,[9] and Nellie Porter.[9]

1085. vi. Sylvanus Porter,[8] b. March 30, 1831; m. Isabel Partridge; resides in Paris, Me. Children: Austin Partridge,[9] Frank Porter,[9] Henry Knox,[9] William C.,[9] and May Isabel.[9]

1085. vii. Lydia Herrick,[8] b. June 2, 1835; m. Smith Dudley, of Paris, Me., Dec., 1836. Children: Charles Smith,[9] James Stearns,[9] Ella Louisa,[9] and Emily Gertrude.[9]

1085A. viii. Mary Susan,[8] b. Feb. 11, 1839; m. James Howe, of Medford, Mass., Aug., 1870. One child: Arthur Stearns.[9]

589

Mary[7] Porter, of Nehemiah[6] Porter, b. Feb. 10, 1800; married Benjamin Cole, of North Yarmouth, Me., 1823; she died Dec. 14, 1838. Children:

1086. i. William,[8] b. 1824; lives Chelsea, Mass.; m. Miss Hanson, of North Yarmouth, Me.
1087. ii. E. Joanna,[8] b. 1826; m. Marston, of North Yarmouth, and has five children.
1088. iii. Emma,[8] b. 1828; m. Hutchinson, of Auburn, Me., and has one son.
1089. iv. Daniel,[8] b. 1837; m. Skillins; lives in North Yarmouth; no children.

590

Seward[7] Porter, of Nehemiah[6] Porter, b. June 3, 1805; resides in Cleveland, Ohio, where he went from Portland, about 1854; married Eliza Daniels, of Paris, Me., Nov. 18, 1830. Children:

1090. i. Clara,[8] m. Barrett, of Boston; died, and left two sons.
1091. ii. Albert,[8] resides Cambridge, Mass.
1092. iii. Eliza,[8] died unmarried, 1874.
1093. iv. Seward W.[8] (?)

593

Mahala[7] Porter, of Benjamin[6] Porter, b. Freeport, July 15, 1790; married Andrew Soule, of Freeport, Me. She died Oct. 26, 1850. Children:

1096. i. Rebecca,[8] b. Aug. 4, 1810.
1097. ii. Desire,[8] b. June 6, 1812.
1098. iii. Martha,[8] b. Aug. 14, 1817.
1099. iv. Benjamin Porter,[8] b. Nov. 19, 1819.
1100. v. Mahala,[8] b. April 21, 1822.
1101. vi. Hannah[8] b. June 10, 1825.
1101½. vii. Andrew Jackson,[8] b. Oct. 12, 1831.

594

Rebecca[7] Porter, of Benjamin[6] Porter, b. Mar. 15, 1792; married Eleazer Pinkham. She died Nov. 18, 1839. No children.

595

Hannah[7] Porter, of Benjamin[6] Porter, b. July 21, 1794; married John Marston, of Falmouth, 1822; she died 1860. Children:

Harriet.[8] Benjamin Porter.[8] Alvin.[8] Caroline.[8]

596

Cyrene[7] Porter, of Benjamin[6] Porter, b. March 8, 1796; married Jonathan Hobbs, of Biddeford; she died Aug. 24, 1858; children:

Isabella.[8] Emeline.[8]

598

Joseph[7] Porter, of Benjamin[6] Porter, b. March 18, 1799; resided Freeport, Me.; m. Eliza Houston, 1823. Children:

1108. i. William,[8] b. Mar. 25, 1824.
1109. ii. Rebecca P.,[8] b. May 1, 1825; married Corydon Walker, 1849. Children: Herbert A.[9] Lester P.[9] Evelyn.[9]
1110. iii. Benjamin,[8] b. Sept. 25, 1827; died young.
1111. iv. Eliza,[8] b. Jan. 13, 1830.
1112. v. Joseph,[8] b. May 3, 1834.
1113. vi. George A.,[8] b. June 8, 1836.
1114. vii. Melissa P.,[8] b. May 23, 1838.
1115. viii. Charles,[8] b. Aug. 25, 1840.
1116. ix. Benjamin.[8]

599

Sarah[7] Porter, of Benjamin[6] Porter, b. Nov. 1, 1801; married 1st, John Hayes, of North Yarmouth, Me.; he died about 1831. Children by Hayes:

Amanda.[8] Francis.[8] John H.[8]

Married 2d, Enoch Morse; she died June 3, 1852. Children by Morse:

Charles.[8] Mellissa.[8] Ellen.[8] Winfield S.[8]

600

Mary[7] Porter, of Benjamin[6] Porter, b. Nov. 1, 1803; married Deacon Edward R. Titcomb, 1830; lived in Durham, Me., and in Freeport. Wife died April 17, 1873. Children born in Durham, except the first, who was born in North Yarmouth:

1109. i. Benjamin Porter,[8] b. June 1, 1832; died Petersburg, Va., June 16, 1864.
1110. ii. Edward P.,[8] b. Nov. 15, 1833; died Feb. 28, 1844.
1111. iii. Joshua M.,[8] b. Sept. 21, 1835; died May 7, 1850.
1112. iv. Augustus,[8] b. May 25, 1837; died July 16, 1837.
1113. v. Mary E.,[8] b. July 24, 1838; died Feb. 18, 1864.
1114. vi. Frances[8] R., b. March 20, 1840; died June 29, 1840.
1115. vii. Frances R.,[8] b. June 20, 1841.
1116. viii. Harriet M.,[8] b. Nov. 22, 1842; died Aug. 15, 1846.

601

Eleanor[7] Porter, of Benjamin[6] Porter, b. April 4, 1805; married Samuel Fogg. She died May, 1877. Children:

Mary E.[8] Fannie.[8] Benjamin.[8]

602

Eliza[7] Porter, of Benjamin[6] Porter, b. Feb. 2, 1807; married Enoch Pratt, 1827-8. Children:

Mellissa.[8] Ellen.[8] Joseph P.[8] Isabella H.[8] Enoch.[8] Edgar G.[8]

603

Patience[7] Porter, of Benjamin[6] Porter, b. Aug. 16, 1809; married Theophilus Herrick, Feb. 28, 1838; he son of John and Rachel Herrick, of Brooklin, Me., b. May 7, 1811. Children:

i. Ellen P.,[8] b. April 21, 1839; married A. B. Ober, Feb. 17, 1863. Children: Lutie G.,[9] b. May 23, 1869. Mr. Ober died Jan. 4, 1874.
ii. Elmira C.,[8] b. Nov. 5, 1840; married William A. Friend, Aug. 16, 1862. Children: Lillia A.,[9] b. Feb. 18, 1864. Charles W.,[9] b. Oct. 13, 1872.
iii. Algernon P.,[8] b. Aug. 16, 1842; died Oct. 28, 1863.
iv. Albertine S.,[8] b. May 18, 1844; died May 8, 1853.
v. Edward P.,[8] b. Jan. 14, 1846.

658

Robert[7] Porter, of Robert[6] Porter, b. Stoughton, Dec. 19, 1798; of Stoughton; farmer and real estate owner; married 1st, Fannie B., daughter of Uriah Capen, of Stoughton,

Aug. 20, 1822; she died Apr. 26, 1832. Married 2d, Eunice Freeman, of Orleans, June 24, 1832. She died April 4, 1874. Married 3d, Mrs. Caroline P. Ames, of Milton, June 5, 1875. He died Nov. 9, 1876, aged 78. Children:

1200. i. Robert,^{8} b. Dec. 6, 1823.
1201. ii. Uriah Capen,^{8} b. Oct. 2, 1826.
1202. iii. Theron Metcalf,^{8} b. Dec. 19, 1828.
1203. iv. Joseph,^{8} b. 1832; died the day he was born.
1204. v. Fannie Capen,^{8} b. June 24, 1833; died Sept. 15, 1833.
1205. vi. Eunice Freeman,^{8} b. Aug. 11, 1834; m. Edward Kinsley, March 30, 1853. One child, Nellie.^{9}
1206. vii. John Murray,^{8} b. Feb. 1, 1837.
1207. viii. Jonathan Freeman,^{8} b. March 23, 1840.
1208. ix. Marcus Morton,^{8} b. May 12, 1841.
1209. x. Horace Mann,^{8} b. June 14, 1844; drowned July 22, 1873.
1210. xi. William Baylies,^{8} b. May 20, 1850; died May 10, 1855.
1211. xii. Fannie Capen,^{8} b. March 23, 1853.
1212. xiii. William Baylies,^{8} b. March 27, 1858.

659

John^{7} Porter, of Robert^{6} Porter, b. Stoughton, Dec. 25, 1800; married Mehetable B. Kingman, of West Bridgewater, Dec. 16, 1828; he died Nov. 7, 1873; his widow resides East Stoughton. Children:

1213. i. Elizabeth,^{8} b. April 12, 1830.
1214. ii. Jonathan K.,^{8} b. Sept. 10, 1832.
1215. iii. Benjamin W.,^{8} b. July 9, 1835.
1216. iv. Weston,^{8} b. March 24, 1841; died Dec. 14, 1861.

660

Joseph^{7} Porter, of Robert^{6} Porter, b. May 11, 1805; of East Stoughton; farmer; married Martha Edson, of North Bridgewater, July 3, 1826; he died Feb. 13, 1848. Children:

1217. i. Martha H.,^{8} b. Nov. 3, 1829.
1218. ii. Lucia C.,^{8} b. Aug. 4, 1832; married Roswell C. Amsden, of Southboro, June 23, 1849; resides Holbrook.
1219. iii. Joseph D.,^{8} b. Mar. 19, 1835.
1220. iv. Susan Crocker,^{8} b. Apr. 10, 1839.
1221. v. Isaac S.,^{8} b. Feb. 23, 1842.
1222. vi. Abbie A.,^{8} b. June 15, 1845; married Warren Thayer, of Holbrook, Nov. 9, 1862; he died Nov. 1, 1874, aged 33 years 9 mos. 11 days. No children.

662

Sally[7] Porter, of Robert[6] Porter, b. Dec. 16, 1806; married Franklin Clark, of Stoughton; both dead. Children: Sarah.[8] Clementine.[8] Franklin.[8] Alice.[8]

663

Joseph Tower was twin son (with Abraham) of Joseph and Betsey Tower, of Randolph, b. Aug. 31, 1804; he lived in Randolph. Married 1st, Eliza Ann, daughter of Shadrach and Hepsibah Thayer, by Rev. Benj. Putnam, in Randolph; she died Jan. 4, 1830. Married 2d, Fanny Wales,[7] dau. of Robert and Elizabeth (Gay) Porter, of Stoughton, Aug. 15, 1832, by Rev. Calvin Hitchcock; she b. Oct. 2, 1808; and died in Natick, Aug. 13, 1872, aged 84. The children, all b. in Randolph:

i. Eliza Ann,[8] b. Sept. 29, 1828; died Oct. 3, 1828.

1227. ii. Abraham William,[8] b. Sept. 10, 1829; mar. in Boston, Sept. 12, 1852, to Lydia Ann, dau. of Benjamin and Lydia Clark, of Randolph, (their son Abraham,[9] b. in Randolph, June 30, 1854. Their daughter,[9] b. New York, 1872.)

iii. Joseph Porter,[8] b. Nov. 17, 1833; died Nov. 25, 1833.

1228. iv. Eliza Ann,[8] b. Mar. 14, 1835; m. in Randolph, by Rev. C. M. Cordley, Oct. 12, 1856, to Benjamin Franklin Springer, son of Stephen and Mary Springer, of Hallowell, Me. Children: Fannie Hinckley,[9] b. Randolph, Aug. 15, 1857. Nellie Kimball,[9] b. Randolph, May 5, 1860. Albertina Colman,[9] b. Natick, Dec. 14, 1862; died in Randolph, Aug. 7, 1864. Frank Hobart,[9] b. April 6, 1865; died Natick, April 22, 1865. Jennie Porter,[9] b. Natick, Sept. 4, 1866. Gertrude Hoyt,[9] b. Natick, Nov. 28, 1868. Freddie Lee,[9] b. Natick, Mar. 3, 1871. Winfield Scott,[9] b. Natick, Jan. 27, 1873. This family reside in Natick, Mass.

v. Ellen Frances,[8] b. Feb. 22, 1837; unmarried.

vi. Ruth Carter,[8] b. Oct. 29, 1840; died Oct. 11, 1841.

1229. vii. Joseph Edwards Carter,[8] b. Aug. 3, 1844; married in New York, by Rev. Dr. Talmage, Sarah Isabella Johnson, Nov. 25, 1868; dau. of Harry and Sarah Johnson, of New York. Their son Harry Durrell,[9] b. Randolph, Apr. 21, 1870. Their dau. Mabel,[9] b. in New York, Dec., 1873.

664

Susanna[7] Porter, of Isaac[6] Porter, b. Middleborough, Apr. 17, 1788; m. Galen Thompson, of William Thompson, Jan. 1, 1807; she died Jan. 16, 1808. Mr. Thompson married 2d, Fanny Marble, and removed to (Jay) Maine. Galen and Susanna Thompson one child:

1230. i. Susanna,[8] b. 1807; married Solomon Beal.

665

Isaac[7] Porter, of Isaac[6] Porter, b. Middleborough, April 20, 1790; was a musician on board U. S. ship Chesapeake, in the war of 1812; was taken prisoner and carried to Halifax; afterward exchanged, and died at the Navy Yard in Charlestown, Aug. 9, 1815, from sickness contracted during his imprisonment.

667

Rhodolphus[7] Porter, of Isaac[6] Porter, b. Middleborough, Jan. 25, 1794; married Sarah F. French, daughter of Sylvanus French, of Braintree, 1820. He died Sept. 16, 1870. Children:

1231. i. Isaac,[8] b. April 19, 1821.
1232. ii. Rhodolphus,[8] b. 1822; died young.
1233. iii. Joseph French,[8] b. April 28, 1824.
1234. iv. Lewis,[8] b. Jan. 26, 1826.
1235. v. Sarah French,[8] b. Oct. 7, 1827; m. David C. Norton; she died May 1, 1864. 1 child.
1236. vi. Lucinda,[8] b. Sept. 11, 1829.
1237. vii. Azubah Ann,[8] b. Jan. 2, 1832.
1238. viii. Rhodolphus,[8] b. Jan. 22, 1834.
1239. ix. Charles F.,[8] b. Jan. 16, 1836.
1240. x. Elisabeth G.,[8] died young.
1241. xi. Elisabeth Guild,[8] b. Sept. 7, 1840.

668

Reuben[7] Porter, of Isaac[6] Porter, b. Mar. 23, 1798; resided East Randolph; married Rhoda Curtis, Mar. 31, 1822; he died Mar. 23, 1873. Children:

1242. i. Flavius,[8] b. Dec. 23, 1823; married Nancy Ford; he died Aug. 15, 1852.
1243. ii. Eliza A.,[8] b. July 21, 1825; died June 14, 1832.

1244. iii. Laura Y.,[8] b. Sept. 17, 1827; married D. Webster Thayer.
1245. iv. Martha,[8] b. Mar. 30, 1830; died May 27, 1857.
1246. v. Lucy C.,[8] b. Apr. 20, 1832; married Henry M. French, of Holbrook, has one child. (1877)
1247. vi. Samuel W.,[8] b. May 5, 1835; died July 2, 1836.
1248. vii. Rhoda E.,[8] b. Jan. 15, 1839; married Richmond T. Pratt, of Holbrook. Has four children:

669

Martin[7] Porter, of Isaac[6] Porter, b. North Bridgewater, July 13, 1800; resided South Braintree; painter; married Rebecca A. Reed, of East Randolph, 1823; she b. July 17, 1803. He died at house of his son Asa, at South Boston, March 8, 1877. Children:

1249. i. Martin R.,[8] b. Jan. 21, 1834.
1250. ii. Rebecca J.,[8] b. Dec. 7, 1826.
1251. iii. Asa R.,[8] b. Feb. 6, 1829.
1252. iv. Susan E.,[8] b. Apr. 4, 1833.

670

Samuel[7] Porter, of Isaac[6] Porter, b. North Bridgewater, May 12, 1796. Married his cousin Sally Gill, of Canton, Sept. 1, 1817, (see No. 677;) she b. July 3, 1795; died St. Louis, Mo., Oct. 18, 1851; he died Canton, Ill., Sept. 13, 1858. Children:

1253. i. Julia Ann,[8] b. Easton, July 18, 1820.
1254. ii. Samuel L.,[8] b. Boston, July 17, 1824.
1255. iii. Benjamin F.,[8] b. Boston, Jan. 31, 1827.
1256. iv. William W.,[8] b. Mar. 31, 1830; unmarried; died Nov. 11, 1863.
1257. v. Hattie,[8] b. Canton, Ill., Dec. 10, 1837.

671

Ira[7] Porter, of Isaac[6] Porter, b. North Bridgewater, Apr. 5, 1803; resides Randolph; married Eulalia Belcher, July 15, 1829; she b. Randolph, Apr. 20, 1803; died there May 5, 1864. Children:

1258. i. Susanna,[8] b. Braintree, June 27, 1830; died Dec. 16, 1830.
1259. ii. Ira W.,[8] b. Braintree, June 17, 1832.
1260. iii. Stephen F.,[8] b. Braintree, Jan, 10, 1835; died Oct. 8, 1836.
1261. iv. Franklin,[8] b. Braintree, Oct. 14, 1836.
1262. v. Mary E.,[8] b. Randolph, March 26, 1840; died Nov. 25, 1840.
1263. vi. Charles H.,[8] b. Randolph, Apr. 8, 1845; died Oct. 25, 1845.

672

Galen T.[7] Porter, of Isaac[6] Porter, b. Nov. 5, 1807; resides Harlem, N. Y.; real estate dealer; married Mary E. Fletcher, Sept. 13, 1829; she daughter of Elisha and Abigail R. (Day) Fletcher, of Lancaster, Mass., and Marblehead; b. Sept. 6, 1810; died White Plains, Westchester Co., N. Y., Oct. 26, 1870. Children:

1264. i. Ellen Adams,[8] b. June, 1830; married William A. Hight, of New York city, Mar. 29, 1853.
1265. ii. John Holmes,[8] b. Feb., 1832; married Louisa J. Ayers, 1858; and died June 5, 1875.
1266. iii. Emma,[8] b. Oct., 1834; died Dec. 17, 1834.
1267. iv. Mary Emma,[8] b. Mar., 1837; m. Marcellus E. Randall, of New York city, Sept. 8, 1854; dry goods dealer.
1268. v. Anna Perkins,[8] b. Nov., 1839; married Lewis W. Stetson, from Taunton, Mass., Mar. 30, 1862; he was an engineer; died Mar. 7, 1869.
1269. vi. Galen Thompson,[8] b. June, 1842; died at St. Thomas, West Indies, Sept. 15, 1866; he was purser's clerk, U. S. Navy.
1270. vii. David Fletcher,[8] b. Dec., 1844; married Fannie E. Leggett, of New York city, Aug. 13, 1869; real estate dealer, New York city.
1271. viii. Harriet Augusta,[8] b. Sept., 1847; m. Elihu L. Tompkins, of White Plains, N. Y., Sept. 27, 1865; farmer; resides New York city.
1272. ix. Frank,[8] b. Apr., 1852; died Feb. 25, 1853.

673

Anna Perkins[7] Porter, of Isaac[6] Porter, b. Apr. 20, 1805; Married William Wales Cushing, Oct. 3, 1827; he son of John and Polly (Wales) Cushing; born Feb. 19, 1806; resides in Abington; boot manufacturer, all of his sons having been co-partners in business with him; has been selectman several years; was postmaster under Amos Kendall; lieutenant of infantry under Marcus Morton. Children:

1273. i. William Henry,[8] b. Mar. 9, 1829; married Anna N. Tanner, 1869.
1274. ii. Susan A.,[8] b. Feb. 20, 1833; married John W. Quinn, 1850; has two sons living,—the oldest in Lewiston, Me.
1275. iii. John,[8] b. Aug. 3, 1837; married Anna M. Cushing, 1864.

1276. iv. Marcus Morton,[8] b. Dec. 2, 1839; died young.
1277. v. Marcus Morton,[8] b. Oct. 27, 1842; died young.
1278. vi. Galen Porter,[8] b. Jan. 7, 1844; married Ellen M. Orcutt, 1867.
1279. vii. Mary Ellen,[8] b. May 23, 1846.
1280. viii. Almira Frances,[8] b. Oct. 11, 1848; died in infancy.

686

Whitcomb[7] Porter, of Lebbeus[6] Porter, b. Stoughton, Mar. 10, 1799; carpenter; merchant; insurance agent; went to Weymouth about 1820; then to Quincy, where he is a much respected citizen; married Susan Bowditch, daughter of Ebenezer and Betsey (Nash) Hunt, of Weymouth, Dec. 7, 1826, by Rev. Jonas Perkins, of Braintree. Mrs. Porter, b. March 16, 1809. Children:

1281. i. John Whitcomb,[8] b. Aug. 2, 1827, in Weymouth.
1282. ii. George Edward,[8] b. Nov. 4, 1828, in Weymouth.
1283. iii. Henry Thomas,[8] July 13, 1832, in Weymouth.
1284. iv. Susan Brastow,[8] b. July 17, 1836, in Weymouth.
1285. v. Ann Maria Hunt,[8] b. Oct. 26, 1838, in Weymouth; died Jan. 23, 1842.
1286. vi. Charles Hunt,[8] b. April 3, 1843, in Quincy.
1287. vii. Helen Maria,[8] b. March 15, 1847, in Quincy.

687

Joseph[7] Porter, of Lebbeus[6] Porter, b. Wrentham, Mass., Dec. 19, 1800; when about twenty-one years of age, he went to Weymouth; in business as carpenter and lumber-dealer with his brother, Whitcomb Porter; in 1824 removed to Milton, where he continued the same business. He was an original member and deacon of the village church, (Orthodox,) at Dorchester Lower Mills; was elected captain of Dorchester Rifle Company, March 8, 1830; elected a member of Ancient and Honorable Artillery Company, Aug., 1832; two of his ancestors having been members of the same company more than *two hundred years ago;* elected colonel of the first regiment of infantry in the first brigade and first division of Massachusetts militia, Sept. 9, 1833. When President Jackson visited Boston, he with his regiment escorted him through Roxbury to Boston line. In

1834 he removed to Brewer, Maine, and about 1840 to Lowell, Maine. Upon the breaking out of the North-Eastern Boundary troubles, in February, 1839, he raised a company of volunteers for the war, and immediately proceeded to the scene of action on the Aroostook river. On the 24th of February he was appointed colonel of the volunteer troops, consisting of twelve companies and nearly one thousand men, which position he held until the arrival of the regular militia. He was several years a County Commissioner for the County of Penobscot, Maine, and a member of the Maine Legislature. He married 1st, Mary Stetson, daughter of Major Amos and Hannah (Hunt) Stetson, of Braintree, Mass., Oct. 22, 1823, by Rev. Jonas Perkins. She born March 27, 1803; died Lowell, Me., June 8, 1866. Married 2d, Mrs. Mary R. Philbrook, of Springfield, Me. He died in Lowell, Maine, Feb. 7, 1878. Children:

1288. i. Joseph Whitcomb,[8] b. Milton, Mass., July 27, 1824.
1289. ii. John Barker,[8] b. Milton, Mass., Mar. 27, 1826.
1290. iii. Mary Stetson,[8] b. Milton, Mass., Oct. 15, 1827.
1291. iv. Susan Fisher,[8] b. Milton, Mass., Dec. 19, 1829.
1292. v. Thomas Williams,[8] b. Milton, Mass., May 15, 1832.
1293. vi. Caroline Elisabeth[8] b. Milton, Mass., Feb. 15, 1834; died Lowell, Maine, March 26, 1872.
1294. vii. Annah Stetson,[8] b. Milton, Mass., June 15, 1836; died Brewer, Me., Aug. 15, 1838.
1295. viii. Elizabeth Burrill,[8] b. Lowell.
1296. ix. Richard Lebbeus,[8] b. Lowell, Mass., March 21, 1875.

688

William G.[7] Porter, of Lebbeus[6] Porter, b. Sept. 24, 1802; resided Wrentham, Mass.; carpenter; married Hannah Torrey, Dec. 2, 1830; he died Feb. 17, 1868, aged 66 years. Children:

1297. i. George William,[8] b. Aug. 8, 1832.
1298. ii. Mary Elizabeth,[8] b. Feb. 7, 1834; married Albert Blake, Jan, 6, 1859.
1299. iii. Sarah Josephine,[8] b. Jan. 27, 1838; married Henry M. Kent, July, 1858; resides Attleboro. Children: Henry Porter,[9] b. Oct. 30, 1859. Frederic William,[9] b. July 7, 1868.

1300. iv. Albert Augustus,[8] b. July 27, 1840; physician; died unmarried, March 26, 1871.

689

Elisabeth B.[7] Porter, of Lebbeus[6] Porter, b. in Wrentham, June 24, 1804, and died there June 24, 1862. Married Ellis Pond, Dec. 5, 1827; son of Jabez Pond. (Rev. Timothy Pond, graduated Harvard College, 1749, and settled in Franklin; in 1774 he sold out and removed to Wrentham, where he died 1804; his son Jabez, b. Franklin, Aug. 8, 1760; married Basmouth Ellis, of Medway, Apr. 29, 1795; she b. March 29, 1772; died in Wrentham, Feb., 1854, he having died in 1849.) Ellis and Elisabeth B. Pond had one child:

1301. i. William Ellis,[8] b. Sept. 1, 1829; he and his father now reside on the old homestead, in Wrentham, to which his great-grandfather removed 1774; he married Mary Stevens Warren, in Foxboro, Mass., Sept. 15, 1853, (she daughter of Samuel Stevens Warren, born in Foxborough, Apr. 14, 1793, who was son of Ebenezer Warren, and nephew of General Joseph Warren, who fell at the Battle of Bunker Hill. Samuel S. Warren, grad. Brown University, 1816; practiced law in Hallowell, Me., China, Me., and Levant, Me.; he m. Nancy, dau. of William Morse, of Hallowell, merchant, in 1820; she died in Levant, Me., Jan. 1, 1837; he resides in Wrentham, Mass. The children of Wm. E. and Mary S. Pond, are: Annie Warren,[9] b. Nov. 3, 1854. Elisabeth Burrill,[9] b. June 8, 1857. Jeannie Thompson[9] b. Oct. 5, 1859. Mary Ellis,[9] b. Mar. 11, 1865. Emily Stevens,[9] b. May 23, 1867. Robert William,[9] b. May 26, 1873.

690

Caroline[7] Porter, of Lebbeus[6] Porter, b. May 7, 1806; m. Rev. William Harlow, March 19, 1829, by Rev. Elisha Fisk, at Wrentham, Mass. He was son of John and Betsey (Torrey) Harlow, of Plymouth, Mass., where he was born Oct. 27, 1805; fitted for college at Milton and Bridgewater Academies; graduated at Yale College, 1826; studied divinity with Rev. Jacob Ide, D. D., of Medway, Mass.; licensed to preach by Mendon (Mass.) Association, March, 1829;

pastor of churches in Canton, Mass., and Waterford, Mass.; afterward supplied vacant pulpits in the vicinity of Wrentham, Mass., where his family now reside in summer, and in winter with his children, in Brooklyn, N. Y. Children:

1302. i. Caroline Elizabeth,[8] b. July 31, 1830; died July 6, 1832.

1303. ii. Caroline Frances,[8] b. Oct. 9, 1834; married Henry M. Messenger, merchant, of N. Y. city, May 18, 1859, at Wrentham, Mass., by Rev. Wm. L. Ropes; he was son of Charles and Harriet (Plimpton) Messenger, b. in Boston, Aug. 31, 1835. Children: Charles Henry,[9] b. Brooklyn, N. Y., April 20, 1863. Caroline Harriet,[9] b. in Brooklyn, N. Y., Apr. 20, 1869.

691

Major Thomas Brastow[7] Porter, of Lebbeus[6] Porter, b. at Wrentham, Jan. 17, 1808; removed from Wrentham to Weymouth, Dec. 16, 1827; carpenter and lumber merchant; dealer in real estate; selectman and assessor of Weymouth; and held other town offices many years; married Emily Vining, of South Weymouth, June 1, 1837. Children:

1304. i. Emily Anna,[8] b. Feb. 12, 1838; married Dr. William C. B. Fifield, May 13, 1856, a successful physician in Dorchester, (Boston) son of the late Dr. Noah Fifield, of Weymouth. Children, all b. in Weymouth: Mary Sanborn,[9] b. Mar. 29, 1857; married Sylvanus F. Freeman, Oct. 19, 1875. George Fordyce,[9] b. July 1, 1859; died Sept. 10, 1860. Charles Bell,[9] b. Sept. 5, 1861; died March 4, 1877.

1305. ii. Susanna Bigelow,[8] b. July 14, 1842; died Aug. 20, 1871. Extract from obituary in Weymouth Gazette: "As a teacher she ranked among the first; her musical powers were charming, and were untiringly cultured; her hands were skilled in all womanly work; and that her heart had large and well filled chambers, is attested by the very large circle of friends who wept around her lifeless form."

1306. iii. Mary Fifield,[8] b. Dec. 29, 1845; married Moses Grant Daniels, July 24, 1872; he son of George Keith Daniels, of Needham, b. in Boston, (Roxbury) Sept. 9, 1836; this was his second marriage. (He married first, Elizabeth Smith Parker, of Providence, R. I., July 26, 1864; she died April 19, 1865.) The children of

Moses G. and Mary F., all born in Boston, (Roxbury) are: Emily Anna,[9] b. Nov. 16, 1873. Lucy Catherine,[9] b. Dec. 18, 1875. Robert,[9] b. Jan. 15, 1877.

1307. iv. Jenny Frances,[8] b. Nov. 18, 1850.

1308. v. Robert Franklin,[8] b. Dec. 31, 1858; died Aug. 9, 1859.

692

Susanna Fisher[7] Porter, of Lebbeus[6] Porter, b. at Wrentham, April 22, 1810; married Isaac B. Warren, of Framingham, March 7, 1833; died without children, Dec. 5, 1848.

693

John H.[7] Porter, of Lebbeus[6] Porter, b. in Wrentham, Feb. 16, 1815; resided in Brewer, Me., and Bangor, Me., also Cambridgeport, Mass.; clerk; married Mehitable H. Parker, of Bucksport, Me., Nov. 5, 1837. He died in Cambridgeport, Aug. 5, 1849, aged 34 years. Children:

1309. i. Stella Richmond,[8] b. Mar. 4, 1839; died April 23, 1860.

1310. ii. John Augustus,[8] b. Nov. 17, 1840; died Feb. 1, 1842.

1311. iii. Ellen Hall,[8] b. Oct. 3, 1843; married Rev. Levi Boyer, May 3, 1870; Episcopal clergyman, now, (1878) of Nantucket.

1312. iv. Hattie Louisa,[8] b. June 1, 1847; married Adams, June 17, 1868; she died May 11, 1873.

694

Nancy K.[7] Porter, of Lebbeus[6] Porter, b. at Wrentham, July 18, 1817; married Dr. Luther W. Sherman, April 26, 1837; he was the "Good Physician;" died in Wrentham, Oct., 1837, aged 31; his widow died Nov. 14, 1846, without children.

696

Samuel K.[7] Porter, of Lebbeus[6] Porter, b. at Wrentham, Dec. 14, 1822; physician; resided in Mercer, Me.; postmaster there; Philadelphia, Penn.; now (1878) of Lowell, Mass.; married Sarah Ann Gilman, of Mercer, Me., Feb. 7, 1850. Child:

1313. i. Harrie Warren,[8] b. in Mercer, Me.

697

. Olive[7] Porter, of Cyrus[6] Porter, b. at Stoughton, Oct. 16, 1800; m. Caleb Copeland, Jr., of West Bridgewater, May 7, 1821; he the son of Caleb and Sally (Byram) Copeland; b. June 17, 1792. She died June 4, 1831 or 1830; he died Feb. 20, 1878. Children:

1314. i. Olive P.,[8] b. Mar. 23, 1822; m. Bela B. Haywood, of Brockton, May 29, 1843. Children: Olive Augusta,[9] b. Feb. 3, 1847. Elmer Baylies,[9] b. Mar. 27, 1849. Edward Byram,[9] b. Jan. 11, 1851.

1315. ii. Caleb,[8] b. Sep. 15, 1823; m. Cordelia F. Hartwell, of West Bridgewater, Oct. 1, 1844; she died Sept. 5, 1875; resides in West Bridgewater; shoe manufacturer; Representative to General Court in 1860. Children: Martha Cordelia,[9] died young. Frank,[9] b. July 7, 1849. Fanny Eveline,[9] b. Aug. 25, 1856.

1316. iii. Martha,[8] b. Sept. 13, 1825; m. William C. Leonard, Oct. 1, 1844; resides in East Stoughton. Children: William.[9] Charles.[9] Edith.[9]

1317. iv. Cyrus Porter,[8] b. June 27, 1827; m. Ann M. Ellis, of New Bedford, Dec. 17, 1848. Children: Cyrus.[9] Ellis Franklin,[9] b. May 21, 1850. Myron Homer,[9] b. July 27, 1856.

1318. v. Almira R.[8] b. May 2, 1830; m. Charles Spear, Dec. 17, 1848; reside at Brockton. Children: Geo. Frederick,[9] b. Dec. 8, 1849; died the same day. Charles Ashton,[9] b. Aug. 3, 1852.

Caleb Copeland, the father, married 2d, Polly, daughter of Perez Southworth, Jan. 21, 1833, by whom he had two children. His wife died July 12, 1862; he died Jan., 1876.

698

Ahira[7] Porter, of Cyrus[6] Porter, b. Stoughton, Nov. 9, (8) 1801, of East Stoughton; mechanic; married Rachel D. Swan, 1826. She died Nov. 4, 1861; he died Dec. 6, 1863. Children:

1319. i. Ahira Swan,[8] b. Jan. 30, 1827.
1320. ii. Rachel D.,[8] b. Dec. 27, 1828.
1321. iii. William,[8] b. Aug. 30, 1831.
1322. iv. Samuel,[8] b. June 27, 1833.
1323. v. James,[8] b. Oct. 4, 1835.
1324. vi. George N.,[8] b. Jan. 30, 1843.

700

Cyrus[7] Porter, of Cyrus[6] Porter, b. June 12, 1807, of East Stoughton; farmer; lives on the old homestead; married Eliza, daughter of Samuel and Betsey Dunbar, of West Bridgewater, April 30, 1837; she born June 19, 1815. Children:

1325. i. Adelaide,[8] b. Feb. 22, 1838, in North Bridgewater; m. Elbridge R. Curtis, of East Bridgewater, Feb. 21, 1868.
1326. ii. Luthera M.,[8] b. North Bridgewater, Dec. 17, 1840; m. William H. Burgess, of Kingston, Jan. 28, 1873.
1327. iii. Cyrus Herbert,[8] b. N. Bridgewater, Dec. 12, 1841.
1328. iv. Lucy Alice,[8] b. E. Stoughton, Dec. 12, 1844; married Franklin B. Upham, of Stoughton, Nov. 18, 1868; he died Aug. 29, 1870.
1329. v. Eliza Ann,[8] b. Aug. 13, 1849.
1330. vi. Mary D.,[8] b. Oct. 14, 1853.

701

Luther[7] Porter, of Cyrus[6] Porter, b. Dec. 18, 1814; resides Stoughton; butcher; married Lucy, daughter of Joel and Lucy Talbot, of Stoughton, June 9, 1836; she born Aug. 15, 1817. Children:

1331. i. Warren F.,[8] b. June 2, 1838.
1332. ii. Helen J.,[8] b. June 28, 1842; m. John H. Bullard, of Boston, June 13, 1867.
1333. iii. Catharine Isabel,[8] b. Mar. 20, 1851.
1334. iv. Charles H.,[8] b. Mar. 25, 1853; died June 25, 1853.
1335. v. Frank M.,[8] b. Dec. 23, 1855.
1336. vi. Alice W.,[8] b. Mar. 11, 1858.

702

Mehetable[7] Porter, of Cyrus[6] Porter; m. Ezra Churchill, of Stoughton; one child:

1337. i. Ezra.[8]

704

William F.[7] Porter, of Cyrus[6] Porter, b. Jan. 23, 1823; married Harriet Sears, of Dorchester, Nov. 11, 1847; she born there Mar. 23, 1825; he died. Children:

1338. i. Lucy Ella,[8] b. Mar. 23, 1848; died May 11, 1853.
1339. ii. George Sears,[8] b. July 24, 1851; died Sept. 4, 1860.

1340. iii. Hattie Louisa,[8] b. July 27, 1853.
1341. iv. Clara Hall,[8] b. Mar. 11, 1857.
1342. v. Ida Amelia,[8] b. June 13, 1858.
1343. vi. Albert DeLancey,[8] b. July 5, 1860.
1344. vii. Willard Sears,[8] b. Oct. 3, 1864; died Sept. 30, 1869.

705

Rebecca[7] Porter, of Cyrus[6] Porter, b. 1805; married Marcus Copeland, of West Bridgewater, June 6, 1826; he was son of Caleb and Sally (Byram) Copeland, born Oct. 27, 1800; wife died Dec. 15, 1869, aged 64 years. Children:

1345. i. Marcus Morton,[8] b. Feb. 15, 1828; m. Mary Ann Cushman, of Middleborough, Oct. 10, 1850; he resides Middleborough. Children: Mark Morton,[9] b. Sept. 28, 1851; died Nov. 21, 1856. Frank Cushman,[9] b. Sept. 29, 1853; died May 12, 1854. Elmer Clinton,[9] b. April 28, 1856. Marcus Morton,[9] b. Dec. 19, 1862.
1346. ii. Jane,[8] b. Jan. 7, 1830; m. John P. Shepard, of Ellsworth, Me., July 18, 1852.
1347. iii. Nahum,[8] b. April, 1831; died Jan. 8, 1834.
1348. iv. Amanda,[8] b. Aug. 9, 1833; m. Luther E. Alden, Dec. 17, 1854; resides Brockton. Children: Frank W.,[9] b. Aug. 14, 1855. Daniel H.,[9] b. Aug. 19, 1857. Frederic S.,[9] b. July 17, 1859. Herman Luther,[9] b. Oct. 21, 1861.
1349. v. Julia A.,[8] b. Aug. 9, 1835; m. Stephen Davis, of Falmouth, Mass., Jan. 1, 1858. Have five children.
1350. vi. Rebecca Porter,[8] b. Nov. 27, 1838; m. Henry L. Bryant, of Brockton, May 11, 1856; she died Nov. 15, 1875; had two sons.
1351. vii. Nahum,[8] b. Oct. 15, 1840; died July 1, 1842.

725

Betsey[7] Porter, of Ebenezer[6] Porter, b. Abington, Oct. 17, 1792; married Christopher Dyer, Jr., of Abington, Jan. 10, 1811; he son of Christopher and Deborah (Reed) Dyer, of Abington; died Sept. 24, 1868, aged 82; she died May 29, 1878, aged 86. Children:

1352. i. Betsey,[8] b. Oct. 29, 1811; died young.
1353. ii. Ebenezer Porter,[8] b. Aug. 15, 1813; clergyman; grad. Brown University, 1833; minister in Hingham, and

other places; now (1878) resides S. Abington; m. Esther Ann Hough, of Canterbury, Conn., Dec., 2, 1838. Children: Ebenezer Porter,[9] b. Nov. 3, 1839; grad. Amherst Col.,1861; m. 1st, Susan M. Fearing, Oct. 19, 1865; she died Feb. 12, 1868; and he m. 2d, Martha A. Fearing, Jan. 12, 1871. Henry Lockwood,[9] b. May 16, 1842; died Aug. 26, 1842. Helen Amelia,[9] b. Mar. 17, 1844; m. Barnard K. Lee, Dec. 6, 1864; post master at Port Royal, S. C.; sailed from New York for Port Royal, Jan. 5, 1865, with her husband, and both lost at sea Jan. 8, 1865. Sarah Elizabeth,[9] b. Aug. 1, 1845; grad. South Hadley; m. Isaac Pierson, Aug. 10, 1877, and sailed as missionary to North China; arrived there Nov. 16, 1877. Mary Lockwood,[9] b. Nov. 25, 1846; m. Henry L. Wyatt, of Cambridgeport, Sept. 8, 1869. Esther Genevieve,[9] b. Aug. 11, 1849; m. James Frank Thomas, Jan. 18, 1877. Edward Norris,[9] b. July 22, 1850; grad. Amherst College; m. Fannie E. Bartlett, Dec. 25, 1876. Frank H.,[9] b. Mar. 4, 1853; died Sept. 23. Samuel Hough,[9] b. Aug. 18, 1855; died Aug. 31, 1855. Martha Louisa,[9] b. Feb. 7, 1859.

1354. iii. Elizabeth Lavinia,[8] b. Aug. 16, 1817; m. Charles Cummings, of Medford.

1355. iv. Christopher,[8] b. Oct. 28, 1819; m. Almira Littlefield, of East Stoughton.

1356. v. Maria Louisa,[8] b. April 9, 1821; m. Rev. Ebenezer Alden, now of Marshfield, April 4, 1848; he son of Dr. Ebenezer and Anne (Kimball) Alden, of Randolph, Mass.; b. Aug. 10, 1819; grad. Amherst College, 1839; installed pastor of Congregational Church, Marshfield, Oct. 30, 1850; where he now resides. Children: Maria Louisa,[9] b. Apr. 30, 1849. Anna Porter,[9] b. Aug. 10, 1851. Ebenezer,[9] b. June 24, 1854; died Feb. 15, 1857. Edmund Kimball,[9] b. Feb. 17, 1858. Mary Kimball,[9] b. May 17, 1860; died Sept. 12, 1860. Alice Elizabeth,[9] b. May 22, 1863.

1357. vi. Sally,[8] b. April, 15, 1823; m. Daniel M. Fullerton, of Abington, May 21, 1843; reside S. Abington. Children: Bradford Morton,[9] by 1st wife; Daniel Waldo,[9] b. Nov. 22, 1845; died Mar. 6, 1857. Helen L.,[9] b. Jan. 9, 1848; m. Bela Alden, of S. Abington, May 21, 1868. Charles Dyer,[9] b. May 5, 1851; m. Elizabeth H. Prince, of Boston, June 6, 1874; two children. Elmer,[9] b. May 8, 1854; m. Anna L. Hunting, of Brighton, Mass.,Nov. 18, 1874; has two children. The sons reside in Brockton.

1358. vii. George Gustavus,[8] b. Aug. 20, 1825; m. Mary A. B. Sampson, of Plymouth.

1359. viii. Edward Loring,[8] b. May 16, 1828; m. Lavinia Gannett, of Hanson; he enlisted in the army for three years, in the war of the Rebellion; before his term of service expired he was taken sick, came home and died, leaving two sons—Edward Oscar,[9] and Ebenezer Alden.[9]

1360. ix. Elihu Francis,[8] b. Dec. 8, 1830; m. Mary Thomas, of Rochester; has two daughters.

1361. x. Helen Amelia,[8] b. April 2, 1836.

726

Lydia[7] Porter, of Ebenezer[6] Porter, b. Abington, Feb. 16, 1800; married Edward Vinton, of East Bridgewater, Feb. 16, 1820; he son of William and Susanna (Robinson) Vinton, born July 14, 1779; was teacher many years; merchant; deputy sheriff; removed to South Abington. Children:

1361. i. Lydia Loring,[8] b. March 8, 1821; m. Theodore Trask, 1840.

1362. ii. Lucia,[8] b. Sept. 12, 1822; m. Charles H. Hardwick, of Quincy, 1846.

1363. iii. Abigail,[8] b. May 5, 1826; unmarried.

1364. iv. Edward,[8] b. Sept. 30, 1828; died a few days old.

1365. v. Edward Porter,[8] b. Jan. 30, 1831; m. Betsey Boldry, of East Bridgewater, Oct., 1855.

1366. vi. Caroline Augusta,[8] b. Nov., 1832; m. William Henry Chamberlain, Oct., 1855.

1367. vii. Susan Elizabeth,[8] b. Sept. 30, 1834; m. William Henry Chamberlain, of East Bridgewater, Sept. 18, 1852. She died March, 1854, leaving one child—William Henry,[9] b. Feb., 1854.

1368. viii. George Warren,[8] b. Aug. 5, 1836.

727

Sarah[7] Porter, of Ebenezer[6] Porter, b. in Abington, Feb. 16, 1803; married Dea. Spencer Vining, of South Abington, Oct. 14, 1824; he was a prominent and worthy citizen; selectman, &c. He died 1875, aged 74 years.

728

Mehetable R.[7] Porter, of Samuel[6] Porter, b. May 6, 1804; married Samuel Norton, of Abington, Sept. 2, 1824; he son of Samuel and Silence (Hersey) Norton, b. Jan. 18, 1790; died Mar. 14, 1871; his widow died June 2, 1873, aged 69 years 26 days. Children, five in number: Samuel[8] and four more.

743

Rebecca W.[7] Porter, of Jonathan[6] Porter, b. in Halifax; married Charles Lincoln, of North Bridgewater, Oct. 13, 1816; he son of Gideon and Martha (Perkins) Lincoln, b. Dec. 27, 1795. Children:

1378. i. Mary Porter,[8] b. Oct. 19, 1816; m. 1st, Samuel Proctor, from Minot, Maine, Oct. 17, 1841; he died Sept. 22, 1846. They had one child,—Samuel Davis,[9]—b. July 19, 1845; widow married again, George Loring, of Portland, Me., May 2, 1850.

1379. ii. Josiah Sears,[8] b. Dec. 1, 1820; m. Almeda A. Wing, Feb. 17, 1846; she died Sept. 1, 1848; he m. 2d, Hannah Holt, May 10, 1850.

1380. iii. Lucy Jane,[8] b. Aug. 24, 1825; m. Ebenezer G. Rhodes, April 30, 1845.

1381. iv. Rebecca Frances,[8] b. Feb. 3, 1831.

1382. v. Charles Beales,[8] b. July 27, 1835; m. Emily A. Stoddard, Nov. 25, 1858.

744

Millicent[7] Porter, of Jonathan[6] Porter; married John Battles, of North Bridgewater, June 2, 1816; he son of Asa and Mary (Pratt) Battles, born July 2, 1792. Children:

1383. i. Harriet Frances,[8] b. April 27, 1817; m. Calvin French, of Randolph.

1384. ii. Adeline Augusta,[8] b. Aug. 21, 1819; m. George M. Taylor, of Boston.

1385. iii. John Otis,[8] b. May 26, 1822; m. Susan Whitman French, Dec. 30, 1849.

1386. iv. Edmund Davis,[8] b. May 21, 1824; m. Isabel Hartwell.

1387. v. Louisa Jane,[8] b. Dec. 17, 1826; m. James W. White, of Mansfield.

1388. vi. Lucien Bradford,[8] b. April 2, 1829; died April 23, 1849.

1389. vii. Lucy Porter,[8] b. Aug. 25, 1831; married James Hill, of Stoughton.

1390. viii. Ellen Maria,[8] b. March 25, 1834; m. William A. Sanford, of East Bridgewater, captain in militia.

745

Bethiah[7] Porter, of Jonathan[6] Porter, b. Halifax; married Apollos Howard, of North Bridgewater—his second marriage. (His first marriage was with Olive, dau. of Major Daniel Cary, April 8, 1802, by whom he had children—Harriet, Noble, George, and Emily.) He died Mar. 5, 1849; the children of Apollos and Bethiah Howard, were:

1391. i. Nancy,[8] died Sept. 8, 1860.
1392. ii. Chloe,[8] m. Walter Chamberlain, of Augusta, Maine.
1393. iii. Amanda.[8]
1394. iv. Charles Henry,[8] m. Sarah Ann Bearce, of Hyannis, Mass. He master of repairs on Cape Cod Railroad; resides in Hyannis.
1395. v. Abbie,[8] m. Orlando Arnold, of Sidney, Me.
1396. vi. Davis Porter,[8] m. Sarah Bacon Perry, of Hyannis, Mass.

749

Chipman[7] Porter, of Oliver[6] Porter, b. Jan 9, 1797; resides Halifax; farmer and real estate owner; owning in 1876, three hundred acres of land in his vicinity. Married 1st, Ruth Hathaway, of East Bridgewater, Jan. 1, 1826; she died Mar. 4, 1835. Married 2d, Cynthia Wood, of Halifax, Sept. 8, 1836; she died Aug. 19, 1863. Children:

1397. i. Oliver Chipman,[8] b. Jan. 26, 1827.
1398. ii. Lucy Tinkham,[8] b. Oct. 30, 1830; died July 9, 1833.
1399. iii. Ruth Hathaway,[8] b. Mar. 3, 1833; died April 4, 1836.
1400. iv. Henry Martyn,[8] b. Nov. 20, 1837.

750

Sarah[7] Porter, of Oliver[6] Porter, b. Mar. 14, 1799; married Seabury C. Hathaway, of East Bridgewater, 1818; she died Jan. 16, 1872; he died Jan. 27, 1877, aged 83 years 3 days. Children:

1401. i. Joseph T.,[8] b. Sept. 29, 1818; m. Mercy T. Wright, of South Scituate; resides East Bridgewater.
ii. Seabury C.,[8] b. June 12, 1825; m. 1st, Almira B. Jones, of Bridgewater; and 2d, Abbie F. Shaw, of Raynham.
iii. Loranus S.,[8] b. Feb. 17, 1827; m. Henriette Germaine, of East Bridgewater; died Sept. 7, 1859.
iv. Ebenezer,[8] b. March 6, 1829; died Jan. 22, 1832.
v. Alonzo L.,[8] b. May 31, 1831; died March 16, 1853.

vi. Julius D. P.,[8] b. July 7, 1833; died Jan. 8, 1834.
vii. Sarah M.,[8] b. May 5, 1836.
viii. Mariette,[8] b. July 28, 1839; died Feb. 22, 1861; married Lysander M. Thompson, of Halifax.
ix. Lorentha B.,[8] b. Feb. 12, 1844; m. Joshua Cook, of South Abington.

751

Cynthia[7] Porter, of Oliver[6] Porter, b. Halifax, Oct. 2, 1803; married Isaac Fuller, of Halifax, 1824. One son:

1402. i. Isaac Porter,[8] b. Jan. 1, 1826; m. Annie B. Vinton, of South Braintree, July 10, 1854; resides in Braintree.

752

Nathaniel[7] Porter, of Oliver[6] Porter, b. in Halifax, June 3, 1805; resides E. Bridgewater; married Phebe Phillips, of E. Bridgewater, 1830. Children:

1403. i. Juliett,[8] b. Nov, 3, 1832; m. Luther Churchill, of E. Bridgewater, 1850.
1404. ii. Abigail Phillips,[8] b. May 28, 1840.
1405. iii. Ellen A.,[8] b. Feb. 17, 1845; died April 16, 1861.
1406. iv. Francis Bartlett,[8] b. Aug. 20, 1835.

762

Dea. Enos[7] Porter, of Asa[6] Porter, b. Cummington, Feb. 2, 1798; was Dea. of the church there from 1828 to 1867. Married 1st, Caroline Priestly, March, 1827. Married 2d, Eunice Stetson, June 24, 1835. Children:

1407. i. Martha P.,[8] b. Nov. 19, 1827; m. William Tinker, of Huntington, Nov., 1849; has had three children; one living in 1876.
1408. ii. Lewis H.,[8] b. March 21, 1830.
1409. iii. Lucius F.,[8] b. April 28, 1833; died Aug. 21, 1834.
1410. iv. Henry M.,[8] b. June 23, 1836.
1411. v. Sarah H.,[8] b. March 26, 1837; m. Lawrence Hatch, of Springfield, 1861; has three children.
1412. vi. Edward A.,[8] b. Sept. 23, 1839.
1413. vii. Abbie O.,[8] b. Jan. 28, 1841: lives in Williamsburg.
1414. viii. Francis E.,[8] b. Dec. 24, 1842; lives in Williamsburg; farmer.
1415. ix. Caroline A.,[8] b. Nov. 27, 1844; died Sept. 7, 1846.
1416. x. William W.,[8] b. Jan. 17, 1847.

17

763

Jonathan[7] Porter, of Asa[6] Porter, b. Cummington, Mar. 13, 1800; hatter; lives Prattville, Mich. Married 1st, Chloe, 1837; 2d, Ann; no children living, 1876.

764

Asa H.[7] Porter, of Asa[6] Porter, b. in Cummington Feb. 7, 1802; resides in Cummington; married Abigail Packard, June 19, 1833; she died Nov. 13, 1834. Married 2d, Hannah Stetson, Dec. 31, 1835. Children:

1417. i. Sarah Thersa,[8] b. Aug. 19, 1834; died Nov. 13, 1835.
1418. ii. Levi Packard,[8] b. Nov. 8, 1836.
1419. iii. Sarah F.,[8] died the year of her birth.
1420. iv. Harlan Page,[8] b. April 23, 1838.
1421. v. Edward Payson,[8] b. Sept. 8, 1841; died Aug. 22, 1843.
1422. vi. Mary E.,[8] b. Oct. 17, 1843; died Oct. 3, 1862.
1423. vii. Alfred E.,[8] b. Feb. 8, 1846; Springfield.
1424. viii. Eliza Ann Clark,[8] b. Mar. 6, 1848; teacher.
1425. ix. Edward H.,[8] b. Sept. 23, 1850; Cummington.

765

Nahum[7] Porter, of Asa[6] Porter, b. Cummington, Jan. 7, 1804; resides in Boston; has lived there over forty years; tailor; during the last twenty-four years he has been employed in carrying religous periodicals over the city of Boston; married Hannah C. Henshaw, Sept. 18, 1837. No children.

766

Milton[7] Porter, of Asa[6] Porter, b. in Cummington, July 26, 1806; resides on the old homestead in C. Married 1st, Lodiska Hume, Feb. 8, 1837-1838; married 2d, Mrs. Clarissa Keep Bisbee, Dec. 23, 1857. Children:

1426. i. Morris Huntington,[8] b. April 28, 1839; Kalamazoo, Mich.
1427. ii. Ralph M.,[8] b. June 2, 1848; lives Springfield (1876.)
1428. iii. Julia H.,[8] b. June 6, 1852; teacher (1876.)

774

Daniel R.[7] Porter, of Jacob[6] Porter, of Worthington, b. March, 1821; resides Worthington, Mass.; married 1st, Dolly A. Geer, June 1, 1848. Married 2d, Sarah Wood, Aug. 24, 1858. Children:

1429. i. Horace,[8] b. April, 1848; lives Epasco, Sedgwick Co., Kan.
1430. ii. Eleanor,[8] b. Jan., 1851.
1431. iii. Carrie Wood,[8] b. 1860.
1432. iv. Arthur C.,[8] b. 1865.
1433. v. Herbert G.,[8] b. May, 1871.

800

Seth J.[7] Porter, of James[6] Porter, b. in Skaneateles, N. Y., Jan. 2, 1803. Grad. Aublum, N. Y., Seminary, 1823; settled minister of the Presbyterian church in New Lisbon, 1824; in 1826, at Jamesville, Onondaga Co., N. Y.; remained there until 1830, when health failing, he removed to Elkland, Tioga Co., Penn., and commenced the practice of medicine; having graduated in the allopathic school, in 1830. In Oct., 1833, he removed to Kalamazoo, Mich., and continued the practice of medicine there up to the date of his death, Aug. 17, 1834. He was a pioneer in Michigan, and is said to have built the first frame dwelling house in the village of Kalamazoo. He also continued to preach from time to time, as health permitted. He was married to Cynthia Maria Haines, Jan. 1, 1821. She was daughter of Stephen (born 1777) and Mary (Cook) Haines, of Morristown, N. J., born April 10, 1804. Mr. and Mrs. Haines died at Allegan, Mich., 1857, aged 81. Mrs. Porter married 1838, Horace Stimson, who died 1862, (and by whom she had children: Mary C., Martha J., Clara C., and Albert S.;) she now resides with her son, James B. Porter, at Lansing, Mich., in the best of health. The children of S. J. Porter, were: (Two dying in infancy.)

1440. i. Edwin Haines,[8] b. at Skaneateles, N. Y., Dec. 17, 1822.
1441. ii. James Bullard,[8] b. at Marcellus, N. Y., Sept. 7, 1824.
1442. iii. Julia Adell,[8] b. at Elkland, Penn., May 10, 1833; married Henry Heydenburk, of Kalamazoo, Mich., 1857; now resides at Olivet, Eaton Co., Mich. Children: William.[9] Frank:[9] Isadore.[9]

812

Sally[7] Porter, of David[6] Porter, b. Sept. 7, 1806; married Oakes P. Brown, 1828; he son of Daniel and Mehetable (Tirrell) Brown, b. Aug. 21, 1796; died Sept. 7, 1868. She died Jan. 4, 1838. Mr. Brown married again, and died Sept. 7, 1868, aged 72. Children:

1443. i. Francis Porter,[8] b. Oct. 22, 1830; resides Hopkinton, Mass., (Woodville P. O.)
1444. ii. N. Porter,[8] b. Aug. 25, 1832; superintendent of Lawrence Industrial School, where he is very successful. M. Sarah Monroe Wight, Nov. 16, 1861. Children: Albert Howard,[9] b. Feb. 23, 1865. Theodore Lyman,[9] b. Sept. 19, 1873.
1445. iii. Daniel,[8] b. 1839; died at two days.

813

Mary[7] Porter, of David[6] Porter, b. Jan. 17, 1809; married Joseph Brown, 1830; he son of Daniel and Mehetable (Porter) Brown, b. Dec. 23, 1801. Children:

1446. i. Charlotte A.,[8] b. Mar. 3, 1830; m. William Noyes.
ii. J. Willard,[8] grad. Amherst College; teacher Emerson School, East Boston.

820

Deborah G.[7] Porter, of Adam G.[6] Porter, b. Cummington, Mass., Mar. 13, 1810; married Stephen French, Feb. 21, 1833; resided in Cummington; she died there Dec. 2, 1851. Children, all born in Cummington:

1450. i. Ellen P.,[8] b. Dec. 29, 1833.
1451. ii. Charles Edward,[8] b. Jan. 31, 1836; m. Marcia Jenkins, Feb. 24, 1859; resides New Jersey.
1452. iii. Clarissa Jane,[8] b. Sept. 20, 1838; m. Henry L. Welch, Nov. 7, 1859; reside Plainville, Conn.
1453. iv. Frances Emeline,[8] b. Aug. 26, 1840; d. Oct. 2, 1866, aged 26.
1454. v. Julia Catharine,[8] b. July 2, 1842; died April 10, 1844, aged 2.
1455. vi. Julia Sophia,[8] b. Nov. 8, 1850; died Jan. 5, 1867, aged 16.

823

Joseph N.[7] Porter, of Adam G.[6] Porter, b. Oct. 24, 1814; grad. Illinois College, at Jacksonville; teacher at South and West; died in Cummington, Sept. 16, 1859.

824

Horatio E.[7] Porter, of Adam G.[6] Porter, b. Mar. 24, 1817; grad. Yale College; studied law at New Haven, Conn.; lawyer; resided at Charlemont, Mass. Married Lucretia L. Burgess, Sept. 4, 1845. He died Feb. 21, 1852, aged 35; his widow married Louis H. Grandgent, Dec. 28, 1854; he born Chatres, France, Oct. 29, 1824.

825

Sophia L.[7] Porter, of Adam G.[6] Porter, b. Oct. 19, 1819; grad. of Oberlin College, 1855; married Rev. M. Henry Smith, June 27, 1857; he son of William and Eliza Smith, born in Westford, N. Y., June 15, 1822; grad. Oberlin College, 1850; tutor at Farmers College, Ohio; minister at Kankakee, Ill.; Four Corners, Ohio; Jefferson, Ill.; Warrensburg, Mo.; four years principal of Lincoln Institute, Jefferson City, Mo.; labored ten years among the Freedmen; now resides at Warrensburg, Mo. Children:

1456. i. Clara Ellen,[8] b. Kankakee, Ill., Oct. 7, 1858; grad. at State Normal School, Warrensburg, June 16, 1876; gives great promise as a teacher.
1457. ii. Sophia Eliza,[8] b. Four Corners, Ohio, Jan. 16, 1860; died there July 9, 1863.
1458. iii. Mary Elizabeth,[8] b. Four Corners, April 12, 1862; died April 19, 1862.
1459. iv. Alice Jane Lottie,[8] b. Jefferson, Ill., June 16, 1864.

829

Edward C.[7] Porter, of Seth[6] Porter, b. Cummington, Sept. 10, 1820; resides in Haydenville, Mass. Married L. Abigail Cleveland, Mar. 17, 1847. Children:

1460. i. Mary,[8] b. Oct. 18, 1851; died Aug. 30, 1855.
1461. ii. Harriet A.,[8] b. Dec. 20, 1856; m. Finley L. Smith, June 10, 1875.
1462. iii. James A.,[8] b. Jan. 30, 1859.
1463. iv. Edward Cobb,[8] b. July 14, 1861.

830

Mary[7] Porter, of Seth[6] Porter, b. July 7, 1822; married Joseph A. Baldwin, Sept. 1, 1841; resides South Deerfield, Mass. Children:

James Goodrich,[8] b. July 27, 1848. Elizabeth A.,[8] b. Oct. 23, 1850. Winfred Alonzo,[8] b. Oct. 8, 1867.

832

Henry[7] Porter, of Seth[6] Porter, b. Jan. 27, 1827; resides Springfield, Mass.; married H. Jane Prince, May 20, 1847. Children:

1467. i. Emma L.,[8] b. Mar. 20, 1849.
1468. ii. Minnie Corinne,[8] b. June 25, 1865.
1469. iii. Ernest Henry,[8] b. Aug. 29, 1870.

833

Elisabeth[7] Porter, of Seth[6] Porter, b. July 23, 1831; married Irving Beals, Dec. 1, 1848. Children:

1470. i. Helen Elizabeth,[8] b. Sept. 26, 1854.
1471. ii. Mary Porter,[8] b. Sept. 17, 1856.
1472. iii. Walter Irving,[8] b. Jan. 31, 1863.

834

Samuel H.[7] Porter, of Nathaniel S.[6] Porter, b. Richmond, Ky., Oct. 13, 1812. Married 1st, Sarah A. Dearinger, at Harrodsburg, Ky., Feb. 5, 1849; she died there April 10, 1859. Married 2d, Elisabeth S. Williams, of same place, Aug. 16, 1860. He died in Williams Store, Casey Co., Ky., where his widow now resides. Children:

1473. i. Nathaniel Huntington,[8] b. April 10, 1868.
1474. ii. John Raymond,[8] b. Jan. 11, 1871.

836

Emily C.[7] Porter, of Nathaniel S.[6] Porter, b. May 15, 1816. Married Christopher Crittenden Ball, Oct. 17, 1839. His father and mother emigrated from Virginia to Kentucky, and were of the same family as Mary Ball, the mother of Washington. He was 12 years police judge of Richmond, Ky.;

removed to Missouri, in Oct., 1867; and in 1868 settled with his family in Carthage, Jasper Co., Missouri, where he now resides on his estate. Children, all born in Richmond, Ky.:

1475. i. Ellen Elisabeth,[8] b. Oct. 14, 1840; m. Alonzo H. Hubbard, Aug. 15, 1865; he was a captain in the 12th Indiana regiment in the last war; lawyer; resides in Green Co., Mo. Post office address, Lawrenceburg, Lawrence Co.
1476. ii. Lewis Huntington,[8] b. Mar. 17, 1843. In the confederate service, second Kentucky Infantry, in last war, and taken prisoner at Fort Donelson; resides Carthage, Mo.
1477. iii. Francis Walker,[8] b. Mar. 14, 1845; is a lawyer at Fort Worth, Texas, where he married Lulu F. Field, April 13, 1875.
1478. iv. Christopher Porter,[8] b. Oct. 12, 1847; m. Emma B. Gates, of Carthage, Dec. 30, 1874; resides at Carthage, deputy county clerk for Jasper County, and dealer in real estate.
1479. v. Caroline Louisa,[8] b. Dec. 30, 1849; teacher.
1480. vi. George Sargent,[8] b. Sept. 7, 1852; farmer.
1481. vii. Sarah Ann,[8] b. April 20, 1855.
1482. viii. Emily Washington,[8] b. Feb. 22, 1857.
1483. ix. William Letcher,[8] b. April 28, 1858.
1484. x. Nathaniel Porter,[8] b. Mar. 17, 1862.

839

Eliza[7] Porter, of Nathaniel S.[6] Porter, b. in Richmond, Ky., July 26, 1823; married Dr. James C. Peacock, Jan. 8, 1840; went to California in 1850, and in 1855 removed his family and settled in San Bernandino. Children:

1485. i. Edwin Roberts,[8] b. July 14, 1842; married Annie Walker, 1865; he is a printer.
1486. ii. William Sargent,[8] b. July 7, 1844; died Nov. 10, 1869.
1487. iii. Martha E.,[8] b. Feb. 28, 1846; married E. P. Bowland, 1862; died Apr. 20, 1871.
1488. iv. Caroline,[8] b. March 10, 1848; died Aug. 1, 1849.
1489. v. James C.,[8] b. April 20, 1850; m. Susan Cochrane, 1876; he is a printer.
1490. vi. Thomas F.,[8] b. Sept. 2, 1856; druggist, in Philadelphia.
1491. vii. Emily,[8] b. June 1, 1858; died July 1, 1860.
1492. viii. Sarah Jane,[8] b. Aug. 26, 1860.
1493. ix. Florence Ellen,[8] b. May 16, 1863; died Jan. 30, 1870.

840

John S.[7] Porter, of Nathaniel S.[6] Porter, b. in Richmond, Ky., Apr. 6, 1826; married Sarah Borland; she died; he died June 16, 1876. Children:

Christopher Ball,[8] died in infancy. Mary Bean.[8] Martha.[8]

847

Laura Stimson[7] Porter, of Oliver[6] Porter, b. at Levant, Me., June 22, 1834; teacher in New York and Brooklyn; married Charles H. Kimball; he was born at Bridgeton, Me.; resided for a time in Rumford, Me.; removed to New York city and Brooklyn, where he was a successful teacher; he has also been an alderman in Brooklyn; he is now a member of the firm of Kimball, Hewell & Co., bankers and stock brokers, of New York city. Children:

1497. i. Charles Henry,[8] b. at Aiken, S. C., where they were spending the winter, Feb. 23, 1871.

1498. ii. Frederic Porter,[8] b. at Plainfield, N. J., July 1, 1872.

848

Huntington[7] Porter, of Oliver[6] Porter, b. at Lynn, Mass., Apr. 29, 1839; clerk in Stoneham, Mass., several years; in the late war, in Co. G, 13th Mass. Regt., and lost a leg at the battle of Gettysburg; after the war, went into business as a currier, at North Woburn, Mass.; now a merchant in Woburn, where he resides. He married Ella Frances Poole, daughter of Rufus Poole, of Woburn, Apr. 6, 1871; they have two children, born in Woburn:

1499. i. Edwin Kimball,[8] b. Sept. 13, 1872.

1500. ii. Florence Stimson,[8] b. Feb. 21, 1877.

849

Eliphalet[7] Porter, of Oliver[6] Porter, b. at Lynn, May 2, 1844; clerk in Boston several years; also in New York city, with his brother-in-law Kimball; now of the firm of Prickitt & Porter, of Farmingdale, N. J.; carrying on grist and saw milling, and flour and meal business. He married Augusta Lydia Wyman, Sept. 18, 1871; she was a daughter of Calvin Wyman, of Woburn, Mass. They have one son:

1501. i. George Wyman,[8] b. at Woburn, July 30, 1873.

873

Rev. Emery H.[7] Porter, of Rev. E. M.[6] Porter, b. Apr. 22, 1844: grad. at Brown University, 1866; rector of Episcopal church, Pawtucket, R. I.; married Delia Dyer Weeden, of Pawtucket, R. I., Apr. 22, 1873.

874

George W.[7] Porter, of Rev. E. M.[6] Porter, b. April 10, 1847; grad. Brown University, 1870; surgeon in Woman's Hospital, N. Y. "Married June 4, 1878, George Whipple Porter, M. D., and Miss Emmogene Louise Hoyt, both of Providence, R. I."

883

Oliver[7] Porter, of Oliver[6] Porter, b. Marshfield; resided in Marshfield or Boston; master mariner; married Ruth Rogers, of Marshfield. Of his children, I can obtain no information, except that he had one son and daughter; he was captain of the ship Atahualpa, of Boston, owned by Théodore Lyman, trading on the North-West Coast, where he was murdered by the Indians, in June, 1805. Prince Lapham, and —— Lapham, of Marshfield, were killed at the same time. Miss M. A. Thomas, of Marshfield, writes April, 1875—that when she was a child, Mr. Richardson, of Billerica, who brought the ship safe home again, called at her father's house. The following account was written by the Hon. John S. Sleeper, and printed in the Boston Journal, of Aug. 17, 1860:

"In the month of June, 1805, the ship "Atahualpa," Capt. Porter, of Boston, on a voyage after fur, entered Sturgis' Cove, in Millbank Sound, in about 50 deg. 30 min. N. lat. Canoes filled with natives came immediately alongside, and the Indians expressed a great wish to trade. Their chief, Caillete, also went on board, and expressed the kindest feelings for white men. He was kindly treated, and seemed grateful for several valuable presents, and the captain believed he had secured his friendship, and congratulated himself on the prospect of a lucrative trade with the natives. In fact the captain was thrown completely off his guard, gave Caillete the freedom of his cabin, and allowed the savages, in large numbers, to roam about the ship. The wily chief was thus enabled to carry his treacherous designs into effect.

The ship had been at anchor several days, and nothing suspicious had occurred, when one morning Caillete came on board accompanied by a number of the natives, and cordially returned the kind greeting of the captain. A number of canoes filled with savages also soon came alongside, all eagerly desirous to trade. The captain and chief mate were on the quarter deck conversing with the Indian chief, and the second mate with a portion of the crew were on the main deck bartering with the Indians. The remainder of the crew were engaged aloft, at work on the rigging. As no suspicions were entertained of treachery, no measures were provided against a sudden attack.

The chief mate having stepped to the other side of the deck, Caillete signed to the captain to look over the quarter rail into the canoes; while he was thus engaged, the designing savage threw the captain's coat over his head, drew a dagger from his garments, and stabbed him twice in the back, and then threw him overboard. He then sounded the terrible war whoop, and the Indians brandished their weapons and threw themselves on the ship's company! The chief mate received a fatal wound from one of the savages, but nevertheless he seized a musket and shot Caillete through the head; but the second mate, the captain's clerk, and seven of the sailors who were on deck were killed or desperately wounded before they could muster arms with which to defend their lives. The cook, a stout African, was in the galley when the struggle commenced; he defended himself bravely with boiling water, which he dealt with a liberal hand, scalding all who approached; but his hot water gave out at last, and the savages split his skull with an axe. Only four men escaped without receiving wounds, and they were at work in the rigging. These men gained the deck by sliding down the backstays, and with others who were wounded, retreated to the forecastle where they found a few cutlasses and muskets, and commenced to fire upon the savages, through loop holes in the break of the forecastle deck. This greatly terrified the natives. a number of whom jumped overboard. This was seen by the sailors, who arming themselves with cutlasses, made a rush on deck. The forescuttle, however, was guarded by a muscular savage, armed with the carpenter's broad axe; as the foremost sailor thrust his head through the scuttle, the Indian aimed a blow which would have laid open his cranium if the axe had not struck the mainstay, a large rope which passed directly over the scuttle. Before the savage could recover himself, the sailor was on deck, and with a sweep of the cutlass laid the Indian dead at his feet.

The seven sailors formed a front, attacked the savages, and fought desperately for their lives. In a few moments they drove the Indians overboard, and cleared the ship. The rascals then came under the bows in their canoes, and tried to cut the cables, that the ship might drift ashore. But the sailors got a swivel from the quarter deck, and loading it with bullets, opened a brisk fire on the canoes, which compelled the savages to paddle ashore with all speed. The sailors had now possession of the ship, and proceeded at once to set the sails, cut the cable and beat out of the bay. In this they succeeded, and steering a course to the northward, the next day reached a roadstead where an American vessel was at anchor, and received assistance."

884

Lemuel[7] Porter, of Oliver[6] Porter, b. Marshfield, Dec. 18, 1777; resided in Boston; master mariner; married Hannah Chellis; she b. in Gloucester, Mass., March 6, 1780; died at Warrenton, Va., 1865. He died in Boston, 1841. Children:

1503. i. Lemuel,[8] b. Boston, May 1, 1809.

1504. ii. Hannah E.,[8] b. Boston, Feb. 17, 1813; died Warrenton, Va., 1855.

1505. iii. Oliver,[8] b. Boston, May 28, 1816.

888

Charles[7] Porter, of Oliver[6] Porter, b. Feb. 25, 1790; lived Marshfield; married Sarah Holmes Walker, 1815; she died in Marshfield; he died in Boston, Dec. 17, 1839. Children:

1506. i. Sarah Ann,[8] b. Dec. 20, 1818; married David Lakin, in Duxbury, Oct. 19, 1836; he born Durham, N. H., Apr. 26, 1811; she died in Duxbury, Apr. 27, 1855. Children: Sarah Holmes,[9] b. Weymouth, Feb. 15, 1838; married David Winslow Burbank, in East Cambridge, July 15, 1860; he b. in Plymouth, Apr. 24, 1835; resides Neponset, Boston. (Children: Louisa Frances,[10] b. Plymouth, Jan. 5, 1861. Annie Winslow,[10] b. Boston, Feb. 7, 1868. Susan Porter,[10] b. Mar. 6, 1875.) John Lakin,[9] b. Randolph, Feb. 18, 1841. Hannah Monroe,[9] b. Duxbury, Feb. 13, 1844; died Plymouth, Aug. 27, 1861. Susan Maria,[9] b. Duxbury, Dec. 22, 1846; died Somerville, May 9, 1870.

892

Peggy[7] Porter, of William[6] Porter, b. May 6, 1788; married John Holmes, of Pembroke, 1809; she died 1866. Child:

Samuel C.,[8] lives on the old homestead.

894

Edward Jarvis[7] Porter, of William[6] Porter, b. Marshfield, 1793; he resided in Scituate, from 1820 to 1839; was a soldier in the war of 1812; also a privateersman; captured and taken to Dartmoor prison. Married Ruth Gardner, of Hingham; (her father was a Revolutionary soldier, served whole time, seven years; was with Arnold in his march through Maine to Canada; and finally discharged at New York, by Gen. Washington.) Edward J. Porter, died 1871; his widow still living. Children prob. all b. Scituate, Mass.:

1509. i. Edward Francis,[8] b. July 21, 1820.
1510. ii. Lucy Gardner,[8] b. Feb. 9, 1822.
1511. iii. Margaretta Parker,[8] b. Apr. 20, 1834.
1512. iv. William,[8] b. Jan. 22, 1827.
1513. v. Charles,[8] b. July 28, 1829.
1514. vi. Perez Gardner,[8] b. Nov. 28, 1831.
1515. vii. Sarah J.,[8] b. Jan. 20, 1834.
1516. viii. Alexander,[8] b. Oct. 16, 1836.
1517. ix. Laura Maxwell,[8] b. Sept. 24, 1839; teacher.

895

Isaac[7] Porter, of Isaac[6] Porter, b. Marshfield, Nov. 1, 1786; lived Mt. Vernon, Me.; married Mary Foster; he died Jan. 1, 1858. Children:

1518. i. Sarah A.,[8] b. June, 1814.
1519. ii. Mary Foster,[8] b. July 20, 1821.
1520. iii. John H.,[8] b. Jan., 1819.
1521. iv. Jane Hall,[8] b. Nov. 22, 1823.

896

Amasa[7] Porter, of Isaac[6] Porter, b. Marshfield, Mass., May 23, 1790; lived Mt. Vernon, Me.; married Lois Stain (?); died Mar. 20, 1878, aged 87 years 10 months. Children:

1522. i. Clarissa,[8] b. May 11, 1811.
1523. ii. Hannah S.,[8] b. July 25, 1813.
1524. iii. Isaac,[8] b. Feb. 8, 1816.
1525. iv. William,[8] b. July 24, 1818.
1526. v. Nathan,[8] b. Aug. 11, 1821.
1527. vi. Laura Ann,[8] b. June 3, 1824.

897

Clarissa[7] Porter, of Isaac[6] Porter, b. Marshfield, June 12, 1788; married John Currier, of Mt. Vernon, Me. Children:

Jane Hatch,[8] b. Oct. 9, 1811. Betsey Porter,[8] b. Feb. 25, 1814. Miriam,[8] b. May 22, 1817. Clarissa Harlow,[8] b. June 24, 1824.

898

Harvey[7] Porter, of Isaac[6] Porter, b. Marshfield, Mass., Nov. 25, 1792; lived Mt. Vernon, Me.; married Polly Hutchins; she died May 8, 1850. Children:

Nancy,[8] b. Aug. 1, 1818. Emily,[8] b. Jan. 3, 1823.

899

Calvin[7] Porter, of Isaac[6] Porter, b. Marshfield, Nov. 10, 1794; lived Mt. Vernon, Me.; married Nancy or Susannah Johnson, 1816; he died May 26, 1859. Children:

1534. i. Mary J.,[8] b. March 14, 1817; in California, 1876.
1535. ii. Charles,[8] b. Aug. 1, 1819; went New Orleans, 1846.
1536. iii. Horace,[8] b. June 13, 1822; died July, 1854.
1537. iv. Almira,[8] b. April 8, 1827; married; resides California.
1538. v. Sarah E.,[8] b. May 15, 1829; married Whittier, of Readfield, Me.
1539. vi. Danforth,[8] b. Oct. 7, 1831; resides California.
1540. vii. Frances,[8] b. July 21, 1836; married; resides California.

900

Betsey[7] Porter, of Isaac[6] Porter, b. June 2, 1798; married Frederick Pishon, of Mt. Vernon, Me. Children:

Caroline.[8] Sarah.[8] Mary Ann.[8] Martha.[8] Emily.[8]

901

Nathan[7] Porter, of Isaac[6] Porter, b. Oct. 28, 1801; lived in Mt. Vernon, Me.; m. Harriet A. Gove; her estate settled 1867. Children:

1546. i. Lemuel,[8] b. Dec. 4, 1834.
1547. ii. Dolly,[8] b. April 2, 1837.
1548. iii. Jane.[8]
1549. iv. Charles Franklin,[8] b. Mar. 8, 1839.
1550. v. George.[8]

1551. vi. Georgianna,[8] b. Nov. 30, 1840; m. Joseph T. Sherburne, both of Readfield, Mar. 31, 1872.
1552. vii. Arvilla,[8] b. Oct. 7, 1844.
1553. viii. Betsey Emma,[8] b. Mar. 16, 1847.
1554. ix. Angie.[8]
1555. x. Frederick E.[8]

902

Sarah[7] Porter, of Isaac[6] Porter, b. Dec. 14, 1803; married Joseph Gile, of Mt. Vernon, Me., March 19, 1829, by Dexter Baldwin; he born May 30, 1802. Children:

Isaac,[8] b. May 28, 1830. Edwin,[8] b. twin of above. Albion F.,[8] b. March 29, 1834. Charles Kelly,[8] b. April 13, 1836. Caroline A.,[8] b. Nov. 17, 1838.

903

Polly[7] Porter, of James[6] Porter, b. Abington, Feb. 25, 1778; married William Fullerton, Nov. 29, 1796; she died Oct., 1848; he died June 30, 1837. This family resided in North Bridgewater, near Abington line. Children:

1561. i. Harvey,[8] b. 1803; died young.
1562. ii. Mehitable,[8] b. 1800; m. David Edson.
1563. iii. Harvey,[8] married Mary Gurney, of Abington.
1564. iv. Almira,[8] b. 1805; m. Moses Dunbar, of Easton.
1565. v. Calista,[8] b. 1807; m. Harrison T. Mitchell, of Easton.
1566. vi. William,[8] b. 1810; m. Mary Johnson, of Sharon.
1567. vii. John,[8] b. 1813; m. Mrs. Rebecca Cobb, of Carver.
1568. viii. James Porter,[8] b. 1815; m. Lemira H. Mitchell, of Easton.
1569. ix. Marcus,[8] b. June 8, 1818; m. Sally Ann Reynolds, of Stoughton.
1570. x. Mary Porter,[8] married James Monroe Holmes, of Easton.

904

Abigail[7] Porter, of James[6] Porter, b. Abington, Dec. 28, 1779; married Levi Keith, Jr., Dec. 28, 1797; lived some time in Augusta, Maine. Children:

Alvin,[8] b. 1799. Clarissa,[8] b. 1801. Samantha,[8] m. Joshua Lowell, of Farmingdale, Me.

905

Hannah[7] Porter, of James[6] Porter, b. Plainfield, Nov. 3, 1781; married Nathaniel Reynolds, Jr., of Sidney, Me., 1811. He b. Dec. 12, 1779; died Mar. 3, 1862; she died July 4, 1831. Children:

1574. i. Julia Ann,[8] b. Jan. 20, 1812; m. W. G. Ellis, of Sidney, Me., 1843; he died July 27, 1864; his widow still lives at West Waterville, Me.—post office, S. Smithfield, Me.
1575. ii. Nathaniel,[8] b. Sept. 1, 1813; died Jan. 6, 1834.
1576. iii. Hannah,[8] b. Oct. 5, 1815; died May 8, 1831.
1577. iv. Cyrus,[8] b. Sept. 25, 1818; unmarried; lives in Georgetown, Me.
1578. v. Bethiah R.,[8] b. May 18, 1821; died Feb. 15, 1832.
1579. vi. Caroline B.,[8] b. Sept. 27, 1823: m. Eliezer Whitman, of E. Bridgewater, Mass., and has a family.

908

Amasa[7] Porter, of Amasa[6] Porter, b. Newton, 1793; married Abigail Frothingham, of Charlestown. Children:

1580. i. Amasa,[8] Jr., unmarried; died aged 25.
1581. ii. Abby,[8] m. Tuft Johnson, of Charlestown; now a widow, residing in Pepperell.
1582. iii. James F.,[8] m. Mary Parker; resides Mt. Benedict St., East Somerville.
1583. iv. Samuel A.,[8] resides in Somerville.
1584. v. Frederick,[8] unmarried; resides in Chicago.
1585. vi. Elizabeth,[8] married Samuel Kimball; resides 407, Shawmut Avenue, Boston.
1586. vii. Charles H.,[8] resides in Somerville.
1587. viii. John Vose,[8] b. 1842; died 1862.

909

Margaret[7] Porter, of Amasa[6] Porter, b. Newton, 1795; Married 1st, Wm. Patterson. Married 2d, Martin C. Sherlock. Married 3d, Herrick. She died 1858. Children:

George Patterson,[8] resides Boston Highlands. Margaret B. Patterson,[8] married Page. Eliza Ann Sherlock,[8] married. Martin Sherlock,[8] died in infancy.

910

Pamelia[7] Porter, of Amasa[6] Porter, b. July 4, 1797; married John Simpson, of Maine. Children:

Thomas,[8] killed in late war. Martha,[8] resides in Boston.

911

Elizabeth[7] Porter, of Amasa[6] Porter, b. Aug. 1, 1799, in Newton; married Amasa T. Thompson, of Conn., who was a pump and block maker in Boston; she died Dec 31, 1860. Children, born in Boston:

Pamelia Porter,[8] m. John T. Ford, of Boston, merchant, Temple Place. Elizabeth,[8] m. Charles W. Little. Lucinda,[8] m. Geo. L. Ford, of Boston, brother of John T. Ford. Otis A.,[8] m. Lottie Smith.

912

William[7] Porter, of Amasa[6] Porter, born 1804; settled in Cambridge; married Elizabeth, daughter of Capt. Charles Porter, of Marshfield. Children:

1598. i. Calvin,[8] m.; died without children.
1599. ii. Ann Eliza.[8]
1600. iii. William,[8] resides at E. Cambridge.
1601. iv. Lizzie,[8] m. Jones; resides at E. Cambridge.

913

James A.[7] Porter, of Amasa[6] Porter, b. 1806; of Charlestown,—No. 38 Bunker Hill street; married Mary Ellingwood, of York, Me. Children:

1602. i. James E.,[8]; wife died Feb. 2, 1878, in Boston.
1603. ii. Rebecca,[8] m. Lane, who resides No. 117 Bartlett street, Charlestown.
1604. iii. Mary E.,[8] married.
1605. iv. Frederick.[8]

914

Sarah[7] Porter, of Amasa[6] Porter, b. Charlestown, 1811; married 1st, Richard Pasquell, of East Cambridge. Married 2d, Donald Melville. Children by 1st husband:

Richard,[8] died in California, 1874. Sarah J.,[8] m. Carroll, an actor; she an actress. Alfred,[8] died at sea, unmarried.

Children by 2d husband:

Donald,[8] died young. Mamie,[8] m. Bates; actress.

915

Alfred H.[7] Porter, of Amasa[6] Porter, b. Charlestown, July 9, 1814; resides No. 285 Gold street, South Boston. Married 1st, Ann R. Scott, of Cambridge; she died Dec., 1848. Married 2d, Clarinda Sackett, July 3, 1849. Children by 1st wife:

1602. i. Sarah E.,[8] b. Dec. 14, 1842; m. Aaron H. Young, of Cushing, Maine.
1603. ii. Abby A.,[8] b. Feb. 17, 1844; m. T. H. Payson, of Rockland, Maine; she died June 20, 1866.

931

Ruth[7] Porter, of John[6] Porter, b. Marshfield, March 11, 1789; married Nathaniel Sampson, of Marshfield; she died May, 1829, aged 42 years. (?) Children:

1604. i. Ruth Briggs,[8] m. Stephen Wright, of Abington.
1605. ii. Judah,[8] lost at sea when about 22 years of age, in schooner Essex, of Cohasset, Aug., 1844.
1606. iii. Mary A.,[8] m. Walter Kidder, of Townsend, Mass.
1607. iv. Warren W.,[8] b. in Pembroke, Feb. 6, 1826; m. Keziah R. Leach; lives in New Bedford, Mass.
1608. v. John,[8] unmarried; lives South Abington,
1609. vi. George,[8] unmarried; lives Plympton.
1610. vii. Charles,[8] m. widow of Pool, of Abington; died Mar., 1874, aged 42 years.

932

Bethiah[7] Porter, of John[6] Porter, b. Marshfield, Sept. 8, 1791; died May 16, 1838; married Prince Lapham; he son of Jesse and Mercy (Randall) Lapham, murdered by Indians on North-West Coast, in June, 1805; was in ship Atahualpa, with Capt. Oliver Porter. (See account of same, page 137.)

933

Sarah[7] Porter, of John[6] Porter, b. Marshfield, Nov. 7, 1792; married Arthur Howland, of Marshfield; she died Mar. 14, 1816, aged 23 years 4 mos. He died April 1, 1816, aged 23 years 8 months. Children:

i. Arthur,[8] died young.
ii. Sarah,[8] b. Feb. 25, 1816; m. Hamilton Moorehead, of

Marshfield, and died July 23, 1869. Children: Arthur,[9] b. April 19; died Mar. 15, 1840. Sarah,[9] b. April 16, 1841; died Mar. 31, 1850. Theodore,[9] b. May 20, 1844; resides in China. Hamilton,[9] b. July 2, 1846; died May 28, 1848. John,[9] b. Mar. 19, 1848; resides Marshfield. Jenny H.,[9] b. Mar. 1, 1851; m. Willard Kent, and resides Woonsocket, R. I.

936

Alvin[7] Porter, of John[6] Porter, b. Marshfield, Aug. 17, 1796. Resided in Marshfield; married Bethiah Ames, June 29, 1820. He died Sept. 18, 1870, aged 74. Children:

1611. i. Louisa,[8] b. June 25, 1821; m. Caleb Bates, of Scituate; had one child; she died Oct. 17, 1842.

1612. ii. Avery,[8] b. May 15, 1823; m. Sarah Cook, of S. Abington; has two children; he died Dec. 8, 1846.

1613. iii. Alvin,[8] b. Aug. 12, 1825.

1614. iv. John,[8] b. Sept. 22, 1827; m. Sarah C. Gilbert, of East Bridgewater; had two children; both dead; he died Oct. 5, 1873.

1615. v. William S.,[8] b. Feb. 22, 1830; m. Abigail B. Williamson, of So. Marshfield; have had five children.

1616. vi. Isaac R.,[8] b. April 19; m. Charlotte A. Steingarelt, of East Bridgewater; lives in South Abington; have seven children.

1617. vii. Calvin,[8] b. Aug. 12, 1834; m. Mary E. Cook; lives in South Abington; has nine children.

1618. viii. Solomon,[8] b. Mar. 4, 1837; died April 14, 1837.

1619. ix. Bethia R.,[8] b. Mar. 26, 1838; m. 1st John F. Steingarelt; one child. M. 2d, James E. Baker, of Marshfield.

1619A. x. Eliza A.,[8] b. Jan. 27, 1841; m. Frank Ford, of Marshfield; have one child.

937

Eliza[7] Porter, of John[6] Porter, b. Marshfield, May 25, 1799; married Lincoln Gould, Oct. 20, 1822, by Rev. Mr. Parish, of Marshfield; he resides at Hingham, Mass.; was born at Hingham, June 5, 1799, and was son of Robert Gould, sometime of Hull and sometime of Hingham. [Robert Gould was son of John, Jr., and Jane (Loring) Gould, of Hull; born there May 29, 1759. Married Mary Lincoln, daughter of Josiah, Jr., and Mary (Holbrook) Lincoln, of

Hingham, Feb. 4, 1783; she b. July 22, 1763; died in Hingham, Nov. 3, 1847; he died there Feb. 26, 1832.] Children:

1620. i. Eliza Porter,[8] b. Jan. 25, 1825; died Mar. 15, 1825.

1621. ii. Josiah Lincoln,[8] b. Nov. 28, 1823; m. Josephine, daughter of Giles and Eliza (Abbott) Gardner, of Hingham, Oct. 19, 1845, by Rev. Joseph W. Talbot; she born Sept. 22, 1826—had one child. Josiah Lincoln,[9] born April 22, 1847; m. Abbie G. daughter of Peter and Sophia (Fearing) Hersey, May 19,1872; by Rev. A. G. Jennings. She born Sept. 27, 1847. Josiah L. Gould, Sen., died Sept. 9, 1849, and his widow married Nathaniel Hunt, of Hingham, May 21, 1858.

1622. iii. Stephen Puffer,[8] b. Aug. 27, 1826; m. Sarah, daughter of Henry and Sarah L. (Barnes) Nye, of Hingham, Oct. 3, 1827. She b. Jan. 7, 1827. Children: Sarah L.,[9] b. Mar. 26, 1848; married Wm. H. Hersey, of Hingham, Aug. 31, 1869, by Rev. Calvin Lincoln; (he son of Warren and Sarah Ann Hersey, b. Nov. 27, 1840.) Augustus S.,[9] b. 1850; unmarried; resides in Lawrence, Mass. Mrs. Sarah N. Gould died May 2, 1861. He married 2d, Nancy Wildes Williams, widow of Samuel L. Williams, Oct. 17, 1869, by Rev. Phebe A. Hannaford. She was daughter of Ezra and Lucy (Cain) Bicknell, of Hingham, b. at Weymouth, Oct. 31, 1839. Children: Hattie May,[9] b. Boston, May 2, 1873; died Hingham, Aug. 17, 1873. Hattie Lincoln,[9] b. Hingham, Sept. 21, 1875.

1623. iv. Mary Lewis,[8] b. April 19, 1832; m. Albert Whiton, of Hingham, Sept. 26, 1861, by Rev. Stephen H. Puffer, of Lunenburg, Mass. Mr. Whiton, son of Isaiah and Martha D. (Easterbrook) Whiton; b. Oct. 10, 1829—her second marriage. They have one child, Eliza Porter,[9] b. Hingham, May 15, 1868.

938

Nicholas[7] Porter, of John[6] Porter, b. Marshfield, Jan. 18, 1801, and resides there; married Mercy R. Holmes, of Marshfield, Jan. 8, 1826; she daughter of Abraham and Ruth (Lapham) Holmes, b. Feb. 10, 1796. They celebrated their golden wedding, Jan. 8, 1876. Children:

1624. i. Marcia R.,[8] b. Oct. 26, 1826; m. Edward Sprague, of Marshfield, June 13, 1848. Children: John G.,[9] m. Emma Thomas. Edward Porter[9]. Frederick Winslow,[9]

m. Lydia Hewett, of Marshfield, Oct., 1877. Marcie Alice[9]. Willie[9]. George Elmer[9].

1625. ii. Nicholas,[8] b. Sept. 6, 1828; m. Deborah P. Bonney, of Marshfield, Mar. 3, 1850; no children.

1626. iii. Lydia,[8] b. Oct. 5, 1832.

1627. iv. Nathaniel J.,[8] b. Jan. 27, 1837; unmarried; resides in Marshfield; in business No. 76 Devonshire St., Boston.

939

Jeremiah[7] Porter, of Isaac[6] Porter, b. Farmington, Dec. 31, 1818; died May, 1866. Mar. Philena Blake, 1840. Children:

1628. i. Charles N.,[8] b. June 21, 1841; married.

1629. ii. Rufus B.,[8] b. Nov., 1843; m. Millie Calden, of Kingfield, Me., at Phillips, Me.

1630. iii. Florence,[8] b. Nov., 1849.

940

William[7] Porter, of Isaac[6] Porter, b. June 26, 1821; married Elisabeth Record, Sept., 1842. Children:

1631. i. Melissa E.,[8] b. Sept. 3, 1843; m. Roscoe Stoddard, resides Minnesota.

1632. ii. Olive L.,[8] b. 1847; m. Henry Gilman, at Farmington, Me.

1633. iii. Ida,[8] b. 1856; unmarried.

941

Selina E.[7] Porter, of Isaac[6] Porter, b. Farmington, Me., Oct. 8, 1824; married Daniel W. Pillsbury, Nov. 17, 1844; he son of Eben and Eliza Pillsbury, of Kingfield, (and brother of Eben W. Pillsbury, Esq., of Augusta;) merchant, of Augusta, Me. Children:

Hanibal E.,[8] b. Sept. 29, 1846; died. Clara R.,[8] died in early life. Ossian D.,[8] b. Aug. 14, 1851; m. Fannie Harris, at Augusta, Me., June 15, 1876; merchant. Lizade E.,[8] b. Mar. 28, 1857.

943

Hiram[7] Porter, of Laban[6] Porter, b. Weymouth; lived in Stoughton; went out in one of Mass. regiments, and served during the war; returned home, and died soon after; married 1st, Lydia. Married 2d, Mary F. Smith, in Stoughton, Jan. 30, 1857. Child:

i. Sarah,[8] by 1st wife; died Stoughton, Nov. 8, 1853.

950

Susanna^7 Porter, of Ezekiel^6 Porter, born May 4, 1785; married Ezekiel Pierce, 1808; lived in Chesterfield, N. H.; she died 1865. Children:

Ezekiel.^{8} Susannah.^{8} Jane.^{8} Lucius.^{8} Julia.^{8} Lafayette.^{8} Horace.^{8} Augusta.^{8}

951

Alexander^7 Porter, of Ezekiel^6 Porter, b. Hallowell, Me., Oct. 10, 1787. He was a miller and farmer, and lived in New Vineyard, Me.; married Hannah J. W. Bray, 1852 (?); died 1853; no children.

952

Thirza^7 Porter, of Ezekiel^6 Porter, b. Hallowell, Me., June 1, 1789; m. Dr. John Cottle, 1807; lived in Mainsville, Ohio; died 1865. Children:

Eliza.^{8} Jane.^{8} Lucius.^{8} Thirza.^{8} John.^{8} Susan.^{8}

953

Ezekiel^7 Porter, of Ezekiel^6 Porter, b. Farmington, Me., July 4, 1791; lived in Strong, Me.; miller and farmer; he died 1867; m. Eunice Hitchcock, pub. Dec. 27, 1816. Children:

1637A. i. Thirza,^{8} b. April 17, 1819; m. Lemuel Crosby, of Phillips, Me., Dec. 20, 1843.
1638. ii. Jeremy W.,^{8} b. Nov. 19, 1820; of Strong, Me.
1639. iii. Eunice H.,^{8} b. April 8, 1823; m. Dr. Edward H. Russell, 1847, of Farmington, Me., now of Lewiston, Me., where he has been Mayor. He has been member of Maine Senate.
1640. iv. Alexander P.,^{8} b. Mar. 6, 1825; married.
1641. v. Elias H.,^{8} b. Jan. 20, 1827; m. Louisa M. Richards, July 17, 1850.
vi. Augusta J.,^{8} died.
vii. Austin T.,^{8} died.
viii. Ezekiel,^{8} died.
1642. ix. Sarah M.,^{8} b. June 21, 1837; m. Albert L. Daggett, of Farmington, Me., April 2, 1857; now of Strong, Me.

954

Jeremy W.[7] Porter, of Ezekiel[6] Porter, born Oct. 3, 1792; petitioner with his mother in 1816, for administration upon his father's estate. Allopathic physician; lived in Waterloo, Ind.; died 1818.

955

Polly[7] Porter, of Ezekiel[6] Porter, born July 26, 1794; m. Joseph Holley, 1833; lived in Farmington; died there, 1874. Children:

Mary.[8] Jeremy.[8] John.[8] Thirza.[8]

956

Zerviah[7] Porter, of Ezekiel[6] Porter, born Mar. 14, 1797; m. James Lunt, of Manchester, N. H., 1819; she died 1855. Children:

Hannah,[8] died. Monroe,[8] died. Daniel.[8] Eliza.[8]

958

Asahel[7] Porter, of Ezekiel[6] Porter, b. May 5, 1802; m. Todd; lived in Warren, Ohio; merchant. Children:

Asahel.[8] Charles.[8]

960

William W.[7] Porter, of Edward[6] Porter, b. Taunton, Jan. 11, 1803; resided there; married Mehetable, dau. of Lemuel and Polly Cobb, of Plympton, Mass., June 1, 1828. She b. Sept. 21, 1805. Children:

1662. i. Edward W.,[8] b. Mar. 11, 1831; m. Sarah Strange.
1663. ii. Polly L.,[8] b. Aug. 1, 1832; m. Manning W. Fox.
1664. iii. Lemuel Cobb,[8] b. June 25, 1839; m Esther G. Austin.
1665. iv. Rhoda C.,[8] b. Sept. 17, 1846; m. David W. Dean.
1666. v. Caroline C.,[8] b. Sept., 1833; died March, 1839.
1667. vi. Rhoda W.,[8] b. Jan. 11, 1835; died.

962

Benjamin[7] Porter, of Edward[6] Porter, b. in Taunton, Sept. 25, 1806; lived there; married 1st, Betsey Williams, 1835; married 2d, Bathsheba Briggs, 1848. Children:

1668. i. Eliza J.,[8] b. 1837; died 1871.

1669. ii. Betsey[8].
1670. iii. Emma,[8] b. 1849.
1671. iv. Benjamin F.,[8] died in infancy.
1672. v. Betsy W.,[8] died in infancy.

963

Mary[7] Porter, of Edward[6] Porter, b. June 7, 180–; married David Osborne, of Camden, N. Y., 1842. Children:

Benjamin P.,[8] died in infancy. Betsey P.,[8] b. 1845; died Mar., 1873. Benjamin L.,[8] b. 1847.

965

Charles[7] Porter, of Jacob[6] Porter, b. Mar. 17, 1788, in Taunton; lived there; died 1855; married Mercy Washburn; she b. Nov., 1792; died Oct. 30, 1866. He died Sept. 8, 1869. Children:

1676. i. Henry Cushman,[8] b. Nov. 9, 1820; m. Sarah E. Pearce, of Providence, R. I.; he died in 1863, from the effects of service in the army; his widow and his sons Charles F.,[9] and William C.,[9] are living in Providence.
1677. ii. Theodore P.,[8] b. Sept. 23, 1823; unmarried; Taunton.
1678. iii. Jane,[8] b. Apr. 15, 1825; m. Charles Foster, May, 1856; resides Taunton; has two sons: Henry E.,[9] b. Feb. 14, 1858. Charles P.,[9] b. May 31, 1860.
1679. iv. Mary,[8] b. Nov. 4, 1828; unmarried.
1680. v. Charles James,[8] b. Dec. 22, 1834; unmarried; died Mar. 23, 1863.

966

Christopher[7] Porter, of Jacob[6] Porter, b. Taunton, Oct. 18, 1789; lived in Boston; died 1824; m. Betsey Miller, of Boston; he left one son,[8] who married Mary N. Washburn, of Taunton; he died in Cannelton, Ind., 1862. No children.

968

John[7] Porter, of Jacob[6] Porter, born Jan. 27, 1793; married Hannah Earle, of Taunton; removed to Dover, N. H.; thence to Fall River, where he died Mar. 21, 1839; had two sons, and two daughters:

Charles B.,[8] m. Annie Williamson, of San Francisco; has three daughters and three sons, and has lived in California since 1848. Sarah K.,[8] m. P. H. Campbell of Boston; removed to San Francisco,

1861; two sons and three daughters. Thomas C.,[8] unmarried. Harriet E.,[8] m. Geo. E. Randolph, of Providence, R. I., 1864, at which time they removed to Central City, Colorado. No children.

970

Sarah[7] Porter, of Zechariah[6] Porter, born in Middleborough, Mar. 10, 1796; m. Dr. Jeremiah Brown. Children:

Priscilla,[8] m. Carpenter, of Elmira, N. Y. Henrietta,[8] m. Lewis Hewlan. Sarah,[8] m. Philo Catlin. Le Haller,[8] probably of Williamsport, Penn.

971

Zechariah[7] Porter, of Zechariah[6] Porter, b. Nov. 7, 1797; married Sarah Follett, Feb. 18, 1829; she b. Dec. 25, 1800; died May 21, 1871; he died May 19, 1848. Children:

1704. i. Henry Lucien,[8] b. Dec. 16, 1829; married and had three children. Sarah.[9] Alice.[9] b. 1855; m. Ford, 1876. Ernest,[9] b. June 2, 1857; resides Missouri.

1705. ii. Sarah E.,[8] b. Nov. 10, 1831; m. Charles Wilson, Sept. 17, 1862; resides Walpole, Mass.; has one son, Clarence Porter,[9] b. July 18, 1867.

1706. iii. George H.,[8] b. Nov. 4, 1833; married; resides New Haven, Conn.; has three children living: George Willis,[9] born Sept. 29, 1865. Edith,[9] b. 1870. Clifford,[9] b. 1877.

1707. iv. Harriet N.,[8] b. June 11, 1836; m. Frank Shaw, of Jersey City; have two children: Frank M.,[9] b. Jan. 1867. Ella H.,[9] b. Oct., 1871.

1708. v. Jefferson B.,[8] b. Nov. 14, 1839; married; has three children living. Harriet H.,[9] b. Oct., 1865. Eugene,[9] b. Sept. 13, 1869. Arthur Le Roy,[9] b. Mar. 31, 1874.

972

Priscilla[7] Porter, of Zechariah[6] Porter, b. Middleborough, Aug. 7, 1799; married Palmer Morey, son of Rev. George and Anna (Palmer) Morey; he b. Walpole, Mass., May 27, 1797, and died Aug. 27, 1867; widow died Aug. 26, 1875. Children:

1709. i. Geo. Palmer,[8] b. Apr. 25, 1826; m. Ann Blakely, Jan. 23, 1873; she b. 1847.

1710. ii. Harriet L.,[8] b. July 15, 1833; m. William Moore, Dec., 1868; and died May 24, 1872.

1711. iii. Sarah Jane,[8] b. June 9, 1837.

973

Jefferson Burr^7 Porter, of Zecheriah^6 Porter, b. Middleborough, July 25, 1801; resided Mansfield, Mass.; married Betsey Knapp; no children. She died Aug. 18, 1835; he died Jan. 16, 1878, in Mansfield, Mass.

974

Jonathan O.^{7} Porter, of Zecheriah^6 Porter, b. Aug. 17, 1811; married Martha J. Clark, of Oldtown, Me., August, 1845; she died Mar. 28, 1871, aged 48. Children, all born in Oldtown:

1712. i. Adrianna,^{8} b. 1846; died in about 11 months.
1713. ii. Albry F.,^{8} b. Sept. 15, 1848; resides Jersey City.
1714. iii. Ada A.,^{8} b. Oct. 15, 1850; m. J. S. Parmenter, of Palermo, Me., Aug. 24, 1868.
1714A. iv. George H.,^{8} b. May 25, 1853; married; he is in the West; wife at present in Lewiston, Me.

992

George S.^{7} Porter, of Sylvanus^6 Porter, b. Middleborough, Jan. 29, 1807; married Rachel Smith, in Charlestown, Mass., May 23, 1833; he died in Alameda, Cal., June 27, 1871; his widow died in Hingham, Mass., Aug. 27, 1872. Children:

1715. i. Georgianna,^{8} b. New York, Jan. 5, 1837.
1716. ii. Amelia,^{8} b. Allegan, Mich., Nov. 26, 1839.
1717. iii. George S.,^{8} b. New Orleans, May 17, 1845.
1718. iv. William,^{8} b. San Francisco, Nov. 23, 1849.
1719. v. John Kirkland,^{8} b. San Francisco, July 22, 1852; resides San Francisco; unmarried.
1720. vi. Louisa,^{8} b. Milwaukee, Wis., Nov. 3, 1841.

993

John K.^{7} Porter, of Sylvanus^6 Porter, b. Middleborough, Mass., Dec. 25, 1808; merchant; resides Boston. Married 1st, Mary Provost Robertson, of N. Y., Sept. 20, 1830; she died Dorchester, Jan. 19, 1848. Married 2d, Elizabeth Rice Bradlee, of Boston, June 10, 1851. Children:

1721. i. John Sylvanus,^{8} b. New York, Oct. 18, 1831; died there May 7, 1833.
1722. ii. Fannie Colden,^{8} b. New York, March 31, 1834.

1723\. iii. Mary Provost,[8] b. Coalsmouth, Kanawha Co., Virginia, Feb. 25, 1838; died in Princeton, Mass., Aug. 21, 1861

1724\. iv. Alexander Sylvanus,[8] b. Princeton, Mass., Aug. 25, 1840.

1825\. v. Florence Virginia,[8] b. Princeton, Mass., Aug. 21, 1843.

1726\. vi. Elizabeth Bradlee,[8] b. Boston, Mar. 18, 1852.

994

Francis E.[7] Porter, of Sylvanus[6] Porter, b. Middleborough, Sept. 8, 1811; married Barnabas Thayer Loring, in Boston, Thanksgiving day, Nov., 1836; she died in Dorchester, Jan. 14, 1857. Children:

1727\. i. Frances E.,[8] b. Boston, July 26, 1840, of Braintree.

1728\. ii. Ellen J.,[8] b. Dorchester, Oct. 15, 1843, of Braintree.

1729\. iii. Alden Porter,[8] b. Dorchester, Jan. 12, 1846, of Braintree.

1730\. iv. Richard Freeman,[8] b. Dochester, July 27, 1847; of Braintree.

1731\. v. George F.,[8] b. Dorchester, Jan. 9, 1851; died Boston, Apr. 6, 1858.

995

Ann W. E.[7] Porter, of Sylvanus[6] Porter, b. Middleborough, Nov. 14, 1812; married Otis Clapp, Aug. 29, 1833, in Boston; she died Oct. 27, 1843. Children:

1732\. i. Otis,[8] b. Boston, Sept. 1, 1834; died Sept. 6, 1834.

1734\. ii. Henry Otis,[8] b. Boston, Sept. 13, 1835; m. Rose Nelson, daughter of Rev. David Nelson, of Quincy, Ill.; he died there of consumption, Aug. 1, 1866.

1735\. iii. Joseph,[8] b. Boston, Aug. 27, 1839; m. Elmira J. Jackson, of Syracuse, N. Y., Feb. 4, 1864; he was Capt. in 8th Illinois Cavalry, in late war; his wife died Nov. 7, 1871; he resides in Evanston, Ill.; his children: Florence P.,[9] b. Dec. 12, 1865; died 1867. Joseph Emery,[9] b. May 2, 1869. Harry Otis,[9] b. June 18, 1871.

997

Andrew W.[7] Porter, of William[6] Porter, born Middleboro', March 2, 1795; died in Monson, Sunday, March 4, 1877. The writer of this was indebted to him for many cheering words and much information; about himself he would write nothing. Rev. C. B. Sumner, of Monson, Mass., his pastor and friend, has at my request prepared the following sketch:

"The first seventeen years of his life were spent on a farm, with the enjoyment of the usual advantages of the common school, and a few terms at Peirce Academy. Leaving home, he spent several years in a country store, first at Wareham, then at Pawtucket, R. I. An apprenticeship of six years at Oxford,* with Mr. Samuel Slater, so intimately connected with the manufacturing interests of this country fitted him to enter a company and take charge of a cotton mill, in Monson. Here he spent the remainder of his life, except six years devoted to manufacturing interests in Stafford, Conn. His business life was very successful; a man of strong constitution, of vast energy, and great power of endurance, he readily overcame obstacles that would have appalled most men. A life long affection of the heart, often very alarming, and a painful lameness the last sixteen years of his life, scarcely diminished his tireless activity. To balance these progressive qualities, he was economical, watchful of details, of good judgment, and conservative. He rapidly accumulated money, and soon acquired a controlling influence in his company, and a business reputation which won many lucrative offers in more important situations. His estate was moderate at his death; but he had doubtless given away many times its amount during his life.

An important event in his life was a deep and thorough christian experience, at the age of thirty-four. He had before been upright, observant of the Sabbath himself, and required its observance by his employees, and who gave regularly one-tenth of his income to charitable objects; but his conversion produced a great change; all the energies of his being were now concentrated in a definite object; henceforth he lived for Jesus Christ, his personal Saviour. Whether he should give up his business, and fit himself for the christian ministry, was at first a perplexing question; he finally decided to remain where God's grace found him, and show himself a christian business man. Beginning at once to live, use his resources, and plan as the Lord's steward, he determined the proper limit of his accumulations for a business capital, purposing to put all beyond that direct into the Lord's treasury.

The same firmness of principle and devotion to his Master, appeared in everything he did. In every form of church work his presence was an inspiration—his zeal, activity and wisdom were an efficient power. The church quickly chose him as deacon, and was never willing to release him. Foremost in devising and planning, he was

*Dea. Porter always understood Mr. Slater as having promised him an interest in the mills at Oxford, but when Mr. Slater's sons became his partners, he did not so understand it. For some reference to Mr. Slater, see in the appendix to this work, an account of the invention of a power loom, by Rev. Jonas Perkins, of Braintree, an intimate and beloved friend of Dea. Porter.

J. W. P.

not less valuable as an executor, whether in the more public or the more private and delicate matters. Among his own employees he was indefatigable in his efforts for the development and growth of christian virtues. Neither were his labors confined to distinctly church matters; they equally embraced every common interest of the community. In the great temperance reform he was especially prominent. The academy in Monson, also found in him a warm and helpful friend.

His abounding benevolence gave a far wider scope to his labors than his own town; much of his charity was dispensed in quiet unobtrusive ways, reaching all over the land, and many missionary homes, churches, and institutions of learning, east and west, north and south, have felt the quickening influence of his sympathy, his prayers and his money. Nearly all the charitable societies of the Congregationalist denomination, and some others, were regularly the almoners of his offerings. Perhaps the A. B. C. F. M., of which he was long a corporate member, shared as large as any during his life, and it was not forgotten in the disposal of his estate. Amherst College, in its darkest days, invited his co-operation, and it was freely given; long a member of the board of assessors of the charity fund and one of the building committee for the erection of the Woods Cabinet and Lawrence Observatory, he devoted much time and thought, as well as contributed freely to the pecuniary necessities of that institution, which to-day holds a place so important to the cause of education, and to the church. But Mount Holyoke Female Seminary claims him as father, and was regarded by him with great affection. Captured by Mary Lyon before ground had been broken, his interest never lessened, nor did he relinquish his thoughtful regard for its welfare so long as his trembling fingers could guide the pencil to convey his messages of love. 'Except Mary Lyon,' wrote the present principal. 'no human being has done as much for the institution as he.' The minute of the trustees, at the meeting subsequent to his death, referring to him whose invaluable services as treasurer and steward they had gratefully acknowledged four years before, contains the following: 'For forty years he has had more or less to do with everything pertaining especially to the finances, buildings, grounds and all the externals of the Seminary; and during the longer part of this time he has had the principal oversight and management of them, and he has managed them with a wisdom, an integrity, and an unselfish devotion which are alike remarkable. For forty years, without any pecuniary reward or emolument, he gave time, thought, money and personal services unsparingly to the institution which he adopted, loved and cared for as a child.'

Mr. Porter was married Jan. 17, 1822, to Hannah Kingsbury, of Oxford, who died Dec. 5, 1869. She was a devoted christian woman, of strong character and cultivated mind, and doubtless had a large influence in moulding his character. They had four children, three of whom died in infancy, and the fourth, Elisabeth, at the age of thirteen. A second marriage was celebrated with Mrs. Mary Sigourney Butler Stafford, of Oxford (cousin of his first wife,) Jan. 17, 1872. This, too, was a very happy union, and she still survives to mourn his loss.

Deacon Porter's home, always abundant in hospitality, was a place of genial rest and enjoyment. Business men, educators, philanthropists, those connected with various benevolent enterprises, a large circle of christian ministers, missionaries, and christian men of other races, who had come to this country for sympathy and help, all found there a cordial, pleasant home.

Deacon Porter was a rare man. His loss is widely felt; but he so lived that, though dead he yet speaketh by his example, by the gracious fruits of his personal ministries, and of his multiplied offerings to the Lord, by the yet unfailing stream of his beneficence."

998

Minerva W.[7] Porter, of William[6] Porter, b. Middleboro', Mass., Dec. 21, 1796; married Lucas Van Dusen, June 19, 1820, in Pittston, N. Y., at the house of her aunt; he born at Kinderhook, Columbia Co., N. Y., April 24, 1790; "he was of Holland Dutch descent;" he learned his trade of tanner and currier, of Peter Van Allen, at Chatham, Columbia Co., N. Y.; and died at Newark, Wayne Co., N. Y., April 16, 1862. Children:

1745. i. John Porter,[8] b. Pittston, N. Y., Mar. 24, 1821; married Annie M. Lay, at Newark, May 22, 1862; have four children; reside in Newark; his busines drying fruit and vegetables by steam.

1746. ii. William James,[8] b. Pittston, July 15, 1822, unmarried; Capt. Co. A, 160th Regt. N. Y. State Volunteers; killed instantly in the battle of Pleasant Hill, Louisiana, in the Red River expedition under Gen. Banks, April 9, 1864.

1747. iii. Peter,[8] b. Pittston, Mar. 14, 1824; married Elizabeth Ann Vanvolkenborgh, Apr. 9, 1856; farmer, has five children.

1748. iv. Edwin,[8] born Dec. 28, 1825; died Sept. 27, 1828.
1749. v. Phillip,[8] born Dec. 28, 1825; died June 9, 1827.

1750. vi. Rebecca,[8] b. Pittston, Mar. 22, 1828; educated Mount Holyoke Seminary, Mass.; married at Newark, Edwin E. Rogers, of Palmyra, N. Y., May 20, 1863.

1751. vii. Henry Martin,[8] b. New Lebanon, N. Y., May 5, 1830; married Emeline Harkness, of Leslie, Mich., Aug. 3, 1858; have two children. Resides Jackson, Mich.; dealer in wood and coal.

1752. ix. Harriet Newell,[8] twin to Henry M.; died in New Lebanon, N. Y., May 10, 1832.

1753. x. Andrew Porter,[8] b. Phelps, Ontario Co., N. Y., April 14, 1836; married Mary Hardy, of Mason, Mich., June 18, 1868. Resides at Mason; dentist.

1754. xi. Harriet Bostwick,[8] b. Phelps, April 10, 1839; unmarried; died Newark, N. Y., July 22, 1859.

999

Mercy[7] Porter, of William[6] Porter, b. Middleboro', Feb. 5, 1799; married Phillip Bostwick, Nov. 29, 1834; he son of Robert S. and Margaret (Rowse) Bostwick, born Pittston, N. Y., Sept. 27, 1799; she died at Albion, Mich., April 5, 1876; he died there July 25, 1877. Children:

i. Margaret L.,[8] b. Pittston, N. Y.; m. John A. Whitbeck, of Newark, N. Y.; resides in Albion, Mich.

ii. Harriet,[8] b. Pittston; unmarried; resides Grand Rapids, Mich.

iii. Rebecca,[8] b. Arcadia, N. Y.; m. John Wessel, of Jackson, Mich.; merchant.

iv. Robert,[8] b. Arcadia; unmarried; of Jackson, Mich.

vi. Jennie,[8] of Albion, Mich.

vii. Jannette,[8] of Albion, Mich.

1000

William[7] Porter, of William[6] Porter, b. Middleboro,' Feb. 20, 1801; married Kline, of Springfield, Ill., where he and his wife both died; they had three children—one son who died at the age of twenty, and two daughters.

1001

Edwin[7] Porter, of William[6] Porter, b. Middleboro', April 26, 1803; resided in Lowell, Mass.; married Paulina Gage, of Pawtucket, R. I., Oct. 19, 1829; she born Sept. 10, 1805; daughter of Anthony and Sarah Bassett Gage, both born in

Harwich, Mass. Edwin Porter died Lowell, Mass., May 1, 1855. Children:

1755. i. Rebecca,[8] b. Mar. 4, 1831.
1756. ii. Abigail,[8] b. Jan. 30, 1833; died Jan. 30, 1833.
1757. iii. Roger Williams,[8] b. Mar. 15, 1834.
1758. iv. Sarah Gage,[8] b. Jan. 2, 1836.
1759. v. Andrew Wood,[8] b. Sept. 30, 1840; died Oct. 9, 1847.
1760. vi. Hannah Elisabeth,[8] b. May 16, 1844.

1002

Rev. James[7] Porter, D. D., of William[6] Porter, b. Middleboro', Mar. 21, 1808; educated at common school and Middleboro' Academy; in 1825 entered a cotton factory, and, spent one year in carding room; then went to Easton and spent some time in the weaving department; experienced religion, and felt called to preach, but thought it impossible; with another man, took a mill for one year, and prospered. At twenty-one years of age, (1829) left Easton and went to Kent's Hill Seminary, Readfield, Me., where he was soon set to preaching, to his great annoyance, as he had hoped to return to his manufacturing business, which he liked very much. He returned to Easton, and was soon at Pawtucket, and Newport, R. I., preaching. The next spring joined the New England Conference on trial. For twenty-six years he took his regular appointment from the Bishops of the Methodist Episcopal church—six years of which he was a presiding elder. Filled four stations in Boston of two years each, and residing there two of the six years of his eldership. He was trustee of Concord Biblical Institute, and of Wesleyan University at Middletown, Conn., which conferred the degree of A. M. on him—as did McKendree Coll. the degree of D. D. Was elected by the legislature of Mass., an overseer of Harvard College several years; was a member of General Conference in 1844; and six following sessions by election of his own conference. In 1856, was elected assistant book agent at New York, and removed to that city—serving twelve years there, until June 1, 1868; has since been preaching in several places. Is also a successful author of religious books. "The Compendium of Methodism"; "The Free Evangelist;"

"The Operative's Friend;" "Chart of Life;" "Winning Worker;" "History of Methodism;" all of which have had a large circulation. He has also written well and much for the religious press; is an able, pious and devoted preacher of the gospel. Is now (1878) living at 133 McDonough street, Brooklyn, N. Y. Married Jane, daughter of Nathaniel and Anna (Tinkham) Howard, of Easton, Mass., June 19, 1833; they had eight children—four of whom died in infancy:

1761. i. James F.,[8] married; resides in N. Y. city.
1762. ii. ——— ———married Wm. H. Chase, of Boston.
1763. iii. George,[8] unmarried; resides in Brooklyn.
1764. iv. Emma,[8] unmarried; resides in Brooklyn.

1003

Rebecca W.[7] Porter, of William[6] Porter, b. Mar. 2, 1810; married Oliver Bostwick; he died about 1870, and his widow Aug. 1, 1877. Children:

1765. i. Victor,[8] b. Pittstown, N. Y.; m. Flora Wilder, of Lee, Mass.; had seven children; was a lawyer; died at Jackson, Mich.
1766. ii. Edward Porter,[8] b. Pittstown, N. Y.; married; resides Jackson, Mich.
1767. iii. William,[8] b. Arcadia, N. Y.; married; resides Detroit, Mich.

1006

John M.[7] Porter, of James[6] Porter, born Pittsfield, Rutland Co., Vermont, Mar. 9, 1797; lives in Naples, Ontario Co., N. Y.; married Daphne Allen Osgood; she born Feb. 14, 1807; died Oct. 18, 1855. Children:

1768. i. Rowena E.,[8] b. April 17, 1828.
1769. ii. James Osgood,[8] b. Nov. 8, 1832.

1007

Zilpah M.[7] Porter, of James[6] Porter, b. Pittsford, N. Y., June 18, 1799; married Gen. Thomas Putnam, Feb. 7, 1828; he of Covington, Tioga Co., Penn., where he came about 1812; he was born in Langdon, N. H., June 19, 1790; he was a surveyor and farmer; he died July 12, 1870; his widow died Aug. 24, 1876. Children, all born in Covington, Penn.:

1770. i. Elijah, born Nov. 15, 1828; died Dec. 22, 1828.

1771. ii. Thomas Burnside,[8] b. Jan. 8, 1830; resides on the old homestead at Covington; m. Elsinore E. Connelly, Dec. 8, 1852. Children: Samuel O.,[9] b. Feb. 19, 1855; resides Porterville, Tulare Co., Cal. Lilly Ophelia,[9] b. Jan. 17, 1857; died Feb. 22, 1864. Thomas Hammon,[9] b. July 21, 1860. John Putnam,[9] born June 15, 1866; died June 16, 1866. Ray,[9] b. Feb. 24, 1868; died Sept. 23, 1868. Martha Helena,[9] b. April 8, 1871.

1772. iii. Samuel Morris,[8] b. Feb. 1, 1834; a government surveyor, of Minnesota; a young man of much promise; died unmarried, at Little Falls, Minn., Oct. 1st, 1857.

1773. iv. Perley Porter,[8] b. Sept. 30, 1835; m. Ellen M. Marvin, May 5, 1859; resides Texana, Jackson Co., Texas, where he went in 1867; has nine children, the first four born at Covington, last five in Texas: Fluella I.,[9] b. Jan. 9, 1860. Perly Porter,[9] b. Nov. 24, 1861. James Ajax,[9] b. Jan. 29, 1864. Hallie Avis,[9] b. Feb. 12, 1866. Samuel Morris,[9] b July 29, 1868. Minnie Io,[9] b. Aug. 11, 1870. Reward Ellen,[9] b. Nov. 10, 1872. Royal Augustus,[9] b. Feb. 10, 1875. Tilly Thomas,[9] b. July 6, 1877. Mr. Porter is a surveyor and farmer.

1774. v. Royal Porter,[8] b. Aug. 5, 1837; went to California in 1858, where he has since resided; he was the first settler on Tule River—and the town bears his name—Porterville, Tulare Co., California; is a merchant, and has been county judge; married Mary J. Packard, of Bainbridge, N. Y., April 4, 1864. Children: Willie Porter,[9] b. June 16, 1865. Samuel Eugene,[9] b. Feb. 9, 1869; died Oct., 1869. Frank Oliver,[9] b. April 10, 1871.

1775. vi. Arthemise Ophelia,[8] b. April 28, 1846; married Aram Brown Lain, Dec. 31, 1872; he was born at Southport, Chemung Co., N. Y., June 9, 1848. Children: Grace Arthemise,[9] b. Oct. 9, 1873; and died Aug. 26, 1875. Zilpha Porter,[9] b. June 28, 1876; resides Canisteo, N. Y.

1009

Sophronia L.[7] Porter, of James[6] Porter, b. Keene, Essex Co., N. Y., Feb. 16, 1809; married Isaac Adams; resides in Tecumseh, Mich.; he born in Tioga, Tioga Co., Penn., Dec. 16, 1802; wife died in Tecumseh, April 2, 1845. Children:

1776. i. Oscar Porter,[8] b. July 30, 1828.

1777. ii. Helen,[8] b. Aug. 31, 1829.

1778. iii. Peter Jerome,[8] b. Oct. 30, 1830; died Dec. 29, 1862.

1779. iv. Rufus,[8] b. Dec. 5, 1832.
1780. v. Mary Amelia,[8] b. Oct. 24, 1834.
1781. vi. Cordelia M.,[8] b. May 23, 1836.
1782. vii. Lydia Ann,[8] b. Jan. 7, 1838; died Aug. 16, 1838.
1783. viii. Rowena Sarah,[8] b. July 2, 1839; died Mar. 12, 1852.
1784. ix. Isaac,[8] b. May 29, 1844; died Aug. 25, 1846.

1010

Sarah R.[7] Porter, of James[6] Porter, b. Keene, Essex Co., N. Y., Mar. 7, 1811; married Asa Stevens, Jr., of Keene, N. H., 1832; she died April 28, 1840. Children:

1786. i. Martha Rowena,[8] married A. T. Guernsey; resides in Lake City, Minn.
1787. ii. Helen A.,[8] b. in Tioga, Penn., Jan. 14, 1836; married 1st, Walter Bartlett Manton, of Providence, R. I., June 4, 1856. He was Lieut. and acting quartermaster of 3d Rhode Island heavy artillery in late war; also 1st lieut. in a company of sharp shooters, attached to the 1st Reg't Rhode Island infantry; he died at Hilton Head, S. C., Oct. 25, 1862. Married 2d, Benjamin M. Jackson, of Providence, R. I., banker, Oct. 13, 1864; he died after a painful illness of nearly three years, Feb. 17, 1869. Married 3d, Newell Clark, of Boston, Aug. 7, 1871, after which they spent one year abroad in foreign travel; they now reside in Boston—Mr. Clark having retired from active business. Mrs. Clark's only surviving child is Walter Porter[9] Manton, now nineteen years of age, and at present a member of the second class in Harvard Medical School. (1877.)
1788. iii. Infant,[8] died young.
1789. iv. Judson A.[8]; married; resides in Maynard, Iowa; proprietor of a large stock farm; has two sons, and one daughter.

EIGHTH GENERATION.

1016

Elizabeth N.[8] Porter, of Joseph[7] Porter, b. Freeport, Me., Sept. 2, 1817; married 1st, Mark L. Means, of Freeport, Sept. 24, 1840; he died May 10, 1843. Married 2d, Samuel Lunt, of Freeport, Nov. 3, 1852; they reside on the old

Porter homestead, at Porter's Landing, Freeport. Children, by first husband:

1793. i. William M.,[9] b. 1841; married Jenny Shurtleff, of Adrian, Mich.; resides Chicago, Ill.

1794. ii. Daniel M.,[9] b. 1843; m. Celia Adams, of Portland, Me.; resides Merrimac, Mass.

1020

Joseph N.[8] Porter, of Joseph[7] Porter, b. Portland, Oct. 31, 1833; resides Freeport, Me.; married Susanna A. Cooper, of Whitefield, Maine, 1861. Children:

1795. i. Joseph W.,[9] b. 1862.

1796. ii. Samuel L.,[9] b. 1869.

1797. iii. Chas. H., b. Jan. 18, 1877.

1021

Delia Ann[8] Porter, of Samuel[7] Porter, b. Dec. 18, 1803; married Joseph L. Dennison, Dec. 15, 1823; daughter, Eliza Freeman,[9] unmarried; one daughter, Delia Ann,[9] married Ansyl Rogers, of Freeport, Me.

1024

Mary[8] Porter, of Samuel[7] Porter, born April 13, 1811; m. Joseph Warren Tucker, Nov. 12, 1856; he son of Elijah and Rebecca (Weatherby) Tucker. No children; they now reside in that part of Boston formerly Roxbury.

1040

George F.[8] Porter, of Seward[7] Porter, b. Portland, Aug. 27, 1819; left home when quite young, following the sea until 1844, when he settled in New Orleans, La., where he now resides, (at No. 182 Felicity street;) he married in New Orleans, Mary Elizabeth Simonds, June 4, 1843; she born Boston, Sept. 10, 1823. Children, all born in New Orleans:

1809. i. Ellen,[9] b. Dec. 9, 1844; died Aug. 22, 1846.

1810. ii. Frank Gordon,[9] b. May 21, 1847; died Dec. 13, 1852.

1811. iii. Eunice Virginia,[9] b. Feb. 7, 1849; died Aug. 4, 1852.

1812. iv. Henry Clay,[9] b. Mar. 4, 1852.

1813. v. Georgie,[9] b. Dec. 25, 1854.

1814. vi. Horace Gray,[9] b. Oct. 26, 1856; died at Brooklyn, N. Y., Dec. 14, 1863.

1815. vii. Geo. Floyd,[9] b. April 30, 1858; died Brooklyn, N. Y., Dec. 23, 1863.

1816. viii. Charles Farley,[9] b. Jan. 25, 1861.

1817. ix. Cornelia W.,[9] b. Mar. 14, 1863; died Sept. 29, 1867.

1818. x. Elizabeth Otis,[9] b. Sept. 3, 1864.

1819. xi. Seward,[9] b. Feb. 24, 1867; drowned in Bay St. Louis, Miss., July 7, 1869.

1045

Mary B.[8] Porter, of Charles[7] Porter, b. April 2, 1818; m. Geo. W. Sumner, New York city, Oct. 10, 1833; he born in Boston, Sept. 20, 1798; died New York, Feb. 19, 1853.

1820. i. Charles Porter,[9] b. New York, Sept. 6, 1834; m. Abigail A. Prince, in Bainbridge, N. Y., Dec. 4, 1871; lives Sparkill, N. Y. Children: Anna Prince,[10] b. Nov. 10, 1873. Charles Porter,[10] b. July 29, 1875; died July 22, 1876. Mary Brown,[10] b. Aug. 6, 1876.

1821. ii. Mary Porter,[9] b. Oct. 5, 1837; d. Mar. 16, 1864.

1822. iii. Martha Ruth,[9] b. April 2, 1840; died June 15, 1841.

1046

Noah B.[8] Porter, of Charles[7] Porter, b. Nov. 21, 1819; lived in N. Y. city; died April 23, 1855; m. Augusta M. Stowe, Oct. 2, 1848; she died Mar. 18, 1850. No children.

1054

Rebecca C.[8] Porter, of Charles[7] Porter, b. Mar. 13, 1836; married Seth E. Geer, July 20, 1859; resides in New York city, where he was born. Children:

1823. i. Harold Sumner,[9] b. New York, April 16, 1860.

1824. ii. Wilson Duryea,[9] b. New York, Aug. 14, 1861.

1825. iii. George Porter,[9] b. in Carmansville, N. Y., May 26, 1863; died Feb. 14, 1869.

1055

Barbour B.[8] Porter, of Sylvanus[7] Porter, b. North Yarmouth, Me., Aug. 4, 1810; resides there; was Major General of Fifth Division Maine Militia, 1853; deputy sheriff; and has held other offices. Married 1st, Mary H. Persons, of N. Yarmouth, Dec. 8, 1831; she died May 13, 1861. Married 2d, Emeline

P. Herrick, of N. Yarmouth, Jan. 21, 1864. Children, all born in North Yarmouth:

1830. i. Helen W.,[9] b. Sept. 7, 1832.
1831. ii. Sylvanus,[9] b. Aug. 23, 1833; m. Sarah P. Jordan, of Saco, Nov. 27, 1857; resides Cumberland, Me. Children: Ella.[10] Bell.[10] Mary.[10] George.[10] Samuel.[10] Chas. B.[10] William O.[10] Frederick S.[10]
1832. iii. David T.,[9] b. Sept. 2, 1834; died Sept. 6, 1834.
1833. iv. George H.,[9] b. July 16, 1836; d. Nov. 16, 1862.
1834. v. Abby C.,[9] b. Mar. 28, 1838.
1835. vi. Caleb H.,[9] b. Dec. 25, 1839; died Sept. 3, 1864.
1836. vii. Charles C.,[9] b. Dec. 5. 1842; died Dec. 7, 1862.
1837. viii. Francis L.,[9] b. Aug. 1, 1844; m. Rose Perley, of Gray, Me., Nov. 29, 1866; resides N. Yarmouth. Children: George M.[10] Della May.[10] Sumner P.[10]
1838. ix. William B.,[9] b. Mar. 6, 1846; died Mar. 30, 1846.

1061

Matilda[8] Porter, of Capt Stephen[7] Porter, b. N. Yarmouth, Me., July 25, 1818; married Anson Jordan, of Raymond, Me. Children:

Abby F.,[9] m. Joseph E. Brown, of Camden, Me. Jedediah Porter,[9] said to be clerk in Boston, and to reside at Mount Wollaston, Quincy.

1063

Hon. William R.[8] Porter, of Capt. Stephen[7] Porter, b. N. Yarmouth, May 20, 1825. Grad. Bowdoin College, 1843. Preceptor of Fryeburg Academy, and engaged in teaching some years. In Maine Senate, from Cumberland county, 1851; member of Board of Education for same county three years. Four years in Portland Custom House, while Ezra Carter was collector; now banker. Married Elizabeth, dau. of James Deering of South Paris, Me., May 21, 1846; she b. Mar. 22, 1824. Children:

1841. i. William D.,[9] born N. Yarmouth, Mar. 9, 1847; resides Chicago, Ill.
1842. ii. Eliza D.,[9] b. Portland, April 6, 1855.
1843. iii. Frances R.,[9] b. Portland, April 24, 1857.
1844. iv. Abby B.,[9] b. Yarmouth, Me., Aug. 17, 1859.
1845. v. James D.,[9] b. Westbrook, Me., Feb. 3, 1865; died Aug. 22, 1866.

1067

Sylvanus[8] Porter, of John[7] Porter, b. Paris, Maine, Mar. 31, 1817; married Esther C. Millett, of Norway, Nov. 10, 1842; resides Paris, Me. Children:

1846. i. John,[9] b. April 27, 1843; died Feb. 27, 1864.
1847. ii. Eliza,[9] b. Nov. 28, 1844.
1848. iii. Fatima M.,[9] b. Jan. 27, 1853.
1849. iv. Ezekiel L.,[9] b. Nov. 13, 1857.

1069

John B.[8] Porter, of John[7] Porter, b. Paris, Me., Aug. 12, 1821, where he now resides: married Maria Horn, of Milan, N. H., Nov. 9, 1853. Children:

i. Harriett,[9] b. Oct. 1, 1854.
ii. Annie,[9] b. July 5, 1858.
iii. Eunice,[9] b. Aug. 31, 1864.
iv. Almon Farwell,[9] b. Dec. 13, 1869.

1070 B

Franklin[8] Porter, of John[7] Porter, born Paris, Me., Oct. 18, 1829; resides in Paris; married Martha M. Millett, of Norway, Me., Sept. 15, 1858. Children:

i. Francis E.,[9] b. Oct. 5, 1861.
ii. James N.,[9] b. May 5, 1865.
iii. Joseph H.,[9] b. Jan. 23, 1869.

1073

William H.[8] Porter, of Charles[7] Porter, b. Paris, Me., May 8, 1822; resides in Paris; married 1st, Emeline Pratt, Nov. 20, 1845; married 2d time. Children:

i. Charles H.,[9] b. 1847.
ii. Survetus P.,[9] b. 1848; died 1875.
iii. George G.,[9] b. 1851.
iv. William N.,[9] b. 1873, by 2d marriage.

1074

Rachel L.[8] Porter, of Charles[7] Porter, b. Paris, Me., Feb. 11, 1824; married Thomas Witt, of Norway, Me., Dec. 9, 1845. Children:

i. Mary Ellen,[9] b. Sept. 23, 1846.
ii. Charles Thomas,[9] b. July 18, 1848.

iii. Elizabeth Porter,[9] b. April 26, 1850.
iv. Sarah Hamilton,[9] b. Dec. 10, 1852.
v. George Herbert,[9] b. May 26, 1856.
vi. Abby Louisa,[9] b. Aug. 11, 1858.
vii. Willie B.,[9] b. June 7, 1862; died Feb. 19, 1863.
viii. Edward Ellsworth,[9] b. Oct. 1, 1864.

1076

Charles N.[8] Porter, of Charles[7] Porter, b. Paris, Me., April 7, 1828; resides in Paris; married Maria L. Millett, Mar. 24, 1852. Children:

1861. i. Millett N.,[9] b. Oct. 7, 1853.
1862. ii. Frank L.,[9] b. June 29, 1855.
1863. iii. Granville H.,[9] b. June 3, 1857.
1864. iv. Willie A.,[9] b. April 7, 1863.
1865. v. Nellie M.,[9] b. Aug. 26, 1866.
1866. vi. Hiram N.,[9] b. Oct. 31, 1870.
1867. vii. Hattie L.,[9] b. Nov. 1, 1872.

1108

William[8] Porter, of Joseph[7] Porter, b. Freeport, Me., Mar. 25, 1824; resides Freeport; married Caroline Merrill, 1845. Children:

1868. i. Ella A.,[9] b. Sept. 14, 1846; died April 7, 1847.
1869. ii. Ella H.,[9] b. Feb. 26, 1849.
1870. iii. Frederick B.,[9] b. Nov. 12, 1857.

1111

Eliza[8] Porter of Joseph[7] Porter, born Freeport, Jan. 13, 1830; married William J. Smith, of Yarmouth, Me. Children:

Clara M.[9] Jerome P.[9] William E.[9]

1112

Joseph[8] Porter, of Joseph[7] Porter, b. Freeport, Me., May 3, 1834; married Laurette Merrill, 1856. Children:

Willis C.[9] Irving S.[9]

1113

George A.[8] Porter, of Joseph[7] Porter, b. June 8, 1836; married Nellie P. Prescott, 1858. Children:

Lucy E.[9] Joseph W.[9] Addie M.[9] George M.[9] Ernest L.[9]

1114

Mellissa P.[8] Porter, of Joseph[7] Porter, born May 23, 1838; married Hon. Charles B. Jordan, May 10, 1857; he born in Lewiston, Me., June 16, 1829; son of James and Deborah (Garcelon) Jordan; now resides in Lisbon, Me.; merchant. Member of Maine Legislature 1873, '76, '77; supervisor of schools, town clerk, etc. Children:

Iva Etta,[9] b. Oct. 29, 1859; died May 8, 1861. Elmar Porter,[9] b. June 19, 1861. Lizzie Beal,[9] b. Oct. 24, 1863. Charles Alton,[9] b. May 7, 1866.

1115

Charles[8] Porter, of Joseph[7] Porter, b. Aug. 25, 1840; married Charity A. Davis, 1840. Children:

Iva Etta,[9] died young. Bertha.[9] Lester N.[9]

1116

Benjamin[8] Porter, of Joseph[7] Porter, b. Freeport, Me., married Angie D. Knight, 1866. Children:

Lizzie H.[9] Benjamin C.,[9] died in infancy. Arthur.[9]

1117

John A. Porter, born Freeport, Me.; married Josephine Allen, 1866. Children:

Howard. Elmer. Burnham.

1200

Robert[8] Porter, of Robert[7] Porter, born Stoughton, Dec. 6, 1823; resides there; farmer, and dealer in coal. Married Mary Holmes Drake, Nov. 16, 1848; she born March 22, 1830. Children:

1800. i. Mary Emma,[9] b. 1849; died Sept 22, 1850.
1801. ii. Mary Emma,[9] b. Dec. 26, 1850.
1802. iii. Theresa Jane,[9] b. Mar. 17, 1853.
1803. iv. Robert Drake,[9] b. July 29, 1856.
1804. v. Ellis Boyden,[9] b. April 28, 1861.
1805. vi. A. St. John Chambre,[9] b. Sept. 27, 1868.

1201

Uriah C.[8] Porter, of Robert[7] Porter, b. Stoughton, Oct. 2, 1826, and resides there; farmer; married Ann E. Gill, Feb. 8, 1850. Children:

1806. i. Clarence Capen,[9] b. Feb. 26, 1851.
1807. ii. Charles Sumner,[9] b. Mar. 3, 1857.
1808. iii. Horace Mann,[9] b. July 6, 1875; died Nov. 9, 1875.

1202

Theron M.[8] Porter, of Robert[7] Porter, b. Dec. 19, 1828. He was a farmer until the age of twenty-five, then went into the employ of the Stoughton Branch Railroad Co. At the opening of Easton Branch Railroad, in 1855, he removed to North Easton, and was station agent there, and in the employ of Oliver Ames & Sons, until 1865, when he established the firm of Porter & Co., wholesale flour dealers, at 613 and 615 Atlantic Avenue, Boston, of which firm he was senior partner at the time of his death, at his residence at North Easton, Feb. 1, 1878, aged 49 years 1 month and 12 days. He was a valued citizen, a kind husband and father, and much respected by all who knew him. He married Betsey M. Bisbee, dau. of John Bisbee, of Easton, Mass., Dec. 27, 1856. (John Bisbee was in the employ of Oliver Ames & Sons, at North Easton, over sixty-two years; he died Dec. 21, 1871, aged 86 years; his widow was living in 1876, at the age of 78 years. She and her husband having lived together fifty years, having had four daughters, now living.) The children of Theron M. and Betsey M. Porter, were:

1809. i. Theron M.,[9] b. June 21, 1858; died Sept. 16, 1858.
1810. ii. Frank B.,[9] b. Aug. 12, 1859; died Sept. 23, 1860.
1811. iii. Helen Maria,[9] b. Aug. 30, 1860.
1812. iv. George,[9] b. Aug. 23, 1862; died Aug. 3, 1863.
1813. v. Fannie Baker,[9] b. Jan. 13, 1865.
1814. vi. Jessie,[9] b. April 6, 1866.
1815. vii. Harry L.,[9] b. May 10, 1867.
1816. viii. Freddie,[9] b. Aug. 14, 1868.
1817. ix. Walter,[9] b. Mar. 28, 1870.
1818. x. Horace Mann,[9] b. Feb. 8, 1874; died Sept. 2, 1874.

1206

John M.[8] Porter, of Robert[7] Porter, b. Feb. 1, 1837; resides No. 290 West Fifth street, South Boston; married Abby N. Leman, of Boston, 1863; she born there, 1837. Children:

1820. i. Avis,[9] b. South Boston, 1865; died 1866.
1821. ii. Eunice F.,[9] b. New Ipswich, N. H., 1867; died 1875.
1822. iii. Abby Leman,[9] b. South Boston, 1869.

1207

Jonathan F.[8] Porter, of Robert[7] Porter, b. Stoughton, Mar. 23, 1840, resides there; farmer. Married Hattie L. Burnham, of Stoughton, April 10, 1864. No children, 1875.

1208

Marcus M.[8] Porter, of Robert[7] Porter, born May 12, 1841; resides East Stoughton; farmer; married Hattie E. Jones, of N. Stoughton, Nov. 28, 1867, she born April 19, 1849. Children:

1823. i. Francis Elam,[9] } twins, b. Mar. 10, 1869.
1824. ii. Francena Ella,[9] }
1825. iii. Emmons Chace,[9] b. Mar. 19, 1871.

1213

Elizabeth[8] Porter, of John[7] Porter, born Stoughton, April 12, 1830; married Daniel F. Baxter of North Bridgewater, Feb. 12, 1860; she died April 6, 1872. Children:

Inez Viola,[9] b. Dec. 3, 1860. John Freeman,[9] b. June 30, 1863. Hiram.[9]

1214

Jonathan K.[8] Porter, of John[7] Porter b. Sept. 10, 1832; resides Stoughton; mechanic; married Sarah E. Gay, Sept. 27, 1856. Children:

Edward W.,[9] b. Feb. 19, 1867. Jonathan K.,[9] b. April, 1869. Bessie C.,[9] b. Feb., 1871.

1215

Benjamin W.[8] Porter, of John[7] Porter, b. Stoughton, July 9, 1835, resides East Stoughton. Married 1st, Frances A. Kelly, of Quincy, Dec. 25, 1865; she died Feb., 1868. Married

2d, Abbie R. Richardson, of Stoughton, Nov. 21, 1869. Children:

Henry E.,[9] b. Feb. 11, 1868. Benjamin W.,[9] b. May 17, 1871. Frederick W.,[9] b. Aug. 5, 1874.

1217

Martha H.[8] Porter, of Joseph[7] Porter, born Stoughton, Nov. 3, 1829; married 1st, Luther French of Stoughton, Jan. 17, 1847. Married 2d, Jeremiah Russell, of East Stoughton. Children, by 1st husband:

Mary Randall,[9] b. Nov. 14, 1849; m. Mark H. Sellers, Feb. 5, 1873; he died Aug. 24, 1875. Martin Luther,[9] b. Mar. 9, 1852. Samuel Chesley,[9] b. Mar. 8, 1855.

1219

Joseph D.[8] Porter, of Joseph[7] Porter, b. Mar. 19, 1835; resides East Stoughton; carpenter; married Sarah Hunt, of West Randolph—she died Jan. 16, 1870. Children:

1840. i. Justina A.,[9] b. July 23, 1857.
1841. ii. Annie S.,[9] b. Mar. 25, 1859.
1842. iii. Davis A.,[9] b. Feb. 5, 1861.
1843. iv. Sarah E.,[9] b. Dec. 30, 1869; died Sept., 1870.

1220

Sarah C.[8] Porter, of Joseph[7] Porter, b. Stoughton, April 10, 1839; married Ira Hunt, of South Weymouth, May 16, 1856. Children:

Susie F.,[9] b. June 24, 1867. Abby Louise,[9] b. Oct. 16, 1869. Joseph Porter,[9] b. Dec. 27, 1874.

1221

Isaac L.[8] Porter, of Joseph[7] Porter, b. Stoughton, Feb. 23, 1842; mechanic, state constable, etc.; married Clara F. Roulstone, of N. Y., Jan. 21, 1866.

1231

Isaac[8] Porter, of Rhodolphus[7] Porter, b. April 19, 1821; resides South Braintree; married 1st, Mary F. Willis,

June 18, 1843; she died April 5, 1853. Married 2d, Adeline Hunt, June 7, 1864; she born April 11. Children:

1856. i. John F.,[9] b. Oct. 11, 1845.
1857. ii. Heman,[9] b. Mar. 30, 1847.
1858. iii. Isaac L.,[9] b. Oct. 9, 1848.
1859. iv. Sylvanus F.,[9] b. Sept. 16, 1850.
1860. v. Mary F.,[9] b. Jan. 28, 1853.
1861. vi. Addie L.,[9] b. Aug. 25, 1867.
1862. vii. Susie E.,[9] b. April 20, 1870.
1863. viii. Sarah L.,[9] b. April 29, 1873.

1233

Joseph F.[8] Porter, of Rhodolphus[7] Porter, born April 28, 1824; resides in South Braintree; butcher; married Mary Arnold, of South Braintree, May 8, 1845; she born Jan. 9, 1823. He died Feb. 8, 1870. Children, one son and three daughters.

1234

Lewis[8] Porter, of Rhodolphus[7] Porter, born Jan. 25, 1826; resides Brockton; boot manufacturer; married Harriet Rainsford Soule, Nov. 26, 1857; she daughter of Oakes S. Soule, of Brockton. Children:

1867. i. Rachel Alma,[9] b. Aug. 26, 1858; m. Frank F. Porter, Sept. 5, 1877.
1868. ii. Harriet Emily,[9] b. Sept. 1, 1861.
1869. iii. Jennie,[9] b. June 12, 1868.
1870. iv. Ella Oakes,[9] b. June 18, 1872.

1236

Lucinda[8] Porter, of Rhodolphus[7] Porter, b. Sept. 11, 1829; married Edward Bailey Packard, May 29, 1845; he son of Ambrose and Esther (White) Packard, born Jan. 8, 1819; resides Brockton; farmer. Children:

1871. i. Edward Ellis,[9] b. Oct. 3, 1848; m. Edith Atherton, Mar. 6, 1877.
1872. ii. Nellie,[9] b. April 16, 1858.

1237

Azubah[8] Porter, of Rhodolphus[7] Porter, b. Jan. 2, 1832; married Nathan Marshall, of Roslindale, Mass., (Ward 23, Boston,) he born in Oxford, Maine, Aug. 1, 1830. Children:

Ada Azubah,[9] b. April 26, 1855; died Aug. 22, 1857. Edgar Nathan,[9] b. Nov. 8, 1857; died Sept. 14, 1858.

1876. iii. Edna Porter,[9] b. Oct. 5, 1860.
1877. iv. Freeland Henry,[9] b. Jan. 9, 1864.
1878. v. Walter Nathan,[9] b. Sept. 6, 1868.
1879. vi. Ada Lucinda,[9] b. Dec. 1, 1872; died April 17, 1873.

1238

Rhodolphus[8] Porter, of Rhodolphus[7] Porter, b. E. Randolph, Jan. 22, 1834; resides South Braintree; merchant in Boston; extensive manufacturer of boots. Married Emily A., daughter of Joel E. Holbrook, Esq., Oct. 1, 1857; she b. Feb. 3, 1840; died Oct. 13, 1860. Married 2d, Mary A. Holbrook, sister of first wife; she born July 13, 1846; died Jan. 16, 1874. One child:

1880. i. Edwin Frances,[9] b. Sept. 29, 1860.

1239

Charles F.[8] Porter, of Rhodolphus[7] Porter, b. Jan. 16, 1836; resides Brockton; boot manufacturer. Married Myra F. Niles, of Braintree, Nov. 30, 1854, by Rev. Richard S. Storrs, D. D. Children:

1881. i. Myra Effie,[9] b. Aug. 5, 1856.
1882. ii. Alice Gertrude,[9] b. Oct. 28, 1864.
1883. iii. Annie Niles,[9] b. Jan. 7, 1870.
1884. iv. Charles French,[9] b. Oct. 4, 1874.

1241

Elizabeth G.[8] Porter, of Rhodolphus[7] Porter, b. Sept. 17, 1840; married Bradford Wilde, of Brockton, Jan. 29, 1862; he born in East Randolph, Mass., now Holbrook. Children:

Hattie Esther,[9] b. Sept. 18, 1864. Mabel Porter,[9] b. Feb. 12, 1871. Lucinda Elizabeth,[9] b. Mar. 22, 1873.

1249

Martin R.[8] Porter, of Martin[7] Porter, born South Braintree, Jan. 21, 1824; married 1st, Mary A. Dyer, 1846; died 1849. Married, 2d, Elizabeth F. Bacon, daughter of Simeon J. and Esther D. Bacon, of South Boston, Dec. 29, 1852; he died April 4, 1859. Mrs. Porter married 2d, Mr. Chas. Messinger, of Brooklyn, N. Y. Children of M. R. Porter:

1888. i. Charles Martin,[9] b. July 24, 1854.
1889. ii. Mary E.,[9] b. June 21, 1856; m. Horam R. Steele, of St. Joseph, Louisiana, Sept. 9, 1877.
1890. iii. William Messinger,[9] b. Mar. 2, 1858; died May 17, 1859.

1250

Rebecca J.[8] Porter, of Martin[7] Porter, b. South Braintree, Dec. 7, 1826; married Theodore D. Randall, South Braintree, 1846. Child:

1891. i. Walter,[9] b. Chicago, 1852; married Lillie C. Harris, 1874; resides Rochester, N. Y.

1251

Asa R.[8] Porter, of Martin[7] Porter, b. Feb. 6, 1829; resides No. 124, F street, South Boston. He is the long well known and popular conductor on the Old Colony and Fall River Railroad; married Sarah C. Daland, Nov. 28, 1850. Children:

1892. i. Geo. Reed,[9] b. South Braintree, Sept. 2, 1851; conductor on the Old Colony & Fall River Railroad; married Carlie J. Tyler, 1875.
1893. ii. Mary Eva,[9] b. South Braintree, July 23, 1853; died 1854.
1894. iii. Asa Herbert,[9] b. South Braintree, Mar. 4, 1855; resides New London, Conn.; m. Sadie H. Ewer, Nov. 16, 1875.
1895 iv. Susie Converse,[9] b. New Bedford, Nov. 13, 1863.

1252

Susan E.[8] Porter, of Martin[7] Porter, b. April 4, 1833; married 1st, Geo. S. Page, of Boston, April 22, 1752; he died in Matanzas, Cuba, Oct. 6, 1860. Married 2d, Leonard C. Baker, of Kingston, April 15, 1869; resides corner of M and Third street, South Boston. Children, by 1st husband:

Jennie D., b. 1853. Susan E.,[9] b. 1855. George M.,[9] b. Girard, Penn., 1857.

1253

Julia Ann[8] Porter, of Samuel[7] Porter, b. Easton, Mass., July 18, 1820; married Hon. Sands Niles Breed, of Canton, Ill.; he son of Jonas and Betsey (Niles) Breed, born Stonington, Conn., Aug. 20, 1810. Children:

1899. i. Child,[9] b. July 30, 1839; died in infancy.
1900. ii. John H.,[9] b. May 29, 1841; died Feb. 22, 1864.
1901. iii. Julia Maria,[9] b. Oct. 29, 1844; m. Samuel P. Cochrane, of Quincy, Ill., Nov. 12, 1871.
1902. iv. Samuel Porter,[9] b. May 12, 1848; died April 21, 1869.
1903. v. Mary Grace,[9] b. Oct. 30, 1851; m. Fred J. Loring, Feb. 16, 1873.
1904. vi. Hattie A.,[9] b. Nov. 19, 1854.
1905. vii. Lucy Emma,[9] b. Nov. 22, 1859.

1254

Samuel L.[8] Porter, of Samuel[7] Porter, b. Boston, July 17, 1824; resides in Canton, Ill.; painter and glazier; married April 1, 1852. Children:

1906. i. Sarah,[9] b. about 1853; m. Charles Cox.
1907. ii. Alice,[9] b. about 1855.
1908. iii. Emma,[9] b. about 1859.
1909. iv. Nettie,[9] b. about 1864.

1255

Benjamin[8] Porter, of Samuel[7] Porter, b. Boston, Jan. 31, 1827; resides Canton, Ill.; married Aug. 19, 1847. Children:

1910. i. Julia S.,[9] b. May 30, 1850; m. John G. Tuttle, Sept. 17, 1868.
1911. ii. Charles L.,[9] b. Jan. 16, 1853.
1912. iii. Blanche J.,[9] b. Aug. 21, 1855.
1913. iv. Benjamin Franklin,[9] b. Jan. 8, 1859.
1914. v. Anna M.,[9] b. April 15, 1862.

1257

Hattie[8] Porter, of Samuel[7] Porter, b. Canton, Ill., Dec. 10, 1837; married William E. Cooper, of Wichita, Kansas, July 4, 1859; served in late war; have six children.

1261

Franklin[8] Porter, of Ira[7] Porter, b. Braintree, Oct. 14, 1836; resides in Randolph; married Eliza R. Woodman, Nov. 25, 1862, daughter of Archibald Woodman; b. Quincy, Aug. 27, 1843. Children:

1921. i. Abbie W.,[9] b. July 16, 1864.
1922. ii. Frank W.,[9] b. Nov. 15, 1868; died Oct. 1, 1869.

1259

Ira W.[8] Porter, of Ira[7] Porter, b. Braintree, June 17, 1832; resides Mobile, Ala.; married Abbie S. Woodman, daughter of Archibald Woodman, Dec. 14, 1859; she born in Randolph, July 4, 1841. Children:

1923. i. Eulalia H.,[9] b. Dec. 23, 1863.
1924. ii. Archie W.,[9] b. Oct. 22, 1866.
1925. iii. Anna,[9] b. Nov. 24, 1868.
1926. iv. Ira W.,[9] b. Oct. 6, 1870.
1927. v. Edith Augusta,[9] b. Nov. 7, 1876.

1281

John W.[8] Porter, of Whitcomb[7] Porter, b. Weymouth, Aug. 2, 1827. Insurance agent, No. 27 State street, Boston; resides at Neponset, Ward 16, Boston. Was for several years a member of the Boston school committee—takes much interest in education. Married Ellen Howland, July 17, 1851, by Rev. Humphrey Richards; she was daughter of Jabez and Dorcas (Jenkins) Howland, of West Parish, Barnstable, born May 10, 1832. Children:

1923. i. Francis Howland,[9] b. June 4, 1854.
1924. ii. John Ilsley,[9] b. Aug. 16, 1856.
1925. iii. William Wallace,[9] b. Mar. 24, 1859.
1926. iv. Ellen Wild,[9] b. July 23, 1861.
1927. v. Henry Herbert,[9] b. Mar. 23, 1865; died Jan. 13, 1866.
1928. vi. Frederick Whitcomb,[9] b. July 14, 1867.
1929. vii. Arthur Butler,[9] b. Nov. 16, 1873.

1282

George E.[8] Porter, of Whitcomb[7] Porter, b. in Weymouth, Nov. 4, 1828; resides in Weymouth; boot manufacturer;

enterprising and successful; married Amanda Cushing, Nov. 13, 1850, by Rev. W. G. Cambridge; she born July 30, 1831. Children:

1930. i. Edgar Cushing,[9] b. Quincy, July 17, 1851; married Emma Jane Sterling, Nov. 28, 1872.
1931. ii. George Whitcomb,[9] b. Weymouth, June 8, 1854; died Dec., 1854.
1932. iii. Edith C.,[9] b. Weymouth, July 4, 1863.
1933. iv. Alice Belle,[9] b. Weymouth, Jan. 24, 1859.
1934. v. Charles Ilsley,[9] b. Weymouth, Nov. 27, 1866.
1935. vi. Susan Hunt,[9] b. Weymouth, Mar. 24, 1868.

1283

Henry T.[8] Porter, of Whitcomb[7] Porter, b. Weymouth, July 13, 1832; resides in Chicago; wholesale lumber merchant; married Mrs. Mary E. Mansfield, of Chicago, Ill., Dec. 15, 1868, by Rev. Robert Collyer.

1284

Susan B.[8] Porter, of Whitcomb[7] Porter, b. Weymouth, July 17, 1836; married John Parker Ilsley, Dec. 21, 1854, by Rev. Wm. P. Lunt; he son of Edward and Ellen (Deering) Ilsley, of Portland, Me., b. Dec. 22, 1826; resides in Germantown, Pa.; is president of St. Paul and Duluth Railroad Company, in Minnesota. Children:

1936. i. Alice Deering,[9] b. Chicago, Jan. 18, 1856.
1937. ii. Susan Porter,[9] b. Milwaukee, Wis., Mar. 24, 1859.
1938. iii. Edward,[9] b. Wilkesbarre, Penn., Feb. 8, 1864.
1939. iv. John Parker,[9] b. Oct. 1, 1876.

1286

Col. Charles H.[8] Porter, of Whitcomb[7] Porter, b. Quincy, April 3, 1843; insurance agent, No. 27 State street, Boston; resides in Quincy. Trustee of Adams Academy there. Member of the 39th Mass. Reg't, in the last war, and has held other positions of usefulness and trust. Married Hannah Almeda French, June 23, 1870, by Rev. John D. Wells. Children:

1940. i. Charles Hunt,[9] b. Oct. 4, 1871.
1941. ii. Henry Whitcomb,[9] b. July 3, 1875.
1942. iii. Robert Brastow,[9] b. Oct. 17, 1876.

1288

Joseph W.[8] Porter, of Joseph[7] Porter, b. Milton, Mass., July 27, 1824; resides Burlington, Me.; farmer and lumberman; after first marriage, resided in Braintree, Mass., where he held several town offices; removed to Weymouth, 1858, and to Braintree again in 1861; thence July, 1862, removed with his family to Burlington, Maine; was appointed aide-de-camp to Governor Coburn, in 1863; messenger of the electoral vote of Maine to Washington, 1864; member of Maine House of Representatives, 1864,-'65,-'68,-'72 and '76; of Maine Senate, 1866 and 1867; Executive Councillor, 1869, 1870; President of Maine State Republican Convention, 1872; Presidential Elector, 1876. Married first, Rhoda Keith, daughter of Rev. Jonas and Rhoda (Keith) Perkins, of (East) Braintree, Mass., Jan. 5, 1851, by her father; she was born Nov. 23, 1826; died in Burlington, Me., Nov. 30, 1875; she was a graduate of Mount Holyoke Female Seminary. 1845, where for the most part of her time she was private secretary to Miss Mary Lyon; taught school in Putnam, Ohio, and in Braintree, Mass. Married second, Mrs. Rose (Brooks) Nickerson, of Orrington, Me., May 4, 1877, at Bangor, Me., by Rev. Prof. Wm. M. Barbour, D. D. She widow of Capt. Henry Nickerson, and daughter of James and Elizabeth Taylor (Bartlett) Brooks, of Orrington, Me.; born April 22, 1840. Children, all born in Braintree:

1943. i. Joseph,[9] b. March 29, 1853; died Sept. 19, 1854.
1944. ii. Rhoda Josepha,[9] b. July 26, 1856.
1945. iii. Mary Stetson,[9] b. June 18, 1858.

1289

John B.[8] Porter, of Joseph[7] Porter, born Milton, Mass.; March 27, 1826; resides in Lowell, Me. Married 1st, Lucinda M., daughter of Colonel Theodore Taylor, of Burlington, Me., Feb. 17, 1851. Married 2d, Mrs. Patience Lambert Pentlen, June 5, 1869. Children, born in Lowell:

1944. i. Lizzie Caroline,[9] b. 1851; married George Edward Rand, April 8, 1868; resides in Hanson, Mass.
1945. ii. Samuel,[9] born Jan. 24, 1853; died Sept. 6.

1946. iii. Samuel Taylor,[9] b. June 29, 1854; married Mary Curtis, July 3, 1878.
1947. iv. Mary Hannah,[9] born Feb. 17, 1856; married George I. Varney, July 24, 1872.
1948. v. Annie Stetson,[9] b. Feb. 9, 1858.
1949. vi. Nellie Frances,[9] b. March 14, 1860; died March 20.
1950. vii. Joseph John,[9] b. June 7, 1863.
1951. viii. Thomas Williams,[9] b. 1870.
1952. ix. Martha Susan,[9] b. Sept. 13, 1871.
1953. x. Rhoda Harriette,[9] b. May 20, 1873.
1954. xi. Esther May,[9] b. May 8, 1875.
1955. xii. Cyrus,[9] b. June 29, 1877.

1292

Thomas W.[8] Porter, of Joseph[7] Porter, b. Milton, Mass., May 15, 1832. Resides Burlington, Maine; unmarried. Was in late war,—Lieut. of Co. F., 14th reg't Maine volunteers; representative to Maine Legislature, 1877,-'78; has held all the town offices, and has been much in the employ of the State surveying on the public lands.

1297

George W.[8] Porter, of William G.[7] Porter, b. Wrentham, Mass., Aug. 8, 1832; resides there; farmer, and dealer in real estate. Married Clara Bradish, July 27, 1857. Children:

1956. i. Isabel E.,[9] b. Dec. 22, 1858.
1957. ii. Eliza Fiske,[9] b. Dec. 23, 1862.
1958. iii. Anna Clough,[9] b. Nov. 3, 1871.

1319

Ahira S.[8] Porter, of Ahira[7] Porter, born Stoughton, Jan. 30, 1827. Resides Brockton; extensive dealer in horses and carriages. Married Louisa, daughter of Josiah Packard, Apr. 22, 1849. Children:

1970. i. Henry Swan,[9] b. May 27, 1842.
1971. ii. Frank Forest,[9] b. Dec. 14, 1856; m. Rachel A. Porter, daughter of Lewis Porter, Sept. 5, 1877.

1320

Rachel D.[8] Porter, of Ahira[7] Porter, b. Stoughton, Dec. 27, 1828. Married Albion P. Richardson, of Worcester, Mass.; no children. She died Aug. 27, 1850. He died Dec. 25, 1875, at his residence in Worcester, after a lingering illness of two years.

1321

William^8 Porter, of Ahira^7 Porter, b. Aug. 30, 1831; resides Randolph, Mass. Married 1st, Ellen, daughter of Sidney French, of Randolph, June 30, 1854; died July 11, 1861. Married 2d, Sarah K. Alden, daughter of Hiram C. Alden, Esq., June 18, 1872. One child:

1972. i. Frederick Arthur,^{9} b. June 24, 1861; died Oct. 2, 1865.

1322

Samuel^8 Porter, of Ahira^7 Porter, b. Stoughton, Mass., June 27, 1833. Resides in Portland, Me.; merchant. Married 1st, Sarah, daughter of Benjamin and Patience Chamberlain, of Marion, Mass., Nov. 26, 1856; she died May 18, 1865. Married 2d, Helen F. Kendall, of Portland, June, 1871. Children:

1973. i. Ada Leslie,^{9} b. July 9, 1859; died.
1974. ii. Walter C.,^{9} b. May 13, 1865.
1975. iii. Marion Kendall,^{9} b. Sept. 28, 1874.

1323

James^8 Porter, of Ahira^7 Porter, b. Oct., 1835. Resides Brockton; mechanic; married Caroline A. Clark, of Brockton, Jan. 14, 1860. One child:

1976. i. William Ellis,^{9} b. Mar. 29, 1861.

1324

George W.^{8} Porter, of Ahira^7 Porter, b. Jan. 30, 1843; resides East Stoughton; mechanic; Married Ellen E., dau. of William and Elizabeth Tucker, of E. Stoughton, Nov. 22, 1866.

1331

Warren F.^{8} Porter, of Luther^7 Porter, b. Stoughton, June 2, 1838, where he resides; mechanic; married Hattie M. Barrows, of Stoughton, Jan. 22, 1859. Children:

1980. i. George A.,^{9} b. Aug. 19, 1864; died Aug. 20, 1865.
1981. ii. Charles F., ^{9} b. Sept. 26, 1867.
1982. iii. Lillia A.,^{9} b. June 6, 1873.

1333

Catharine I.[8] Porter, of Luther[7] Porter, b. Mar. 20, 1851; married Francis L. Clapp, of Boston, July 1, 1869. Children:

Arthur W.,[9] b. July 19, 1871. Luella W.,[9] b. Mar. 30, 1874. Charles H. P.,[9] b. Mar. 25, 1875; died June 25, 1875.

1397

Oliver C.[8] Porter, of Chipman[7] Porter, b. Halifax, Mass., Jan. 26, 1827; family reside Middleboro'; married Malanza Phillips, of East Bridgewater, Nov. 19, 1863; he died Feb. 18, 1873. Children:

1989. i. Lucy Blanchard,[9] b. April 2, 1865.
1990. ii. Franklin,[9] b. May 12, 1869.

1400

Henry M.[8] Porter, of Chipman[7] Porter, born Halifax, Nov. 20, 1837; resides there. Married Harriet G. Hathaway, of E. Bridgewater, Sept. 19, 1865. Children:

1991. i. Cynthia Wood,[9] b. Oct. 22, 1867.
1992. ii. Hattie Hathaway,[9] b. Feb. 11, 1869.
1993. iii. John Chipman,[9] b. Oct. 4, 1870.
1994. iv. Gertrude,[9] b. July 7, 1872.
1995. v. Annie,[9] b. Jan. 8, 1876.

1404

Abby F.[8] Porter, of Nathaniel[7] Porter, b. E. Bridgewater, May 28, 1840. Married Samuel Foster, of South Abington, Oct. 15, 1857; he son of Hector and Mary (Churchill) Foster, born 1835. Children:

Child,[9] died young. Austin Powers,[9] b. June 9, 1859. John Albert,[9] b. June 15, 1866. Mabel Amanda,[9] b. April 18, 1873.

1406

Francis B.[8] Porter, of Nathaniel[7] Porter, b. Aug. 20, 1835; resides East Bridgewater; married Abbie A. Hartwell, of N. Bridgewater, 1860; she dau. of Charles A. and Abigail (Copeland) Hartwell, born Aug. 12, 1838. Children:

Charles Frazier,[9] b. Feb., 1863. Ellen A.,[9] b. Feb., 1869. Grace H.,[9] b. Nov., 1870.

1408

Lewis H.[8] Porter, of Enos[7] Porter, born Cummington, Mar. 21, 1830. Resides in Williamsburg, Mass.; merchant; married Phebe Byram, of Waterville, N. J.; she born 1835. Children, all born in Waterville, N. J.:

2007. i. Frances Enos,[9] b. May 30, 1854.
2008. ii. Lucius E.,[9] b. Oct. 8, 1857.
2009. iii. Theodore Priestly,[9] b. Oct. 9, 1859.
2010. iv. Watson Byram,[9] b. Dec. 12, 1860.

1410

Henry M.[8] Porter, of Enos[7] Porter, born June 23, 1826; resides in Williamsburg; merchant; married Mary E. Tileston, Oct. 23, 1862.

1412

Edward A.[8] Porter, of Enos[7] Porter, born Sept. 23, 1839; resides in Williamsburg; married Jennie Warner, June 19, 1873. One child:

2011. i. Charles Warner,[9] b. May 28, 1874.

1418

Levi P.[8] Porter, of Asa H.[7] Porter, born Cummington, Mass., Nov. 8, 1836; widow and children reside there; married Cornelia E. Wilbur, Dec. 18, 1860; he died Jan. 23, 1871. Children:

2012. i. Fannie Maria,[9] b. April 13, 1862.
2013. ii. Delia Alice,[9] b. Jan. 9, 1865.

1420

Harlan P.[8] Porter, of Asa H.[7] Porter, born Cummington, Apr. 23, 1838; resides Brooklyn, N. Y.; in the army two years; married Mary J. Bailey, of Brooklyn, N. Y., July 14, 1868. Children:

2014. i. Emma Maria,[9] b. May, 1869.
2015. ii. Jennie E.,[9] b. May 14, 1871.
2016. iii. Alfred Eugene,[9] b. July 9, 1874.

1423

Alfred E.[8] Porter, of Asa H.[7] Porter, b. Cummington, Feb. 8, 1848; resides Springfield; house builder.

1426

Morris H.[8] Porter of Milton[7] Porter, born Cummington, April 28, 1839; resides Kalamazoo, Mich.; married Mary R. Barnard, Nov., 1863. Children:

Gertrude,[9] born Mar. 9, 1865. Harry,[9] and Nora,[9] twins, born June 28, 1872.

1427

Ralph M.[8] Porter, of Milton[7] Porter, born Cummington, June 2, 1848; resides Springfield, Mass.

1440

Edwin H.[8] Porter, of Seth J.[7] Porter, born Skaneateles, N. Y., Dec. 17, 1822; was for five years deputy commissioner of the state land office, Michigan; married 1st, Adaline E. Walter, at Kalamazoo, Mich., Dec. 23, 1845; she died June 15, 1866. Married 2d, Emma E. Nash, of Lansing, Mich., July 26, 1867. Children:

Harry W.,[9] b. 1849. Alice E.,[9] b. 1852. Charles E.,[9] b. 1856. Nellie R.,[9] b. 1859.

1441

Hon. James B.[8] Porter, of Seth J.[7] Porter, b. Marcellus, N. Y., Sept. 7, 1824; elected register of deeds and county clerk of Allegan Co., Mich., in 1850, which office he held until June 1, 1861, at which time he entered upon the duties of secretary of state of Michigan, and held that position until Jan. 1, 1867; since that time he has been engaged in the real estate and general insurance business, at Lansing, Mich. Married Eunice Johnson House, at Otsego, Allegan Co., Mich., Aug. 17, 1845; she daughter of Eleazer and Apphia A. Johnson House, b. Moreux, N. Y., 1824; Mr. House died at Otsego, Mich., 1852; his widow died in Lansing, Mich., 1872. Children:

2017. i. Aristun,[9] b. 1849; died.
2018. ii. Edgar Seth,[9] b. May 10, 1851; grocer; Lansing, Mich.

2019. iii. William Hubbard,[9] b. May 9, 1853; of the firm of Baker & Porter, furniture dealers, Lansing, Mich.; m. Elvira A. Morehouse, at Litchfield, Ohio, Feb., 1872. Children: Florence,[10] b. Aug. 28, 1875. Walter Ford,[10] b. Aug., 1877.

2020A. iv. James Ballard,[9]; died.

2020B. v. Rosie A.,[9] b. 1862; died.

1503

Rev. Lemuel[8] Porter, D. D., of Lemuel[7] Porter, born in Boston, May 1, 1809; his father being in China, did not see him until he was three years old; at an early age he was clerk in a store on Central wharf, Boston; after a while he fitted to go supercargo of a vessel to the East Indies. In the spring of the year in which he was to sail he became interested in religion and joined the Baldwin Place church, of which his mother and sister were members; he felt it his duty to preach the gospel, and fitted for college, graduating at Waterville, Me., in 1834, and Newton Theological Institute; settled over a Baptist church in Lowell, Aug., 1835, where he has preached for sixteen years with remarkable success. In 1851 he removed to Pittsfield, and settled there as pastor of the Baptist church, of which his beloved friend Governor George N. Briggs, was a member; after preaching there thirteen years, the death of his dearly loved daughter seemed to almost crush him, and his health failed; he resigned his pastorate and was appointed Secretary of the American Tract Society, at Chicago, Ill. His physicians thought the climate would be beneficial, but it was not so to be; he was attacked by a bilious fever which terminated in a typhoid fever, of which he died Oct. 17, 1864. His remains were interred at Mount Auburn, beside his father and sister. His mother, whom he dearly loved, never spoke but once after hearing of his death, but swoomed away and died. He was one of nature's noblemen, of commanding personal appearance, possessed of ardent affections and of amiable disposition; he was beloved by all who knew him. Rev. Baron Stow, D. D., in an obituary notice of him, says:

Dr. Lemuel Porter, died in Chicago, Oct. 17; he was a native of Boston. In childhood he was one of Dr. Baldwin's catechetical class; at the age of eighteen he was baptised; at twenty-six he was settled over a Baptist church in Lowell, where in a pastorate of sixteen years, and a pastorate of twelve years at Pittsfield, Mass., he baptised over one thousand and two hundred christian converts. I have been acquainted with him thirty-seven years, most of the time intimately, and I can say that I have never known, either in the pulpit, or out of it, a nobler specimen of christian manhood. I have yet to meet the first person who ever suspected him of actions or motive bordering on meanness in any department of life. His heart was large, generous, and true; his ministerial life was stained by no folly; his friends were never ashamed of him; the vilest never could speak ill of him. His character was harmoniously and beautifully developed; he commanded universal respect; he was an illustration of what a christian mother's fidelity, and a thorough intellectual training, and the sanctifying grace of God combined, could make of a human being. His record is without a blot. In Pittsfield he had the confidence and co-operation of the late Gov. Briggs, and when that great and good man departed he felt the blow as one of unusual severity. Soon his elder daughter, a young lady of uncommon worth, was suddenly removed; two such dispensations nearly crushed him. He had no ambition for literary distinctions; his great aim was to be a good preacher and pastor; in that line he had few superiors. He resorted to no expedients to secure popularity; he kept his character unimpeached, and did well his work. He held steadily on his way, a uniform light that had no eclipse. He was not perfect, but very few at the age of fifty-four retire from life leaving so unblemished a history. His labors were eminently blessed in the conversion of sinners, and the healthy growth of churches. He gradually sank a martyr to a climate to which his temperament was not adapted. At early dawn on the Sabbath his spirit passed to its home on high. He died among friends, who did their utmost to save him. His mind was peaceful when not shattered by the terrible typhoid in his brain. He spoke composedly and firmly of his trust in a Redeemer, and his apprehension that his earthly mission was near its conclusion."

He married W. Maria Skinner, Nov. 24, 1835. Mrs. Porter was of Windsor, Vt. where she now resides. Children:

2020. i. Clara Maria,[9] b. Lowell, Mass., Oct. 12, 1837; died at Pittsfield, Mass., Nov. 24, 1861. She was a most beautiful woman, in person, character, and everything which makes completeness. She had a fine education and splendid poetical talents. Her death was a severe blow to her relatives and friends. From an obituary of her by Rev. John Todd, D. D., of Pittsfield, I take the following: "Twenty-four years ago, a beautiful child was placed in the arms of these parents; the great question was, what manner of child shall this be? to-day it is answered. None but her parents can know how much that was bright, pure and lovely, dwelt in that casket which has been so suddenly crushed. With a disposition of unalloyed sweetness, with an education for which no expense was spared, seven years were spent in our excellent institution, (Maplewood, Pittsfield, Mass.;) with a memory that gave her a full mind; with a taste that selected nothing which was not refined, graceful and beautiful; with powers of mind and heart that had made her pen known very extensively; with poetical talents that were fast bringing her into notice and admiration; with a love of music, and ability to execute, that made her home like a nest of singing birds on the bough that is rocked in sunshine; her hand engaged to one to walk the journey of life, how could this young timid girl meet death, and go away from all this into eternity, without terror or regret? Clara Maria Porter, at twenty, knelt at the cross, gave her heart to Christ in an everlasting covenant, so that on her dying bed, she could speak calmly, tell her father of her firm trust in the Saviour, so that the day before she died, could sing several hymns with great sweetness, and recite with touching eloquence, her own requiem for Governor Briggs."

2021. ii. Helen Gertrude,[9] b. Lowell, Nov. 6, 1840; married James N. Edminister, Esq., of Windsor, Vermont, Nov. 5, 1867. They have a son, Lemuel Porter,[10] b. April 12, 1869.

1504

Hannah E.[8] Porter, of Lemuel[7] Porter, b. Feb. 17, 1813; died at Warrenton, Va., Nov. 3, 1858. She was a lady remarkable for her personal beauty; loveliness of features, delicacy of form, and grace of carriage united to add a peculiar charm to her person; sprightly and amiable of character, which made her universally beloved; pious, conscientious and devoted to every good work; an affectionate wife and mother, and a useful member of society and the church. She married Rev. Joel Smith Bacon, of Georgetown, Ky., Dec. 1, 1831;

he was born in Cayuga Co., N. Y., Sept. 3, 1802; in 1822 entered Homer N. Y., Academy; grad. Hamilton College, N. Y., 1826, and at Newton Theological Seminary, 1831; taught school in Virginia; afterwards taught a classical school in Princeton, N. J., where he enjoyed the society of its literary *elite*, and was recognized as a gifted and scholarly man; installed pastor of First Baptist church, Lynn, April 7, 1837; resigned Dec. 13, 1839; for the next few years an efficient member of the Baptist Triennial Convention, having in charge foreign and domestic missions, with his location at Boston. In 1842 visited the Shawnee missions; in 1843, he accepted the office of President of Columbian College, Washington, D. C., where he continued with great success, until July 14, 1854, when he resigned; he spent one year in southern Georgia, another in Louisiana; afterward removing to Warrenton, Va.; and in 1859 removed to Tuscaloosa, Ala., where he was president of a female institute, in connection with his son-in-law. Prof. Latham; the war coming on, he returned to Warrenton, Va., 1860. Here he was at the head of the Fauquier Female Seminary, until 1866. For several years after this he was in the employ of the American and Foreign Bible Society. He was an earnest, devoted, christian minister, of unusual abilities; as an extemporaneous preacher and debater, not excelled; a fond, affectionate, and beloved father and husband. He died in Richmond, Va., Nov. 9, 1870. His funeral, on the 11th, was attended by ministers of all denominations; Rev. Dr. Barrows preached on the occasion, and Rev. Dr. Jeter spoke of his character and labors: "In its intellectual characteristics Dr. Bacon's mind was versatile without being superficial; popular rather than profound in its views of principles; practical, and yet fond of speculation * * fond of the study of men and things rather than of books * * ready for the defence of the established truth, yet tolerant of views manifestly erroneous, from charity toward human infirmity. Children:

i. Ida,[9] b. Hamilton, N. Y., July 10, 1834; m. Prof. R. P. Latham, of Alexandria, Va., Dec. 26, 1854; he died in the Confederate service, 1862. Children: Florence M.,[10] born Richmond, Va., Oct. 8, 1855. Josie B.,[10] b. Alexandria, Va., July 29, 1858. Richard P.,[10] b. Warrenton, Va., 1861; died 1862. Mrs. Latham m. 2d, Rev. H. W. Dodge, D. D., a Baptist clergyman, of Lynchburg, Va., July, 1864; he afterwards minister in Loudon Co., Va., Austin, Texas, and now has charge of a church in Columbia, Mo. Children: Clarence Porter,[10] b. Lynchburg, Va., Mar., 1867. Willie Ruggles,[10] b. Nov. 23, 1871. (Florence Latham,[10] m. John Hollingsworth, of Austin, Texas; now living in Graham City, Young Co., Texas. Children: Ida M.,[11] b. Mar., 1875. Mary,[11] b. Nov., 1876.)

ii. Josie,[9] b. Boston, Feb. 28, 1837; m. L. R. Spilman, Esq., attorney at law, Richmond, Va., Dec. 24, 1866. Children: Ida,[10] b. Oct. 6, 1867. Arthur Ruggles,[10] b. Aug. 21, 1869. Allan Lester,[10] b. Aug 17, 1876; died same year.

iii. Lemuel Porter,[9] b. Lynn, May 24, 1839; died May 26, 1851.

iv. Albert J.,[9] May 1, 1842; died Washington, July 17, 1851.

v. Gertrude,[9] b. Boston, Sept. 18, 1840; died there Nov. 16, 1840.

vi. Gertrude Ruggles,[9] b. Washington, D. C., Aug. 8, 1848.

vii. Alice Preston,[9] b. Washington, D. C., May 15, 1851; m. S. G. Sneed, of Austin, Texas, Feb., 1876; died Feb., 1876.

1505

Oliver[8] Porter, of Lemuel[7] Porter, b. Boston, May 28, 1816; grad. Hamilton College, and at Harvard Law School; was in the Mexican war in the U. S. Army, and died at Jalapa, Mexico, Jan. 22, 1848. Married Mary Ann Russell, of West Cambridge. One son:

2022. i. Herbert Oliver,[9] b. about 1847.

1509

Hon. Edward F.[8] Porter, of Edward J.[7] Porter, b. Scituate, July 21, 1820; resides West Newton: manufacturer of dye woods and extracts; was member of the General Court from Boston, 1857, 1858, 1859, and of the Boston city government 1855, 1856, 1865, 1866; state liquor commissioner from 1859 to 1866. Married Phebe Damon, 1842; she born 1820. Children:

2023. i. Francis E.,[9] b. Aug. 28, 1844; physician; resides at Somerville; married Christine Taylor, Oct. 14, 1876.

2024\. ii. Damon Clarke,[9] b. Oct. 29, 1846; graduated Wesleyan University, Conn.; clergyman; married Helen A. Fuller, April 9, 1873; spent a year and a half in Europe and Palestine, and soon after returning home he fell in the barn, December 1, 1874, killing him instantly. He was thoroughly devoted to his sacred calling, and much beloved by all who knew him.

2025\. iii. Henry Sumner,[9] b. June 28, 1851; married Louisa F. Ives, Nov. 30, 1871, and has one child, Ruth Bassett,[10] b. Dec. 1, 1872; resides Indianapolis, Ind.

2026\. iv. Wendall Lee,[9] b. Dec. 18, 1852; married Nettie Rose, Oct. 27, 1874,—has one child, Damon Lee,[10] b. Oct. 28, 1876; resides Sedalia, Mo.

2027\. v. Lewis Bates,[9] b. Jan. 27, 1856.

2028\. vi. Willie Doane,[9] b. Oct. 31, 1858.

2029\. vii. Annie Phebe,[9] b. Aug. 5, 1861.

1510

Lucy Gardner[8] Porter, of Edward J.[7] Porter, b. Feb. 9, 1822; married W. H. Jenkins, of New York, 1843; merchant. Children:

i. Theodore Parker,[9] b. 1847.

ii. Arthur Chauncy,[9] b. 1848.

iii. William Porter,[9] b. 1854.

iv. Charles E.,[9] b. 1856.

v. Isabel S.,[9] b. 1858; died 1859.

1511

Margarette[8] Porter, of Edward J.[7] Porter, b. April 20, 1824; married Perez Jenkins, of Lexington, Mass., 1862; farmer and master mariner.

1512

William[8] Porter, of Edward J.[7] Porter, born Jan. 22, 1827; resides Cincinnati, Ohio; printer; married Lucy J. Ives, 1849. Children:

2035\. i. Edward Jarvis,[9] b. 1850.

2036\. ii. Alice Ives,[9] b. 1852.

2037\. iii. Jessie May,[9] b. 1857.

2038\. iv. William,9 b. 1860.

2039\. v. Mary Mansfield,[9] b. 1864.

2040\. vi. Helen Augusta,[9] b. 1866.

1513

Charles[8] Porter, of Edward J.[7] Porter, b. July 28, 1829; resides Miamiville, Ohio; farmer; married Mary Buxton, 1869.

1514

Perez G.[8] Porter, of Edward J.[7] Porter, b. Jan. 20, 1834; resides Cambridge, Mass.; merchant in Boston, (No. 23 Broad street;) married Helen A. Burchstead, May 24, 1852; she daughter of Benjamin and Mary Noyes (Childs) Burchstead, born July 9, 1829. They have one son:

2041. i. Harry Gardner,[9] b. Dec. 6, 1857.

1515

Sarah J.[8] Porter, of Edward J.[7] Porter, b. Jan. 20, 1834; married Thomas H. Kendrick, of Lexington, Mass., merchant. Children:

2042. i. Carrie Fletcher,[9] b. 1852.
2043. ii. Julia Fremont,[9] b. 1856; died 1857.
2044. iii. Frederick Parker,[9] b. 1858.
2045. iv. Laura Maxwell,[9] b. 1861.
2046. v. Charlotte,[9] b. 1863.

1516

Alexander[8] Porter, of Edward J.[7] Porter, b. Oct. 16, 1836; resides New York city; merchant; married Elizabeth F. Jenness, 1856; she died April 12, 1872. Children:

2047. i. Walter Howard,[9] b. 1856.
2048. ii. Mary Lizzie,[9] b. 1858.
2049. iii. William Henry,[9] b. 1860; died 1862.
2050. iv. Lucy Gardner,[9] b. 1862.
2051. v. Lucy Gardner,[9] b. 1864.
2052. vi. Jennie Kendrick,[9] b. 1868.

1546

Lemuel[8] Porter, of Nathan[7] Porter, b. Mount Vernon, Me., Dec. 4, 1834; married 1st, Nellie E. Bartlett, of Belgrade, Me., pub. April 26, 1867; she died May 16, 1868. Married 2d, Lydia A. Dudley, of Readfield, Me., pub. Nov. 3, 1868. Child:

2053. i. Hattie D.,[9] b. Oct. 18, 1870.

1525

William[8] Porter, of Amasa[7] Porter, b. July 24, 1818; resides Mt. Vernon, Me.; married Sarah H. Children:

2054. i. Lester,[9] b. April 13, 1850.
2055. ii. Ida Aurissa,[9] b. Dec. 13, 1854.
2056. iii. Alice Rosamond,[9] b. Oct. 28, 1856.
2057. iv. Ellsworth Amasa,[9] b. Dec. 31, 1865.

1613

Alvan[8] Porter, of Alvan[7] Porter, b. Marshfield; resides E. Bridgewater; married Mehetable, daughter of Jacob Reed, of E. Bridgewater, 1844. Children:

2058. i. Almira C.,[9] b. Sept. 1, 1846; died April, 1848.
2059. ii. Louisa M.,[9] b. Oct. 17, 1848.
2060. iii. Frank S.,[9] b. Aug. 5, 1852; died Aug. 9, 1853.
2061. iv. Ellen F.,[9] b. June 6, 1854.
2062. v. Edith M.,[9] b. April 9, 1857.
And five others.

1638

Jeremy W.[8] Porter, of Ezekiel[7] Porter, born in Strong, Me., Nov. 9, 1820; resides in Strong; manufacturer; member of Maine Senate; Trustee of State Reform School. One son:

2063. i. James E.[9] Relating to him, I subjoin an article from Portland Maine Press: "JAMES E. PORTER.—Lieut. James E. Porter, one of the officers of Gen. Custer's command who fell in the Big Horn massacre, was a son of the Hon. Jeremy Porter, of Strong, in this state. He graduated at West Point in the class of 1869; received his commission as second lieutenant, and at once joined Gen. Custer's force at Fort Levenworth, Kansas. He was transferred to North Carolina, and thence to Fort Lincoln, having meanwhile been promoted to a first lieutenancy. At the time of his death he was acting captain of Company I, 7th Cavalry. He was thirty-two years old, leaves a wife and two children. His family is now at Fort Lincoln. Lieut. Porter was an officer of much promise, and cordially esteemed by all who knew him."

1662

Edmund W.[8] Porter, of William W.[7] Porter, born Taunton, Mass., Mar. 11, 1831; resides in Aurora, Ill.; superintendent of Aurora Silver Plate Manufacturing Company; married Sarah E. Strange, April 6, 1852, by Rev. E. Maltby; she daughter of Jirah and Sally Strange, of Taunton, born Sept. 12, 1832. They have had one child:

2064. i. Warren S.,[9] b. Oct. 3, 1857; died Sept. 1, 1861.

1663

Polly L.[8] Porter, of William W.[7] Porter, born Aug. 1, 1832; married Manning W. Fox, of Taunton, May 21, 1850. Children:

William A.,[9] b. 1851; died 1853. Caroline P.,[9] b. 1853. William M.[9] Horace E.[9] Adeline E.[9]

1664

Lemuel C.[8] Porter, of William W.[7] Porter, b. June 25, 1839; resides Aurora, Ill.; britannia worker; married Esther G. Austin, of Taunton, Sept. 14, 1859. Children:

2065. i. Lillias,[9] b. June 3, 1860.
2066. ii. Jennie B.,[9] b, Mar. 19, 1865.
2067. iii. Anna A.,[9] b. Mar. 1, 1868.

1665

Rhoda C.[8] Porter, of William W.[7] Porter, born at Taunton, Sept. 17, 1846; married David W. Dean, of Taunton. Children:

Ruth A.[9] Edmund P.[9]

1715

George S.[8] Porter, of George S.[7] Porter, born New Orleans, May 17, 1845; resides New Durham, N. J.; married Sarah M. Nichols, of New Durham, May 8, 1872. One child:

i. Josephine,[9] b. Feb. 19, 1874.

1718

William[8] Porter, of George S.[7] Porter, born San Francisco, Nov. 23, 1849; resides there; married Sarah Andrews, July, 1870.

1720

Louisa^{8} Porter, of George S.^{7} Porter, born Milwaukee, Wis., Nov. 3, 1841; died Nov. 8, 1868; married John De Camp Bluxem, of Brooklyn, N. Y., May 26, 1858. Children:

i. Sarah,^{9} b. Aug. 23, 1859.
ii. Georgianna,^{9} b. Feb. 14, 1861.
iii. Louisa,^{9} b. Feb. 25, 1863; died 1863.
iv. Mary,^{9} b. May 20, 1864.
v. George Porter,^{9} b. Dec. 10, 1866.

1724

Alexander S.^{8} Porter, of John K.^{7} Porter, born Coalsmouth, Va., Aug. 25, 1840; resides in Boston; merchant; married Mary Otis Cushing, in Boston, Apr. 27, 1865. Children:

2090. i. Mary Otis,^{9} b. Feb. 25, 1866.
2091. ii. James Otis,^{9} b. Feb. 25, 1870.
2092. iii. Alexander Robertson,^{9} b. Feb. 6, 1873.
2093. iv. Catharine Cushing,^{9} b. Feb. 3, 1876.

1755

Rebecca^{8} Porter, of Edwin^{7} Porter, born Mar. 4, 1831; married Henry J. Coop, July 14, 1857; he son of John and Rose Coop, of Messina, Italy, born Nov., 1822; resides No. 390, Magazine street, New Orleans, La. Children:

Louis F.,^{9} b. Jan. 8, 1858. Sarah P.,^{9} b. April 26, 1865.

1757

Roger W.^{8} Porter, of Edwin^{7} Porter, born March 15, 1834; resides Nashua, N. H.; married Clara Amelia Baldwin, Sept. 13, 1864; she daughter of Josephus and Nancy (Blanchard) Baldwin, born Dunstable, Mass., July 20, 1845. (Mr. Baldwin, born Oct. 15, 1803; Mrs. Baldwin born Milford, N. H., Feb. 23, 1804.) Children of Roger W. and Clara A. Porter:

2100. i. Clara Grace,^{9} b. Oct. 15, 1865; died June 21, 1866.
2101. ii. Paulina Elisabeth,^{9} b. Feb. 24, 1867.
2102. iii. Edwin,^{9} b. April 30, 1869; died June 22, 1869.
2103. iv. Annie Baldwin,^{9} b. Aug. 23, 1872.

1768

Rowena E.[8] Porter, of John M.[7] Porter, born Naples, N. Y., April 7, 1828; married James H. Macomber, April 19, 1849. She died Feb. 18, 1865. Children:

Daphne M.,[9] b. Nov. 16, 1850. Claritra L.,[9] b. April 4, 1852. Royal Porter,[9] b. Nov. 7, 1854. Arthemise R.,[9] b. Aug. 5, 1857. Emma O.,[9] b. Mar. 1, 1859. Zilpha T.,[9] b. Oct. 25, 1861. Evaline A.,[9] b. June 26, 1863.

1769

James O.[8] Porter, of John M.[7] Porter, born Nov. 8, 1832; lives Naples, N. Y.; married Hannah Jerusha Holland, Sept. 14, 1860; she born June 22, 1843. Children:

2104. i. Flora Elsina,[9] b. Dec. 8, 1861.
2105. ii. Cora A.,[9] b. June 8, 1863.
2106. iii. Willie I.,[9] b. Aug. 6, 1865.
2107. iv. Viletta A.,[9] b. April 18, 1867; died Aug. 23, 1874.
2108. v. John M.,[9] b. April 1, 1868.
2109. vi. James O.,[9] b. Mar. 28, 1870.
2110. vii. Almira J.,[9] b. Jan., 1872; died Aug. 16, 1874.
2111. viii. Eric David,[9] b. Feb. 19, 1874.
2112. ix. Mina Belle,[9] b. July 5, 1876.
2113. x. Nini Adel,[9] b. July 8, 1877; died Sept. 3, 1877.

RICHARD PORTER APPENDIX.

Richard[1] Porter was a good writer. His signature to his will was written when he was very aged.

5

ZACHARY[5] BICKNELL came from England, in 1635, with Rev. Joseph Hull and others, and probably died the next year, for the General Court ordered March 9, $163\frac{6}{7}$, "that William Reed, having bought the house and twenty acres of land at Weymouth, unfenced, which was Zachary Bicknell's, for seven pounds thirteen shillings and four pence, of Richard Rockett and wife, is to have the sale confirmed by the child when he cometh of age, or else the child to allow such costs as the court shall think meet." Zachary and Agnes appear to have had but one child, John.[2]

The widow Agnes Bicknell, married Richard Rockett, of Braintree, (now Rockwood,) by whom she had one child, John, b. in Braintree, Dec. 1, 1641, who was the ancestor of a large portion of the Rockwoods in New England. Mrs. Agnes Rockett died in Braintree, July 9, 1643, aged forty-five years.

87

COL. AARON[5] HOBART was son of Isaac[4] and Mary (Harden) Hobart, born 1729; resided in South Abington; a distinguished man in his day; he owned a township of land in Maine, now Edmunds, in Washington county, where his sons Nathaniel and Isaac settled. Married 1st, Elizabeth, daughter of Jacob and Ann (Dingley) Pillsbury, Nov. 5, 1753.

Married 2d, widow Thankful Adams, Nov. 25, 1777; she widow of Elihu Adams, of Braintree, brother of John Adams. Children:

- i. Jacob,[6] b. Aug. 5, 1754; died Dec. 20, 1772.
- ii. Seth,[6] b. Sept. 4, 1755; m. Esther, of Jona Allen, of Braintree, 1782; settled in East Bridgewater; he died 1813; his widow 1814. Children: Betsey,[7] b. 1783. Jacob,[7] b. 1784. Jonathan,[7] b. 1786. Seth,[7] b. 1788. Polly,[7] b. 1790. Eunice,[7] b. 1795. Joseph,[7] b. 1796. Esther,[7] b. 1798.
- iii. Nathaniel,[6] b. Oct. 15, 1758; married; died June 23, 1838, aged 80.
- iv. Elizabeth,[6] b. Oct. 5, 1761; m. Dr. David Jones, Feb., 1777; he b. at Wrentham, Mar. 26, 1749; came to Abington with his father; removed to North Yarmouth, Me., Oct. 17, 1783. Children: Mary,[7] m. John Hall, and had eight children (one of whom, Mary Jones,[8] m. Albert W. Paine, Esq., attorney at law, Bangor, Me.) Jacob H.,[7] m. Hannah Bisbee. Betsey,[7] m. John Lawrence. Sarah,[7] m. Henry Scott. David,[7] m. Elizabeth L. Chase. Esther,[7] m. Stephen Hall. Abigail G.,[7] m. Isaac Hobart. Jane T.,[7] m. Isaac Hobart. Elias,[7] unmarried.
- v. Aaron,[6] b. Aug. 9, 1764; m. Susanna Adams, niece of President John Adams, b. Dec. 7, 1766; died Dec. 31, 1826; he died Jan. 9, 1818. Children: Elihu,[7] b. Dec., 1785; died Sept., 1842; m. Sally Dyer. Aaron,[7] b. June, 1787; M. C. from Massachusetts; resided East Bridgewater; m. Maria Leach.
- vi. Noah,[6] b. Mar. 17, 1767; m. Deborah W. Thomas, of East Bridgewater, Nov. 5, 1789; she b. Duxbury, May 18, 1767; removed to Foxboro, 1804, where he died Jan. 24, 1854; wife died Dec. 3, 1834. Children: Henry,[7] b. Abington, Sept. 13, 1790. Albert,[7] b. Abington, Nov. 8, 1792. Nathaniel,[7] b. Abington, Aug. 30, 1794. James Thomas,[7] b. Abington, July 12, 1801. Aaron,[7] b. Abington, Oct. 8, 1803. Deborah A.,[7] b. Foxboro, Jan. 29, 1806. Jane T.,[7] b. Foxboro, June 28, 1808.
- vii. Isaac,[6] b. Sept. 1, 1771; m. Joanna Hersey, July 17, 1794; settled in Edmunds, Me., 1792, on land given him by his father; he died in Eastport, Me., Feb. 26, 1847; his widow died in Edmunds, Me., May 21, 1858; she b. at Hingham, Mass., Mar. 1, 1776. His sons Aaron,[7] Isaac,[7] and Benjamin,[7] and his son-in-law,

Daniel Kilby, have been members of the Maine Legislature; his grandson, Daniel K. Hobart,[8] Representative, Senator, and Executive Councillor; now U. S. Vice Consul at Windsor, N. S.; his grandson, William Henry Kilby,[8] of Eastport, member of Maine Legislature; now resides in Boston; agent of Boston and St. John steamers. Children: Aaron,[7] b. July 31, 1795; m. 1st, Mary Kilby; m. 2d, Catharine Eastman; had nine children. Isaac,[7] b. Aug. 13, 1797; married 1st, Abigail Jones; m. 2d, Jane Jones; nine children. Joanna,[7] b. July 12, 1799; m. Daniel Kilby; seven children. Eliza,[7] b. May 13, 1801; m. William H. Brooks; six children. Benjamin,[7] b. Apr. 11, 1803; m. 1st, Emily Hayward; m. 2d, Mary Mayhew; had seven children. Sarah Jones,[7] b. Sept. 16, 1806; m. Rev. Heman Nickerson; had eleven children.

92

JAMES PINNEO was a French protestant, who fled to this country after the revocation of the edict of Nantes, 1685—arrived at Bristol, R. I., probably about 1700; he had a companion by the name of James Sullard, (or Soulard.)

"Robert Jolls, of Bristol, for one hundred pounds sold land in Bristol, to James Penneau, weaver, April 2d, 1713. "Witness, John Soulard."

"James Penneo, of Bristol, weaver, sold house and land in Bristol for 200 pounds, to Edward Bosworth, Jr., April 17, 1717, being same tract of land lately purchased of Robert Jolls."

About this time he removed to Lebanon, Conn. "July 27, 1717, James Pinneo, of Bristol, R. I., bought land in Lebanon. (See Lebanon records, vol. 3, page 100.) This land was in south part of Second parish, called "The Crank," now Columbia.

"James Pinneo baptised at Bristol, Feb. 7, 1707, and owned the covenant."

"James Pinneo and Dorothy B.—were married together, (by Mr. Sparhawk) May 9, 1706." He and wife both died in Lebanon. Children:

i. James,[2] b. Bristol, April 19, 1707; died June 6, 1707.
ii. Elisabeth,[2] b. Bristol, Feb. 22, 1709.

iii. James,[2] b. Bristol, 1709-10; m. Priscilla Newcomb, June 16, 1731; lived in Lebanon Second Parish, Conn.; he died April 16, 1789, aged 81; she died Jan. 15, 1793, in her 82d year.

iv. Sarah,[2] b. Dec. 19, 1712; m. Joseph Porter, of Taunton. Married 2d, Sullard, Oct. 11, 1735; as Sarah Sullard, she quit-claims to her brother James, all her interest in her father's, James Pinneo, estate.

v. Daniel,[2] b. Bristol, July 28, 1715.

vi. Submit,[2] b. probably in Lebanon, Oct. 19, 1717; m. Silas Newcomb, 1739.

vii. Joseph,[2] b. probably in Lebanon, June 14, 1720.

viii. Peter,[2] b. probably in Lebanon, May 4, 1723; m. Polly Samson, and removed to Nova Scotia, about 1763; her son Jonathan,[3] probably living in Machias, Me., about 1774.

ix. Dorothy,[2] b. probably in Lebanon, Dec. 6, 1725; m. Capt. John Reed, of Taunton, Dec. 30, 1746; he was son of William and Mary (Richmond) Reed, b. 1722; he was a blacksmith; a man of sturdy honest character; selectman of Taunton, 1772 and 1773, and one of the committee of correspondence during the revolutionary war. She died in 1770. He m. 2d, Mrs. Hannah Austin, Jan. 9, 1771, and died Dec., 1788. The children of John and Dorothy Reed, all born in Taunton:

i. Ruth,[3] b. Nov. 20, 1747; m. 1st, Job Knapp, of Douglass; m. 2d, James Whitney, of Uxbridge, Mass.

ii. Lois,[3] m. Daniel Drake, Oct. 4, 1764, and went to Grafton, N. H.

iii. John,[3] b. Mar. 29, 1752; m. Mary Godfrey, Nov. 21, 1775. Children: John,[4] b. Aug. 11, 1776. William,[4] b. Oct. 6, 1778. Polly,[4] b. Aug. 31, 1782; died Nov. 2, 1796. Dolly,[4] b. May 31, 1785. Marshall,[4] b. Jan. 17, 1788. Hodges,[4] b. June 3, 1790; m. Clarissa Hodges, May, 1813; he died 1864; (they parents of Edgar H. Reed,[5] Esq., now of Taunton). Sophia,[4] b. Sept. 2, 1792. Zilpah,[4] b. Dec. 22, 1796; died May 24, 1798.

iv. Mary,[3] b. June 4, 1754; m. Richard Cobb, of Putney, Vt., 1776; she died Aug. 9, 1822.

v. Dorothy,[3] b. Mar. 1, 1759; m. Paul Dudley, of Douglass, Mass., July 16, 1782; she died Sept. 20, 1847.

vi. Hannah,[3] b. April 4, 1761; m. 1st, Abiathar Hull, of Raynham, May 24, 1787; m. 2d, Stephen Deane, of Raynham, 1807.

vii. Zilpah,[3] b. Dec. 1, 1763; m. Gershom Gulliver, Mar. 8, 1803, and died Mar. 7, 1841.

viii. Enos,[3] b. Nov. 22, 1765; died in Boston, of small pox.

ix. Lydia,[3] b. May 20, 1768; m. Ebenezer Deane, Jr., of Raynham, Mar. 6, 1791.

156

NOAH[5] PORTER, of Jacob[4] Porter, born Abington, Aug. 16, 1744; married Mary Norton, in Abington, Feb. 2, 1766. Children:

394A. i. Noah,[6] b. Abington, April 17, 1767; was one of the earliest pioneers of Palmyra, N. Y.—emigrating there in 1789; he m. Ruth Rogers. Children: Cynthia.[7] Norton.[7] William.[7] Noah,[7] now living. John,[7] now living at Lewiston, Niagara Co., N. Y.

394B. ii. Norton,[6] b. Abington, 1771.

iii. Mary,[6] b. May 18, 1769; m. Dr. John Pomroy, in Abington, 1789; he b. in Middleborough, April 9, 1764; died in Burlington, Vt., Feb. 19, 1844; she died Oct. 2, 1846. Children: Cassius.[7] Francis.[7] Rosamond Porter.[7] John Norton,[7] now living at Burlington, Vt.

iv. William,[6] baptised at Abington, Oct. 4, 1773; (church records.) Adam Porter, guardian of Wm. Porter, minor, empowered to sell real estate in Hampshire County, 1793.

NOTE.—Some of this family claim that Adam[5] Porter, brother of Noah[5] Porter, was their ancestor. The record of births of Adam[5] Porter's children, on page 48, is a copy of his own record.

306

RUTH[6] PORTER, of Josiah[5] Porter, b. Weymouth, May 27, 1773; married Benjamin Haynes, Canaan, N. H.; he son of Samuel Haynes (who died May 26, 1824, of Sudbury family,) born Nov. 2, 1769; died Canaan, N. H., Oct. 26, 1836; widow died Oct. 3, 1852. Children:

i. Sally,[7] b. April 7, 1795; died in Corfu, N. Y. (?)

ii. George H.,[7] b. Nov. 16, 1797; died May 18, 1804.

iii. Increase Sumner,[7] b. June 2, 1800; died in Plymouth, N. H., about 41 years ago.

iv. Josiah Porter,[7] b. Oct. 1, 1802; resides in Monson, Me.; one daughter,[8] m. Burnham, at one time mayor of Biddeford, Me.

v. Francis Asbury,[7] b. Nov. 21, 1807; resides Hanover, N. H.; m. Fanny Balch, of Lyme, N. H., Oct. 2, 1833. Children: Charles W.,[8] b. Aug. 6, 1834. Edgar Kittridge,[8] b. Aug. 10, 1836. Adna B.,[8] b. Aug. 20, 1839. Albert Sumner,[8] b. Dec. 13, 1841; died Mar. 17, 1873. Charlotte F.,[8] b. Dec. 13, 1843; m. Rev. Alexander Wiswell, graduated at Dartmouth College, 1874—now preaching at Monmouth, Me.

vi. John H.,[7] b. Sept. 19, 1810; resides Farmington, N. H.

vii. George H.,[7] b. May 16, 1813; resides South Royalton, Vermont.

310

ELIAS[6] PORTER, of Micah[5] Porter, of Weymouth, removed to Canaan, N. H. Deacon of the Congregational Church there. Removed from Canaan to Raymond, N. H., or Warner, N. H. Said to have had four children—two sons and two daughters—Ephraim[7] and William,[7] who married Sallie Withington, (see 307A) and removed to Boston; daughters married and moved away.

320

David[6] Porter, of Micah[5] Porter, born Weymouth, Mass., March 3, 1784; died in Jackson, Mich., April 11, 1860; was "mason by trade, and a master mason of the secret order." Went to Enfield, N. H.; thence in 1813, to Newport, N. Y.; thence to Boonville, N. Y., 1823; and in 1837, removed to Jackson, Mich. Married in Jan. 1800, in Enfield, N. H., to Sarah, daughter of Col. William Johnson; she born in Haverhill, Mass., Nov. 7, 1779; died in Jackson, Aug. 3, 1854. Children:

i. Maria,[7] born Oct. 13, 1806, in Enfield, N. H.; married, Nov. 19, 1836, in Boonville, New York, to Francis Woodbury, of Beverly, Mass.; she died in Beverly, Jan. 16, 1842.

ii. Mary S.,[7] b. in Enfield, N. H., Jan. 14, 1809; married April 7, 1828, to Charles Johnson; now living in Kalamazoo, Mich.

iii. Sarah H.,[7] b. in Enfield, N. H., June 30, 1810; married Oct., 1832, Ichabod Cole, (?) of Oswego, N. Y.; she died April 23, 1877, in Jackson, Mich.

iv. Eliza M.,[7] b. Newport, N. Y., Nov. 3, 1814; died Jan. 31, 1830.

v. Clarissa A.,[7] b. Newport, N. Y., Oct. 5, 1817; married Sept. 20, 1842, in Jackson, Mich., to Francis Woodbury, of Beverly, who died in Cincinnati, Ohio, Jan. 17, 1878; widow now resides Walnut Hills, Cincinnati.

vi. George W.,[7] b. Newport, N. Y., Oct. 15, 1820; died Oct. 27, 1840.

vii. Harriet N.,[7] b. Boonville, N. Y., Nov. 24, 1829;(?) married Sept. 30, 1850, in Jackson, Mich., to Eli F. Hollister, of Detroit,—now of Chicago, Ill.

322

Hon. Reuben[6] Porter, of Micah[5] Porter, b. in Weymouth, 1790; lived in Warner, N. H.

386

ELIAS[6] PORTER, of John[5] Porter, b. Abington; had sons—Daniel[7] and Fuller,[7] (a Presbyterian minister,) Zeruiah.[7] Lois.[7] Mary.[7]

388

NOAH[6] PORTER, of John[5] Porter, born in Abington, Jan. 11, 1775; when a young man settled in New Hartford, Oneida Co., N. Y.; in his old age he removed to Lisbon, Ill., where he died, Feb. 10, 1851, aged 76 years 1 month. He carried and kept with him through life his old fashioned religious principles, which he imbibed in early life. He married Sarah, daughter of Ezekiel Williams, of New Hartford, N. Y., Feb. 20, 1799; she died Sept. 22, 1860, aged 80 years 8 months and 2 days. Children:

i. Francis D.,[7] b. Mar. 12, 1801; married 1st, Olive Barker, of New Hartford, who died 1831, by whom he had son Truman H.,[8] who died 1878, aged 50, leaving one child, Margaret,[9] of Orange, N. J. Married 2d, Eliza Gridley, of Clinton, N. Y.; three children. Adeline,[8] m. Rev. Mr. Peck; both dead, leaving one son Henry,[9] who graduated Amherst College, 1878. Olive,[8] married D. W. Hammond, of Independence, Iowa. They had a son and daughter.

ii. William N.,[7] b. Oct. 1, 1804; removed and settled in Warren, Ohio; m. Mary Ann Higby, of Canandaigua, N. Y. Children: Charlotte,[8] married Dr. Jameson, of Warren, Ohio; they have two children. William F.,[8] died in 1877, leaving a wife and two sons, now residing in Warren, Ohio.

iii. Julia Ann,[7] b. Feb. 2, 1809; married Horace Bigelow, of Waterville, N. Y., Feb. 2, 1830; he died July 29, 1871. Children: Horace P.,[8] grad. Hamilton College, 1861; teller and director in National Bank. Laura A.,[8] m. C. C. Bigelow, Esq., her cousin, attorney at law, New York city; reside in Mt. Vernon, N. Y., and have two daughters. Dana W.,[8] grad. Hamilton College, 1865; pastor of West Utica Presbyterian Church, of Utica, N. Y.; m. Catharine Huntington, of Auburn, N. Y. They have four daughters and one son.

iv. Edwin,[7] b. Sept. 20, 1814; resides in Morris, Ohio; m. 1st, Cordelia Church. Married 2d, Harriet Spencer, One daughter, Carrie.[8]

549

SAMUEL[7] PORTER, of Seward[6] Porter, born Falmouth, Me., April 10, 1779; married Ann Stover, 1802; he died Nov. 11, 1847. Children:

1021. i. Delia Ann,[8] b. Dec. 15, 1803; m. Joseph Lufkin Dennison, Dec. 5, 1823; she died Aug. 11, 1829. Children: Eliza Freeman,[9] b. Nov. 22, 1824. Samuel Porter,[9] b. Feb. 27, 1826; died July 9, 1850. Delia Ann,[9] b. June 6, 1828; m. Ansel K. Rogers, Oct. 21, 1852.

1022. ii. Jane Mayo,[8] b. Oct. 9, 1805; m. Dr. H. A. C. Prescott, (about 1830); he died Nov. 11, 1832; she died April 29, 1857. Children: Caroline C.,[9] died May, 1832, aged 3 months. Henry,[9] died June, 1850, aged about 20. Charles P.,[9] died Sept. 16, 1854, aged 21.

1023. iii. Eliza Freeman,[8] b. Aug. 31, 1808; died Nov. 2, 1828.

1024. iv. Mary,[8] b. April 3, 1811; m. Joseph W. Tucker, of Boston.

1025. v. Caroline,[8] b. Aug. 3, 1814; m. Randolph A. L. Codman, Esq., attorney at law, of Portland, Me., about 1840; she died about 1853; he survived his wife but a short time. Children: Annie C.,[9] m. Charles Shaw, who died in the south, 1876; she m. 2d, Dr. Swan. Grace,[9] who m. Clinton Furbush, and has four children.

1026. vi. Charles Henry,[8] b. Dec. 6, 1816; died in New Orleans, of yellow fever, about 1841; he entered Bowdoin College in same class with Gov. John A. Andrew, but did not graduate, owing to financial difficulties; he was quite remarkable as a scholar, with fine literary and poetical tastes.

680

JOSEPH P.[7] BROWN, of Joseph[6] Brown, b. Dec. 13, 1801; m. Mary Porter. Children:

i. Charlotte,[8] b. Mar. 3, 1830; m. William E. Noyes. She died Jan. 28, 1859. He married 2d, Alice Wood, and has five children; he is a Baptist minister in Stetson, Maine.

ii. Mehetable J.,[8] b. 1834; m. Arthur W. McKenney, in Abington; she died Aug. 8, 1872; and he has married again.

iii. Willard,[8] b. Jan. 13, 1837; died May 28, 1838.

iv. Joseph Willard,[8] b. Mar. 2, 1839; teacher in Boston; m. Lucia E. Reed.

v. George A.,[8] b. Oct. 14, 1842; m. Ella Reed, and has two children; has a stock farm in Osborn, Mo.

687

MAJOR AMOS[6] STETSON was son of Amos[5] and Experience (French) Stetson, born in Braintree, Mass., Feb. 25, 1777, and resided there; he was a merchant; captain and major of militia; selectman of Braintree from 1814 to 1833, except one year; representative to General Court 1824, 1825, 1830. He was an honest man, and a good citizen; he married Hannah, daughter of Caleb and Mary (Thomas) Hunt, of Weymouth, Jan. 8, 1800; she born 1776; died Jan. 28, 1834, aged 57; he died May 8, 1859, aged 82. Children:

i. Caleb,[7] b. Jan. 6, 1801; the well known merchant and banker of Boston and Braintree; m. Susanna, dau. of Dea. Ebenezer and Susannah, (Bowditch) Hunt, of Weymouth, in 1824; she died.

ii. Amos Warren,[7] b. April 27, 1802; resides Braintree; m. Susanna, dau. of Noah Curtis, Esq., of Quincy, in 1828.

iii. Mary,[7] b. Mar. 27, 1804; m. Joseph Porter, Oct. 22, 1823; she died June 8, 1866; he died Feb. 6, 1878.

iv. **James Aaron,[7] b. 1806; physician, of Quincy, Mass.; m. Abby Brigham, dau. of Josiah Brigham, 1842.**

v. **Rhoda,[7] b. 1808; died 1811.**

vi. **Rhoda Wild,[7] b. Oct. 21, 1812; m. Dea. Henry Hill.**

1288

REV. JONAS[6] PERKINS, an Orthodox clergyman, born in North Bridgewater, Mass., Oct. 15, 1790; son of Josiah[5] and Anna (Reynolds) Perkins; [he a blacksmith, son of Josiah[4] and Abigail (Edson) Perkins, born Oct. 9, 1762; he a blacksmith, and son of Mark[3] and Dorothy (Whipple) Perkins, of Bridgewater, born Jan. 4, 1727; he a blacksmith, and son of Luke[2] and Martha (Conant) Perkins, born Sept. 17, 1695, of Plympton, Ipswich, Wenham, Beverly, Marble-head, and Hampton, N. H.; he a blacksmith, and probably youngest child of Abraham and Mary Perkins, of Hampton, N. H., born 1664.] He was a man of remarkable ingenuity and mechanical talent. Old Capt. Thomas Thompson, the next neighbor of his father, who made spinning wheels, large and small, for cotton and flax, for all the country around about Bridgewater, used often to tell that when "Jonas was just out of petticoats, all the little brooks near his father's house run all sorts of mills, and all sorts of gear were attached to innumerable wind mills, which buzzed so loud that no one could sleep in a windy night." His father thought his son wasted too much time, but when he believed that his "perpetual motion was sure to succeed," he gave up to the boy to operate as much as he pleased.

In 1804, *he invented a power loom.* In 1806 he wove his mother some towels by only turning a crank. His inventions were the wonder of every one in the vicinity of his home. In 1807, when about to leave home, he packed his machinery in a barrel, making his mother promise not to show it to any one. Not long after two *very* polite gentlemen rode up in a nice chaise, and overpersuaded her to show them the proofs of her son's genius. She finally consented, and they spent nearly two hours in looking it over. Years after, when she told the circumstances to her son, she said that at the time "she thought it took them a good while!" When in college, which he entered as a sophomore, in 1810, he called on Mr. Slater, the great manufacturer, at Pawtucket, and talked with him about the importance of such a loom. After some conversation, during which Mr. Slater asked him where he lived, and the names of his parents, Mr. Perkins began to declare that he had accomplished the fact, and invented a power loom; whereupon Mr. Slater drew himself up to his full height, and said, "Do you think you, a little Yankee, can do what all England has been trying to do for centuries?" Upon this the young man felt insulted, and left. Whether Slater or some other man sent emissaries to discover the secret of the invention is not known; but Mr. Perkins always said that the first power loom he saw in operation *had some clumsy and homely attachments, he had on his only because he had not the materials or means to employ any others*," which he esteemed as proof positive that the looms he saw were patterned directly from his. He never applied for any patent, because the country was in such a confused condition, and he had determined to fit himself for a preacher of the gospel.

I have given the story of his invention, much of it as he used to tell it occasionally to his intimate friends. Thirty years ago it was a matter susceptible of absolute proof. It is not now too late to give him the credit due him for his invention. Judge Mitchell, in his History of Bridgewater, page 59, says:

"The Hon. Hugh Orr, * * * invited Robert and Alexander Barr, brothers, from Scotland, to construct carding, spinning and roping machines, at his works in East Bridgewater; and the General Court, Nov. 16, 1786, (Mr. Orr himself then being one of the Senate,) allowed them two hundred pounds for their ingenuity. * * * These were the first machines of the kind ever made in this country. Mr. Slater, with the late Mr. Moses Brown, of Providence, came to examine them on Mr. Slater's first arrival in the country, and before he had commenced any establishment of the kind. The circumstances of the visit were communicated to the writer, (Judge Mitchell,) by Mr. Brown himself, who at the same time added that these were the first machines of the kind ever made in the United States."

So that it is possible that not only the spinning machine, but the power loom also, came from Bridgewater. At the age of seventeen, Mr. Perkins commenced fitting for college at Phillips Academy, Andover; having from the time of his conversion, at ten, intended to devote himself to the christian ministry. He graduated with distinguished honor at Brown University, in 1813; studied theology with Rev. Otis Thompson, of Rehoboth; was licensed by Mendon Association, Oct. 11, 1814. On the second day of January, 1815, he was engaged to preach for the Union Religious Society, of Weymouth and Braintree, for three months, at the rate of five hundred dollars a year salary. His ministrations were so acceptable that before his time of service expired, the church and society gave him a unanimous call for settlement, which he accepted, and was ordained June 14, 1815.

"The pastorate of Rev. Mr. Perkins, covering as it did, forty-six years of active service, with fifteen added years upon the retired list, was long and successful; resulting in great good to the church and society, increasing largely their material as well as spiritual strength, adding to the membership of the church, principally during three powerful revivals, three hundred and twenty-two members.

Consecrating his whole powers to the work of the gospel ministry, uniting in himself ripe scholarship, excellent judgment, with firmness of purpose, and the strictest integrity, his was a character of the most admirable proportions. A wise and faithful pastor, he was eminently a peacemaker—and when at the full age of seventy years, in accordance with long expressed plans, he resigned his office and retired from its duties, he carried with him the affection and respect, not only of his own church and society, but that of the whole community where he lived.*"

Sept. 16, 1860, he offered his resignation, to take effect on Oct. 15 following,—and Oct. 21 he preached his farewell sermon,—taking for his text, Ephesians IV: II. "He gave some apostles, and some prophets, and some evangelists, and some pastors and teachers."

He was twice offered a professorship of mathematics in one of the colleges of New England, but declined because he thought it his duty to continue in the ministry.

---

* Church Manual.

He continued to live at the old homestead in East Braintree, until his death, June 26, 1874.

Upon the monument which his children erected over his remains, in the Weymouth cemetery, is inscribed the following, taken from his written farewell to his family:

"With great satisfaction I testify, that, in the doctrines of grace which I have uniformly preached during all my ministry, I have unswerving faith as being taught in the Holy Scriptures."

And also the following:

"Descended from a pious ancestry, he became a hopeful subject of divine grace at the age of ten years, and ever after maintained a consistent religious character; was pious and gentle, self denying and generous in private life; and wise, faithful, loving, earnest and successful as a minister of Christ." "He walked with God."

He married Rhoda,[6] daughter of Simeon and Molly[5] (Cary) Keith,* of Bridgewater, June 12, 1815; she was born Feb. 16, 1790, and died at the old homestead, in Braintree, Mar. 22, 1878. She was in every situation the model woman, wife, mother and friend. Her husband, in a note preliminary to his will, wrote:

"With devout gratitude I reflect on the many years I have lived with my beloved wife, whose fidelity and kindness, counsels and labors, have done me good all the days of my life; with whom I have so many times walked to the house of God in company, and enjoyed sweet communion at the table of our blessed Lord." Children:

i. Mary Ann,[7] b. April 2, 1816; m. Rev. Daniel Wight, Jr., of Scituate, April 28, 1851; died Oct. 26, 1853.

ii. Martha Bond,[7] b. Dec. 20, 1817; married 1st, John Vickery, March 31, 1841; resided in Weymouth, Mass., Fishkill, and Rochester, N. Y., where he died Feb. 3, 1863. She married 2d, Hon. John W. Loud, of Weymouth, Mass., Aug. 24, 1865; he died April 22, 1874. She now resides at the old homestead in East Braintree, Mass.

---

*NOTE.—Her father was the son of Nathan[3] and Hannah (Snell) Keith, born Jan. 19, 1749. He the son of Timothy[2] and Hannah (Fobes) Keith, b. Dec. 16, 1714. He the son of Rev. James[1] and Susannah (Edson) Keith—Mr. Keith being the first minister of Bridgewater. Her mother was the daughter of Col. Simeon[4] and Mary (Howard) Cary, born July 7, 1755. He son of Dea. Recompense[3] and Mary (Crossman) Cary, born Dec. 6, 1719. He son of Jonathan[2] and Sarah (Allen) Cary. He son of John[1] and Elizabeth (Godfrey) Cary, born Sept. 24, 1656—all these being of Bridgewater.

iii. Josiah,[7] b. Dec. 31, 1819; resides Weymouth; married Hannah Ayers Kingman, Nov. 20, 1850.

iv. Jonas Reynolds,[7] b. Feb. 18, 1822; grad. Brown University, 1841; studied law with Timothy Coffin, at New Bedford, and practiced law there; Sept., 1849, he sailed from Boston for California; returning, arrived at New York, July 1, 1852; resumed practice of law at North Bridgewater, (now Brockton,) Mass; appointed Judge of First District Court, Plymouth County, June 16, 1874. Married 1st, Jane Avery Holmes, of New Bedford, June 22, 1854; she died July 31, 1858. Married 2d, Mary Elisabeth Sawyer, of Boston, Oct. 26, 1859.

v. Nahum Simeon Cary,[7] b. June 19, 1824; married Mrs. Mary Moon, of Providence, R. I., Nov. 25, 1845; machinist and manufacturer; resides Norwalk, Ohio; elder in the Presbyterian church.

vi. Rhoda Keith,[7] b. Nov. 3, 1826; grad. Mount Holyoke Female Seminary; m. Joseph W. Porter, Jan. 5, 1851; died in Burlington, Maine, Nov. 30, 1875.

vii. Sidney Keith Bond,[7] b. April 14, 1830; grad. Amherst College, 1851; studied theology at Bangor, Me., Theological Seminary, graduating 1857; Congregational clergyman; a successful pastor at Glover, Vermont, 18 years; removed to South Royalton, Vt., 1876. Married Laura L. Brocklebank, of Meriden, N. H.

117

Micah[5] Porter, of Richard[4] Porter, born Dec. 21, 1742; he died in Canaan, N. H., 1811; his widow died in Jan., 1830. Children, all born in Weymouth:

312. iv. Noah—— (Mrs. Harriet Withington, West Newton, Mass.)
315. vii. Betsey, m. Brackley Shaw; (Mrs. Dorinda Shaw, Rockland, Mass.)

310

Elias[6] Porter, of Micah[5] Porter, born Weymouth, Jan. 14, 1769; he removed to Canaan, N. H., between 1797 and 1800; thence to Raymond, N. H., 1832–3; thence to Hanover, Mich., in 1846; he died at the home of his son Micah, in Sharon, Mich., about 1848; he married Sarah Bates, of Weymouth, 1792; she died in 1847, aged about 80. Children, as near as I am able to give them:

i. Micah,[7] born S. P., Weymouth, Nov. 10, 1793.
ii. Daniel,[7] born S. P., Weymouth, Sept. 6, 1796; settled in Hanover, Mich., and afterward removed to Iowa.
iii. Alfred,[7] born S. P., Weymouth, Oct. 8, 1797.
iv. William,[7] lived in New York.
v. Sarah,[7] died young; unmarried.
vi. Mary,[7] married Daniel Willard, in Raymond, N. H., and died there.
vii. Elisabeth,[7] married Hiram Sargent, in Raymond, N. H.; she died August, 1846; they had four children, of whom Mr. W. H. Sargent, of Portland, Me., is the only one now living.

319

William[6] Porter, of Micah[5] Porter, born June 11, 1782; died in Pleasantville, Venango county, Penn., very aged. Sons:

i. Rev. Samuel[7] Porter, of Crete, Ill.
ii. William[7] Porter; has a son, William.[8]

322

Hon. Reuben[6] Porter, of Micah[5] Porter, born Weymouth, Mass., Aug. 2, 1790; was in Warner, N. H., 1812; studied medicine with Dr. Moses Long, which he practised for a few years; then went into trade; removed to Sutton, N. H., in March, 1822, and went to farming; he was a representative to the Legislature from Sutton, 1826, 1827 and 1828, and a senator in 1833 and 1834; returned to Warner in 1850, where he now resides; married in Warner, Aug. 24, 1813, Abigail Evans, born April 30, 1796. Children:

i. Mary Stockbridge,[7] b. Jan. 15, 1814.
ii. Susan Evans,[7] b. Nov. 10, 1816; died in Sutton, N. H., Mar. 8, 1853.
iii. William,[7] b. June 30, 1819; resides at Warner, N. H.
iv. Benjamin Evans,[7] b. April 19, 1821; died in Mexico, Aug. 22, 1847.
v. Reuben,[7] b. April 6, 1823; died in Sutton, Feb. 10, 1830.

vi. Edward Granville,[7] b. July 7, 1825; died in Sutton, Aug. 12, 1858; m. Sophia G. Harvey, of Sutton, about 1848. Children: Benjamin E.,[8] and Sarah G.,[8] of Lynn, Mass.

vii. Abigail Evans,[7] b. Jan. 4, 1828; died at Springfield, N. H., Jan. 5, 1856; m. Valentine Manahan, M. D., of New London, N. H. No children. Dr. Manahan now resides in Enfield, N. H.

viii. Margaretta Rowan,[7] b. Sept. 28, 1830; died in Lynn, Jan. 23, 1874; m. Joseph Brackett, of Lynn. One daughter.

ix. Hannah Loud,[7] b. Sept. 21, 1832; m. Robert Wadleigh, of Sutton, 1857; he died in Louisiana, 1863. One son, Thomas Edward,[8] b. July 4, 1858; died Sept. 12, 1878.

x. Micah,[7] b. Jan. 6, 1835; died Sutton, Oct. 17, 1856.

xi. Harriet W.,[7] b. June 10, 1838; died June 8, 1875, in Warner; m. J. B. Philbrick, of Deerfield, N. H., Oct. 21, 1862. They had one daughter Meribah,[8] now residing at Nottingham, N. H. He died at Warner, Oct. 2, 1863. She married 2d, Harrison W. Bartlett, of Nottingham, Oct. 31, 1869. They had one son: Jerome B.,[8] b. Aug. 26, 1870; died Mar. 8, 1872.

xii. Henrietta W.,[7] b. June 10, 1838; died in Lebanon, Me., Aug. 9, 1878; married James W. Baker, of Epping, N. H., Feb., 1875. One son, James Edward,[8] b. June 16, 1878.

xiii. Reuben Benton,[7] b. May 31, 1840; found dead in the woods, near Windham Junction, N. H.; probably died March, 1878; m. Fanny Carner, of Greenbush, N. Y. Children: Abby,[8] and Sarah,[8] living in Concord, N. H.

xiv. Jerome Bonapart,[7] b. April 18, 1844; died in Warner, June 25, 1870.

626

Hon. Micah[7] Porter, of Elias[6] Porter, born in Weymouth, Aug. 23, 1793, and baptised at South Parish church, Nov. 10, 1793; his father soon after removed to Canaan, N. H.; he left home at the age of twenty, with eleven dollars, to fight his way through life for himself; and the first money he earned was for teaching school, in Herkimer county, New York. He was a mason by trade, and in March, 1819, removed to Toronto, Canada West, going around Lake Ontario from Rome, N. Y., in a cutter. At Toronto he erected the Parliament buildings, and many elegant private residences. At Rome, New York, he had with his uncle erected the United States Arsenal. From Toronto he removed to the village (now city) of Rochester, N. Y., in 1821–2, where he continued until June, 1832, when he removed to the Territory of Michigan, and settled on a farm in Dexter, (now Sharon,) in that State. He was one of the first justices of the peace appointed by the Governor of the Territory; supervisor of the town, 1842; and a member of the Legislature in 1843. In the language of "the craft," he was a "speculative mason," besides being an "operative mason;" while a resident of Toronto, he made the entire circuit of

Lake Ontario as a visiting member among the lodges of the fraternity, during which time he presided at the initiation of a son of Brant, the noted Indian chief.

While in Rochester, in 1827, occurred the abduction of William Morgan, followed by the anti-masonic excitement. It was a reign of terror in that region. Wives left their husbands, children their fathers; fathers disinherited their sons; churches dismissed their pastors; masons were excluded from juries, and from participating in public business. During all these times, Mr. Porter, living in the vicinity and knowing all the circumstances, steadfastly adhered to the sublime teachings of the order, and connected with it the graces and virtues of a Christian life. He united with the Presbyterian church in Rochester, N. Y., in 1826. His life of discipleship was not a passive one; to his faith he added works; he seemed to realize fully that he was a steward here below, and that God's visible church needed systematic business members. He and his first wife were of the seventeen original members of the Presbyterian church, at Manchester, Mich., founded Dec. 26, 1835. He afterwards worshipped at Grass Lake, Mich. Finally, feeling the need of a church nearer home, and as the town became populated, he made it his delight and pleasure to put his whole heart to the work of erecting the Congregational church in Sharon, Mich., which was finished from turret to foundation stone, paid for and dedicated to the worship of God, before there was a society organized to worship in it. That edifice, close to where he now sleeps, is the best and most sacred monument that could be erected to his memory, and stands there as a testimony of his untiring energy and Christian activity. He was strong without anger, decided without dogmatism, firm without obstinacy, and earnest without fanaticism. After arriving at the age of seventy, feeling the burden and care of a large farm too much for him, he sold it, and moved to the village of Manchester, near Sharon, in 1863, where he worshipped in the church of which he was an original member. During his long and painful sickness, he evinced an abiding and clear faith in Christ Jesus as his only hope of eternal life. He died July 7th, 1870, and on the 9th of July his remains were taken to Sharon, where, after an impressive discourse by his pastor, Rev. J. Gordon Jones, his Masonic brethren committed them to the grave "in due form." He was married first, in 1817. Children:

i. Charles B.,[8] dentist, Ann Arbor, Mich.
ii. Byron R.,[8] resides Foristell, Miss.
iii. George,[8] settled in Valparaiso, Ind., and died there, Feb. 20, 1870, leaving two daughters and a son.

RICHARD PORTER.

ALTERATIONS AND ADDITIONS.

Page 88, No. 406—Dillaway, not Dilloway.

Page 88, No. 408—Mr. Adams graduated Bowdoin College. Mrs. Adams still living.

Page 89—Mrs. Hall resides at West Newton.

Page 89, No. 411—Studied theology at Yale Divinity School; resides near Lonsdale, R. I.; married Betsey W. Arnold.

Page 90, No. 414—Was a Presbyterian minister.

Page 90, No. 415—Elvina, not Elvira. Dr. Weeks graduated Bowdoin College.

Page 120, No. 1304—Sylvanus P. Freeman.

Page 120, No. 1306—Daniell, not Daniels. He born in Boston, not Roxbury.

Page 140, No. 1517—Teacher Boston Grammar School, 19 years; graduated New York Female College, 1878; resides Boston.

Page 183, No. 2017—Aristeen A., not Aristun.

Page 183, No. 1440—First child's name, Harvey W.

Page 184, No. 2020—James Bullard.

Page 183, No. 2018—Married Marietta Story, of Lansing, October 15, 1878.

Page 184, No. 2019—William Hubbard,[9] born Aug. 23, 1852; of firm of Baker & Porter, furniture dealers, Lansing; married Elnora L. Morehouse, at Litchfield, Ohio, Feb. 4, 1872. Children: Florence,[10] born Aug. 28, 1875. Walter Ford,[10] b. Sept. 8, 1877.

Page 188, No. 1509—Resides Auburndale.

Page 188, No. 2023—Graduated Wesleyan University, Conn., 1869; graduated Harvard Medical School, 1873; went to Europe to pursue his studies in Vienna, Paris, London, and Edinburgh; returned in 1874, and settled in Somerville; now resides in Newton; married Christine W. Taylor, Oct. 14, 1876.

Page 189, No. 2027—Lewis B. Porter, manufacturer of patent needle machinery, Auburndale, Mass.

Page 190, No. 1515—Not of Lexington.

Page 190, No. 2046—Lotta, not Charlotte.

Page 190, No. 2050—Agnes Jarvis, not Lucy Gardner.

Page 207—7th and 8th lines, read "unwavering" for "unswerving"; and 12th line, read "was *pure* and gentle."

4

JOHN VINING,—(Page 14.)

Cooper; lived in Weymouth; selectman several years. In 1660, cut thatch contrary to law; in 1672, administrator with his sister Sarah, on Thomas Porter's estate; in 1676, testified that he was about 40 years old. Married 1st, Margaret, daughter of William Reed, 11th 3d mo., 1657, by Capt. Torrey; she died Aug. 6, 1659. Married 2d, Mary, daughter of Phillip Reed, 22d 11th mo., 1659; probably cousin of his first wife. He died 1685; his will dated Jan. 18, proved Feb. 17; witnessed by Deliverance Porter, James Lovell, and Thomas Dyer. Names in it wife Mary, oldest son John, George, Samuel, Benjamin, Jane, Sarah, Hannah, and Margaret; John Holbrook, kinsman, and Joseph Dyer, overseers. Some of children under age. "Widow Mary Vining, died Sept. 2, 1717." Children, the last not in order:

2. i. John,[2] born April 15, 1662.
3. ii. Mary,[2] born June 18, 1664; died before her father.
4. iii. Thomas,[2] born Oct. 30, 1667; died before his father.
5. iv. Samuel,[2] born Oct. 2, 1670.
6. v. Jane,[2] born July 2, 1672; married Jacob Turner, 1692; he died Nov. 29, 1728; widow probably married Samuel Allen, July 12, 1728.
7. vi. Margaret,[2] born March 19, 1682.
8. vii. Benjamin,[2] born July 22, 1684.
9. viii. George.[2]
10. ix. Hannah.[2]
11. x. Sarah,[2] married Nicholas Whitmarsh, Jr., 1700.

2

John[2] Vining, Jr., b. April 15, 1662; died Jan. 11, 1737; lived in Weymouth; married Naomi——; she died Sept. 11, 1719. He admitted S. P. ch., June 18, 1732. Children:

12. i. John,[3] b. Feb. 17, 1688.
13. ii. Mary,[3] b. March 25, 1690; m. Ephraim Richards,—pub. Oct. 1, 1715; she died April 22, 1718. He married 2d, Sarah Bates, 1719, and died 1751.

5

Samuel,[2] of John,[1] born Feb. 2, 1670; lived in Weymouth; married Sarah——; she died Feb. 3, 1721. Children:

14. i. Samuel,[3] b. Oct. 25 1701.
15. ii. Sarah,[3] b. July 4, 1704.
16. iii. Ann.[3]

9

George,[2] of John,[1] born——; died Mar. 27, 1723; lived in Weymouth; married Hannah Judkins, Oct. 10, 1700, by John Wilson, Esq. Children:

17. i. Thomas,[3] b. Sept. 14, 1703.
18. ii. Elisha,[3] died Abington, 1799, aged 85.
19. iii. Hannah,[3] she or mother died April 14, 1820.
20. iv. George.[3]

12

John,[3] of John,[2] born Jan. 17, 1688; died July 27, 1746; lived in Weymouth; selectman, 1729, '35, '38, '45. Married Elisabeth, dau. of James Richards,—great granddaughter of Richard[1] Porter, 1710. Children:

21. i. Benjamin,[4] b, Feb. 24, 1711.
22. ii. John.[4] b. April 16, 1713.
23. iii. Richard,[4] b. Sept. 12, 1715.
24. iv. Mary,[4] b. April 9, 1717; m. Gideon Parkman, Aug. 21, 1734; removed to Abington.
25. v. Joseph,[4] b. June 23, 1723; died Jan. 27, 1724.
26. vi. Ruth,[4] b. Nov. 1, 1725; m. Jonathan Joy, Dec. 12, 1745.
27. vii. Lydia,[4] b. Nov. 27, 1728; m. John Hunt, March 17, 1748.
28. viii. Betty,[4] b. Jan. 9, 1721.

17

Thomas,[3] of George,[2] born Sept. 14, 1703; lived in Weymouth; m. Hannah, of John Randall, July 25, 1727. Children:

29. i. Susanna,[4] b. July 9, 1728.
30. ii. Josiah,[4] b. Dec. 8, 1729; m. Abagail Dawes, of Bridgewater, 1751.
31. iii. Hannah,[4] b. Nov. 10, 1731.
32. iv. Mary or Mercy,[4] b. April 5, 1734.
33. v. John Randall,[4] b. July 4, 1736.
34. vi. Benjamin,[4] b. Nov. 16, 1738,—probably of Durham, Me.
35. vii. Sarah,[4] b. Nov. 9, 1741.
36. viii. Jonas,[4] b. March 17, 1744; (?) bap. N. P., Mar. 18, 1743.
37. ix. Elisabeth,[4] b. Sept. 21, 1746.

20

George,[3] of George,[2] lived in Weymouth, and Norton; m. Ruth, dau. of Jonathan Darby, Dec. 3, 1741. Children:

38. i. Abner,[4] b. Weymouth, Oct. 20, 1742; died Jan. 20, 1743.
39. ii. Abner,[4] b. Weymouth, Nov. 16, 1743.
40. iii. Ruth,[4] b. Weymouth, Feb. 7, 1745; probably m. Lemuel Bicknell, Sept. 4, 1760.
41. iv. Leah,[4] b. Weymouth, Feb. 17, 1747; died in Norton, June 29, 1750.
42. v. Eli,[4] b. Weymouth, Feb. 17, 1749; died in Norton, June 30, 1750.
43. vi. Eli,[4] b. Norton, Jan. 23, 1752.
44. vii. George,[4] b. Norton, Dec. 24, 1754.

21

Benjamin,[4] of John,[3] born 1711; lived South Weymouth; married Hannah, daughter of Samuel[3] Pratt, Nov. 30, 1732. Children:

45. i. Benjamin,[5] b. Feb. 27, 1734; died the same day.
46. ii. Abner,[5] twin with Benjamin; b. Feb. 27, 1734; died the same day.
47. iii. Hannah,[5] b. May 19, 1735.
48. iv. Naomi,[5] b. Feb. 12, 1738; married Thomas Bates, Jan. 23, 1755.
49. v. Lucy,[5] b. April 10, 1741; m. William Loud, published June 4, 1761.
50. vi. Joseph,[5] b. May 6, 1744.
51. vii. Benjamin,[5] b. June 14, 1747.
52. viii. Betty,[5] b. March 23, 1751.

22

Major John,[4] of John,[3] born April 16, 1713; lived in South Weymouth; married Sarah, daughter of James Beal, July 20, 1735. She died Oct. 24, 1764. Children:

53. i. Sarah,[5] born Oct. 5, 1736; m. Jona. Hunt, July 2, 1761.
54. ii. Elisabeth,[5] born Oct. 30, 1738.
55. iii. Jerusha,[5] born Aug. 3, 1742; married Abner Holbrook, Nov. 3, 1763; she died 1819, aged 79; he died May 31, 1788, aged 48.
56. iv. James,[5] born Aug. 15, 1744; died Aug. 17, 1746.
57. v. Miriam,[5] born March 18, 1747.
58. vi. Mary,[5] born Nov. 19, 1749.
59. vii. John,[5] born June 6, 1752; died Sept. 13, 1765.
60. viii. Sarah,[5] born April 16, 1765.
61. ix. Lydia,[5] died June 9, 1761.

23

Richard,[4] of John[3] b. Sept. 12, 1715; lived S. Weymouth; m. Lydia, dau. of Benj. Allen, of Bridgewater, Feb. 17, 1737. He probably died 1790; she 1800. Children:

62. i. Mehetable,[5] b. Aug. 9, 1738; died young.
63. ii. David,[5] b. Sept. 25, 1740.
64. iii. Richard,[5] bap. S. P., 1748.
65. iv. Hitty,[5] b. Oct. 13, 1751; died young.
66. v. Hitty,[5] b. Nov. 24, 1752; died young.
67. vi. Lydia,[5] bap. S. P., June 3, 1753.
68. vii. Nehemiah,[5] b. July 3, 1765; m. Deborah Ward, 1785.
69. viii. Mehetable,[5] m. Samuel Porter, July 6, 1783.

30

Josiah,[4] of Thomas,[3] born Dec. 8, 1729; lived in Norton; joined church there, 1764. Married Abigail Dawes, of Bridgewater, 1751. Children:

70. i. Josiah,[5] b. July 21, 1759.
71. ii. John Randall,[5] b. July 26, 1761.
72. iii. Child,[6] b. Jan. 16, 1764.
73. iv. Abigail,[5] b. Jan. 2, 1766.

50

Joseph,[5] of Benjamin,[4] born May 6, 1744; m. Olive Torrey, Jan. 9, 1766. Children, born Weymouth:

74. i. Joseph,[6] b. Nov. 26, 1766; married Susanna, of Matthew Porter, Sept. 25, 1787; removed Plainfield.
75. ii. Betty,[6] b. Feb. 4, 1770.
76. iii. James,[6] b. Feb. 10, 1779; m. Lucy Cushing, Nov. 4, 1799.

63

David,[5] of Richard,[4] b. Sept. 25, 1740; died 1830; aged 90; lived South Weymouth; m. Lydia Torrey, Nov. 25, 1762. Children:

77. i. Vashti,[6] b. July 1, 1764; died July 15.
78. ii. Olive,[6] b. May 16, 1765; died aged 85.
79. iii. Richard,[6] b. Oct. 13, 1766; prob. m. Susan Pratt, Aug. 29, 1793.
80. iv. Asa,[6] b. Jan. 12, 1769.
81. v. David,[6] b. Jan. 22, 1771; m. Lydia Hunt; published July 10, 1796.
82. vi. Bela,[6] bap. S. P., July 21.
83. vii. Sally,[6] b. June 13, 1773; prob. m. Lewis Hayden, Nov. 12, 1805.
84. viii. Bela,[6] b. Mar. 26, 1775. (?)
85. ix. Bela,[6] b. Aug. 8, 1776; m. Content Pratt, Mar. 20, 1799.
86. x. John,[6] b. July 30, 1777; m. Hannah Reed, Dec. 25, 1800.
87. xi. Noah,[6] b. July 30, 1781; died aged 79; m. Mary L. Stoddard, of Hingham, July 16, 1806; parents of Noah, Jr.
88. xii. Lydia,[6] b. Jan. 12, 1783.
89. xiii. Warren,[6] b. Apr. 23, 1785; m. Mary Holbrook, Nov. 24, 1812.
90. xiv. Polly,[6] b. 1787; m. Bela Thayer, Nov. 27, 1806.

NOTE.—John[1] Vining, was probably ancestor of all of the name now in New England. George[2] Vining moved to Abington, where his widow died 1774, aged 100; his descendants now live there.

BROOKS FAMILY.

1288

GEORGE[1] BROOKS, was born in Bradford, (near Yoville,) England, about eighty miles from London, 1754. His brothers and sisters were John, James, Thomas, Elisabeth and Mary. In 1771, his father being dead, and his mother living, he left England and went to Newfoundland, into the fishing trade; he spent the next winter there, and the next summer commenced whaling with Capt. Doane, of Cape Cod—afterward living at Wellfleet, Mass. March 4th, 1776, he married widow Mary (Atwood) Thompson. She was widow of John Thompson, to whom she was married Oct. 11, 1768, and daughter of Richard and Mary Atwood, of Eastham, Wellfleet part, born Aug. 16, 1749. She had by Thompson, three children:

- i. Hannah, m. Wm. Murch, of Hampden, Me.; grandparents of T. H. Murch, M. C. from 5th Me. District.
- ii. Nancy, m. Ezekiel Cobb, of Hampden, Me.
- iii. Mary, m. 1st, Nath. Harding; and 2d, Levi Young, both of Hampden, Me.

Mr. Brooks removed to Orrington, Maine, 1776-7, where he died Dec. 5, 1807; his widow married, third, Deacon Mark Hatch, of Castine, July, 1814, and died there Sept. 2, 1817, aged 68. The children of George and Mary Brooks, all born in Orrington, were:

- 2\. i. Elisabeth,[2] b. Dec. 14, 1777; m. Capt. Daniel Snow, Oct. 13, 1793.
- 3\. ii. John Thompson,[2] b. Dec. 4, 1778; m. Sallie Dean, Jan. 1, 1801.
- 4\. iii. Martha,[2] b. Dec. 4, 1780; m. Henry Dillingham.

5. iv. Joanna,[2] b. Mar. 8, 1783; m. Capt. Jeremiah Simpson, June 1, 1801.

6. v. Abigail,[2] b. Mar. 4, 1785; m. Ellen Hodges, Mar. 10, 1805.

7. vi. Deborah A.,[2] b. April 10, 1887; m. Thos. Snow, Esq., of Frankfort, May 19, 1817.

8. vii. James,[2] b. Feb. 14, 1789; m. Elisabeth T. Bartlett, Aug. 18, 1814.

9. viii. Thomas,[2] b. April, 1791; died 1793.

10. ix. Lucy,[2] b. April, 1793; died 1794.

8

James[2] Brooks, of George[1] Brooks, b. Feb. 14, 1789; lived in Orrington, Me. A most worthy, upright, estimable man, who had the confidence and respect of all who knew him. He married Elizabeth Taylor Bartlett, Aug. 18, 1814; she daughter of Capt. Samuel and Joanna (Taylor) Bartlett, of Orrington, b. Nov. 24, 1794.* He died March 16, 1868, aged 80 years. Children, all born in Orrington:

i. George,[3] b. June 21, 1815; married.

ii. Joanna Bartlett,[3] b. Mar. 31, 1817; died June 19, 1834.

iii. Mary Hatch,[3] b. Aug. 11, 1819; m. Atkins R. Nickerson, of Orrington, Oct. 29, 1839; he died.

iv. Elizabeth Taylor,[3] b. Oct. 29, 1821; m. Capt. Simeon E. Fowler, of Orrington, July 14, 1845; he died. Married 2d, Dr. Lewis Watson, of Bangor, June 23, 1857.

v. Susan Bartlett,[3] b. Dec. 1, 1823; m. Capt. Albert B. Wyman, at Orrington, Jan. 6, 1848; he died in Brooklyn, N. Y., 1877.

vi. Caroline Smith,[3] b. Aug. 15, 1825; m. E. Newton Fowler, of Orrington, Dec. 31, 1848.

vii. Hannah Jane,[3] b. Jan. 19, 1829; m. Robert Hatton, of Hampden, Dec. 22, 1846; he died. She married 2d, Jeremiah S. Paine, at Orrington, April 21, 1853; resides Brewer, Me.

viii. Edward James,[3] b. Dec. 27, 1830; m. Belle M. Sackett, of New Albany, Ind., June 8, 1869; resides there.

ix. Emily Prudence,[3] b. Nov. 25, 1832; m. Joseph H. Kaler, of Belfast, Me., Nov. 23, 1854; resides there.

---

*Samuel Bartlett was son of William and Mary (Bartlett) Bartlett, of Plymouth, Mass., born there July 24, 1757; died in Orrington, Mar. 24, 1836, aged 78 years and 8 months; his wife, Joanna Taylor, b. in Plymouth, Mass., daughter of Jacob and Jemima (Sampson) Taylor, b. Aug. 11, 1761; died in Orrington, Oct. 4, 1844, aged 83 years.

x. Alonzo Scudder,[3] b. Feb. 7, 1835; m. M. C. Wilson, of Bardstown, Kentucky, June 20, 1861; and died there.

xi. Samuel Bartlett,[3] b. Nov. 19, 1837.

xii. Joanna Bartlett,[3] b. Nov. 19, 1837; died Jan. 3, 1838.

xiii. Rose Abby,[3] b. April 22, 1840; m. Capt. Henry B. Nickerson, of Orrington, at Chelsea, Mass., July 16, 1865; he lost on coast of South America. Married 2d, Joseph W. Porter, at Bangor, Me., May 5, 1877, by Prof. W. M. Barbour.

George[3] Brooks, of James[2] Brooks, born June 21, 1815; resides Orrington; married 1st, Corilla Nickerson, Oct. 13, 1842; died Aug. 19, 1843, aged 27. Married 2d, Mrs. Lydia B. Hopkins, Jan. 22, 1845; died Oct. 20, 1856, aged 41. Married 3d, Caroline J. Nickerson, May 18, 1858; died Nov. 14, 1860, aged 31. Married 4th, Priscilla Nash, of Addison, Me., March 5th, 1862. Children:

i. George Henry,[4] b. Nov. 14, 1860; died Nov. 25, 1860.

ii. George Willis,[4] b. Jan. 3, 1863; died 1876.

iii. Edward Alonzo,[4] b. July 30, 1865; died Sept. 8, 1865.

iv. Harrison Nash,[4] b. Sept. 10, 1867.

v. James,[4] b. Feb. 13, 1872.

vi. Bartlett,[4] b. 1874.

CHRISTIAN NAMES

OF

RICHARD PORTER'S DESCENDANTS.

A

B

C

D

E

F

G

H

T

U

W

Z

SURNAMES OF PERSONS

WHO HAVE

INTERMARRIED WITH THE PORTERS, (OF RICHARD.)

A

Adams, 408, 1312, 1009, 1794. Alden, 195, 344, 1321, 1348, 1356, 1357. Allen, 1072, 1117. Ames, 431, 936, 658. Amsden, 1218. Andros, 249. Andrews, 525, 1718. Arnold, 411, 1395, 1233. Atherton, 308, 1871. Atwood, 56, 1013. Austin, 1664. Ayers, 1265.

B

Bacon, 1396, 1249, 1504. Bailey, 3, 1420. Bates, 37, 70, 93, 233, 271, 310, 378, 506, 641, 914, 979. Baker, 186, 1252. Badlam, 276. Ball, 836. Baldwin, 830, 1757. Barker, 652, 790. Barbour, 266, 266, 1056. Barber, 76, 211. Barrows, 152, 365, 1331. Barnes, 864. Barrett, 1090. Bartlett, 580, 987, 1353, 1546. Barnicoat, 753. Barnard, 1426. Battles 338, 744. Beal, 45, 113, 114, 346, 152, 210, 791, 833, 1230. Bean, 587. Bearce, 1394. Bellinger, 775. Bennett, 530. Belcher, 671. Bicknell, 5, 134, 504, 648. Bisbee, 99, 766, 1202. Blake, 654, 939, 1298. Blakely, 972. Bluxsom, 1720. Boldry, 1365. Borland, 840, 1487. Bostwick, 999, 1003. Bonney, 1625. Boyd, 1043. Boyer, 1311. Bradlee, 993. Bradish, 1297. Bradford, 61. Bradbury, 294. Brastow, 343. Bray, 951. Briggs, 371, 962. Breed, 1253. Brown, 557, 812, 813. Brooks, 880, 1288. Bryant, 206, 1350. Buchanan, 1066. Burbank, 1506. Burchstead, 1514. Burnham, 1207. Burgess, 824. Burrill, 82, 130, 138, 213, 296. Burr, 381. Bullard, 385, 1332. Butler, 440. Buxton, 1513. Byrum, 2, 1408. Byington, 961.

C

Calden, 939. Campbell, 968. Carroll, 914. Capen, 337, 658. Catlin, 970. Carver, 515. Chandler, 431. Champney, 782. Chase, 582. Chipman, 145. Chellis, 884. Chamberlain, 1322, 1366, 1367, 1392. Churchill, 702, 1403. Cheesman, 64, 204. Cochrane, 1489. Cole, 589. Collier, 230. Comstock, 399. Colson, 236, 290. Conant, 294.

D

E

F

G

H

P

Q

R

S

T

V

W

Y

JOHN PORTER,

Of Hingham and Salem, (Danvers) tanner, was born in England, probably in Dorset, in 1596. In what ship or at what date he came to New England, I have not learned. Before settling at Hingham, he may have lived for a short time in Boston or Dorchester. Hon. Solomon Lincoln, in his History of Hingham, 1827, page 43, says he was a settler there in 1635. No grant of land is found to him at that date; only the fact, that in one grant made that year at Weary-all (Otis) hill, it was described as "bounded on land of John Porter." Mr. Quincy Bicknell, who is authority in such matters, suggests that the description may have been written at a later period. In the early settlement of Hingham, there were two sets of records—town and proprietors'; the town records gave dates when the votes were passed making a grant; and the proprietors' records, the date when it was completed by the person appearing and taking the same. The first lots were house-lots, thirty in number, and were drawn or granted, Sept. 18, 1635, O. S. In the names of grantees * of these lots, the name of John Porter does not appear. After the house-lots, grants of land for other purposes followed. The house-lots were laid out so as to make as compact a settlement as possible, as a safeguard against Indian attacks. There was a system in laying out the lots: Commencing at a point near the harbor, and laying off on a street called Town Street—(North Street, in 1827) extending westward from the place of beginning, about one mile, and skirting the north side of an

*Of the early grantees of land in Hingham, Edmund Hobart, Sen., Thomas Hobart, Andrew Lane, in 1635, Thomas Josselyn, in 1637, and James Buck, in 1638, were ancestors of the compiler of this work.

irregular swamp, until reaching the head of it, on which they made a short street extending to the south side of the swamp; and then returning on the south side of said swamp to within one-quarter of a mile of the place of beginning, where the street stopped on an arm of the sea. Of the first, twenty-eight were on the north side of the swamp, and two on the head. The office of Quincy Bicknell is now (1878) on the 29th lot. The extent of the street is about one mile in length. The lots on the south side of the swamp were allotted in 1636. Near the easterly termination of the south street, they laid out a street at right angles thereto; and near the junction, on a slight eminence, the first meeting house was built. This last street was extended about one mile from the meeting house. About midway on the street, commenced a plain, and here they laid out an open square, of about fifty acres, which was left for a common or training field. This was in what is now Centre Hingham. On the south and east side of the common, house-lots were granted in 1637 and 1638; on the west side, lots were granted in 1638; on the north-east corner of the common, two house-lots were granted Sept. 1, 1637, the first to William Carlyle, and the second to John Porter. Both these lots, or nearly all of them, are now the property of the Hingham Agricultural and Horticultural Society—the hall of the society being on the Carlyle lot; the John Porter lot fronts on East street, and is probably where he built his first house in New England.

September 2, 1637, there were laid out to John Porter, for a house-lot, 7 acres; 5 acres for a planting lot; 38 acres for a great lot, on the east side of the river; 4 acres of salt marsh at Layford's Liking Meadows; 3 acres of fresh meadow at Crooked Meadows; for a small planting lot, 5 acres at the Plain Neck; 2 acres of salt meadow at Wear Neck; and 2 acres of fresh meadow at Turkey Meadow.

The proprietors of Hingham claimed a portion of Nantasket lands, and made grants of land there March, 1637-8. The ninth lot was granted to John Porter, and contained four acres of upland, and twenty acres of meadow. Nantasket contested the legality of this appropriation of lands, and the General Court, in Sept., 1643, voted that, "The former grant to Nantascot was again voted and confirmed, and Hingham were willed to forbear troubling the Court any more about Nantascot." Hingham afterward made compensation to those who suffered loss by this decision, by granting other lands. In 1640, John Porter was one of a committee to divide Cohasset lands remaining. May 13, 1640, he was appointed by the General Court to value horses, mares, cows, oxen, goats, and hogs, for Hingham. "June 2, 1641, the fine of John Porter, James Ludden, and John Gurney, which they forfeited for want of gunpowder, was remitted by the General Court. Ludden and Gurney were of Weymouth. In 1641, he with others, was chosen to make a rate in Hingham. Also, constable of Hingham. He was deputy to General Court for Hingham, May 20, 1644. He removed to Salem, now Danvers, 1644. A Mary Porter, supposed to be his wife, joined the church there May 5, 1644; but his own name does not appear in the list of members until 1649. May 10, 1643, John Porter, of Hingham, bought of Rev. Samuel Sharp, of Salem, his farm in Salem, lying north of Mr. Skelton's, for 110 pounds, and agreed to pay for it in three installments, viz: May 20, 1643, fifty pounds; May 1, 1644, thirty pounds; May 1, 1645, thirty pounds—but did not pay the last until Jan. 20, 1652.

"John Porter, of Salem, grants unto Nathaniel Baker, of Hingham, his house and lot in Hingham, with all the barnes and outhouses, &c., and all the several parcels of land in Hingham, bought by the said Porter, or granted by the town, date 15, (1) 1648—sealed and delivered in presence of Wm. Aspinwall."

(Suffolk Records, vol. 1, page 101.)

June 29, 1648, he bought of Simon Bradstreet, of Boston, one-third of a farm containing one hundred and eighty acres, which was bought of Abraham Page, late of Boston, tailor. Also, same day, bought of William and Richard Haynes, of Salem, two-thirds of Bishop's farm. In 1650, he bought the farm of Emanuel Downing, in Salem, 500 acres, which in 1663, he gave his son Joseph as a marriage portion. He also made other purchases of lands, so that at the time of his death, he was the largest land holder in Salem village,* his lands lying in what is now Danvers, Salem, Wenham, Topsfield, and Beverly. In a deposition given by him, Nov. 23, 1674, he states that "about 30 years ago I came to live at Salem; that then and ever since, the hemlock tree at the head of Crane's river, was accounted Mr. Bishop's bound." It was near the hemlock bound that Mr. Porter and Mr. Endicott, at some time, built a saw mill, as testified to by Isaac[2] Porter—Mr. Endicott being desired "to speak with Nathaniel Putnam, to give them liberty to droun his land by making use of the saw mill, which was assented to, and the said hemlock by the saw mill was accounted Mr. Bishop's bound." The house which he built and lived in, probably stood on the plains in Danvers, on Sharp's farm, near the site of the Unitarian church, and is said to have been destroyed by fire twenty or thirty years since.

Mr. Porter was a man of energy and influence,—well known in the Colony, and held many official positions,—among which was deputy to General Court, in 1668. He died in Salem village, (now Danvers,) Sept. 6, 1676. In a deposition given in 1669, he stated his age to be 73; in another in 1674, he gave it as 79. His widow Mary, whom he probably married in England, is said by Judge Savage to have died Feb. 6, 1684; while Perley Derby, Esq., eminent authority in Essex county matters, says she was living in 1685.

I give a copy of will of John Porter, from Essex County Records:

In the Name of God Amen. I John Porter of Salim Senr. in the Coun of Essex in New England Yeomn. Do declare and make my last will and testament in manner and forme following. Impr. my imortall soul I do desire humbly and beleiveingly to comitt unto ye everlasting

*Salem was incorporated into a town June 24, 1629. Wenham, part of Salem, incorporated May 10, 1643. Topsfield probably included part of Salem, incorporated Oct. 18, 1650. A part of Salem annexed to Beverly, 1753. Danvers, the village and middle parishes of Salem, and the oldest part thereof, incorporated into a district, Jan. 28, 1752, and a town June 16, 1757.

mercyes of God, Father, Sonne and Holy Ghost, my body I commit to ye earth to be decently buried at the discretion of my x'ian friends. And my outward estate I do dispose thereof in manner following. Impr. I do constitute and ordeine my loveing wife Mary Porter, sole execcutrix of this my will, unto whome I do give the one halfe of all my goods, debts, chattills, & cattell etc. and also during her life I do give her one third pt. of the yearly vallew of all my houses and lands or the thirds thereof as the law directeth. To my Sonne John Porter who by his Rebellious & wicked practises hath been a great greife to his parents, & hath greatly wasted my estate, on condiccons hereafter expressed, I do give unto him one hundred & fifty pounds, in currant pay of ye Country at three paymts annually i. e. fifty pounds p ann. Provided alwayes before the paymnt of any pt. thereof he ye said Jno. Porter shall make, signe, & seale unto my sonnes Joseph, Benjamin & Israell, their heyres & assignes, or to some one of them in behalfe of ye rest of my children an absolute & full release of any further clayme to any pt. of my houses and lands whereof I am now possessed, and in speciall to any pt. of yt necke of land yt was sometime Mr. Skeltons, & in ye meanetime shall not directly or indirectly make or signe any alienation thereof to any other, and in case ye sd. Jno. Porter shall faile in yeformance of this condiccon for more than one yeare after my decease, then the above named legacy of one hundred and fifty pounds shall be utterly voyd, and in lew yr of I do give him five pounds to be payd in country pay within three yeares after my decease at the discreccon of my Excecutrix. Item. I do give and bequeath to my Sonne Benjamin Porter these following parcells of land, namely all that parcell of land commonly called Bishop's farm also two hundred acres of land more or less, lying in blind hole, given mee by the towne, also one hundred acres of land purchased of Mr. Broadstreet also five acres of fresh meadow purchased of Jaffery Massey, also eight acres of meadow & upland more or less purchased of Wm. Nicholls & formly was a pt. of Bishop's farme, also ten acres of upland bought of John Hawthorne of Linn, & was formly appteyneing to Wm. Baily also one hundred pounds to be pd. in Country pay at two equall paymts annually within two yeare next after my decease. To my daughter Mary the wife of Thomas Gardiner to whom I have already done for according to my ability, I do give to her three children forty shillings apeece and also I do give to my daughter Mary and to my daughter Sarah to be equally divided between them, the farme called Smith's farme conteyneing eighty acres more or less & one hundred & twenty-five acres lying between the farm yt was sometime Kenistones & Laurance Leaches, also ten acres purchased of Mr. Gotte and is lying next to Putmans agt. mr. Downeings farme, also the above named Kenistones farme, conteyneing two hundred acres more or less, with twenty acres of meadow appteyneing thereunto.

Item. I give and bequeath unto my Sonne Joseph Porter five pounds to be payd. with in two yeares after my decease and forty shillings apeece to each of his children to be pd. at ye same time.

To John Porter Sonne of my sonne Samuel Porter I do give ten pounds to be payd him at 21 yeares of age. It. I do give & bequeath to my sonne Israel Porter, my now mansion place with all ye housing thereupon; orchard & lands adjoining vizt. so much as was by mee purchased of Mr. Sharp viz. with all ye appurtenances to ye same belonging, also I do give him sixty acres of Skeltons necke i. e. that pt. wh. I purchased of Mr. Skeltons daughters.

It. I do give and bequeath to Joseph, Benjamin & Israel Porter the remainder of Skelton's neck of land, conteyneing 150 a[cre]s more or less, and I do order them to make payment of the one hundred & fifty pounds by mee bequeathed unto my sonne John Porter.

To my sonne Benjamin I do give a parcel of land wh. I purchased of Mr. Gott, conteyneing eighty acres, more or less, and thirty acres purchased of Jacob Barney junr. and forty acres purchased of Jafery Massey and forty acres purchased of Gm. Watson & forty acres purchased of Jno. Pickard and my will is that he shall pay to my two daughters Mary & Sarah fifty pounds apiece, virt. in five years time, ten pounds pr ann. to each of them.

It. I do give to my sonne Israel Porter my interest in the saw mill near Skeltons neck.

It. I give & bequeath to the Reverend Mr. John Higgison forty shillings, and to the poor of Salim five pounds, to be distributed by my overseers as they shall in their discreccon judge meet.

To my wife over & beside wt. is before given her, I do give her my best feather bed, with all appurtenances necessary to compleat ye same, and also five pounds in money and it is my will yt. wt. shee shall spare of yt. pt. of my estate yt. I have above bequeathed to her that shee do in speciall wise consider my two daughters and be helpfull to them in confidenc whereof I have disposed to her and to my sonnes my estate as is above expressed.

To Cornelius Baker & Jno. Glover I do give forty shillings apiece, to be payd. within twelve mos. after my decease in country pay. *

Finally. I do nominate & intreate my loveing friends Mr. Edmund Batter & Mr. Hilyard Veren to be the overseers of this my will. To whome I do give full power & authority to determine any doubt or difference yt. may arise concerneing the trew meaning of this my will

& in case any legatee shall refuse to submit thereunto, hee or they shall loose all ye. interest therein, and as a toaken of my love and respect to my overseers, I do give them forty shillings ap. to be pd. in money.

In witness hereof I do hereunto put my hand and seale this 28th day of Aprill 1673.

JOHN PORTER, Sen'.

Sealed & published
In presence off
Samuel Danforth
Peter Olliver
Thomas Brattle Junir.

seal.

*And the residue of my goods & chattels not a[ready] disposed of, I do give and bequeath to my sonnes Joseph, Benjamin & Israel, & my two daughters Mary & Sarah, to be equally divided between them.

Children of John[1] and Mary Porter:

2. i. John[2].
3. ii. Samuel[2].
4. iii. Joseph,[2] bap. Hingham, Sept. 9, 1638, by Rev. P. Hobart.
5. iv. Benjamin,[2] bap. Hingham, Nov., 1639, by Rev. P. Hobart.
6. v. Israel,[2] bap. Hingham, Feb. 12, 1643, by Rev. P. Hobart.
7. vi. Mary,[2] m. Lieut. Thos. Gardner, April 22, 1669.
8. vii. Jonathan,[2] bap. Salem, Mar. 12, 1647-8; died before 1676.
9. viii. Sarah,[2] bap. June 3, 1649, in Salem; m. Daniel Andrews.

2

John[2] Porter, of John[1] Porter, unmarried. Mariner; was in prison in 1665, for abuse of his parents; in fact he was a bad fellow. His case was taken up against the colony by the royal commissioners, which made a great stir among the people at that time. He died Mar. 16, 1684. In 1683, June 2, when giving evidence in court, he stated his age to be sixty-five. In 1681, he gave it as fifty-two; and his counsel before the royal commissioners, in 1665, stated his age to be about thirty, which was probably correct. His estate was administered upon by his brothers Joseph and Israel.

3

Samuel[2] Porter, of John[1] Porter, mariner, of Wenham, where he owned a house and a large farm, near Wenham pond. He married Hannah, dau. of William and Elisabeth Dodge, of Beverly, (who married after his decease, Dec. 2, 1661, Thomas Woodbury, of Beverly, by whom she had nine children, and died Jan. 2, 1689, aged 45.) Samuel Porter died 1660. His will, dated 10th, 12 mo., 1658, "being bound to the Barbadoes."

"Imp. I give to my dearly beloved wife, Hannah Porter, the one-half of my farme during her life. Item, I give to my son, John Porter, the other half of my farme at Wenham; and after the death of my wife, the other half to returne unto him, more or less. I desire my ffather Porter, and my father-in-law, William Dodge, and Edmund Batter, to be my overseers."

SAMUEL PORTER.

Witnessed in the presence of us Edmund Batter, Sara Batter. Allowed by Court, 28th, 4 mo., 1660, at Salem. Inventory by Roger Conant and John Rayment. (Query? Rayner) same date.

One child:

10. i. John,^{3} b. 1658.

4

Joseph^2 Porter, of John^1 Porter, baptised in Hingham, Sep[illegible] 1638, by Rev. Peter Hobart. He was of Salem, Dan[illegible] part. Sept. 17, 1678, he bought of Hilliard Veren, Jr., 40 pole of land in Salem. Nov. 24, 1696, bought of Sarah Williams, (widow of Joseph,) and her son Daniel, about 20 [illegible]s of land on south side Ipswich river, in Topsfield, bounded south on Benjamin Porter. June 5, 1704, bought of Ben Marston, of Salem, 100 rods land on the road that leads along North river. He married, Jan. 27, 1664, Anne, dau. of Major William and Ann Hathorn, baptised first church, Salem, Dec. 17, 1643. The marriage contract is taken from registry of deeds, Essex county, book 3, page 139:

"Joseph Porter, Salem,—agreement between his father, Serg't John Porter, and Wm. Hathorne, concerning the marriage of said Joseph with Anna, daughter of said Wm. Hathorne,—wherein said Hathorne agrees to give his daughter £50 within two years from date of their marriage; and said John Porter engages to give his son Joseph that farm known as the Downing farm, with one-half an acre of land in the town, near Mr. George Keazer, both which shall be given Joseph on day of marriage. And also £50, to be paid in horses, neate cattle, hides, cider, some corn, and some money, within one year after marriage, Jan. 2, 1664."

His wife died before him. He died Dec. 12th, 1714. His will, dated July 15, 1713; proved Jan. 8, 1715:

"Gives son Joseph all my homestead yt I now live upon; my dwelling house and barn, with all other housing, together with my whole farm, (known formerly by ye name of Mr. Downing's farm,) excepting so much as I shall see cause hereafter otherwise to dispose of, which farm is bounded on ye east or easterly by a lot of lieutenant Perkins, of Topsfield, as also by Topsfield common land, and by Wenham meadows; south or southerly by Leache's meadow, and Daniel Andrews, his land, as also by Raye and Putnam's meadow land; west or westerly by Salem common land; and north or northerly by land of Michael Dunnell, of Topsfield, to ye bounds first mentioned.

2d. I do give my son Samuel ye land which he now lives upon and hath improved, together with the dwelling house or housing standing on said land where he now dwells, together with an hundred acres of land adjoining to ye land he now lives upon, it being ye southerly part of my farm, bounded as aforesaid—and also another lot of meadow land, ten acres on Salem and Wenham line.

3d. I do give my son Nathaniel, 20 acres of land, which I bought of widow Williams, of Salem, joining to Isaac Esty's land—also ten acres of meadow land adjoining what I shall give my son William.

4th. I give my son William 20 acres of land, be it more or less, lying west of land he now has in possession; also ten acres of meadow adjoining to Samuel's meadow. * * * Also my four sons before mentioned shall have an equal share in my upland or marsh which I have in Skelton's neck. * * * Also my will is that my sons aforesaid together with my daughters shall have an equal share therein * * * of what Leather I have, they all paying an equal part for ye dressing of what hides there be in ye tan vats to make it leather. To son Joseph my negro boy. * * daughters Anna, Mary, Abigail, Hephzebah, Ruth and Mehetabel to have 50 pounds each besides what they have had—to be paid by Executors. * * * Gives to Margaret King that hath been a faithful servant to me five pounds.

Children:

11. i. Joseph,[3] b. Oct. 30, 1665; died young.
12. ii. Anna[3] b. Sept. 5, 1667; m. Dr. Samuel Wallis.
13. iii. Samuel,[3] b. Aug. 4, 1669.
14. iv. Nathaniel,[3] b. Mar. 8, 1670-1.

15. v. Mary,[3] b. Dec. 18, 1672; m. William Dodge, of Beverly, maltster. Children: William,[4] baptised Dec. 14, 1701. Anna,[4] baptised Oct. 13, 1706.

16. vi. William,[3] b. Aug. 30, 1674.

17. vii. Eliezer,[3] b. May 23, 1676; probably died before his father.

18. viii. Abigail,[3] b. twin above; m. Samuel Symonds, of Boxford, Jan. 8, 1698.

19. ix. Hepsibah,[3] b. Apr. 11, 1678; m. Joseph Andrews, June 7, 1711.

20. x. Joseph,[3] b. April, 1681.

21. xi. Ruth,[3] baptised Sept., 1682; m. Jesse Dorman.

22. xii. Mehetable,[3] baptised Sept., 1682; m. Thos. Cummings of Boxford, Mar. 20, 1705.

5

Benjamin[2] Porter, of John[1] Porter, bap. Hingham, Nov., 1639, by Rev. Peter Hobart; died Jan. 7, 172 2-3, aged 83. (Beverly Second Church records.) He was unmarried, and after death of his parents, lived with his brother Israel, to whom he gave most of his estate, "in consideration of his maintenance, in food, washing, and lodging for many years," Feb. 17, 1701. He inherited the most of his property by his father's will, including the Bishop farm of two hundred acres in "Blind Hole," on the Topsfield line, and the one hundred acres his father bought of Mr. Bradstreet. He deeded Joseph and Nathaniel Porter, sons of his brother Joseph, one-third of his right in Skelton's neck, fifty acres, which he had by his father's will; also same day to same, a parcel of land at "Blind Hole," and Bishop's farm on north side of Topsfield line. Jan. 3, 1700, he gave brother Israel the land bequeathed him by his father, called Gott's corner. No settlement of his estate after his decease is recorded, as he appears to have disposed of it all previously.

6

Israel[2] Porter, of John[1] Porter, bap. Hingham, Feb. 12, 1743, by Rev. Peter Hobart. He was one of first tax payers in old Salem, (now Danvers,) 1682. Member of first Church, where all his children were baptised. In 1676, he bought of his brother Benjamin, his one-half of land which they had of their father, nine score acres, which was bought of Mr. Gott, Jacob Barney, Jeffrey Massey, William Watson, and Jno. Pickard, all of which was bounded on Jacob Barney's, Sharp's farm, Josh Ray, and Capt. John Corwin, formerly Mr. Peters. "30th, 11 mo., 1677, Israel Porter, aged thirty-two, or thereabouts, testifies that eighteen or twenty years since his father was desired by Topsfield to show the bounds of his land which lie within their township, (I being present,) my father showed three bounds belonging to that part of his Downing farm, within Topsfield line; also three bounds belonging to his land in "Blind Hole," all which bounds were accepted and approved of by Topsfield." Apr. 15, 1681, he was agent and trustee for Salem village. Feb. 20, 1689, he and his brother Benjamin signed a petition to form a distinct town out of Salem village. Oct. 11, 1686, he with other selectmen and trustees of Salem, purchased of the Indians for £20, all the tract of land "lying to the westward of Bass River, whereupon the town of Salem is built." He married Nov. 20, 1672, Elisabeth, daughter of Maj. Wm. and Ann Hathorn, sister to his brother Joseph's wife; she born July 5, 1649. He died Nov., 1706. His will, dated Nov. 7, 1706, proved Nov. 28, of same year, gives to two eldest sons, John and Israel, "all that part of Sharp's farm lying to the westward of the county highway, going from Salem to Ipswich, to be equally distributed between them." Also Bishop's farm, excepting 50 acres which he gives to his youngest daughter, Anna Porter, to his three eldest daughters, Elisabeth, wife of Joseph Putnam, Sarah, wife of Abel Gardner, and Ginger, wife of Sam Leach, "all that land I bought of Topsfield, together with all my right which I had of my brother Benjamin Porter, lying in Blind Hole. To William, the land that was formerly Mr. Gott's, together with all the additional grants adjoining thereto, lying at the head of Frostfish river, lying by Sharp's farm, commonly known by the name of Gott's Corner; also a little piece of land off Sharp's farm, lying on east side of Frostfish brook, and so to end of bridge, that he may come to ye salt works for a landing place." To his beloved wife, Elisabeth, "one-half of housing and lands,—part of Sharp's farm, of Skelton's neck, and also the other half of above during son Benjamin's minority, or till he comes to age of 21. Son William not to enjoy his portion till 21 years of age." Provides that "brother Benjamin shall live with my wife and son Benjamin, and be comfortably maintained during his life." Inasmuch as his daughter Ginger Leach had deceased, he gave her share to her husband, Samuel Leach, who had been a kind husband to her. His wife to be sole executrix of his will.

Children:

23. i. Elisabeth,[3] b. Oct. 2, 1673; her will proved Oct. 27, 1746; married, Apr. 21, 1690, Joseph Putnam, of Lieut. Thomas[2]; he born Sept. 14, 1669; will proved May 25, 1733; yeoman. Children: Mary,[4] b. Feb. 2, 1691. Elisabeth,[4] b. April 12, 1695. Sarah,[4] b. Sept. 26, 1697. William,[4] b. Feb. 8, 1700; died May 19, 1720. Rachel,[4] b. Aug. 7, 1702. Anna,[4] b. April 26, 1705. David,[4] b. Oct. 25, 1707. Eunice,[4] b. April 13, 1710. Son,[4] died April 14, 1713. Huldah,[4] b. Nov. 29, 1716. Israel,[4] b. Jan. 7, 1718; General in revolutionary war; died Brooklyn, Conn., May 19, 1790. Mehetable,[4] b. Jan. 13, 1720.

24. ii. Sarah,[3] b. Aug. 24, 1675; died Sept. 24, 1728; m. Abel[2] Gardner, of Samuel,[1] b. Salem, Sept. 1, 1763; died Nov. 10, 1739, aged 66; merchant. Children: Samuel,[4] b. Mar. 7, 1696. Jonathan,[4] b. Feb. 23, 1698; d. Nov. 27, 1783. Thomas,[4] b. Feb. 21, 1700; d. Apr. 13, 1700. Elisabeth,[4] b. Mar. 30, 1701. Thomas,[4] baptised Oct. 14, 1705. Israel,[4] baptised Oct. 5, 1707. Sarah,[4] baptised May 21, 1710. Abel,[4] baptised May 10, 1713. Hannah,[4] baptised May 1, 1715. Mary,[4] baptised Oct. 28, 1716. Joseph,[4] baptised Sept. 28, 1718.

25 iii. John,[3] b. Sept. 24, 1674; died before 1715; he was a mariner, and removed to Boston; made his will Dec. 22, 1709, in which he empowers his wife Elisabeth, "to sell his land in Salem for the benefit of their child or children." July 15, 1715, she sold to Timothy Lindall, of Boston, 130 acres of land in Salem, on Ipswich road, by the gate that led to the house of the late Israel Porter's homestead, bounded on Frost Fish brook and land of Wm. Porter; also fifty acres by Nath. Porter; a piece of 11 acres, and another of 14 acres.

26. iv. Ginger,[3] b. Oct. 6, 1679; died 1706; m. Sept. 25, 1699, Samuel Leach, of John and Elisabeth (Flint) Leach. Children: Baptised First Church in Salem, John[4], Nov. 8, 1702. Eunice,[4] Sept. 10, 1704.

27. v. Mary,[3] b. Sept. 22, 1681; died June 28, 1682.

28. vi. Israel,[3] b. April 4, 1683; died 1729.

29. vii. Benjamin,[3] b. Sept. 4, 1685; died Aug. 22, 1691.

30. viii. Anna,[3] b. June 17, 1687.

31. ix. William,[3] b. Feb. 12, 1689; living in 1750.

32. x. Benjamin,[3] b. May 17, 1693; died Dec., 1726.

7

Mary[2] Porter, of John[1] Porter, baptised in Salem, Oct. 12, 1645; died Nov. 27, 1695; m. April 22, 1669, Lieut. Thomas Gardner, son of Thomas and Margaret (Frier) Gardner, born May 25, 1645; died in Salem, Nov. 16, 1695. Children:

Mary,[3] b. Feb. 14, 1670; d. 1724. Thomas,[3] b. Oct. 25, 1671. Habbakuk,[3] b. Feb. 25, 1673. Joseph,[3] b. Aug. 29, 1677. Hapscott,[3] (daughter) b. July 22, 1679.

9

Sarah[2] Porter, of John[1] Porter, baptised Salem, June 3, 1649; married Daniel, son of Thomas and Rebecca Andrews, of Cambridge, b. Watertown, 1643; died in Danvers, of small pox, Dec. 3, 1702, aged 59; she died 1731. Administration granted on her estate May 19, 1731, to her son Israel. Children:

Daniel,[3] baptised Sept. 2, 1677; d. young. Thomas,[3] b. 1678; died of small pox Jan. 6, 1703. Samuel,[3] b. 1683; died of small pox, Jan. 12, 1703. Elisabeth,[3] baptised Aug. 9, 1685; died before 1702. Daniel,[3] baptised Sept., 1686; died 1728. Israel,[3] baptised Oct., 1689; died 1771. Mehetable.[3] Sarah.[3]

THIRD GENERATION.

10

John[3] Porter, of Samuel[2] Porter, of John[1] Porter, of Wenham; probably born there in 1658,—his father's farm, which he inherited and upon which he lived and died, being in that town; his lands extended from Wenham Lake to Pleasant Pond. In May, 1716, he and wife Lydia, gave a deed to John Ober and als., of Beverly, of three-eighths of third division in east part of Wenham, laid out to said Porter. May 28, 1741, by deed of gift to son Samuel, of three acres; April 23, 1723, deed of gift to son John, of forty acres in his possession, and four acres of meadow called Denman's lot, seven acres meadow called Fiske's lot, and one common right in great swamp. "May 20, 1746 for five shillings, to son Jonathan four acres salt marsh, ten acres wood land, west side Wenham Pond, all other lands bought of John Newman, all my other lands joining what was part of Mr. Fiske's farm; one common right in great swamp; also £100." July 2, 1739, "deed of gift to sons Benjamin, of Boxford, and Nehemiah, of Ipswich, eighteen acres upland and meadow, on the river running out of Wenham pond, on condition they pay their six sisters, Lydia, Hannah, Elisabeth, Mehitable, Mary and Sarah, £5 each within twelve months after my decease." Aug. 1, 1738, to son Samuel his house and homestead on west side of road leading to Wenham meeting house; five acres salt marsh, ten acres north part of my land on west side of Wenham pond, on condition he pay his six sisters £30 each within two years after my decease." April 23, 1723, to son Nehemiah, of Ipswich, gift of forty-six acres of land in his possession. In 1692, during the witchcraft delusion, he and his wife Lydia were witnesses at court, and testified against one Goody Bibber, who accused Sarah Wildes of bewitching her, "and that said Bibber was an unruly, turbulent woman, would have strange fits when crost, was double tongued, very idle in her calling, mischief making, very much given to speaking bad words against her husband, obscene in her language, and could fall into fits when she pleased, etc." He was a man of high respectability; representative to General Court 1712, '24, 26; moderator of town meetings, 1723, '24, '27, '28, '29; maltster and farmer; he married Lydia,[3] daughter of Henry[2] and Lydia Herrick, of Beverly; born 1661; died Feb. 12, 1737, in the seventy-seventh year of her age. He died March 8, 1753, in the ninety-fifth year of his age. No will or administration on his estate, it being divided among his children during his lifetime. Children:

33. i. Samuel,[4] b. Feb. 17, 1681; died Sept. 13, 1770, aged 92.
34. ii. John,[4] b. 1683; died about 1775, aged 92.
35. iii. Hannah,[4] b. Nov. 24, 1687; she died at age of 100; married Thomas Kimball, of Wenham; pub. Jan. 8, 1708.
36. iv. Elisabeth,[4] married Daniel Gilbert, of Ipswich, Dec. 1, 1710; died at age of 100.
37. v. Benjamin,[4] b. 1692; died June 30, 1781, aged 89.
38. vi. Jonathan,[4] b. Sept. 11, 1696; died Oct. 9, 1759, aged 63.
39. vii. Nehemiah,[4] married; died at age of 92.
40. viii. Mehetable,[4] b. Oct. 11, 1698; died, aged 88; married Caleb Kimball, Jr., of Wenham, Feb. 15, 1718.
41. ix. Sarah,[4] b. Jan. 6, 1706; died age of 89; married Thomas Dodge, of Wenham, June 23, 1724.
42. x. Mary,[4] b. July 20, 1700; she died 1790, at age of 90; married 1st, Robert Cue, of Wenham, 1718; he died Jan. 7, 1737; she probably married 2d, Samuel Tarbox, April 20, 1737; "a daughter by Cue, married Col. Hutchinson, of Danvers, whose dau. married John Brown, father of Bartholomew Brown, whose son George married Harriet, dau. of Captain John Porter, of Sterling." (Williams Latham.)
43. xi. Lydia,[4] died at age of 60; married William Lamson, of Ipswich; pub. Oct. 26, 1706.

The ages of eleven children at death, 955 years; average, 87 years.

13

Samuel[3] Porter, of Joseph[2] Porter, born Aug. 4, 1669; of Salem (Danvers.) May 9, 1722, sold to Samuel West, saddler, one common right belonging to him, by virtue of his (Porter's) dwelling house, where he then lived; 1722, deeds to sons Eleazer and Samuel, one-half his homestead, to be divided between them after his decease; said farm on the border of Salem, next to Wenham. September 8, 1737, for £1580, sold his son Samuel 86 acres 30 poles land, with dwelling house, barn buildings, live stock, and husbandry improvements; said farm beginning at a black oak, which is a bound between said Samuel Porter and Daniel Andrews, and between Salem and Wenham; also, 11 acres at lower end of Skelton's neck; also, deed of gift to son Eleazer for the duty he has done and legacies he has had, 82 acres, being farm he now lives on. March 19, 1739, being about 71 years old, he testifies in a deposition that 54 years since he had known the reputed bounds of Porter's farm at Blind Hole, in Topsfield, and was present when the commissioners of Topsfield received the bounds. June 25, 1750, after his decease, his widow Love, in a deed conveys to her son Eleazer, her right of dower for fifty pounds. He married Love Howe; she made her will July 12, 1759, proved Sept. 13, 1762, in which she names her brothers Abraham and Mark Howe, and her grandsons Israel and Edmund Putnam. Children:

44. i. Samuel,[4] owned covenant Oct. 15, 1738.
45. ii. Eleazer.[4]
45A. iii. Lydia,[4] m. John Putnam, and had sons Israel,[5] and Edmund,[5] named in their grandmother's will.

14

Nathaniel[3] Porter, of Joseph[2] Porter, b. March 8, 1671; lived in Topsfield; probably died 1756; farmer and tanner. In 1720, Mar. 17, he and the Esteys divided land; in 1701, Mar. 24, he and wife Eleanor, sold Joseph Waters and John Felton, of Salem, eight acres of land in Topsfield. March 16, 1726, sold land in Salem to Ebenezer Bachelder, of Wenham. May 18 1741, sold sons Nathaniel and Elijah, tanners, for ten pounds, one-half acre of land, tan house and tan yard, being part of a farm said Porter now lives on, to carry on tanning; also to same, for £110, 17 acres bounded on Porter's farm. Also, in 1743, twenty acres of upland and marsh, in Salem, at the end of a fence at North river, dividing said land from John Hubbard, Israel Wood, Jno. Jacobs, to said river; also, five acres bounded on Joseph Porter, Ebenezer Bachelder, and William Porter, deceased. "The 10th day of Nov., 1744, Nath. Porter was ordered by William Foye, Esq., Treasurer of His Majesty's Province of Lord George the Second, of Great Britain, etc., King, to collect a tax in Topsfield." (Old paper.) Jan. 30, 1747, deed of gift to son Nathaniel, four acres; Sept 9, 1747, deed of gift to son Elijah, twenty-three acres. He married, Dec. 16, 1701, Eleanor Dorman, probably sister of his brother William's wife; she died Jan. 5, 1752. Children, born in Topsfield:

46. i. Mehetable,[4] b. April 14, 1702; m. Estey.

47. ii. Nathaniel,[4] b. Dec. 22, 1703; died June 22, 1758.

48. iii. Mercy,[4] b. Sept. 23, 1705; m. Aug. 11, 1730, Israel, son of Daniel and Damaris Clark, b. Topsfield, Sept. 28, 1701; will pro. March 1, 1790. Children: Elijah,[5] b. Mar. 9; died May 9, 1731. Israel,[5] b. Apr. 11, 1732; living 1790. Mercy,[5] b. Dec. 28, 1734. Sarah,[5] b. Nov. 5, 1736; died Feb. 7, 1738. Sarah,[5] b. Jan. 31, 1739; died before 1790. Samuel,[5] b. Mar. 13, 1741. Bathsheba,[5] b. Apr. 6, 1743. Jacob,[5] b. Aug. 8, 1744; living 1790. David,[5] b. Jan. 1, 1748.

49. iv. Abigail,[4] b. Jan, 19, 1709; m. Dorman.

50. v. Thomas,[4] b. Jan. 5, 1712; died March 4, 1774.

51. vi. Elijah,[4] b. Apr. 22, 1713; died Dec. 17, 1775.

52. vii. Joseph,[4] b. Sept. 22, 1715.

53. viii. Eleanor,[4] b. Oct. 21, 1717; m. Abbot.

53A. ix. Mary,[4] b. Oct. 2, 1720; m. Clarke.

16

Deacon William[3] Porter, of Joseph[2] Porter, b. Aug. 30, 1674; lived in Topsfield; removed to Norton, between 1720 and 1730; he bought land of Joseph Elliott, in Norton, Feb. 8, 1732; "William Porter and Phebe Dorman were married Dec. 25, 1706;" (Topsfield records.) He died in Norton, May 7, 1732; his will, (Bristol records,) dated July 29, 1731, probated June 30, 1732, names "wife Phebe, four sons, Benjamin, Seth, Jonathan and Jabez, to whom he gives to be divided equally, his lands in Salem and Topsfield; daughters Judith Hewins, and Anna Porter." "Phebe, widow of William Porter, of Norton, died in Braintree, June 21, 1736, aged 55." (Braintree rec'ds.) Children, all b. in Topsfield:

54. i. Ruth,[4] b. Aug. 28, 1707.

55. ii. Judith,[4] b. July 6, 1710; m—— Hewins.

56. iii. Benjamin,[4] b. Feb. 4, 1712; married Dorothy Curtis, June 1, 1738.

57. iv. Seth,[4] b. Feb. 15, 1714; married Abigail Herrick, Mar. 27, 1746.

58. v. Anna,[4] b. Feb. 21, 1716; married Dea. Peter Thayer, of Braintree, June 1, 1732; he removed to Peterboro, N. H., where he died Sept. 27, 1798. Children, all born in Braintree: William,[5] b. July 26, 1733; died same day. Peter,[5] b. May 5, 1735; died July 6, 1736. Peter,[5] b. April 3, 1737. William,[5] b. Jan. 26, 1739. Ephraim,[5] b. Feb. 16, 1740; married Phebe Porter, of Benjamin, 1762. Zacheus,[5] b. Dec. 27, 1742. Anna,[5] b. Sept. 29, 1744; died Nov. 25, 1744. Anna,[5] b. April 9, 1746. Jabez,[5] b. July 7, 1748. Phebe,[5] b. Feb. 11, 1750; m., 1781, Abraham Cummings, of Topsfield. Ruth,[5] b. Aug. 23, 1753. Bartholomew,[5] b. July 15, 1757; married Elis Blanchard, of Braintree, 1789.

59. vi. Phebe,[4] b. June 18, 1718; died July 3, 1718.

60. vii. Jonathan,[4] b. Dec. 11, 1720, (or July 17, Topsfield record says.)

61. viii. Jabez,[4] b. Feb. 1, 1723.

20

Joseph[3] Porter, of Joseph[2] Porter, born Danvers, April, 1681; yeoman; June 11, 1712, he of Salem village, and his brother Nathaniel, of Topsfield, sons of Joseph, senior, confirmed to John Curtis, of Topsfield, seven acres their father bought with his brother Israel, about twenty years previous. He married, May 3, 1709, Mary ———, (who after his decease married Geo. Bixby, Aug. 6, 1718.) He died 1713. Administration granted his widow, Jan. 3, 1714. Children:

67. i. Joseph,[4] baptised Aug. 13, 1710; died February, 1747.

68. ii. Priscilla,[4] baptised May 12, 1712.

69. iii. Mary,[4] baptised May 29, 1715, after her father's decease.

26

Ginger[3] Porter, of Israel[2] Porter, b. Oct. 6, 1679; died 1706; m. Sept. 25, 1699, Samuel Leach, son of John and Elisabeth (Flint) Leach, b. Salem, April 28, 1677. Children, bap. 1st church, Salem:

i. John,[4] bap. Nov. 8, 1702; m. Rachel:—His daughter, Ginger,[5] m. Dr. Benj. Jones, of Beverly—his 2d wife; "she died Dec. 13, 1756, about three-quarters of an hour after 6 o'clock, in the evening, in the 30th year of her age. The children of Dr. Benj. and Ginger Jones, were: Hannah,[6] b. June 17, 1750; m. Henry Herrick, Jr., 1772; she departed this life Sept. 27, 1786, about half after 7 of the clock in the morning, aged 36 years three months, wanting—days." William,[6] b. Dec., 1752; died Jan. 11, 1761, "about 3 o'clock in the afternoon." John,[6] b. Sept. 10, 1755—"my dear son John, we have reason to fear and believe, was lost in a cartel from Halifax to Boston, having been taken prisoner by the British, in the armed ship Starks, in 1781, and sailed in a cartel from Halifax, in Dec., 1781, for Boston, and never has been heard of." (Dr. Jones' family record.)

ii. Eunice,[4] bap. Sept. 10, 1704.

iii. Hepzibah,[4] bap. Nov. 8, 1702.

iv. Samuel,[4] bap. July 15, 1713.

v. Mary,[4] bap. Aug. 1, 1714.

28

Israel[3] Porter, of Israel[2] Porter, born April 4, 1683; died 1729; will made April 8, 1729; proved Oct. 20, 1729; wife Sarah executrix, who had land coming to her from her brother, Nathan Putnam. He was member of the church, Salem village; clerk 1710, 1718, and 1723. Married, Sept. 12, 1706, Sarah, daughter of James and Sarah Putnam, baptized 1st Church, Salem, June, 1686. Children:

70. i. Ginger,[4] baptised Aug. 17, 1707; married Jan. 1, 1727, Elisha, son of Joseph and Rebecca (Knight) Hutchinson, of Salem village, who died before 1730; they were received into church, Oct. 28, 1727. Child by Hutchinson: Israel,[5] baptised Nov. 12, 1727; died Mar. 15, 1811, from the effect of a fall in his mill, where he lived at Danversport; in 1762, was part owner of a saw and grist mill on Crane river; he bore a prominent part in the Revolutionary war, and for his bravery received a Lieutenant Colonel's commission. She married 2d, Sept. 20, 1730, Daniel Andrews, Jr., son of Daniel and Hannah (Peabody) Andrews, b. Sept. 28, 1704; died 1756. Children, by Andrews: Sarah,[5] b. Aug. 5, 1731; died Mar. 1. 1776. Daniel,[5] b. July 13, 1734; died Aug. 3, 1755. John,[5] b. Feb. 28, 1737; died Oct. 12, 1756. Nathan,[5] b. Sept. 30, 1739; died Jan. 23, 1768, unmarried. Samuel,[5] b. April 11, 1741. Widow married 3d, Herrick, before 1767.

71\. ii. Sarah,[4] baptised Feb. 10, 1710; died before 1729.

72\. iii. John,[4] baptised Mar. 12, 1713; died 1742, unmarried; will probated Oct. 11, 1742, gives sisters Ginger, Elisabeth, Anna, and Mary, the land on the plains given him by his father; to brother Israel, part of saw mill, &c.; his mother to have improvement of all his other land as long as she lived; brother Daniel Andrews, ex'r; inv. £743, 9s, 3d.

73\. iv. Israel,[4] baptised June 24, 1716; married Mary Batchelder, of Wenham, Dec. 28, 1737, (who survived him and married 2d, Aug. 27, 1747, Jona Kettle, formerly of Charlestown, who married 1st, Dec. 2, 1725, Edith Moore, of Beverly.) Adm. granted in his estate widow Mary, June 9, 1746. One child, Sarah,[5] b. Aug. 20, 1739, married ——— Williams.

74\. v. Elisabeth,[4] bap. April 26, 1719; died about 1772; married March 13, 1737, John Andrews, son of Daniel and Hannah (Peabody) Andrews. Children: Elisabeth,[5] bap. May 28, 1738. John Porter,[5] bap. Sept. 29, 1745.

75\. vi. Anna,[4] bap. Sept., 1722; married ——— Faxon.

76\. vii. Mary,[4] bap. Apr. 24, 1726; married Jan. 31, 1745, Joseph, son of Joseph and Lydia (Flint) Putnam, bap. Apr. 26, 1724; yeoman; his will made Mar. 3, 1781, proved April 17. Children, all bap. Salem village: Lydia,[5] bap. July 27, 1746; died young. Sarah,[5] bap. Jan. 29, 1749. Joseph,[5] bap. April 21, 1751. Israel,[5] bap. June 24, 1753. Mary,[5] bap. Sept. 14, 1755; died young. Lydia,[5] bap. Feb. 26, 1758. John,[5] bap. Jan. 18, 1761. Elisabeth,[5] bap. Oct. 30, 1763. Mary,[5] bap. Jan. 26, 1767. Porter,[5] bap. Mar. 25, 1770.

31

William[3] Porter, of Israel[2] Porter, born Feb. 12, 1688-9; was of Salem village (Danvers); yeoman; married 1st, Feb. 1, 1708-9, Edith, daughter of Joseph and Mary (Endicott, 2d, wife) Herrick; she born Feb. 20, 1690; died Beverly, March 13, 1723-4; member of Second church, Beverly. Married 2d, Dec. 8, 1725, Mary, widow of John Kettle, of North Beverly, and daughter of Josiah and Mary (Raymond) Batchelder, born Nov. 5, 1701. (John Kettle was son of James and Elisabeth Kettle, born in Beverly, July 3, 1696; died Feb. 1, 1723-4. Married 1st, June 17, 1718, Mehetable Brown, who died Sept. 15, 1718. Married 2d, June 25, 1719, Mary

Bachelder; his grandfather was John Kettle, of Beverly, who died Oct. 12, 1685.) June 22, 1722, William[3] and wife Edith sold to Samuel Fisk, clerk, land belonging to the house on his farm given him by his father. May 1, 1728, sold Nathaniel Tompkins, of Salem, house and six poles of land near the meeting house, middle precinct, (now Peabody.) Jan. 29, 1740, deed of gift of one and one-half rods of land at Royal Side, for erection of school house near Barney's gate; April 19, 1750, he and wife Mary sold to Robert Hooper, of Marblehead, for £1843 4s, "my farm of 246 acres, 76 poles, beginning at south-west angle of highway leading through Royal Side, and near Frost Fish brook, where it joins land of Timothy Lindall; also 61 pole 4-10 butting on middle of the river, and by south side of Frost Fish bridge, with dwelling houses, barns, &c., excepting the land where the school house stands, which I gave the proprietors." He probably removed to Woburn. His estate was administered in Middlesex county, 1755. Widow Mary. Children: William.[4] Benjamin.[4] Jonathan.[4] Nathan.[4] George.[4] Mary Brown.[4] Josiah.[4] Joseph.[4] Ginger,[4] and Mary,[4] named therein. Children:

77. i. Israel,[4] baptised Aug. 20, 1710; probably d. Beverly, 1744.
78. ii. William,[4] baptised June 21, 1713.
79. iii. Benjamin,[4] baptised June 19, 1715.
80. iv. Joseph.[4]
81. v. Anna.[4]
82. vi. Josiah.[4]
vii. Jonathan,[4] baptised Nov. 4, 1733.
viii. Edith,[4] baptised Nov. 4, 1733.
ix. Nathan,[4] baptised Oct. 3, 1736.
x. George,[4] baptised Aug. 13, 1738.
xi. Ginger,[4] baptised Oct. 4, 1741.
xii. Mary,[4] baptised Feb. 5, 1745.

32

Benjamin[3] Porter, of Israel[2] Porter, born Salem village, May 17, 1693; married April 3, 1712, Hannah, daughter of Samuel and Hannah (Felton) Endicott, born 1691—(after decease of Samuel Endicott, his widow married Thorndike Proctor.) He died Dec., 1726; will made Dec. 15, 1726, proved Jan. 18, 1727, names wife Hannah, daughter Hannah, about fourteen years old; her uncle, Sam Endicott, appointed guardian, Mar. 23, 1729-30; sons, John and Benjamin, Samuel, Bartholomew. Father-in-law, Thorndike Proctor, and brother-in-law Sam Endicott, overseers of will. Children:

88. i. John,[4] b. about 1712-13; died 1759.
89. ii. Hannah,[4] b. 1716; d. before Dec. 2, 1746; m. Joseph Fowles, Feb. 6, 1733. Children: Benjamin.[5] Sarah.[5] Hannah,[5] offered by Apphia, wife of her uncle John, at the ch., middle precinct, July 3, 1743, after decease of her mother.
90. iii. Benjamin,[4] died 1794.
91. iv. Samuel,[4] b. about 1722.
92. v. Bartholomew,[4] b. about 1726.

FOURTH GENERATION.

33

Samuel[4] Porter, of John[3] Porter (Samuel,[2] John,[1]) born in Wenham, Feb. 17, 1681, and lived there on the old homestead, bequeathed him by his father. Feb. 10, 1719, he and wife Sarah, of Wenham, with Simon Bradstreet, Samuel Bradstreet's guardian, and Dorothy Bradstreet, and children of John Bradstreet, of Topsfield, divide a meadow left them by their father; same day he and wife Sarah deed to their brother, Samuel Bradstreet, of Topsfield, all their right in the farm given them, the children of Jno. Bradstreet, by their grandfather, Simon Bradstreet." Feb. 14, 1754, he and wife Sarah, deed to their sons, Samuel, Jr., of Wenham, housewright, and Ebenezer, of Danvers, cordwainer, for £1000, "my homestead and house where I now dwell, with all appurtenances, except three acres I sold Ebenezer, where his house stands, in Wenham, on west side of county road leading to meeting house; also five acres of salt marsh my father bought of Edward Bishop, etc." He was published March 22, 1706-7, to Sarah, daughter of John and Sarah (Perkins) Bradstreet, of Topsfield, granddaughter of Gov. Simon Bradstreet. He probably married 2d, Experience Batchelder, of Wenham, Mar. 25, 1733. "September 13, 1770, died Sergeant Samuel

Porter, who was born Feb. 17, 1681, ætatis 89 years and seven months, lacking four days. What man is he yt liveth and shall not see Death." (Wenham records.) Children:

93. i. Samuel,[5] b. Nov. 14, 1711; married.
94. ii. Ebenezer,[5] b. 1716; of Beverly, Wenham, &c.
95. iii. John,[5] b. July 9, 1717; of Littleton.
96. iv. Anna,[5] b. Aug. 13, 1719; m. Nath. Brown, May 27, 1738.

34

John[4] Porter, of John[3] Porter, b. 1683, of Wenham; moved to Ellington, Conn., about 1740; married Elisabeth, dau. of John Putnam, of Danvers, pub. Dec. 9, 1708; she b. Feb. 2, 1687; he died about 1775, aged 92. Children, all born in Wenham:

100. i. John,[5] b. Apr. 16, 1710; died Jan. 27, 1722.
101. ii. Jonathan,[5] b. Apr. 1, 1712; died July 5, 1783.
102. iii. Elisabeth,[5] b. Aug. 14, 1714; died Jan., 1715.
103. iv. David,[5] b. Mar. 10, 1716; died Apr. 22, 1716.
104. v. Lydia,[5] b. Sept., 1717; probably m. Samuel Burroughs, of Windsor, Oct. 30, 1745.
105. vi. Ruth,[5] b. Oct. 28, 1719; probably m. Samuel Bowles, Jan. 1, 1743.
106. vii. Daniel,[5] b. Sept. 19, 1721; died Jan. 5, 1760.
107. viii. John,[5] b. Jan. 17, 1723.
108. ix. Jerusha,[5] b. Nov. 8, 1724.
109. x. Elisabeth,[5] b. May 23, 1726.

37

Benjamin[4] Porter, of John[3] Porter, born Wenham, 1691–2; carpenter; lived in Boxford; died there June 30, 1778, aged 87; (another account says 1781, aged 89.) "Jan. 8, 1735, Benjamin Porter and John Chadwick, of Boxford, sold for £200, to Ebenezer Steward, all right and title in two lots of land belonging to said Chadwick, and three lots belonging to Moses Tyler, deceased, father-in-law to said Benjamin Porter." Married Sarah, daughter of Moses Tyler, Jan. 30, 1716; she born 1696; died January 27, 1767, aged 71. Children:

110. i. Moses,[5] b. Nov. 18, 1719; married Mary Chadwick, Dec. 3, 1741.

111. ii. Mary,[5] married Deacon Thomas Chadwick, of Boxford, June 12, 1738. (He was son of John and Mehetable (Hazeltine) Chadwick, of Boxford,—they m. 1706.) Children: Molly,[6] b. March 1, 1742; married Peter Russell, of Salisbury, Nov. 26, 1761. (Marriage recorded in Boxford and Salisbury, but no further record of him or wife in either town.) Benjamin,[6] b. Mar. 26, 1745. Thomas,[6] b. April 15, 1751. Samuel,[6] b. 1755. [Primus, the man servant of Mrs. Mary Cue, of Wenham, and Flora, the woman servant of Deacon Thomas Chadwick, of Boxford, were pub. in Wenham, Jan. 28, 1753.]

112. iii. Benjamin,[5] b. Oct. 21, 1721; died May 15, 1784.

113. iv. Sally,[5] b. March, 1726.

114. v. Lucy.[5]

38

Jonathan[4] Porter, of John[3] Porter, born Sept. 11, 1696; lived in Wenham; innholder; citizen of more than ordinary distinction. Representative to General Court 1745, '46, '47. Married Lydia, daughter of Moses Tyler, published Aug. 30, 1724; she born in Boxford, 1702; died in Wenham, Nov. 2, 1785, aged 83; he died Oct. 8, 1759. Children:

120. i. Benjamin,[5] b. Mar. 12, 1726.

121. ii. Mary,[5] b. June 29, 1728; m. Joseph Low, of Newbury, Jan. 1, 1756.

122. iii. Ruth,[5] b. Jan. 5, 1731; m. Dr. Caleb Rea, and others.

123. iv. Jonathan,[5] b. June 20, 1733.

124. v. Tyler,[5] b. Nov. 23, 1735.

125. vi. Billy,[5] b. Aug. 23, 1739.

126. vii. Lydia,[5] b. Feb. 9, 1741; m. Joseph Emerson, of Topsfield.

39

Nehemiah[4] Porter, of John[3] Porter; born in Wenham; weaver. Removed to Ipswich, where he was living in 1724, and 1739. Married Hannah, daughter of Hazadiah Smith, of Beverly; he died 1784, aged 92; will dated Oct. 9, 1782, proved Oct. 5, 1784. Children, probably not in order:

127. i. Nehemiah,[5] b. Nov. 20, 1720.

128. ii. Ebenezer,[5] b. 1732.

129. iii. Samuel,[5] died before his father.

130. iv. Hannah,[5] living in 1784.

131. v. Sarah,[5] living in 1784.

132. vi. Hazadiah,[5] living in 1784; prob. removed to Nova Scotia.

133. vii. Lydia,[5] living in 1784.

45

Eleazer[4] Porter, of Samuel[3] Porter, of Joseph[2] Porter, born Danvers, and lived there. Dec. 11, 1735, he bought of Jno. Wildes, and wife Phebe, of Topsfield, for twenty-eight pounds, one right in a tract of land in Souhegan west, or township number three, lately granted by General Court to ye Narragansot soldiers drawn by such living at or near Salem, of which Sam Perkins was one, and which said right was granted him. Nov. 1, 1739, he and wife Abigail, sold to John Jacobs, of Salem, eleven acres of upland, near lower end of Skelton's Neck, given him by his father, for two hundred sixty pounds. Jan. 19, 1740-1, he sold Israel Wood of Beverly, for two hundred and eighty pounds 11 acres 26 poles upland and marsh—bounded on North river—said Eliezer, Nathaniel and William Porter, and John Jacobs. He married 1st, Mary—probably 2d, Abigail—he died 1756; his will dated Sept. 25, 1756, proved Nov. 8, 1756, gave wife Abigail all indoor goods his first wife brought with her. Son Samuel under 22; daughters Mary and Abigail, over 14. Guardianship granted to Elijah Porter, of Topsfield Nov. 8, 1756. Sons David and Asa, executors; widow died 1758; adm. granted on her estate to Tarrant Putnam, Mar. 6, 1758. Children:

134. i. David,[5] baptised May 9, 1731.
135. ii. Asa,[5] baptised May 26, 1734; adm. granted on his estate to Tarrant Putnam, Jan. 6, 1758.
135A. iii. Mary,[5] baptised Aug. 22, 1736.
135B. iv. Abigail,[5] baptised Dec. 17, 1738.
135C. v. Samuel,[5] baptised Jan. 30, 1742-3.

47

Nathaniel[4] Porter, of Nathaniel[3] Porter, born Dec. 22, 1703; lived in Topsfield; tanner. Sept. 22, 1731, he and wife Mary, for £43 15s., sold their brother, Luke Averill, of Topsfield, their one-tenth part of real estate of their father, Ebenezer Averill, deceased. April 12, 1743, he and brother Elijah Porter, from Joseph Porter of Topsfield, all his (Joseph's) right in estate of his father Nathaniel, (he) is now in possession of in Topsfield, bounded by Jno. Baker,

Porter's farm, Joseph Herrick, Nichols' meadow, and Timothy Lindall. May 1, 1744, same from Amos Dorman and wife Mary, of Coventry, Conn., for £7 10s., two and one-half acres in Topsfield, bounded on meadow of Lydia Curtis, Emerson, and Jabez Towne. Dec. 5, 1751, he and Elijah, with their wives Abigail and Dorothy, for £55 7s, sold five and one-fourth acres land, salt marsh, Porter's Neck, to John and John Felton, Jr. Dec. 16, 1752, he and wife Abigail, for £57, sold Elijah Porter sixteen acres thirty-three poles, bounded on David Towne, Felton, Samuel Perkins, and Porter's farm. Dec. 20, 1752, to brother Elijah, for £5, twenty-two acres, also one-half acre land and one-half of tan house and tan yard on said land. Nath. Porter, Jr., of Topsfield, was appointed Lieutenant, July 2, 1754, by Wm. Shirley, "Capt. General and Governor in chief over His Majesty's Province, in the 28th year of the reign of His Majesty King George the Second." Married 1st, Mary, daughter of Ebenezer Averill; she died Dec. 23, 1736. Married 2d, May 25, 1738, Abigail, daughter of John and Abigail Waters Jacobs; she baptised First Church, Salem, Sept. 1, 1706; living in 1767. (John Jacobs was son of George Jacobs, hung for witchcraft, in 1692.) He died Jan. 22, 1758; inventory of estate, Oct. 10, 1758. Children, all born in Topsfield:

136. i. Daniel,[5] b. Jan. 6, 1731; died Dec. 19, 1736.

137. ii. Nathaniel,[5] b. Dec. 15, 1733; died Dec. 24, 1736.

138. iii. Mary,[5] b. Dec. 23, 1736; died Dec. 31, 1736.

139. iv. Mary,[5] b. March 24, 1739; married Asa Kinney, of Middleton, and had no children. In old age she married Asa Pingree, of Georgetown. She died in Middleton, March 12, 1823, having been blind about five years.

140. v. Phebe,[5] b. March 31, 1741; died April 26, 1745.

141. vi. Daniel,[5] b. Feb. 3, 1743; died Jan. 28, 1831; married.

142. vii. Nathaniel,[5] b. Jan. 3, 1745; died 1836, aged 92.

143. viii. Phebe,[5] b. May 12, 1746; married Joshua Willard, of Hubbardston, and had sons.

144. ix. Abigail,[5] b. Sept. 24, 1748; died June 6, 1820; married Henry,[5] son of Simon,[4] and Anna (Flint) Bradstreet, born Topsfield, Nov. 30, 1741; died Sept. 7, 1818. Children: Dr. Nathaniel,[6] born Oct. 4, 1770–71, of

Newburyport; died Oct. 6, 1828. Daniel,[6] born Feb. 12, 1773, of Franklin, Warren county, Ohio; died 1832. William,[6] born March 13, 1775; removed to Royalton, Vt. Nabby,[6] b. June 6, 1778; m. Joseph Killam, of Boxford.

50

Thomas[4] Porter, of Nathaniel[3] Porter, born in Topsfield, Jan. 5, 1712; removed to Danvers about 1755; mariner; afterwards a merchant; representative to General Court, 1760-1-2-3-5; town clerk 1763 and '67; lived in what is now Peabody. Married Mercy Clark, of York, Me.; certificate of marriage given, Danvers, Oct. 7, 1755; he died March 4, 1774. Children:

154. i. Thomas,[5] b. Aug. 6, 1756; died June, 1796.
155. ii. Mercy,[5] b. Nov. 15, 1758; died Nov. 4, 1763 or '73.
156. iii. James,[5] b. July 6, 1761; died Jan. 9, 1830; unmarried.
157. iv. Daniel Clark,[5] b. Oct. 9, 1766; died Sept. 9, 1767.
158. v. Mercy,[5] b. July 7, 1768; m. May 18, 1802, Samuel Foster, of Boston, merchant.

52

Joseph[4] Porter, of Nathaniel[3] Porter, born Sept. 22, 1715. In 1743, April 12, he sold his brothers Nathaniel and Elijah, all his right in estate of his father, Nathaniel, lying in Topsfield.

In East Randolph, (Braintree) 1746—Dr. E. Alden says "he was owner of first vehicle used for conveyance of persons ever used in town (Randolph;) was a rudely constructed chaise without a top, called a chair; he resorted to its use from necessity, being afflicted with a lameness which prevented him from mounting a horse, or going a long distance on foot. He was a considerable land owner." Dr. Alden says he "was son of Dea. William[3] Porter, of Norton, and brother of Benjamin,[4] Jabez,[4] and Seth,[4] of Braintree." But as there is no mention of any Joseph's birth on Topsfield records, or in will of Dea. William[3] Porter, I place him as son of Nathaniel[3] Porter, where he no doubt belongs, his age at death agreeing with date of Nathaniel[3] Porter's son Joseph's birth.

He married Ruth Towne; he died in East Randolph, Mar. 8, 1797, aged 81; his widow died April 14, 1799, aged 80; they had four children, one son and three daughters, who all lived and died in East Randolph, and were remarkable for the strength and accuracy of their memories.

159. i. Ruth,[5] born 1747; married Joseph[5] White, Jr., Esquire, of Randolph, June 16, 1766. He was son of Joseph[4] and Ruth (Nash) White, born in Braintree, (Randolph.) Nov. 22, 1742; died July 18, 1816. He was a descendant of Richard[1] Porter, of Weymouth. He was justice of the peace and selectman many years; also representative to the General Court. Widow died March, 1830. Daughter, Ruth,[6] born April 12, 1769; married Zenas French, of Randolph, blacksmith—his second wife; daughter Relief,[6] b. Jan. 7, 1772; married Bailey White, 1792, her cousin. (Joseph[5] White's sister Thankful, m. 1st, Elihu Adams, brother of President John Adams, Sept. 20, 1765; and 2d, Col. Aaron Hobart, of Abington.)

160. ii. Joseph,[5] b. 1754, of East Randolph; lieutenant; m. Rachel Thayer, daughter of Zach Thayer; pub. Nov. 5, 1785; he died Nov. 18, 1833, aged 79; she died June 22, 1841, aged 83. Children: John,[6] b. 1786; "school master many years; carpenter when not otherwise engaged; representative to General Court two years; selectman several years; and in every situation fully competent for his employment, and much respected." Elijah,[6] b. 1788. Alvin,[6] b. 1790; died 1796. Jabez,[6] b. 1792; grad. B. U., 1818; student of divinity; died Quincy, Ill., 1820. Asa,[6] b. 1793. Lucy,[6] b. 1795; m. Nathan Blanchard. Ruth,[6] m. Jeremiah Stockbridge. Rachel,[6] b. 1797; m. Ira Beal.

161. iii. Mary,[5] b. 1758; m. Nathaniel Spear, 2d, of Randolph; pub. April 13, 1785.

162. iv. Elisabeth,[5] b. 1761; m. John Whitcomb, May 30, 1790.

51

Elijah[4] Porter, of Nathaniel[3] Porter, b. Topsfield, April 22, 1713; lived there; died Feb. 17, 1775. He was useful in the church, and active in town affairs; more than once a representative to General Court; and when he died clerk and treasurer of the town. His will, July 17, 1775, proved Feb. 5, 1776, names wife Dorothy, to whom he gives negro woman, Tamar. Children: Anna Hale.[5] Sarah.[5] Dorothy.[5] Hannah,[5] and Thomas[5]. Inventory, £1628; negro man and woman servant, and mulatto girl included. Married Dorothy. Children:

163. i. Anna,[5] m. Hale.
164. ii. Sarah.[5]
165. iii. Dorothy.[5]
166. iv. Hannah;[5] one account says she was unmarried in 1785, another that she married Rev. Daniel Breck, who began his ministry at Topsfield, in 1779; removed to Hartland, Vt., where he settled, and where he died. He was a man of fair talents and a good writer. His son Daniel Breck, was M. C. from Kentucky, in 1850.
167. v. Thomas,[5] m. Ruth Allen, of Salem.

56

Benjamin[4] Porter, of William[3] Porter, born in Topsfield, Feb. 4, 1712; lived in Braintree (Randolph part;) clerk of the precinct; wrote an excellent hand, and was much in the public business; selectman in 1756, '57, '58, '59, '60, '64, '65, and '66; removed to Wendell after 1766. Married 1st, June 1, 1738, Dorothy, daughter of Moses[3] and Dorothy (Ashley) Curtis, born Dec. 24, 1719; died April 10, 1743. Married 2d, Mary or Mercy, daughter of Seth and Sarah (Thayer) Dorman, of Braintree, Nov. 20, 1744; she born Sept. 7, 1720; died Dec. 28, 1811. He and wife Dorothy admitted to church in Braintree, (probably 2d,) 1739; he died in Wendell, Mass., Oct. 28, 1793. Children:

168. i. Benjamin,[5] b. Mar. 9, 1739.
169. ii. Phebe,[5] b. Aug. 14, 1740.
170. iii. Moses,[5] b. Apr. 6, 1743.
171. iv. Micaiah,[5] b. Apr. 26, 1745.
172. v. Eli,[5] b. Mar. 25, 1746.
173. vi. Ruth,[5] b. Oct. 26, 1748.
174. vii. William,[5] b. Aug. 15, 1750.
175. viii. Job,[5] b. Apr. 24, 1753; lived in Montague; had a son Seth,[6] who has a son Cephas,[7] living in Leverett, Mass.
176. ix. Seth,[5] b. Feb. 6, 1755; died same year.
177. x. Daniel,[5] b. Oct. 21, 1757.
178. xi. Noah,[5] b. July 21, 1760.

57

Seth[4] Porter, of William[3] Porter, born Topsfield, Feb. 15, 1714; lived in Braintree (Randolph.) Married Abigail Herrick, in Topsfield, Mar. 27, 1746. Children:

179. Seth,[5] b. Apr. 2, 1748 or 1747.
180. Abigail,[5] b. July 10, 1749.
181. Elisabeth,[5] b. Nov. 20, 1751.
182. Judith,[5] b. Sept. 8, 1756.

60

Doctor Jonathan[4] Porter, of Dea. William[3] Porter, born in Topsfield, Dec. 11, 1720. Physician; lived in Braintree and Malden; married Hannah, daughter of Jonathan[3] and Sarah[3] (Copeland) Hayden, of Braintree, Sept. 14, 1742; she born Dec. 4, 1724; died in Malden, June 20, 1811; he died in Malden, Jan. 1, 1783; his will filed for probate, Jan. 15; oldest son William appointed executor. There is a paper dated April 14, 1783, which purports to be the assent of the widow and children to the probate of the will, signed by "Hannah Porter, widow," Jona. Porter, Hannah Hills, Jabez Porter, Phebe Porter, Mary Porter, Joseph Porter, and Benjamin Porter, and some vacant places between the names, which look as though some of the children did not sign—these were all the children then living except John and Samuel, who were probably in South Carolina. Children:

183. i. William,[5] b. Braintree Sept. 19, 1743; m. Lamb; d. in Boston, Sept. 28, 1813.
184. ii. Jonathan,[5] b. Braintree, Mar. 12, 1745; m. Medford, 1773; m. Phebe Abbott, of Andover; died in Medford, Nov. 4, 1817.
185. iii. Hannah,[5] b. Braintree, April 4, 1748; d. Malden, Aug. 17, 1785.
186. iv. Sarah,[5] b. Braintree, Feb. 4, 1750; d. Malden, Sept. 31, 1775.
187. v. John,[5] b. Braintree, Dec. 28, 1751; d. Malden, Aug. 9, 1798.
188. vi. Jabez,[5] b. Braintree, Sept. 26, 1753; died S. Carolina, 1796.
189. vii. Phebe,[5] b. Braintree, Mar. 4, 1756; d. Malden.
190. viii. Polly,[5] born Braintree, Apr. 17, 1758; died Malden, July 12, 1762.

191. ix. Samuel,[5] b. Sept. 30, 1761; d. S. C.
192. x. Polly,[5] b. Malden, Sept. 27, 1762; d. Salem, Feb., 1838.
193. xi. Joseph,[5] b. Malden, Sept. 3, 1764; d. St. Stephen, N. B., June 19, 1822.
194. xii. Benjamin,[5] b. Malden, Mar. 16, 1767; d. in S. Carolina.

61

Jabez[4] Porter, of Dea. William[3] Porter, b. Topsfield, Feb. 1, 1723; grad. Harvard College, 1743; lived in Braintree; school master—taught school in Braintree, in the North, Middle and South Precincts, in 1767, '68, '69, '70, '71, '72, '84, '85; a part of the time the school is spoken of in town records as the "Latin School." He fitted Jonathan, Huntington, and Eliphalet Porter, three sons of Rev. John Porter, of North Bridgewater, for college, all of whom graduated at Harvard, in 1777. Married Ruth Wadsworth; she died May 17, 1792, aged 55; he died Jan. 28, 1792, aged 70. Children, born in Braintree (Randolph:)

195. i. Ruth,[5] b. 1759; teacher; died Mar. 17, 1793, aged 34.
196. ii. Samuel,[5] b. April 10, 1763.

67

Joseph[4] Porter, of Joseph[3] Porter, baptised at Salem village, Aug. 3, 1710; lived in Danvers; yeoman. Married Mary; he died Feb., 1747; (the widow married again, Joseph Perkins, of Malden.) Children:

200. i. Elisabeth,[5] baptised May 14, 1732; died young.
201. ii. Joseph,[5] baptised Mar. 16, 1736; died young.
202. iii. Mary,[5] born Feb. 28, 1739; died April 24, 1739.
203. iv. Joseph,[5] born April 4, 1740; died Feb. 12, 1805.

77

Israel[4] Porter, of Wenham—probably son of William[3] Porter, baptised Aug. 20, 1710. Married in Wenham, Abigail Batchelder, of Beverly; published Sept. 26, 1741. Children, from Wenham records:

204. i. Israel,[5] b. Feb. 16, 1743.
205. ii. Abigail,[5] b. June 10, 1745; probably married Charles Dodge, July 18, 1763.

78

William[4] Porter, of William[3] Porter, baptised June 21, 1713. He was executor of will of Jonathan Batchelder, Sen., of Salem, Mar. 22, 1740. "William Porter, Jr., yeoman, and Lydia his wife, of Salem, in the county of Essex, April 28, 1747, relinquish to Jona. Batchelder all right and title to the estate of their father, which her brother then occupied; was of Beverly Mar. 21, 1757, administrator of his brother Benjamin's estate, and was living there, in the part nearest to Salem, in 1759; probably soon after removed to Woburn; married Lydia Batchelder, July 5, 1738. Children:

210. i. **Ebenezer,[5] baptised Oct. 8, 1738, 2d church, Beverly.**
211. ii. **Asa,[5] baptised July 13, 1740, 2d church, Beverly; probably married in Wenham, April 14, 1768, Mary Batchelder, of Salem.**
212. iii. **Lydia,[5] baptised Dec. 26, 1742, 2d church, Beverly.**
213. iv. **Anna,[5] baptised Jan. 12, 1746, 2d church, Beverly.**
214. v. **Elisabeth,[5] baptised June 12, 1748, Salem village.**
215. vi. **William,[5] baptised April 21, 1751, Salem village.**
216. vii. **Jonathan,[5] baptised Oct. 14, 1753, 2d church, Beverly.**
216A. viii. **Asahel.[5]**

79

Benjamin[4] Porter, of William[3] Porter, baptised June 19, 1715; lived in Beverly and Danvers. Married 1st, Hannah Giles, April 27, 1737; died 1750. Married 2d, Anna, (or Emma;) he died 1757; adm. granted on his estate to his brother William, of Beverly, Mar. 21, 1757. His children were:

217. i. **Rufus,[5] baptised Sept. 21, 1740, 2d church Beverly; m. April 18, 1758, Jerusha, daughter of Boanerges and Jemima Raymond, baptised July 1, 1739—one child Hannah,[6] baptised after her father's decease, May 1, 1763; widow m. Ezra Fluant, May 22, 1764.**
218. ii. **Hannah,[5] baptised Oct. 18, 1742, 2d church Beverly.**
219. iii. **Abigail,[5] baptised Oct. 6, 1745, 2d church Beverly.**
220. iv. **Anna,[5] b. Danvers, Oct. 18, 1753.**
221. v. **Mary,[5] b. Danvers, May 4, 1755.**
222. vi. **Benjamin,[5] b. July 10, 1757, after father's decease.**

80

Joseph[4] Porter, of William[3] Porter, baptised 2d church, Beverly, Aug. 18, 1717; tailor; of Beverly; removed to Bedford prior to 1754. October 18, 1754, Joseph Porter, of Bedford, and wife Bethiah, sell for £26 13s 4d, to our brother William Batchelder, of Beverly, cooper, two acres and one hundred poles of land, in Beverly, and is part of the estate of our father, John Batchelder, late of Salem, deceased; also one-ninth part of two-thirds of a house and barn belonging to the estate. Probably married in Beverly, April 21, 1741, Bethiah Batchelder, daughter of John, senior, and Sarah Batchelder, who was baptised 2d church Beverly, with several others of her father's family, Dec. 24, 1727.

82

Josiah[4] Porter, probably of William[3] Porter, mentioned in settlement of his father's estate (Middlesex records,) of Woburn, 1755. I give account of the family, not vouching for its entire correctness. Married Sarah Waterman. Children:

222A. i. Dudley.[5]
B ii. Asa.[5]
C iii. Josiah,[5] estate probably adm. 1782, Middlesex county.
D iv. Betsey.[5]
E v. Polly.[5]
F vi. Nancy.[5]
G vii. Edith.[5]
H viii. Susan.[5]

88

John[4] Porter of Benjamin[3] Porter, (Israel,[2] John,[1]) born about 1712-13; lived in Danvers; inn-holder. Married Apphia, (who survived him and married 2d, Aug. 12, 1762, Asa Perly, of Boxford.) He died 1759. Jan. 11, 1762, Apphia, admin'x of her husband, John Porter, of Danvers, for £205, sells to Daniel Putnam, twenty acres of said Porter's estate, bounded on Benjamin Porter, and Frost Fish river. Children:

223. i. Elisabeth,[5] baptised Oct. 12, 1735, middle precinct; m. Asa, son of John and Rachel Leach, of Beverly; he baptised 2d church, Dec. 4, 1737. Children: Ginger,[6] bap. Sept. 19, 1762. Elisabeth,[6] bap. Sept. 19, 1762. Rachel,[6] bap. Sept. 26. Asa,[6] and Nathan,[6] twins, bap. Mar. 11, 1770, all at 1st church.
224. ii. John,[5] bap. June 13, 1736; died 1774.
225. iii. Benjamin,[5] bap. Oct. 22, 1738, middle precinct.
226. iv. Abigail,[5] bap. Mar. 22, 1740-1.
227. v. Ezra,[5] bap. July 1, 1744.
228. vi. Nathan,[5] cooper and mariner; m. Lydia Goodridge, Mar. 23, 1773; in revolutionary war.
229. vii. Anna,[5] m. Aug. 12, 1762, Eliphalet, son of Major Asa and Susana Perly, of Boxford, born Nov. 22, 1747. (?)
230. viii. Apphia,[5] bap. Oct. 20, 1754.
231. ix. Mary,[5] bap. May 30, 1756.

90

Benjamin[4] Porter, of Benjamin[3] Porter, (Israel,[2] John,[1]) born Danvers; of Danvers; potter. He and five sons said to have served in revolutionary war. Married 1st, Eunice, daughter of Samuel Nurse, Jr., Dec. 13, 1739; she baptised at Salem village church, Sept. 28, 1718. Married 2d, Abigail Osborne, April 21, 1778; born 1734; died South Danvers, Feb. 14, 1817. Administration granted on his estate to Israel Porter, potter, July 10, 1794. Children by Eunice:

232. i. Benjamin,[5] b. Oct. 28, 1740.
233. ii. Hannah,[5] b. Mar. 29, 1742; said to have married Com. Loring, of the British navy. (?)
234. iii. Eunice,[5] b. Sept. 22, 1744; married Nath. Webb, for his 1st wife; she died 1786. (He married 2d, Eunice Dale, and died Oct. 13, 1831.) Children: Nabby,[6] b. Sept. 6, 1770. Nathaniel,[6] b. Mar. 21, 1772. Benjamin,[6] b. July 23, 1779. Nathan,[6] b. June 23, 1782.
235. iv. Israel,[5] b. Oct. 3, 1746; m. Huldah Smith, 1771.
236. v. Francis,[5] b. Sept. 22, 1748; living in 1794.
237. vi. Sarah,[5] b. Aug. 11, 1752; m. John Page, Nov. 25, 1773; died before 1794.
238. vii. James,[5] b. Jan. 13, 1755; living in 1794.
239. viii. Peter,[5] b. May 9, 1757; soldier in revolutionary war.

240. ix. Huldah,[5] b. Mar. 20, 1759; m. Thomas Kimball.

241. x. Allen,[5] b. May 13, 1761; living 1794.

242. xi. Phebe,[5] b. Mar. 10, 1763; m. Ephraim Smith, May 12, 1781; he son of Nathan Smith, Jr.; bap. May 19, 1758; she died July 19, 1828. Children: Eunice,[6] b. Aug. 5, 1782. Mary,[6] b. Apr. 28, 1785. Ephraim,[6] b. Mar. 25, 1788. Phebe,[6] b. Dec. 13, 1790. Nathan,[6] b. Apr. 14, 1794. John,[6] b. Aug. 28, 1796. Thomas,[6] b. Feb. 11, 1799; died young. Thomas,[6] b. Sept. 17, 1801. William C.,[6] b. Jan. 20, 1805. Sally P.,[6] b. June 9, 1807.

93

Samuel[5] Porter, of Samuel[4] Porter, born Nov. 14, 1711; was of Wenham; housewright. Married Anna ——; she born 1715; died March 22, 1805, aged 90. He died 1786; will dated Nov. 29, 1784; proved July 3, 1786. Children:

250. i. Anna,[6] born Dec. 4, 1736; married John Dodge, Jr., May 15, 1760.

251. ii. Samuel,[6] born Jan. 15, 1739.

252. iii. Asa,[6] born Feb. 11, 1741; married Mary Batchelder, of Salem, April 14, 1768.

253. iv. Sarah,[6] born Jan. 2, 1743; died Jan. 23, 1743.

254. v. Dudley,[6] born Jan. 23, 1744.

255. vi. Isaac,[6] born May 1, 1746; died young.

256. vii. Mehetable,[6] born May 1, 1748; married Samuel Bean, of Beverly, Feb. 19, 1765.

257. viii. Isaac,[6] born July 1, 1750; died March 21, 1837.

258. ix. Jacob,[6] born Oct. 26, 1752.

258A. x. Sarah,[6] died July 27, 1757.

259. xi. Benjamin,[6] born Feb. 15, 1758; drowned in Wenham pond, Oct. 14, 1773.

260. xii. Nathaniel,[6] born Jan. 29, 1762.

94

John[5] Porter, of Samuel[4] Porter, born Wenham, July 9, 1717; lived Wenham; removed to Littleton after 1744. Married 1st, Mary Kimball, Nov. 30, 1738; she born Nov. 26, 1721; married 2d, Lydia ——, May 24, 1750, of Littleton. He sold for £93, to his brother Ebenezer, of Danvers, his house, barn, and seventeen acres of swamp and land in Wenham. He died March 12, 1802. Children:

261. i. Bial,[6] (dau.,) born Jan. 3, 1740; married Joseph Woodbury; pub. March 27, 1774.

262. ii. John,[6] born April 18, 1742; was of Littleton, Mass.; major in the revolutionary war; died 1834, aged 92.
263. iii. Mary,[6] born Nov. 28, 1744.

96

Ebenezer[5] Porter, of Samuel[4] Porter, born Wenham, 1716. After his marriage he went to Beverly, where, March 20, 1743, he sold Samuel Woodbury, for £180, a messuage situated partly in Salem and Beverly, consisting of eighteen acres land, house and barn, reserving a privilege unto our father, Josiah Creesy, and family. Between the above date and May 24, 1750, he removed to Danvers, where he bought of his brother John, of Littleton, his homestead. About June, 1763, returned to Wenham. Married April 2, 1741, Hannah Creecy, daughter of Joseph and Sarah (Dodge) Creecy, born July 25, 1721. He died in Wenham, March 3, 1800. His will dated Nov. 24, 1799; proved April 8, 1800. Children:

264. i. Sarah,[6] baptised 2d Church, Beverly, May 29, 1743.
265. ii. Ebenezer,[6] born Jan. 25, 1745.
265A. iii. Joseph,[6] born Danvers, Jan. 20, 1751.
265B. iv. Nathaniel,[6] born Danvers, Dec. 9, 1753.

101

Jonathan[5] Porter, of John[4] Porter, (of John,[3] of Samuel,[2]) born in Wenham, April 1, 1712; removed to Ellington, Conn., 1740; married Elizabeth Bachelder, of Wenham, May 5, 1737. He died July 5, 1783, aged 72; she died 1793, aged 81. Children:

266. i. John,[6] born 1738; baptised in Ipswich, July 2.
267. ii. Betsey,[6] born 1739; baptised in Ipswich, Dec. 30, 1739.
268. iii. Reuben,[6] b. 1742.
269. iv. Lydia,[6] b. 1744.
270. v. Jonathan,[6] b. 1748.
271. vi. Jerusha,[6] b. 1752.
272. vii. David,[6] b. 1754.

106

Daniel[5] Porter, of John[4] Porter, born Wenham, Sept. 19, 1721; died Wenham, of small pox, Jan. 5, 1760; married

Eunice Cue, of Wenham, April 17, 1745. She probably daughter of Robert and Mary (Porter) Cue. Children:

273. i. Ruth,[6] born Feb. 19, 1746.
274. ii. Lettice,[6] died April 5, 1749.
275. iii. Eunice,[6] born March 3, 1750.
276. iv. Abel,[6] born Dec. 31, 1751.
277. v. Elizabeth,[6] born Dec. 31, 1751; twin; died Jan. 29, 1752.
278. vi. Benoni,[6] died May 8, 1753.
279. vii. Elizabeth,[6] born July 9, 1754; probably married Ben Vernum, Feb. 12, 1775.
280. viii. Lydia,[6] born Oct. 24, 1759.

110

Moses[5] Porter, of Benjamin[4] Porter, of John,[3] of Samuel,[2] of John,[1] born Nov. 18, 1719; lived in Boxford; died there, town records say Nov. 3, 1711, (family record says Nov. 7;) he and first wife helped form the first church in the upper parish, and joined it Mar. 11, 1742, and remained members until their death; he was a member 69 years and 7 months. Married 1st, Mary, dau. of Edmund Chadwick, of Bradford, Dec. 3, 1741, (town records;) she born 1720; died Mar. 7, 1781, aged 61. Married 2d. Probably married 3d, his cousin, Mrs. Mary Low, widow of Joseph Low, of Newbury, and daughter of Jonathan[4] Porter. (See No. 121.) Children: Dates of birth by town records:

281. i. Asa,[6] b. May 26, 1742.
282. ii. William,[6] b. April 27, 1744; family record says May.
283. iii. Mary,[6] b. 1748; died 1752.
284. iv. Moses,[6] b. Jan. 18, 1750; married Ann Kay.
285. v. Aaron,[6] b. Mar. 28, 1752; of Biddeford.
286. vi. Mary,[6] b. July 20, 1754; m. Joseph Hovey of Boxford; died July, 1818, aged 64.
287. vii. Lucy,[6] b. Oct. 1, 1756; family record says September; m. Col. Benj. Towne, of Methuen; she a widow; died in Belfast, Me., May 11, 1836, aged 81.
288. viii. James,[6] b. Dec., 1758; died 1761.

112

Benjamin[5] Porter, of Benjamin[4] Porter, born Boxford, Oct. 6, 1721; lived there; died May 15, 1784. Married 1st, Ruth Foster, of Andover, Nov. 8, 1744; she died November,

1760, aged 38. Married 2d, Mary Sherwin, (?) Aug. 28, 1760. Children:

289. i. Lydia,[6] born Nov. 4, 1745; married Daniel Varnum.
290. ii. Mehetable,[6] born Dec. 24, 1747; published Asa Sherwin, April 26, 1764.
291. iii. David Foster,[6] born Sept. 4, 1749.
292. iv. Lucy,[6] born Oct. 3, 1751; married Asa Barker.
293. v. Sarah,[6] born Nov. 13, 1753; married Samuel Kimball.
294. vi. Benjamin,[6] born Sept. 29, 1754.
295. vii. Ruth,[6] born Oct. 27, 1756; died Feb., 1779.
296. viii. Tyler,[6] born April 27, 1758.
297. ix. Susanna,[6] b. May 9, 1763; m. Thomas Chadwick, May 22, 1796.
298. x. Jonathan,[6] b Aug. 29, 1765; died June 27, 1782.
299. xi. Mary,[6] b. July 25, 1767; died Mar. 5, 1824, aged 57.
300. xii. Mehetable,[6] b. Aug. 21, 1769; m. Stephen Peabody, of Boxford, 1792.

120

Benjamin[5] Porter, of Jonathan[4] Porter, of John[3]; born Wenham, Mar. 12, 1726; tanner; he removed to Danvers, prior to 1756, where he died, Feb. 12, 1810; he married Mar. 27, 1755, Sarah, widow of Bartholomew Brown, of Danvers, and daughter of Zerubbabel Rea, sister of his brother Jonathan's wife. Children:

301. i. Moses,[6] b. Mar. 20, 1756.
302. ii. Aaron,[6] b. Oct. 24, 1757; died Danvers, Dec. 3, 1843.
303. iii. Zerubbabel,[6] b. Sept. 4, 1759; died Nov. 11, 1845.
304. iv. Lydia,[6] b. Mar. 30, 1762; m. her cousin.
305. v. Sarah,[6] b. Nov. 25, 1763; unmarried Nov. 23, 1835.
306. vi. Benjamin,[6] b. April 27, 1766; taught school in Danvers, Beverly and other places; settled in Randolph, Vt.; had sons Benjamin,[7] and Aaron,[7] who had daughter Eunice,[8] (who m. Edward Brown; she died 1836;) he died in Rochester, Vt., 1854, aged 65; shoe-maker and Universalist preacher.
307. vii. Daniel,[6] b. Oct. 1, 1771.

122

Ruth[5] Porter, of Jonathan[4] Porter, born Wenham, Jan. 5, 1731; married Dr. Caleb Rea, of Gloucester, June 5, 1751; he was son of Zerubbabel and Margaret (Rogers) Rea, born in Danvers, July 17, 1727. (This was his second marriage; he married 1st, widow Abigail Sargent, Nov. 14, 1748, in Gloucester, who died 1749, leaving a daughter Abigail, born Aug. 23, 1749.) He was a physician; removed back to his native place Danvers, 1757. He was surgeon in Col. Bagley's Massachusetts Regiment, which was in the expedition against Ticonderoga, in 1758; he died in Danvers, Jan. 10, 1760. Children of Ruth and Caleb Rea:

i. Ruthy,[6] b. in Gloucester, April 8, 1752.

ii. Peirce Rogers,[6] b. in Gloucester, April 24, 1754; was in the battle of Bunker Hill, at the age of 21; died in Tewksbury.

iii. Caleb,[6] b. Danvers, Mar. 8, 1758; physician; traveled in Europe and Asia; surgeon in Continental army; first commenced practice of his profession at Ipswich, then Topsfield, and in Windham, Me., where he had a large practice; he died in 1796; he married Sarah, daughter of Capt. John White, of Salem, Oct. 4, 1781. F. M. Ray, Esq, attorney at law, of Portland, Me., is his great-grandson, and has his papers.

iv. Jonathan Porter,[6] b. Danvers, Mar. 25, 1760.

Mrs. Ruth Rea, married 2d, Johnson Proctor, of Danvers, and had children. Mrs. Ruth Proctor, married 3d, ——— Marsh, and died Mar. 12, 1819.

123

Jonathan[5] Porter, of Jonathan[4] Porter, born July 14, 1733, in Wenham; married Mehetable, daughter of Zerubbabel and Margaret (Rogers) Rea, Jan. 23, 1760; (?) removed to Exeter, N. H., Jan. 28, 1760; afterward to Salem, Topsfield, Bridgton, Me., Londonderry, N. H., and to Danvers, where he died at the "old homestead," Dec. 21, 1824, aged 91. Child:

308. i. Jonathan,[6] b. Exeter, N. H., May 1, 1763.

124

Tyler[5] Porter, of Jonathan[4] Porter, of John,[3] of Samuel,[2] of John,[1] born Wenham, Nov. 23, 1735; lived there; physician; distinguished in the revolutionary war as a patriot; married

Dorcus Emerson, of Topsfield; published Sept. 7, 1760; he probably died July, 1811. Children:

809. i. Mehetable,[6] b. Aug. 26, 1761; probably married Ben. Shaw, of Pembroke, N. H.; published Feb. 14, 1784.
810. ii. Tyler,[6] b. Aug. 31, 1764.
811. iii. Emerson,[6] b. Oct. 16, 1767.
812. iv. Jonathan,[6] b. April 28, 1771; had son Dr. John,[7] (who had daughter Elisabeth Winslow,[8]) and a daughter Harriet S.,[7] m. ——— Dodge.

125

Major Billy[5] Porter, of Jonathan[4] Porter, born Wenham, Aug. 23, 1739; lived there; he served in the army during the entire period of the revolutionary war, and rose to the rank of Major in the Continental troops. He was the first representative chosen by the town after the revolution, and again in 1793; soon after this he removed to North Beverly, where he died, Saturday, Nov. 20, 1813; his remains buried in Wenham. He married Mary, daughter of Dr. Benjamin and Mary (Woodbury) Jones, of Beverly; published in Wenham, Oct. 3, 1762; she born Feb. 8, 1742; died Oct. 15, 1763. Child:

813. i. Benjamin Jones,[6] born Sept. 20, 1763; educated at Byfield Academy; studied medicine with his uncle, Dr. Jones, who was a surgeon in the revolutionary army; in 1780, April 10, surgeon in Col. Tupper's regiment; in 1783, in Col. Jackson's regiment; practised medicine in Scarboro', Me., Westbrook, Me., and Portland. Became a partner in the extensive lumbering business of his brother-in-law, Governor Wm. King, at Topsham, Me.; A. M. Bowdoin College, 1809; Fellow and Treasurer of Bowdoin College from 1806 to 1815; member of the Supreme Executive Council of Massachusetts, and Senator from Lincoln County prior to separation. In the fall of 1829, removed to Camden, Me., where he died, August 18, 1847, aged 84. Married Elizabeth L., daughter of Hon. Richard and Mary (Black) King, of Scarboro', Me., born Jan. 7, 1770; sister of Hon. Rufus King and Governor Wm. King. Children were: William King.[7] Charles R.[7] Rufus K. Jones.[7] Mary.[7] Benjamin Jones.[7]

124

Dr. Tyler[5] Porter, of Jonathan[4] Porter, born in Wenham; lived there; physician; an eminent citizen and distinguished as a patriot in the Revolutionary War; m. Dorcas Emerson, of Topsfield; published Sept. 7, 1760. He died June 27, 1811, aged 76; his widow died Aug. 13, 1821, aged 81.

309

Mehetable[6] Porter, of Dr. Tyler[5] Porter, born Aug. 26, 1761; m. Benjamin Shaw, of Pembroke, N. H.; published Feb. 14, 1784. Children:

i. Tyler,[7] of Northport, Me.
ii. Jones,[7] of Northport, Me.
iii. Benjamin,[7] settled in Frankfort, now Winterport. One daughter, Mary E.,[8] m. Hon. Nathaniel H. Hubbard, of Winterport, Me., a successful lawyer.

310

Tyler[6] Porter, of Dr. Tyler[5] Porter, b. Aug. 31, 1764; he was a physician, and died Dec. 13, 1789, at the age of 25.

311

Emerson[6] Porter, of Dr. Tyler[5] Porter, born Oct. 16, 1766; m. Rebecca Story, dau. of Isaac Story, of Gilmanton, N. H. He died there, April 22, 1815, leaving a widow, but no children.

312

Jonathan[6] Porter, of Dr. Tyler[5] Porter, born April 28, 1771; lived in Wenham; m. Martha, dau. of Dr. William Fairfield; published Oct. 14, 1792; he died July 14, 1829; she died Sept. 1, 1862, aged 92. Children:

i. Harriet Shaw,[7] born April 13, 1793; married John Thorn Dodge, of Wenham, April 13, 1811; he died suddenly, Feb. 26, 1836, aged 46; his widow died May 1, 1876, aged 83. Children: Emerson Porter,[8] born April 3, 1815; m. Priscilla Rust, of Hamilton. Martha,[8] born Nov. 10, 1817; died Nov. 5th, 1820, aged 3 years. Harriet Gerrish,[8] b. Oct. 26, 1819; died Nov. 7, 1820. John Thorn,[8] b. Oct. 25, 1824; m. Mary Libby of Newfield, Me. Elisabeth Ann,[8] born Jan. 28, 1830; m. Andrew Dunn, of Wenham.

ii. John,[7] b. Oct. 27, 1799; studied medicine; practiced for several years in South Danvers, now Peabody. After the death of his father he returned and settled on the old homestead, in Wenham. Afterwards engaged in mercantile pursuits, in Boston, and continued in active business until his death, always returning at night to the old homestead, to which he was strongly attached. He was for many years one of the most prominent, useful, and respected citizens of his native town, filling all the offices of importance in the gift of the town; also representative to general court for several successive years; a man of superior judgment, stern integrity, and universal kindness. He died suddenly of heart disease, in the midst of active life, Nov. 19, 1866, aged 67. He married Elisabeth Averill, of Topsfield, Nov. 13, 1834; his widow is now living. One child, Elisabeth Winslow,[8] b. Aug. 13, 1835; m. George H. Tilton, of Boston, March 22, 1860; merchant. Mrs. Tilton is now the owner of a part of the original farm, which in the days of Samuel,[2] John,[3] and Jonathan,[4] extended from Wenham Pond to Pleasant Pond. Her house, with seven acres of land—adjoining other lands of John[3]—was deeded him April 15, 1703, and has been occupied successively by John,[3] Jonathan,[4] Dr. Tyler,[5] Jonathan,[6] and Dr. John[7] Porter.

iii. Tyler,[7] born Sept. 4, 1802; died Nov. 8, 1864; lived in Hamilton—farmer; m. Mary Quarles, of Hamilton; published Sept., 1823; widow is still living. Children: Martha Ann,[8] born Jan. 17, 1824; unmarried. Lucinda,[8] born Sept. 12, 1825; died Mar, 17, 1830. Oliver,[8] born May 26, 1827; married and resides in Hamilton. Lucinda,[8] born Mar. 29, 1830; died Aug. 9, 1850. Octavius,[8] now Otis,[8] born Nov. 1, 1832; unmarried; resides Dubuque, Iowa. Olive Maria,[8] born Aug. 3, 1835; m. —— Nelson, of Philadelphia, Miss. Frank,[8] born Oct. 15, 1837, resides in Chicago, Ill. Emily Clara,[8] born April 19, 1840; married Charles Lunn, of Marshall, Wis. Sylvanus,[8] born Sept. 15, 1842; m. Mary E. Lovering, of Hamilton; resides North Beverly. Charles,[8] born Feb. 16, 1845; m. Mary Trefrey, of Hamilton; resides North Beverly.

iv. William Fairfield,[7] b. April 18, 1806; he was a man of enterprise and spirit; had a passion for the ownership of land, inherited perhaps, from his earliest ancestors. In early life he settled in Newton, where he laid out many streets, ornamented them with trees, and erected tasteful residences. Subsequently he removed to Bradford, Mass. In 1835 went west, and purchased several hundred acres of land in the vicinity of Madison, Wisconsin; erected buildings, and remained there until 1865, when he returned to the vicinity of Boston, spending his winters in Florida. There he purchased several orange plantations, and also with other gentlemen, St. George's Island, in St. John's River, near Jacksonville, where they erected a hotel, laid out drives, etc., intending to make it in the future a popular resort. He died suddenly at Jacksonville, Fla., Nov. 20, 1878, aged 72. Married 1st, Clarissa Lummus, of Union, Me., Jan., 1830; she died at Bradford, Sept. 23, 1854. He m. 2d, Elisabeth Lane, of Haverhill, Mass., Oct. 13, 1856; his widow is still living. Children: William Henry,[8] born Nov. 10, 1830; resides in Marshall, Wisconsin, a leading and prominent citizen. He m. 1st, Elisabeth M. Bell, (?) April 26, 1870; she died Oct. 26, 1874. He married 2d, Nettie Page, Dec. 26, 1876. (He has one son, William Fairfied,[9] b. Nov. 20, 1877.) Martha,[8] born April 1, 1833; died in Bradford, Jan. 23, 1855, aged 22.

v. Henry,[7] b. Sept., 1809; died Jan. 22, 1851, aged 42. He was the inventor of "Porter's Patent Burning Fluid," so universally used before the introduction of kerosene. He received a patent for his invention, and established himself in business, in New York city, and afterwards in Boston; he acquired a handsome fortune. He married Louise Sanborn, of Portland, Me.; she died Jan. 4, 1859, aged 55, leaving no children.

vi. Edward,[7] b. March 30, 1812; resides in Weston, Mass.; m. Mary L. Knowlton, of Manchester, Feb. 26, 1843. One daughter,[8] married Henry Dodge, of Weare, N. H.

Ipswich. Married Lydia, daughter of Thomas Cummings; removed to Little Hockhocking, Ohio, where she died, March 28, 1814; and he died Feb. 24, 1827. Children:

314. i. Ebenezer,[6] born May 22, 1757; married Hannah Head.
A. ii. Lydia,[6] born Dec. 14, 1759.
B. iii. Solomon,[6] born May 30, 1762.
C. iv. Sarah,[6] born Feb. 18, 1766.
D. v. David,[6] born March 25, 1768.
E. vi. Joseph,[6] born March 18, 1770.
F. vii. Hannah,[6] born May 19, 1772.
G. viii. John,[6] born May 29, 1774.
H. ix. Rebecca,[6] born Aug. 4, 1776; married David White, Little Hockhocking, Ohio.
I. x. Cummings,[6] born Sept. 27, 1778.
J. xi. Priscilla,[6] born April 19, 1783.
K. xii. Samuel,[6] born Jan. 27, 1784.
L. xiii. Mary,[6] born March 12, 1787.

129

Samuel[5] Porter, probably son of Nehemiah[4] Porter, of Ipswich; lived in Boxford; married Sarah ———; he died May 10, 1750, aged 27. Children:

315. i. Samuel,[6] born May 8, 1746.
316. ii. John,[6] born March 10, 1747.
317. iii. Nehemiah,[6] born Dec. 15, 1749; married Susanna Robinson, of Andover, Jan. 7, 1772.

132

Hazadiah[5] Porter, of Nehemiah[4] Porter, lived in Ipswich; perhaps removed to Nova Scotia; married Anna ———. Children:

i. Hazadiah,[6] born Dec. 30, 1756.
ii. Anna,[6] born March 13, 1758; probably married Jacob Manning; published June 10, 1776.

135A

Mary[5] Porter, of Eleazer[4] Porter, of Samuel[3] Porter, born in Danvers; baptised Aug. 22, 1736; married Tarrant Putnam, Jan. 19, 1758; he born in Bedford, Sept. 2, 1733; son of Israel and Sarah Putnam; lived in Danvers; removed to Newbury, Vt., about 1789, where he died, 1804. Children, by first wife:

A. i. Eleazer Porter,[6] born Dec. 7, 1758; married Rebecca Smith, of Topsfield; she born June 29, 1760; died April 15, 1816; he died May 3, 1814, at Corinth, Vt. Children: Samuel,[7] physician, of Newbury, Vt.; died 1817; married ——— Bailey. (Child: one son, Samuel Porter;[8] went west.) Israel,[7] born March 25, 1785; physician; married Charlotte Safford; died in 1835. (Children: Betsey Smith,[8] born April 9, 1812. Israel,[8] b. 1813. Charlotte S.,[8] b. 1815; married W. C. Gardiner; died 1862. Silas Safford,[8] born 1817; died young. Harriet Newell,[8] born 1818; died young. La Fayette,[8] born 1820; died 1852. Silas Safford,[8] born 1822; resides Neponset; m. ——— Whitmarsh. Samuel P.,[8] b. 1823; died 1851. Fanny Loraine,[8] m. ——— Stockman, of Roxbury.) Benjamin,[7] born Sept. 1, 1788; minister; preached in Randolph and other places; married Joanna Weaver. (Children: Maria Louisa,[8] born 1816; married Rev. R. K. Bellamy, of Chicopee Falls. Hiram Smith,[8] born 1817; died young. Julia Ann,[8] born 1819; married Rev. E. B. Cross; died in Burmah, India, in 1875. Harriet L.,[8] born 1820; married Wm. S. Packer; resides in Brooklyn, N. Y.; founder of Packer Institute. Benjamin Porter,[8] born 1822; died 1848. Joseph Elliot,[8] born 1824; of Foxcroft, Me.; unmarried.) Harriet Smith,[7] married ——— Ormsby, of Fairlee, Vt.; four children. Sally,[7] b. 1799; m. ——— Raymond; died 1850. Louisa,[7] born 1805; married E. C. Scott, 1837; lives at Atlantic, near Boston.

B. ii. Israel,[6] born Nov. 22, 1760; of Topsham, Vt.

C. iii. Asa,[6] born Dec. 28, 1763; of Essex, N. Y.

D. iv. Daughter,[6] baptised Jan. 5, 1766.

E. v. Abigail,[6] born July 13, 1768; married cousin, Joseph Putnam.

F. vi. Mary,[6] born April 5, 1771; married Wyman Smith. Six children.

Tarrant Putnam married second, Eunice Porter, (No. 275,) daughter of Daniel Porter, (No. 1[illegible]) who died of small pox, Jan. 5, 1760; she born in Wenham, March 3, 1750. "May, 1777, Eunice Porter, widow, of Wenham, and Tarrant

Putnam and wife Eunice, and als., sell to George Crownshield 19 acres 12 poles land in Wenham, bounded on Daniel Porter, deceased, and others." Children, by second wife:

Sarah.[6] David.[6] Tarrant.[6] Eunice.[6] Ruth.[6] Elisha.[6] Elisabeth,[6] born Feb. 16, 1786.

135c

Samuel[4] Porter, of Eliezer[3] Porter, born in Danvers, Jan. 30, 1743; graduated at Harvard College, 1763; lawyer; lived in Ipswich and Salem. March 30, 1764, Samuel Porter, gent., for thirteen pounds six shillings and eight pence, bought from Tarrant Putnam and Mary his wife, thirty-seven acres fifty poles of land that Abigail Porter (his youngest sister) died seized of, in which said Tarrant and Mary quit-claim their right. June 5, 1771, Samuel Porter, of Ipswich, gent., for 658 pounds 10 shillings, L. M., sold Archelaus Rea, of Topsfield, 5 3-4 acres 16 poles meadow, dwelling house and barn, in Danvers, bounded on Israel Andrews, Jonathan and David Putnam, Tarrant and Benjamin Putnam, said Samuel Porter, heirs of Daniel Gott, John and Archelaus Rea, and right to use cider mill, on land standing to right of Mary, wife of Tarrant Putnam. Samuel Porter, of Ipswich, 1772, bought land of Elijah and Thomas Porter, of Topsfield. April, 1774, Samuel Porter, esquire, of Salem, for 100 pounds, sold Joseph Porter, of Danvers, twenty acres of land bounded on Tarrant Putnam and others. He was a loyalist, and fled to England during the revolutionary war. Sabine, in his History of American Loyalists, says his name occurs among the barristers and attorneys who addressed Gov. Hutchinson, on his departure for England in June, and among the Salem addressers of Gov. Gage, on his arrival, June, 1774; and is to be found in the banishment act of 1778. He died in London, 1798; lived in Wormwood street. His will, dated Sept. 29, 1797; proved March 9, 1798. Administration granted to Thomas Graham, executor of the will in London, and Jacob Ashton, executor and administrator in Salem, Mass. To the children of his sister Mary, (wife of Tarrant Putnam,) deceased, he gives one hundred dollars each. To Mr. Ashton, for his friendship, "whatever money or effects he may happen to have in hand for me at my decease, and wherein such money may be short of 200 dollars, (pounds ?) * * I would have it made up." To Mr. Novello, "with whom I for the most of a dozen years resided, in Oxford street, ten pounds for his friendly and honest demeanor." "To my friend Thomas Graham, of Lincoln's Inn, I leave the rest he may owe me, with any justice he may obtain of this nation *for my losses and ruin on its account*, excepting what may be pretended so thereunto me on pension of eighty pounds, assigned some time in 1788," &c., &c. The mourning ring for my friend, Richard Saltonstall, esquire, with another provided by Mr. Graham, I wish to be sent to Mr. Ashton, the former to be by him handed over to my said friend Saltonstall's half-brother, Nathaniel Saltonstall, of Haverhill, in the county of Essex; and the other to be kept by Mr. Graham. (Ashton ?)

141

Daniel[5] Porter, of Nathaniel[4] Porter, b. Feb. 3, 1743; lived in Topsfield; died Jan. 28, 1831, aged 87 years 11 months and 11 days. He married, April 9, 1769, or as another account says Mar. 29, 1770, Sarah Peabody, daughter of Matthew and Mehetable Peabody, born Mar. 31, 1733. Children:

318. i. Nathaniel,[6] b. Oct. 25, 1771.
319. ii. David,[6] b. July 29, 1773.
320. iii. James,[6] b. Apr. 19, 1775; died in fourth year.
321. iv. Sarah,[6] b. Mar. 6, 1777; died in second year.
322. v. Allen,[6] b. June 23, 1779.
323. vi. Polly,[6] b. Jan. 16, 1782.
324. vii. Sally,[6] b. April 1, 1786; m. David Cummins, Aug. 13, 1812; born in Topsfield, Aug. 14, 1785; graduated D. C., 1806; died in Dorchester, March 30, 1855, aged 69. He was Judge of Court of Common Pleas, 1848 to 1855. Married 2d, Katharine Kitteredge, 1815.
325. viii. Ira,[6] b. July 8, 1791; resides in Topsfield, 1878; m. Dolly Coburn, of Fairlee, Vt., Dec. 28, 1834; she died May 7, 1838, aged 42; had three children, died young.

Married 2d, Harriet Towne, Mar. 13, 1839. Children: Ira Coburn,[7] born April 16, 1840. Francis Leverett,[7] b. June 13, 1842; died Aug. 11, 1869. Harriet Sophia,[7] b. Jan. 31, 1849.

142

Nathaniel[5] Porter, of Nathaniel[4] Porter, born Topsfield, Jan. 3, 1744; "died 1836, aged almost 92 years." Grad. Harvard College, 1768; clergyman, first at New Durham, N. H., where June 4, 1777, he sold for £30, his part of his father's estate; afterward removed to Conway, N. H.; married—— of Portsmouth, N. H., the mother of his children and afterwards Mrs. Page of Conway. Children were probably:

326. i. Nathaniel,[6] went to sea; died in West Indies.
327. ii. Tobias Lear,[6] was captain of the brig Success; eighty-four days from St. Petersburg, struck Branch Rock, Marshfield beach; were all lost but the cook and cabin boy, Nov. 20, 1811; the captain was about 33 years old, and had a wife in Salem.
328. iii. Sally,[6] b. about 1776; m. D. Davis.
329. iv. Mary,[6] b. 1781; m. Jonathan Webster.
330. v. Patty Mumford,[6] b. 1786; m. Joseph Durgin.
331. vi. Nabby,[6] b. 1788; m. Samuel Plumer.
332. vii. James Stilson,[6] b. Sept., 1791.
333. viii. John,[6] b. Jan 26, 1794; died Aug. 22, 1814.
334. ix. Daniel T.,[6] b. 1798.
335. x. Stephen,[6] b. 1800.

154

Thomas[5] Porter, of Thomas[4] Porter, of Nathaniel,[3] born in Danvers, August 6, 1756; died there, June, 1796; married Martha Whartt, (?) June 13, 1776. Children:

336. i. Thomas,[6] born June 29, 1776. (?)
337. ii. John,[6] born Feb. 14, 1778; sailed out of Salem as master of a vessel, in 1812; was taken by a privateer, and died in Dartmoor prison.
338. iii. Patty,[6] born Oct. 15, 1779; married first, John Lewis, of Lynn; and second, Wm. P. K. Ramsdell.
339. iv. James,[6] born Oct. 8, 1781.
340. v. Betsey,[6] born March 21, 1784; married John Lowe, of Lynn.
341. vi. Samuel,[6] born Aug. 3, 1788.

167

Thomas[5] Porter, of Elijah[4] Porter, born Topsfield; he held a military commission in the first years of the revolutionary war; married Ruth, daughter of Edward and Ruth (Hodges) Allen, of Salem. She died June, 1849, aged 90. Cleveland's Topsfield Centennial Address says: "This charming old lady lived to see around her a numerous and prosperous race, and certainly could feel, as she looked upon them, that some, at least, of the Porter family, had effectually fought their way out of 'Blind Hole.'" Children:

342. i. Mary,[6] born March 29, 1786; married Seth Low.
343. ii. Edward Allen,[6] born Jan. 25, 1788; died unmarried, in Salem, Dec. 31, 1819.
344. iii. Thomas,[6] born Dec. 31, 1790; died in New Orleans.
345. iv. Elijah,[6] born Sept. 27, 1792.

168

Capt. Benjamin[5] Porter, of Benjamin[4] Porter, born Braintree, (Randolph,) Mar. 9, 1739; went from Braintree to Assonet village, Freetown, and learned blacksmith trade with Samuel Tisdale. In 1758, he enlisted to fill quota of Freetown, in French and Indian war; in 1788 captain of infantry; he acquired a moderate competence, and was much respected by his fellow townsmen. Married Rebecca, daughter of Samuel Tisdale, of Freetown, Jan. 30, 1763; she died Nov. 16. 1798; he died Mar. 28, 1817; will proved, April 4. Children:

352. i. Betsey,[6] b. Nov. 16, 1763; m. Daniel Douglas, of Freetown, July 22, 1782. Children: Robert.[7] Benjamin.[7]
353. ii. Robert,[6] b. Aug. 6, 1765; m. Ruth Reed, of Freetown, Mar. 22, 1792. Children: Betsey.[7] Joseph.[7] Rowena.[7]
354. iii. Benjamin,[6] b. May 3, 1767; m. Betsey Hathaway, of Freetown, Oct. 27, 1796. Children: Hanford.[7] Bradford.[7] Benjamin.[7] Thomas.[7] Lewis.[7] Mary.[7] William.[7] Anna.[7] Eliza.[7] Delany.[7]
355. iv. Tisdale,[6] b. April 29, 1769; m. 1st, Betsey Tobey, of Berkley, Jan. 12, 1794; m. 2d, Rebecca Hathaway, of Berkley, Mar. 10, 1799. Children: Rebecca.[7] Henry.[7] Phillip.[7] Emma.[7] He died Mar. 25, 1850.
356. v. Mary,[6] b. Mar. 5, 1771; m. Capt. Benj. Lawton, of Freetown, Oct. 9, 1803. Children: Rebecca.[7] Harriet.[7] William.[7] She died Oct., 1836.

357. vi. Sarah,[6] b. Aug. 23, 1773; m. James Valentine, Mar. 16, 1806; she died April 30, 1848. Children: Rebecca.[7] James.[7] Ann.[7] William.[7] Helena.[7]

358. vii. Henry,[6] b. Jan. 29, 1776; m. Elisabeth Tisdale, Feb. 7, 1807. Ensign in Capt. Lynde Hathaway's company, 1814; lieutenant, 1816; captain, 1818; discharged in 1822; died Freetown, the oldest man in town, Mar. 9, 1866, aged 90. Children: Rebecca,[7] died young. Betsey,[7] died young. Robert.[7] Henry.[7] William,[7] drowned. Rebecca.[7] William.[7] Benjamin.[7] Mary.[7] Bradford.[7]

359. viii. Lewis,[6] b. Nov. 10, 1781; died unmarried, Sept. 19, 1807.

360. ix. Rebecca,[6] b. Mar. 5, 1784; m. James Phillips, July 11, 1805; she died Nov., 1806.

360A x. Phebe,[6] b. Sept. 29, 1778; (?) m. James Phillips, Dec. 20, 1812; she died Aug. 29, 1861. Children: Rebecca.[7] Phebe.[7] James.[7]

361. xi. William,[6] b. April 10, 1786; unmarried; died Jan. 18, 1811.

171

Micaiah[5] Porter, of Benjamin[4] Porter, born in Braintree, April 26, 1745; grad. B. U., 1775; studied theology with Dr. Levi Hunt, of Preston, Conn.; traveled through the south as a preacher; ordained minister at Voluntown, Conn., 1781, where he remained until Aug., 1800; afterward settled at Plainfield, July 17, 1805. He married Elisabeth, daughter of Capt. Isaac Gallup, of Voluntown, Conn., Nov., 1781, the evening after his ordination; she was a descendant of Capt. John Gallup, who was killed in the "Narragansett swamp fight," 1675. Children:

362. i. Isaac,[6] b. Oct. 11, 1783; grad. B. U., 1808; commenced practice of medicine at Lebanon, N. H., 1816; removed thence to Charlton; and in 1825, to Boston; he m. Amey, daughter of Capt. William Potter, of Cranston, R. I., June 11, 1817. Children: William M.,[7] b. Mar. 18, 1818. Joseph K. P.,[7] b. July 25, 1819. Phebe R.,[7] b. April 5, 1824. Isaac G.,[7] b. Aug. 21, 1827.

363. ii. William,[6] b. Feb. 11. 1785; he was school master; taught at Freetown four years; died at his father's house, in Plainfield, Nov. 13, 1816, at the age of 32.

364. iii. Benjamin,[6] b. May 11, 1788; commenced practice of medicine at Northfield, Vt., 1816; m. Sophia K. Fullerton, June 9, 1822; she born July 3, 1801. Children: Elisabeth P.,[7] b. Mar. 17, 1823. Edward,[7] b. April 24, 1826. Ewen,[7] b. April 24, 1826. Benjamin F.,[7] b. April 20, 1833.

365. iv. Phebe,[6] b. Mar. 11, 1790; "an eminent and devout christian;" died unmarried June 24, 1819.

366. v. John,[6] b. Jan. 25, 1795; physician; received his medical degree at D. C.. 1820; settled at Duxbury, Mass.; m. Ann, daughter of John and Lucy Thomas, of Marshfield, July 19, 1829. Children: John Thomas,[7] b. Aug. 27, 1830. George K.,[7] b. Feb. 9, 1833.

367. vi. Jabez,[6] b. Dec., 1797; unmarried, 1835.

368. vii. Martha,[6] b. Feb., 1799; died July 30, 1834; m. Rev. Charles Walker, Aug. 8, 1827; he born at Rindge, N. H., Nov. 21, 1795; graduate D. C., Aug., 1823; ordained minister New Ipswich, N. H., Feb. 28, 1827. Children: Charles Porter,[7] b. Nov. 12, 1828. Henry Lankton,[7] b. April 29, 1830; died June 11, 1833. Henry Lankton,[7] b. Mar. 23, 1833.

177

Daniel[5] Porter, of Benjamin[4] Porter, born Braintree, Oct. 21, 1757; physician; removed Wendell, Mass.; town clerk there many years; late in life, removed to Whitestown, N. Y.; married Rachel Weatherbee, 1782; she born April 9, 1763; died June 19, 1845. Children:

369. i. William Dorman,[6] b. June 15, 1783; died Sept., 1870; he m. Nabby Jones, Nov. 29, 1804; she died Aug. 31, 1847. Children: Augustina S.,[7] b. Aug. 31, 1805; died 1841. Julia,[7] b. Sept. 10, 1807. William L.,[7] b. Nov. 11, 1814. Benjamin Willard,[7] b. Aug. 10, 1821; now of 202 Lasalle street, Chicago. Mary Jane,[7] b. Dec. 28, 1824.

370. ii. Katy Willard,[6] b. Oct. 17, 1788; died April 17, 1838.

371. iii. Polly,[6] b. April 15, 1792; died April 25, 1838.

372. iv. Samuel,[6] b. Feb. 19, 1796; died 1874.

373. v. Amy,[6] b. March 5, 1801; living 1878.

178

Noah[5] Porter, of Benjamin[4] Porter, born July 21, 1760; lived in Wendell, Mass.; married Asenath Smith; he died April 12, 1830, aged 70; she died Aug. 11, 1836. Their son:

374. i. Noah,[6] b. Sept. 26, 1792; died Oct. 8, 1855.

187

John[5] Porter, of Dr. Jonathan[4] Porter, born in Braintree, Mass., Dec. 28, 1751; died in Malden, Aug. 9, 1798. He lived in Malden and Charleston, S. C., but the time in which he lived in either of them, I am unable to give; he married Elisabeth, dau. of James Lamb,* of Boston—(after his death widow m. Vincent; and 3d, Normand McLeod, planter, of Edisto Island, S. C.; he outlived his wife, she dying in 1819, at age of 53.) Children of John[5] Porter:

390. i. William Lamb,[6] b. Charleston, S. C., 1786.
391. ii. Elisabeth,[6] b. in Mass.; m. Moses Wheeler, of Boston, and died 1825, aged 38.
392. iii. Frances,[6] b. in Mass.; m. Moses Wheeler, her sister's husband; she died about 1829; their daughter Mary,[7] m. William Rea, of 48 Chestnut St., Boston.
392A. iv. Hannah,[6] b. in Mass.; died unmarried.

193

Joseph[5] Porter, of Jonathan[4] Porter, born Malden, Sept. 3, 1764; in 1786, he went to Robbinston, Me., in the employ of Gov. Robbins, of Mass. In 1788 he removed to Calais, Me., and went into trade on Ferry Point, and kept the first store there; in 1785 he removed to Saint Stephen, N. B., just over the river St. Croix, where for many years he lived a useful, active and respected citizen. He married, Sept. 18, 1793, Betsey Marks, daughter of Capt. Nehemiah Marks, of St. Stephen, N. B., (loyalist) she born Derby, Conn., Sept. 18, 1774; died St. Stephen, Jan. 4, 1870; he died there June 19, 1822. Children, all born in St. Stephen, except the first, were:

383. i. William,[6] born Feb. 2, 1795; married; died St. Stephen, May 30, 1861.
384. ii. Betsey Ann,[6] b. May 17, 1796; m. James P. Bixby, of New Hampshire; now living, 1878.
385. iii. Hannah Hayden,[6] b. Feb. 2, 1798; m. Jonathan Williams, of Mass.; died Jan. 7, 1828.

*James Lamb, of Boston, said to have had a family of 20 children: one dau. m. Wm. Porter; one m. John Porter; one m. Hastings; one m. Twing; two m. Wadsworths; one m. Woodbridge; and among other sons, Thomas Lamb, of Boston.

386. iv. John,[6] b. Aug. 20, 1802; m. 1st, Louisa McAllister; m. 2d, Ann Whitney; he died Boston, Feb., 1852.

387. v. George Marks,[6] b. June 24, 1804; resides St. Stephen; a gentleman of standing and character; m. 1st, Mary B. Topliff; and 2d, E. A. Housley.

388. vi. Mary,[6] b. July 12, 1806; m. Parker Bixby, of Litchfield, N. H.; now living.

389. vii. Eliza,[6] b. twin with above; m. Joseph Stuart; she died St. Stephen, Mar. 4, 1828.

390. viii. Joanna Brewer,[6] b. Sept. 13, 1808; m. David Upton, of St. Stephen; now living, 1878.

391. ix. Joseph Nehemiah,[6] b. Oct. 19, 1811; m. Janette Grant, of St. Stephen; he died New York, Feb. 23, 1852.

392. x. James,[6] b. Mar. 18, 1816; m. Anna Maria Christie, of St. Stephen; he died Dec. 8, 1859.

196

Samuel[5] Porter, of Jabez[4] Porter, b. Braintree, (Randolph) April 10, 1763; lawyer of eminence; grad. Dartmouth College, 1790; lived in Dummerston, Vt.; represented the town in the legislature several years; Chief Judge of the County Court in Windham County, and several years Judge of Probate; he died Feb. 10, 1810, aged 46. He married Mehetable, daughter of General Samuel and Mehetable (Hazeltine) Fletcher, of Townshend, Vt. Children, all born in Dummerston, except the oldest:

393. i. Samuel Wadsworth,[6] b. Nov. 4, 1792.

394. ii. Henry Lee,[6] b. Dec. 28, 1794; died May 17, 1862.

395. iii. Frederick Augustus,[6] b. Sept. 5, 1796.

396. iv. Sophia Charlotte,[6] b. Aug. 26, 1798; m. Marshall Miller, of New Fane, Vt.; her husband deceased; she now resides with her son, Samuel Miller, at New Fane.

397. v. George Washington,[6] b. July 28, 1800.

398. vi. Lorena Stella,[6] b. June 8, 1802; m. Phillip Goss.

399. vii. Aurelia P.,[6] b. July 25, 1804; m. David Goss; deceased.

400. viii. Charles Edward,[6] b. Sept. 2, 1806; m. Lydia Ann Emerson; he died in Springfield, Vt., April 10, 1859. Son, Charles Emerson,[7] b. Dec. 16, 1847.

203

Joseph[5] Porter, of Joseph[4] Porter, of Joseph[3] Porter, of Joseph[2] Porter, of John[1] Porter, born Danvers, April 4, 1740;

died there Feb. 12, 1805; lieut. in revolutionary war; married 1st, Sarah, daughter of Benjamin and Sarah Putnam, May 17, 1745; she died Sept. 10, 1766; married 2d, Elisabeth Herrick (1767;) she died 1816; her will made April 13, 1816, not executed, probably owing to same informality; in it she names daughter Ruth Gould, of Joseph, grand-daughter Betsey, of late daughter Betsey Gould, and daughters of the late daughter Polly Bradstreet; Joseph Porter, executor. Children:

410. i. Joseph,[6] b. June 22, 1763; died June 3, 1820; m. Ruth Hartwell, June 3, 1788; she died Danvers, Nov. 24, 1843; no children.

411. ii. Sarah,[6] b. Feb. 5, 1765; died Newbury, Vt., Feb. 13, 1834; m., Jan. 27, 1789, Daniel Putnam, son of Daniel and Elisabeth Putnam; b. Danvers, Oct. 3, 1762; died Newbury, Vt., Dec. 19, 1802. Children: Betsey,[7] b. Jan. 22, 1791; died Aug. 29. Daniel,[7] b. Jan. 9, 1792; m. Rebecca G. Carlton, b. Dec. 26, 1796. Betsey,[7] b. May 12, 1794. Joel,[7] b. July 28, 1796. Sally,[7] b. Mar. 17, 1800.

412. iii. Elisabeth,[6] b. Jan. 10, 1768.

413. iv. Phebe,[6] b. Aug. 20, 1769; m. Cornelius, son of Joseph Gould. Children: Clarissa.[7] Phebe.[7] Betsey.[7] Porter.[7] Fanny.[7]

414. v. Polly,[6] b. Jan. 20, 1771; m. Capt. Dudley Bradstreet, of Topsfield, who came down and settled on the old Downing Porter place, in Danvers. Children: Colonel Porter.[7] John,[7] m. Sarah Rea; she now living in Topsfield, over 80 years of age. Polly.[7] Dudley.[7] Eliza P.[7] Joseph.[7] Albert G.[7] Jonathan.[7] (?) Sarah.[7] Lydia,[7] (probably Thomas Jefferson.[7])

415. vi. Lydia,[6] b. June 7, 1772; m. Nathaniel Gould, probably Jan., 1793. Children: Henry.[7] Betsey.[7]

416. vii. Ruth,[6] b. May 12, 1774; m. Joseph Gould, brother of Cornelius. Children: Harriet.[7] Joseph.[7] Ruth.[7] Elisabeth.[7] Lydia.[7] Emerson.[7] Angelina.[7] Ariel.[7]

417. viii. Jonathan,[6] b. May 24, 1776; m. Eunice Boardman, sister of Nathaniel Boardman; no children; she m. 2d, Capt. Jeremiah Putnam, of Danvers—his 2d wife; she born Jan. 8, 1778; died May 2, 1851, aged 73.

215

William[5] Porter, of William[4] Porter, (?) b. Apr. 21, 1751; of Woburn; m. Hannah, dau. of William and Rebecca (Locke) Munroe, of Lexington, 1774; she born 1751. Children:

420. i. Rufus,[6] b. Mar. 27, 1775; m. Abigail Grover, 1796.
421. ii. Lydia,[6] b. Dec. 15, 1776; died unmarried, 1849.
422. iii. Rebecca,[6] b. June 28, 1779; living unmarried in W. Cambridge, 1852.
423. iv. James,[6] b. Aug. 17, 1782; died without issue.
424. v. Hannah,[6] b. July 18, 1785; m. Wm. Locke.
425. vi. Apphia,[6] b. Mar. 30, 1788; m. 1st, Ward Locke, of Lexington; m. 2d, Richard Cummings. Children—by 1st husband: Maria,[7] b. Oct. 6, 1808; m. 1st, David Mellen, 1825; 2d, Orrin Rawson, of Nashua, N. H. John Franklin,[7] b. Jan. 20, 1814; m. Sarah Thomas, 1845, of New Orleans. Sarah Ann,[7] b. Apr. 30, 1816; m. John Bowen, 1838, of Hillsboro, N. H. Elisabeth,[7] b. Dec. 29, 1817; m. Benjamin F. Reeves, 1837, of Salem and Boston.
426. vii. Frederick,[6] b. July 8, 1790; m. Sarah B. Hume, of New Jersey; lived in Philadelphia; Secretary of American Sunday School Union.

216A

Asahel[5] Porter, probably of William[4] Porter, of Woburn; killed by British troops at Lexington, April 19, 1775; about twenty-three years of age. John Munroe in his deposition, Dec. 28, 1824, (Elias Phinney's His. of Battle of Lexington,) says "Asahel Porter, of Woburn, who had been taken prisoner by the British, on their march to Lexington, attempted to make his escape, and was shot within a few rods of the common." Hon. Charles Hudson, of Lexington, says he was a non-combatant, taken without arms. Sewall's History of Woburn, page 362, says in connection with the Lexington fight, "of these who went from Woburn, two did not return, viz: Mr. Asahel Porter, son of William Porter," etc. A marble stone erected to his memory, in Woburn cemetery, April 21, 1875, just one hundred years after his burial. "Married at Seabrook, N. H., Oct 3, 1773, by Rev. Samuel Perley, Mr. Asahel Porter and Mrs. Abigail Brooks, both of Salem." I suppose this to be this man.

Asahel[6] Porter, whom I suppose to have been son of above, bought of ——— Mason, a farm in Reading and removed from Stoneham. Married Betsey Atwell, 1796; she died 1869. Children:

i. Asahel.[7]
ii. Mary,[7] m. Capt. Geo. Bancroft, 1819.
iii. George,[7] m. Emily Bancroft, July 23, 1827; she b. April 26, 1809; died Mar., 1868. Their daughter Elisabeth, m. John Laurie, of Galesburg, Ill.; and son George resides in Reading with his father, unmarried.
iv. Daughter,[7] m. Wyman Damon, of Reading; now of Andover; she died.

222A

Dudley[5] Porter, of Josiah[4] Porter, or Josiah[5] Porter, (I give this family here, but have some doubt about its being the right place, but with no doubt as to their being descendants of John[1] Porter, of Danvers.) He removed to Yarmouth, Nova Scotia, where several Porters removed from Essex county, during and after the revolutionary war. He is said to have married Mary Brown, in New York. Children, born in Yarmouth, Nova Scotia:

423. i. Benjamin,[6] m. Eleanor Dodge.
424. ii. Josiah,[6] m. Edith Corning.
425. iii. Sarah,[6] m. James Crosby.
426. iv. Mary,[6] m. Wm. Corning.

A Dudley Porter, married Sarah, first daughter of Dr. John Hay, of Reading, Mass., part now Wakefield—Nov. 5, 1780, she born 1762. They removed to Yarmouth, Nova Scotia, where she died in 1800, aged 38.

224

John[5] Porter, of John[4] Porter, bap. June 13, 1736; lived in Danvers; died there, 1774; married Hannah ———; administration granted widow Hannah, May 2, 1774; guardianship of son John, aged 18, Hannah, over 14, Nathan, aged 8 years, granted Asa Leach, Oct., 1781. Jan. 20, 1783, Hannah, adm'x of her husband and John Porter, mariner, deceased, sells two acres of land on Porter's Plain, being part of the thirds of Apphia, widow of John Porter (father of said John,) innholder. Children, baptised middle precinct:

427. i. John,[6] baptised July 1, 1764.
428. ii. Rebecca,[6] baptised July 1, 1764; died young.
429. iii. Hannah,[6] baptised Sept. 27, 1767.
430. iv. Nathan,[6] baptised Nov. 22, 1772.

225

Benjamin[5] Porter, of John[4] Porter, baptised Oct. 22, 1738, middle precinct of Danvers; lived there and was a potter; Mar. 21, 1783, he and wife Eunice, (probably Osborne) for £46, sold Gideon Putnam, innholder, three pieces of land "which was my father John Porter's," first containing one and one-fourth acres "bounded on Ipswich road, and land set off to Mehetable, now wife of Sylvester Procter, formerly widow of my brother, Ezra Porter, as her right of dower, and on land which Gideon Putnam lately bought of my brother Nathan, and land belonging to my sister Anna, wife of Eliphalet Perley, containing in all four acres; probably removed to Wiscasset, Maine, in 1790, with son Ezra, aged 20 years, and two daughters; he died Wiscasset, Me., 1805; administration granted on his estate, Sept. 17, 1805, Lincoln county; married Eunice Osborne. Children:

431. i. Jonathan,[6] b. Feb. 1, 1764.
432. ii. Ezra,[6] probably b. 1769, of Wiscasset; died there, 1847, aged 78; married three times; had son John,[7] b. Mar. 25, 1800; who had son John W.,[8] b. Oct. 6, 1836; now living in Wiscasset. These men were all potters by trade.
433. iii. Andrew,[6] b. Oct. 22, 1774; m. Eunice Dwinel, (?) Apr. 12, 1802; born Apr. 23, 1773. Children: Apphia,[7] b. Oct. 1, 1801; m. Mar. 7, 1824, John Barnes. (Child: John,[8] b. Apr. 21, 1824.) David,[7] b. Jan. 30, 1806; m. April 10, 1832, Melinda Wells; born Boxford, May 5, 1810. (Children: Alonzo Dwinel,[8] b. Jan. 1, 1833. Edward Everett,[8] b. Sept. 6, 1836. Daniel Webster,[8] b. Sept. 22, 1834. Leonidas King,[8] b. Feb. 1, 1842.) Joseph,[7] b. Mt. Vernon, N. H., Feb. 1, 1809.

227

Ezra[5] Porter, of John Porter, baptised July 1, 1744; lived in Danvers; mar. Mehetable; no children; adm. granted his widow Mehetable, May 5, 1766; his mother's right paid to Asa Perley; names brothers John, Benjamin, Nathan; sisters Anna and Elisabeth; widow m. (for his 3d wife,) Sylvester Proctor, Oct. 22, 1772. He died June 6, 1814; (he married 1st, Hannah Buffington, Dec. 3, 1761; and 2d, Abigail Gale, Jan. 18, 1763.)

235

Israel[5] Porter, of Benjamin[4] Porter, (of Benj.,[3] of Israel,[2] of John,[1]) born Danvers, Oct. 3, 1746; married Dec. 13, 1771, Huldah, daughter of James Smith, baptised Oct. 22, 1752; he was living 1794. Children:

434. i. Israel,[6] b. Mar. 27, 1773; pub. Sally Nurse, Dec. 12, 1795. Children: Huldah,[7] b. Apr. 20, 1796. Sally,[7] b. Oct. 16, 1797. Rocksena,[7] b. Oct. 28, 1799.

435. ii. Abijah,[6] b. Aug. 2, 1776; died Oct. 15, 1854; m. 1st, July 31, 1800, Sarah Dodge, of Wenham.

436. iii. Benjamin,[6] b. Sept. 7, 1786; died May 16, 1856.

236

Francis[5] Porter, of Benjamin[4] Porter, born Danvers, Sept. 22, 1748; lived there 1794; married Martha Gott, of Wenham, April 12, 1772.

238

James[5] Porter, of Benjamin[4] Porter, born Jan. 13, 1755; tailor; m. Hannah, daughter of Rev. Phillip and Elisabeth (Bass) Curtis, of Sharon, Mass.; she born Nov. 21, 1748; died Nov. 4, 1805, aged 57. He died in Peterboro', N. H., Dec. 2, 1843, aged 88. The History of Peterboro' says his oldest child was born there; and other authority says son James was born in Wenham, but he without doubt removed from Wenham or Danvers, to Peterboro, N. H., in 1776, where his children were born:

440. i. Peter,[6] b. Dec. 5, 1777; died Mar. 22, 1802, aged 25.

441. ii. Hannah,[6] b. Feb. 9, 1779; died July 10, 1804; m. James Cunningham, May 6, 1802. No children.

442. iii. Zacheus,[6] b. Oct. 25, 1780.

443. iv. Sally,[6] b. Oct. 28, 1782; m. Asa Gibbs, July 4, 1815; died Oct. 24, 1859, aged 77.

444. v. James,[6] b. June 18, 1785.

445. vi. Nancy Curtis,[6] b. April 12, 1787; m. 1st, Abel Gibbs, Mar. 13, 1816; he died Savannah, Ga., 1819, aged 32; she m. 2d, Dea. Samuel Maynard.

vii. Roxanna,[6] b. Aug. 18, 1792; died June, 1874, aged 82.

SIXTH GENERATION.

251

Samuel[6] Porter, (third) of Samuel[5] Porter, b. in Wenham, Jan. 15, 1739; lived ~~there~~ in ~~part now~~ Hamilton; marriage pub. June 27, 1762, Anna, dau. of Stephen and Ruth (Waldron) Patch, of Ipswich; b. Dec. 3, 1733; he died September 27, 1821. His will, 1821, names all his children except Dudley. Children, not in order:

i. Anna,[7] b. Sept. 17, 1762-3; married Thomas Adams, of Hamilton, and had son George.[8]

ii. Samuel,[7] settled in Worcester.

iii. Dudley,[7] m. Martha Smith; had son Dudley,[8] who m. Edna Dane; and Samuel,[8] died young.

iv. John,[7] settled in Hampton Falls, N. H.

v. Allen,[7] twin with John; light-house keeper, Portsmouth, N. H.

vi. Willard,[7] deacon.

vii. Elisha.[7]

viii. Joshua,[7] b. April, 1782; carpenter and sexton, of Hamilton; died Nov. 18, 1832; m. Hannah, of Benj. and Lucy (Whipple) Peck; she born March 13, 1784; died Sept. 5, 1858. Children: Joshua,[8] b. Oct. 20, 1808; physician; settled North Brookfield, June 12, 1834; died there Jan. 6, 1874. He married Martha Lee, dau. of Stephen and Abigail Crafts Hooper Lee, May 6, 1835; she born Jan. 4, 1809. (Their son Charles A.,[9] resides at Windsor Locks, Conn.; m. Mellissa E. Denslow, Jan. 11, 1871; and Ernest,[9] merchant, in Boston, resides at Malden.) Benjamin,[8] born 1810.

Lucy Ann,[8] b. 1815; died unmarried. Nathaniel,[8] died young. Eliza,[8] b. 1823; m.——Webber, of Wenham, George,[8] b. 1828.

ix. Mercy,[7] married Aaron Patch, of Hamilton.

x. Sarah,[7] married John Boies.

xi. Betsey,[7] married Reuben Smith, of Topsfield,

xii. Hannah,[7] married —— Tuck, of Beverly.

254

Dudley[6] Porter, of Samuel[5] Porter, born in Wenham, (Hamilton,) Jan. 23, 1744; died in Andover, Nov. 3, 1816; lived in Haverhill; merchant. A gentleman of the highest honor and capacity; m. Sally; she died Sept. 19, 1792, aged 43. Children, all born in Haverhill:

i. Dudley,[7] died Sept. 17, 1839, aged 69; of Haverhill; married "in Salem, Dudley Porter, to Miss Polly Austin, June, 1793." (Mass. Magazine.) Children: Dudley,[8] died of consumption, at the age of 25. Eleazer A.,[8] of Haverhill; died in 1861; he was a citizen and merchant of New York, from 1824 to 1837, and was quite successful until the crash of 1837, when he with many others, embarked in eastern land speculations, which proved ruinous. He returned to Haverhill, and was, until a few years before his death, cashier of the Merrimac Bank. He was a man of singular rectitude of character, and remarkable financial ability; he left an honorable name as a citizen, and the pleasantest of memories as a father and friend. He m. Harriet, dau. of Dr. Dan'l Brickett, of Haverhill. (Children: Charles,[9] died in infancy. Harriet B.,[9] m. Dr. James C. Nichols, of Haverhill, and died in child birth at the age of 24. Dudley,[9] merchant of Haverhill; now at the age of 41; married and has two daughters, and one son.) Mary,[8] m. Thomas Tileston, an eminent merchant of New York; she is still living and enjoys remarkable health, at the age of 81.

ii. Greenleaf,[7] master mariner, died at sea of yellow fever, Aug. 10, 1823, age 44. He married Elisabeth Barrett, of Danvers, (or Salem.) Children, John,[8] printer; formerly proprietor of Rockland, Me., Gazette; resides there; married and has two children. Mary Ann,[8] unmarried, resides in Haverhill. Charles G.,[8] the well known and highly esteemed Baptist clergyman, of Bangor, Me., who died there 1877, aged 65. (His widow and daughter reside in Bangor.)

iii. Job D.,[7] master mariner; died in Havana, of yellow fever, Nov. 15, 1822, at age of 36. Married Catharine Holt, of Reading. Children: Job D.,[8] died young. Sarah,[8] married —— Marston; died aged about 50. Catharine,[8] m. —— Heath; now lives in San Francisco. Charles,[8] resides in Cambridge, Mass.

iv. Ann,[7] m. Ezra C. Ames; she died at the age of 50; two children now living.

v. Charles,[7] unmarried; a successful merchant in Boston, and New York, for many years; he died at Haverhill, Oct. 25, 1858, aged 72; was a man of remarkable intellectual capacity, and business ability, and of great dignity and integrity of character.

vi. John,[7] died Mar. 26, 1873, aged 89; a gentleman of the old school, a man of the most uniform courtesy, and most generous impulses. He was remarkably handsome in person, and very genial and pleasant in all his relations; universally beloved and respected. He retained possession of his faculties until within a year or two of his death. He married Harriet, daughter of William Bartlett, a prominent and successful merchant of Newburyport. Children: Elizabeth,[8] married Dr. Noyes, and died at middle age, leaving children. William B.,[8] resides in the west. Catharine B.,[8] m. Lambert; resides West Newton; had five children. Charles,[8] died at sea at age of about 40. John,[8] drowned at age of 35 or 40. Mariana,[8] living, unmarried.

vii. Samuel,[7] died early of consumption.

257

Isaac[6] Porter, of Samuel[5] Porter, born Wenham, July 1, 1750; lived and died there, Mar. 21, 1837; married Mary, dau. of Thomas and Mary Kimball, Sept. 13, 1772; she born Dec. 7, 1753; died Oct. 11, 1837, aged 86. His will names grandchildren Mary, Nancy, Betsey, Sarah and Lucy, children of his daughter Lydia Kimball; grandsons Isaac Porter, Jr., (?) and William Porter; gives to son Paul, silver tankard. Children:

452. i. Lydia,[7] b. April 28, 1774.
453. ii. Paul,[7] b. April 21, 1776.

260

Nathaniel[6] Porter, of Samuel[5] Porter, born Wenham, Jan. 29, 1762; lived in Wenham and Beverly; married 1st, Anna Dodge, of Wenham; published Oct. 25, 1783. "Anna, wife of Nathaniel Porter, died Dec. 9, 1789, 27th." Married 2d, Mary Cleves, of Beverly, Sept. 13, 1792; he died in Beverly, April 15, 1817. Children:

455. i. Nancy,[7] b. Nov. 11, 1784; died Nov. 5, 1803.
456. ii. John,[7] b. July 10, 1786.
457. iii. Billy,[7] b. Dec. 23, 1788; died at sea.
458. iv. Nathaniel,[7] b. Dec. 11, 1793; died Nov. 8, 1796.

262

John[6] Porter, of John[5] Porter, (of Samuel,[4]) born Wenham, April 18, 1742; lived in Littleton, Mass.; major in the revolutionary war; died 1834, aged 92; married probably Lydia Lambert, of Ipswich, Apr. 16, 1761. (?) Children:

459. i. Joseph Lombard,[7] b. Jan. 7, 1762. (?)
460. ii. John,[7] lived in Sterling, Mass.; married Mary Kendall, (sister of Rev. Dr. Kendall, for many years a distinguished and beloved minister in Plymouth, Mass.;) their daughter Augusta,[8] b. July 31, 1809; died Eastport, Me., Jan. 8, 1876; married Rev. Eliphalet Porter[6] Crafts, June 13, 1832; he was grand-son of Rev. John[4] Porter, of North Bridgewater, and a descendant of Richard[1] Porter, of Weymouth, 1635.

270

Jonathan[6] Porter, of Jonathan[5] Porter, born in Ellington, Conn., (part of ancient Windsor,) Nov. 24, 1748; m. Mercy Foote, of Ellington, June 3, 1785. He died Mar. 25, 1825; she died April 22, 1835. Children:

460A i. Sally,[7] b. Mar. 27, 1786; died Dec. 7, 1792.
460B ii. Louisa,[7] b. Nov. 24, 1788.
460C iii. Marilda,[7] 3d child, born May 21, 1790; married Meletiah Martin, July 29, 1812. Their 2d child Horace,[8] b. Dec. 11, 1814; resides in Corning, Holt Co., Missouri; physician; he writes me a letter, dated Nov. 4, 1878, in which he says he had in his possession an old parchment deed, given by Indians, conveying title to land about Salem, to Capt. John Putnam, father-in-law of Lieut. John[3] Porter, which he donated to the Western

Reserve Historical Society, of Cleveland, Ohio, some years since; also a book, "The History of the Colony of New Plymouth," printed about 1664, on the fly leaf of which was the autograph of John[3] Porter, which his mother willed to his son Horace N.[9] Martin, who was killed in the late war, which Dr. Martin presented to the Baptist Historical Society, of Philadelphia, Penn.; the president of that society writing him that the book was "a priceless acquisition;" also he has now in his possession, a book the title of which is "Chronicles of the Kings of England," printed 1661, upon the fly leaf of which the autograph of John[3] Porter, was written. Also, he says he has seen a silver headed ebony cane, with the name of Lieut. John[3] Porter, date from 1680 to 1688. The Indian deed was probably given to John[1] Putnam, original settler; there has been some difference of opinion as to which family Jonathan Porter, who m. Mercy Foote, belonged; the possession of Lieut. John[3] Porter's books, cane, etc., would seem to clearly indicate that he was of the Salem family. J. W. P.

460D iv. Lemuel,[7] b. Mar. 19, 1792; of Ellington, Conn.; m. Lucinda Jennings, Sept. 21, 1817; she b. Aug. 11, 1798; d. Sept. 18, 1828. Married 2d, Welthy Willobee, Feb. 11, 1830; b. Mar. 10, 1796; he died Jan. 3, 1841; (she m. 2d, James Worden, Aug. 1, 1844, and died Mar. 4, 1873.) Children: Sally,[8] b. Aug. 4, 1818; died Feb. 7, 1826. Lucy Foot,[8] b. July 15, 1820; m. Geo. W. Neff, July 7, 1839; died Sept. 3, 1870. Lemuel C.,[8] b. April 14, 1823; banker; resides Winona, Minn; m. Adele Horton, of Skeneateles, N. Y., Mar. 3, 1852. (Children: Carrie H.,[9] b. Feb. 6, 1853; died Nov. 11, 1853. Clark Horton,[9] b. Mar. 10, 1854. Adelbert,[9] b. Apr. 4, 1861. Lillie Maud,[9] b. Aug. 28, 1864.) Eliza,[8] b. Feb. 13, 1825; m. L. Van Anden, Jan. 6, 1847; resides Mantorville, Minn. Lucinda,[8] b. Feb. 26, 1827; died Oct. 13. Horace D.,[8] b. Sept. 8, 1828; died Oct. 28. Louisa,[8] b. Jan. 1, 1831; m. John Young, May 27, 1868, of Kasson, Dodge Co., Minn. (Children: Frank P.,[9] b. Nov. 5, 1869; d. Nov. 10, 1869. Albert John,[9] b. Jan. 24, 1873; d. Jan. 30.) Lucinda,[8] b. Mar. 27, 1832; m. Lafayette Stout, Oct. 28, 1852; resides Winona, Minn.; no children. Allen L.,[8] b. Mar. 25, 1835; m. Adelphia Mellen, Jan. 26, 1863; resides in Kasson, Minn. (Children Fannie M.,[9] b. Oct. 28, 1864. Frank Proctor,[9] b. Feb. 18, 1865.) Wife died June 19, 1870; he m. 2d, Vira S. Baldwin, Dec. 17, 1874. (Son Roy Baldwin,[9] b. Jan. 2, 1878.)

v. Sally,[7] b. Dec. 23, 1793; died Jan. 1, 1794.

vi. Betsey,[7] b. Aug. 13, 1795.

vii. Jerusha,[7] b. May 5, 1797.

viii Horace,[7] b. May 7, 1799; died at sea off Sandy Hook, Aug. 21, 1824.

ix. Dolly,[7] b. May 16, 1801; died June 30, 1823.

x. Guy,[7] b. June 27, 1803.

xi. Philo,[7] b. June or Jan. 27, 1806; resides in Windsorville, Conn.; m. Clarissa B., daughter of Daniel Skinner, of Windsor, Conn., Mar. 28, 1838. Children: Horace Philo,[8] b. Feb. 6, 1839; physician; resides Claremont, Dodge Co., Minn.; m. Margaret Smith Blakeslee, of New Haven, Conn., Jan. 27, 1861. (Children: Ida Louisa,[9] b. Nov. 23, 1864, in New Haven, Conn. Effie May,[9] b. June 20, 1868, Wayland, Mich. Maud Alice,[9] b. April 21, 1870, in Wayland.) Louisa Clarissa,[8] b. Aug. 24, 1842; died June 23, 1849. William Emerson,[8] b. July 16, 1836; resides Kasson, Minn.; m. Delia K. Allen, of East Windsor, Conn., May 1, 1875. (Children: Allen Putnam,[9] b. April 5, 1876. Ethyl Kate,[9] b. Dec. 31, 1877.) Emma H.,[8]; died young.

281

Asa[6] Porter, of Moses[5] Porter, born Boxford, May 26, 1742; grad. Harvard College, 1762; settled in Newburyport, as a merchant; a gentleman of the old school; during the revolutionary war, he was a devoted loyalist; he removed to Haverhill, N. H., before 1780; where he was a large landholder. Sabine's History of the Loyalists, page 198, says: "He suffered in person and property, in consequence of his adherence to the royal cause, and was compensated by grants of crown land in Canada. He was on terms of intimacy with Gov. Wentworth, and other gentlemen of rank, and was himself a person of highly respectable character." He died Aug. 2, (or Dec. 28,) 1818, aged 76; he married Mehetable Crocker, of Newburyport; his children, as near as I have been able to get them, were:

461. i. Asa,[7] grad. Dartmouth College, 1787; died at Broome, Canada East.

462. ii. Moses,[7] grad. Dartmouth College, 1798; died at Haverhill, N. H., Jan. 14, 1819, aged 38.

iii. John.[7]

v. Benjamin.[7]
vi. Mary,[7] m. Judge Farrand.
vii. Elisabeth,[7] m. Hon. Thomas W. Thompson.
viii. Sarah,[7] m. Hon. Mills Orcutt.

"The late Wm. T. Porter, of the New York Spirit of the Times, who died in 1858, was a grand-son; and the wife of Rufus Choate, a grand-daughter."

282

William[6] Porter, of Moses[5] Porter, born May 27, 1744; lived in Boxford; married there, Mary Adams; he died July 26, 1822. Children, all born in Boxford:

467. i. Hannah,[7] b. Jan. 26, 1769; m. at Boxford, Zecheriah Bacon.
468. ii. William,[7] b. Mar. 26, 1770; m. Lettice Wallace; afterward moved to Haverhill, N. H., and to Danville, Vt., where he died.
469. iii. James,[7] b. Aug. 28, 1771; m. at Haverhill, to Margaret Tilton.
470. iv. Aaron,[7] b. June 7, 1773; m. Rebecca Blanchard, Nov. 2, 1807; lived in Danville, Vt.
471. v. Mary,[7] b. June 3, 1775; m. at Haverhill, to Amos Carlton; their daughter, Mary[8] Carlton, m. Thomas Bishop, June 14, 1827, at St. Johnsbury, Vt.
472. vi. Sarah,[7] b. April 22, 1777; m. John Osgood, at Haverhill.
473. vii. Isaac Adams,[7] b. Mar. 22, 1779; m. 1st, Catharine Buel; 2d, May, 1816, to Mary Norman; 3d, in Concord, N. H., 1818.
474. viii. Elisabeth,[7] b. Nov. 29, 1782.
475. ix. Pamelia,[7] b. Feb. 5, 1785; m. Luther Clark, in Danville, Vt.; their daughter, Mary,[8] m. in 1831, Geo. B. Mansur, of Bennington, Vt.

285

Aaron[6] Porter, M.D., son of Moses[5] Porter, born in Boxford, Mass., Mar. 28, 1752; d. in Portland, Me., June 30, 1837; a physician of eminence in his profession; first at Biddeford, Me., and afterward at Portland, Me.; married Paulina King, April 30, 1777; she born Mar. 1, 1759; died Feb. 27, 1833; she was daughter of Richard King, of Scarborough, Me., and sister of the Hon. Rufus King, the first U. S. Senator from N. Y., minister to England, &c.; and half-sister of Hon. William King, the first Governor of Maine. Children:

485. i. Rufus King,[7] b. June 14, 1778; died July 9, 1791.

486. ii. Moses,[7] b. Sept. 26, 1780; grad. Harvard College, 1802, and died in June of the same year, at Biddeford, of yellow fever.

487. iii. Mary,[7] b. at Biddeford, Me., Aug. 19, 1782; died at Batavia, Ill., 1866; m. Nathaniel Coffin, Nov. 18, 1804; he was son of James and Martha Coffin, born at Saco, Oct. 26, 1781; grad. D. C., 1799; lawyer; resided at Bath, Me., and Wiscasset, Me., clerk of courts for Lincoln County, Me., many years; removed to Jacksonville, Ill., 1836; treasurer of Illinois College, twenty years; died at Wataga, Ill., April 7, 1864, aged 82. Children: Egbert Benson,[8] born Bath, Me., July 29, 1805; grad. Bowdoin College, 1823; died Oct. 21, 1827. Harriet Porter,[8] b. Bath, April 25, 1807; died April 6, 1865; m. Prof. Wm. Smyth, of Bowdoin College, 1827; he died April 9, 1868. Sarah Leland,[8] b. Wiscasset, Me., Apr. 23, 1810; d. Feb. 11, 1811. John Huntington Crane,[8] b. July 17, 1812; died Aug. 18, 1813. John Huntington Crane,[8] b. Sept. 14, 1815; grad. Bowdoin College, 1833; Prof. of Mathematics, in U. S. Navy; retired at Washington, 1878; m. Louisa Harrison, of Washington, D. C., April 10, 1845; she died 1874. Sarah Leland,[8] b. twin with above; m. Rev. Charles Beecher, of Georgetown, Mass., July 23, 1840. (Children: Charles McCulloch,[9] of Bridgeport, Conn., and Mrs. Mary[9] Noyes, of Georgetown.) Mary Boynton,[8] b. Wiscasset, Dec. 11, 1817; now living at Batavia, Ill.; m. Rev. Charles E. Blood, Sept. 1, 1840; he grad. at Illinois College, and Lane Seminary; minister at Manhattan, Kansas, and at Wataga, Ill., where he died, March 25, 1866, aged 56. Helen Olcott,[8] b. May 3, 1820; died Nov. 30, 1833. William,[8] b. Wiscasset, Jan. 19, 1822; grad. Ill. Col., 1842, and at Andover; Prof. of Mathematics, at Illinois College until 1853; moved to Batavia, Ill.; banker there twenty years; m. June 19, 1847, Mary, daughter of Hon. S. D. and Mary (Nash) Lockwood; she born May 18, 1828; died July, 1877. (Children: Samuel D. Lockwood,[9] born April 24, 1848; m. 1873, Harriet Bean. William King,[9] b. Aug. 9, 1850; m. Mary Gove Burroughs, 1873. Mary Ellen,[9] b. July 22, 1855; m. Aug. 14, 1877, Rev. John W. Bradshaw, of Batavia, Ill.

Charles Porter,[9] b. April 23, 1858; in Ripon Col., Wisconsin. Martha O.,[9] b. May 12, 1863. Francis Drake,[9] b. Oct. 31, 1860. John Nash,[9] b. Dec. 29, 1865.)

488. iv. Richard King,[7] b. July 20, 1784; ship master; for many years in the employ of "the Pattens" of Bath, Me.; m. Mary Clapp, of Mansfield, Mass., Mar. 6, 1815; she sister of Judge Ebenezer Clapp, of Bath, born 1789; died in Portland, Me., June 15, 1847, aged 54; he died in Westbrook, Me., July 25, 1859, and was buried in Eastern cemetery, Portland. Children: Mary King,[8] b. 1818; died unmarried, 1850. Isabella Homes,[8] b. 1820; m. Rev. Edwin E. Bliss, 1842, and has ever since resided near Constantinople. (Children: One dau.,[9] m. —— Dwight, missionary. Laura,[9] m. Langdon S. Ward, treasurer A. B. C. F. M. Edward.[9]) Arixene Southgate,[8] b. 1821; m. (1842) Hon. Wm. Aspinwall, of Brookline, Mass. (Children: Thomas.[9] Mary.[9] William.[9]) Elisabeth Clapp,[8] born 1823; m. Alexander W. Longfellow, 1842; a most estimable gentleman; of the U. S. Coast Survey, and a brother of Henry W. Longfellow, the poet; resides in Portland, Me. (Children: Mary King.[9] A. Wadsworth,[9] grad. Har. Col. Elisabeth Porter,[9] m. in Portland, Oct. 16, 1878, Edward Sherman Dodge, of Cambridge. Richard King.[9])

489. v. Paulina,[7] b. May 26, 1786; died Jacksonville, Ill., 1842; m. Enoch Jones, merchant, of Bath, Me., Dec. 9, 1804; he died 1810. Children: Ann King,[8] unmarried. Isabella Porter,[8] b. July 10, 1807; m. Oct. 27, 1829, Rev. Edward Beecher; resided in Boston, Jacksonville, Ill.; president of Illinois College; Boston, Galesburg, and now in Brooklyn, N. Y. (Their children: Edward Lyman,[9] b. May 5, 1831; d. 1873. Frederick William,[9] b. Feb. 3, 1835; Congregational minister at Wellsville, N. Y. Isabella King,[9] died 1861. Eugene Francis,[9] b. Mar. 7, 1846; editor of Brooklyn Monthly. Albert Louis,[9] b. Jan. 26, 1847; drowned with two cousins, at Georgetown, Mass., Aug. 27, 1867. Alice Cornelia,[9] b. Sept. 16, 1849, unmarried; besides four who died in infancy.)

490. vi. Isabella Bragdon,[7] b. April 25, 1788; m. Henry Homes, of Boston, Sept. 20, 1814; merchant of the firm of Homes & Homer. Children: Miranda,[8] b. Dec. 11, 1818; m. Geo. F. Homer, esq., of Brookline, Sept. 26, 1843; he died April 14, 1876. (Children: William B.,[9] b. June 7, 1846. Julia L.,[9] b. June 5, 1848. Isabella,[9] b. 1851. Mary B.,[9] b. Aug. 4, 1853. Hattie R.,[9] b. June 27, 1855.

Frederic H.,[9] Oct. 10, 1857.) William B.,[8] b. 1820; graduated Illinois College, and Lane Seminary; minister Presbyterian church, St. Louis. Frederic,[8] b. 1822; resides St. Louis. Mary,[8] b. 1825; m. Frederick Ray; resides Andover, Mass. Francis,[8] b. Oct., 1827; grad. Amherst College; Orthodox clergyman. Henry A.,[8] who is State Librarian of New York, at Albany. Dorcas,[8] who m. Philander Washburn, (?) of Middleboro; they parents of Rev. Geo. Washburn, of Roberts College, Constantinople. (?)

491. vii. Harriet,[7] b. April 25, 1790; died July 6, 1835; m. Rev. Lyman Beecher, of Litchfield, Conn., Oct. 29, 1817; his 2d wife. Children: Frederic,[8] b. 1820; died in infancy. Isabella,[8] b. Feb. 22, 1822; m. John Hooker, esq., of Hartford, Conn.; lawyer. (Children: Mary,[9] m. Eugene Burton, esq. Alice,[9] wife of John Day, esq. Edward.[9]) Thomas K.[8] b. Feb. 10, 1824; grad. Illinois College, 1843, and Lane Seminary; Congregational minister at Elmira, N. Y.; twice married. James C.,[8] born Jan. 8, 1828; clergyman.

492. viii. Almira,[7] b. Jan. 7, 1792; living 1878; m. John H. Goddard, of Nobleboro, Me., and Portsmouth, N. H., Jan. 27, 1812; he died in Groton, Mass., 1876. Children: John Heath,[8] b. April 7, 1813; grad. Col.; m. Catherine, daughter of Rev. Bennett Tyler, D. D.; he d. about 1842, leaving one son, Dr. John Tyler Goddard,[9] who died in New York city, Sept. 14, 1878. Susanna,[8] b. Sept. 25, 1816; m. Rev. Lemuel Phillips, of Groton, Mass.; (has three children: Catherine,[9] m. Wm. Shedd. Helen.[9] John,[9] m. ——— Nightengale.)

493. ix. Rufus King,[7] b. Sept. 3, 1794; m. twice.

494. x. Lucy,[7]
495. xi. Elisabeth,[7] } twins, b. Sept. 9, 1795; d. 1796.

496. xii. Lucy Elisabeth,[7] b. Aug. 23, 1797; m. John P. Brace, of Hartford, Conn., Nov., 1819; she died 1841, leaving two sons and one daughter.

291

David F.[6] Porter, of Benjamin[5] Porter, b. Boxford; removed from Boxford to Denmark, Me.; thence to Dixmont, Me.; married Susan Towns, of Boxford. Children, all born in Boxford:

David.[7] Asa.[7] Benjamin.[7] Tyler.[7] Ruth.[7] Sally.[7]

Isaiah,[7] of David,[6] b. Boxford, 1775; lived in Dixmont, Me; m. Children, all born in Dixmont: Benjamin.[8] Isaiah.[8] Joshua.[8] Mary.[8] Asa.[8] Nancy.[8] John.[8] Lucy.[8]

Benjamin,[7] of David,[6] b. Boxford; lived in Hampden, Me.; died there 1853; will proved Sept. 2; married Polly—— Children:

i. Andrew J.[8]
ii. Alphonso.[8]
iii. Matilda M.[8]
iv. Horace B.[8]
v. Dudley G.[8]
vi. Mellissa.[8]
vii. Louisa G.[8]
viii. Sarah J.,[8] married Andrew Mabury.
ix. Mary M.,[8] married John Knowles.
x. Julia,[8] married —— Hardy.

294

Benjamin[6] Porter, of Benjamin[5] Porter, born in Boxford, Sept. 29, 1754; removed to Winthrop, Me., 1780, and to Vienna, Me., 1788, where he died about 1837; married 1st, Polly Sargent; married 2d, Pamelia Barton, July 17, 1782. Children:

506. i. Betsey,[7] born 1779; m. Barnard Kimball, of Vienna, Me.; killed by lightning in his field; his widow long survived him, and died at the age of 80. No children.

507 ii. John,[7] b. 1780; m. Mary Robinson; had five children, and died in Vienna, many years since.

508. iii. Benjamin,[7] b. 1782; died young.

Children, by 2d wife:

509. iv. Mary,[7] or Polly, b. 1788; m. James Chapman, esq., of Vienna, Me.; both died several years since; they had twelve children.

510. v. Jonathan,[7] died unmarried.
511. vi. Dolly,[7] m. Abel Whittier.
512. vii. Stephen,[7] m. Miriam Whittier.
513. viii. Tyler,[7] m. Mary Whittier.
514. ix. Benjamin,[7] m. Phebe Gould.
515. x. Byron,[7] m. Eliza J. Morse.

516. xi. Parthenia,[7] b. 1805; m. 1st, Rufus H. Folsom; 2d, Ira Seavey of Mt. Vernon, Me. Children: Benjamin.[8] James.[8] Julia,[8] and two others.

517. xii. James,[7] b. 1805; twin with Parthenia.

518. xiii. Caroline,[7] died young.

519. xiv. Caroline,[7] m. Jonathan Poor; she died at the age of 30. Children: Leander O.,[8] of Sebago, Me. Russell.[8] Caroline.[8] Martha.[8]

520. xv. Julia Ann,[7] m. 1st, Daniel Barton; now lives at N. Oxford, Mass. Children: Ida,[8] and Ada,[8] twins. Mary.[8] Stephen.[8] Probably all married but Mary.

296

Tyler[6] Porter, of Benjamin[5] Porter, born in Boxford, Apr. 27, 1757; he sold his grandfather's (Benjamin[4] Porter's) farm, which he owned in Boxford, in 1801, and removed to Sebago, Me., where he died Sept. 15, 1842; married Abigail Johnson, of Andover, Jan. 7, 1772. Children, all born in Boxford, (not in order:)

521. i. Tyler,[7] b. Nov. 27, 1784; married and living in Weston, N. Y., in 1853.

522. ii. Jonathan,[7] b. Sept. 13, 1782; lived in Boxford; m. Mary Ross, of Rowley, June 14, 1807; he died April, 1854; Children: Jonathan James,[8] b. June 13, 1808; now living West Boxford, the last of his family. Mary Pitman,[8] b. Dec. 29, 1809. Abigail Johnson,[8] b. Oct. 19, 1810.

523. iii. Ruth,[7] b. June 27, 1780; m. Jonathan Poor, of Sebago, Me.; she d. April 7, 1846.

524. iv. Stephen,[7] b. Feb. 11, 1788; died in Portland, Me., Nov. 3, 1851; dau., Mrs. H. B. Newbegin, 94 Kneeland street, Boston.

525. v. Benjamin,[7] b. Boxford, Mar. 12, 1790; m. Sarah Runnels, May 20, 1820; she b. in Methuen, Mass., May 18, 1791; they settled in Merrimac, N. H.; afterward, 1833, removed to Sebago, Me., and in 1850, to Buxton, Me. Children: Stephen Runnels,[8] b. Merrimac, N. H., Oct. 27, 1826; formerly of Sebago, Me., now of Portland, Me.; member of Maine Legislature, 1854, '55, '57, '58; m. Sarah W. Osgood, of Sebago, Oct. 15, 1846. (Children: Millard Fillmore,[9] b. May 18, 1849. Abbie Jane,[9] b. June 5, 1853; m. Osceola Jackson, Mar. 25, 1869. Ada Florence,[9] b. June 12, 1855; died Feb. 20,

1856. Mabel W.,[9] b. May 18, 1865.) John Tyler,[8] b. Dec. 18, 1826. Sarah,[8] b. Aug. 26, 1828. Martha,[8] b. June 4, 1830.

526. vi. Rufus,[7] b. Boxford; resides New Haven, Conn., 1878. "Of the members of the Portland Light Infantry, who served in the war of 1812, only two survive, Benjamin Ilsley, of Portland, now in his 84th year, and Rufus Porter, of New Haven, Conn., 86 years old this month. Mr. Ilsley though somewhat infirm, appears to share a good degree of health. Mr. Porter writes that he has good health, and walked seventeen miles the 3d inst."

527. vii. Henry,[7] died in Portland, May, 1870.

301

General Moses[6] Porter, of Benjamin[5] Porter, born in Danvers, Mar. 26, 1756. (The house he was born in is still standing, and one of the great Porter hives, it having been occupied after it was the home of Zerubbabel Rea, 1715, 1739, by Benjamin[5] Porter, his sons Gen. Moses,[6] and Zerrubabel.[6]) He died in Cambridge, April 14, 1822, unmarried. I copy from the History of Danvers. "General Moses Porter, was one of the bravest and best of the officers in the revolutionary army; distinguished himself at Bunker Hill; was under Washington through the war; wounded after the battle of Brandywine, in the fight on the banks of the Delaware; was in the service many years on the western frontier, and superintended the line of surveys for fortifications along the coasts of Maine and Mass. He was actively engaged in the war of 1812, at various places, being at the taking of Fort George, and commanding at Niagara, where he held the rank of brigadier general. In winter of 1813, he accomplished a march from Niagara to New Orleans, in five months, through a trackless wilderness, and accompanied Wilkinson's expedition against Montreal, in 1814, and was stationed at Norfolk, until the close of the war; all his life in the service of country; longer than any officer of his grade, and won the confidence and admiration of all as an able, courageous soldier, and a high disciplinarian."

302

Aaron[6] Porter, of Benjamin[5] Porter, born Oct. 24, 1757; died Danvers, Dec. 3, 1843; m. Eunice Hathorne, of Salem, Feb. 5, 1788; she daughter of Daniel and Rachel (Phelps) Hathorne. Children:

528. i. Samuel Hathorne.[7]
529. ii. Aaron.[7]
530. iii. Eunice.[7]
531. iv. Mary E.[7]
532. v. Sarah,[7] and Sarah[7] 2d.
533. vii. Andrew S.[7]
534. viii. Israel P.[7]
535. ix. Cynthia.[7]
536. x. Alfred Rea.[7]

303

Zerubbabel[6] Porter, of Benjamin[5] Porter, born Danvers, Sept. 6, 1759; died Nov. 11, 1845; "yoeman, tanner and manufacturer of all kinds of leather, and the first shoe manufacturer in the United States; that is to say, he was the first to conceive of the idea of making up a large lot of shoes and sending them off to find a market; he began by sending them packed in barrels, by vessels to the southern states, and taking in return, corn and other southern products. He was one of the early Universalists; he had positive elements of character; was of rare intelligence; a ready and most influential speaker at town meetings and elsewhere, when called upon to address his fellow citizens; also wrote much and well for the newspapers, especially upon political subjects; he was at one time U. S. assessor, and collector of internal revenue. Married, Dec. 16, 1788, Mary, daughter of Elias and Eunice (Andrews) Endicott; she born Oct. 8, 1762; died Mar. 17, 1842. Children:

537. i. Warren,[7] b. Sept. 30, 1789.
538. ii. Alfred,[7] b. May 1, 1792.

307

Daniel[6] Porter, of Benjamin[5] Porter, born Danvers, Oct. 1, 1771-3. Married Ruth Mecam, of Beverly, 1794. "In

Topsfield, Daniel Porter, of Danvers, to Miss Ruth Mecam, March, 1795." (Salem Gazette.) Children:

539. i George Washington,[7] midshipman in the war of 1812; d. New York harbor, 1814.
540. ii. Sarah,[7] d. Beverly, Oct. 19. 1815.
541. iii. Eliza Robinson,[7] b. Danvers, April 28, 1799; now residing in Canaan, N. H.
542. iv. Ruth Maria,[7] m. Royal Abbott; died Brookfield, Vt., Apr. 23, 1877.
543. v. Clarissa,[7] m. Stillman S. Clark; d. in Canaan, N. H., Mar. 4, 1863.
544. vi. Thomas Jefferson,[7] d. Canaan, N. H., Mar. 14, 1876.
545. vii. Daniel Rea,[7] d. Canaan, N. H., May 11, 1837.
546. viii. Benjamin W.,[7] drowned in Lake Michigan, Sept. 24, 1856.
547. ix. William H. H.,[7] d. Canaan, N. H., Dec. 3, 1845; m. 1840, Almira Bliss, of Lyme, N. H. Child: Dr. Daniel Rea Porter,[8] of Long Island, N. Y., who m. Sarah M. Skidmore, at Great Neck, N. Y. (Children: Mary H.[9] Elisabeth L.[9] George R.[9] James S.[9])
548. x. George Washington,[7] b. Beverly, Mass., June 21, 1817; Episcopal clergyman; rector of St. Thomas church, at Hamilton, N. Y.; received honorary degree of D. D., 1861, from Hobart College, of Geneva, N. Y.; m. Elisabeth Eustis Langdon, of Portsmouth, N. H., April 9, 1849.

308

Jonathan[6] Porter, of Jonathan[5] Porter, born Exeter, N. H., May 1, 1768; went to Marblehead to learn sail maker's trade of Robert Devereux; he remained there until the 19th of April, 1775; then went to Boxford, and spent more than three years with Mr. David Kimball; in 1778, a soldier of the revolution, going to Rhode Island, and serving for six months in Capt. Simeon Brown's company, and Col. Nathaniel Wade's regiment; afterward spent two or three months with his father, at Bridgton, Me.; and then in 1779, again in R. I., under Capt. Jeremiah Putnam, and Col. Nathan Tyler; afterwards went privateering; taken prisoner and carried to Halifax, N. S.; escaped and went to see his father again, at Londonderry, N. H.; remaining there until 1784, when he removed to Danvers; shoe-making for about a year; then several voyages to West Indies, and as he says in his autobiography which he left his family, "after which, I set up my trade in my cousin Zerrubabel Porter's shop, with whom I boarded two years." Married, Feb. 15, 1789, his cousin Lydia Porter, sister of Zerrubbabel and Gen. Moses; he died Oct. 13, 1851, at the age of 88; wife born Mar. 30, 1762; died Oct. 30, 1838. Children:

549. i. Cynthia.[7]
550. ii. Lydia.[7]
551. iii. Moses;[7] his widow died in Danvers, 1877.
552. iv. Sarah Rea.[7]
553. v. William Rea,[7] now living in Salem.

310

Tyler[6] Porter, of Tyler[5] Porter, born Wenham, Aug. 31, 1764. Children:

554. i. Oliver,[7] living 1876, with family.
555. ii. Octavius.[7]
556. iii. Sylvanus.[7]
557. iv. Frank.[7]
558. v. Charles.[7]
And daughters.

313c

Nehemiah[6] Porter, of Rev. Nehemiah[5] Porter, born Jan. 12, 1753; married Mary Tardy, at Yarmouth, Nova Scotia. One son:

558a. i. George Rowland,[7] b. at Yarmouth, Jan. 13, 1803; m. at Conway, Mass., Feb. 13, 1823, Elisabeth, daughter of Russell Rossin and Mehetable (Porter) Chauncey, born Canaan, Columbia Co., N. Y., Sept. 17, 1806. Children, first three born in Conway—the last two in Sidney, N. Y.: Wealthy Ann,[8] b. Oct. 18, 1824; m. S. Le Roy Wattles, 1848. Mary M.,[8] b. Mar. 11, 1831; m. Rinaldo M. Southwick, 1852. William Redfield,[8] b. May 26, 1834. Elisabeth Sarah,[8] b. Aug. 23, 1840. George Chauncey,[8] b. Feb. 24, 1850.

313d

John C.[6] Porter, of Rev. Nehemiah[5] Porter, born May 11, 1754; married Mabel Flower, at Ashfield, Mass., May 29, 1777, by his father. Children, born at Ashfield:

559. i. Mabel,[7] b. 1778, (or Mehetable) m. R. R. Chauncey, at Ashfield, 1802.

560. ii. Ebenezer,[7] b. 1780; m. Anna Phillips.
561. iii. Elizabeth N.,[7] b. Mar. 18, 1783; m. Elias Currier, 1808.
562. iv. John.[7]
562A. v. Hannah,[7] b. Mar. 17, 1786; m. Hezekiah Warner, May 27, 1817; he b. at Hawley, 1786. Children: Justin,[8] b. Mar. 5, 1818. Edwin,[8] b. May 10, 1819. Benjamin Leonard,[8] b. Sept. 15, 1820. Hezekiah Ryland,[8] b. July 22, 1822. Henry A.,[8] b. Sept. 21, 1824.
562B. vi. Rebecca,[7] m. Josiah Browne.
562C. vii. Sarah,[7] m. Moses Pollard.

313F

Samuel[6] Porter, of Rev. Nehemiah[5] Porter, b. May 6, 1757; m. Miriam Fuller, daughter of Julius Fuller, by his father; she b. Chebacco Parish, Ipswich. Children, born in Ashfield:

563A. i. Chipman,[7] m. Sophia Porter.
563B. ii. Hannah,[7] m. Caleb Cranston, at Ashfield, 1805.
563C. iii. Sarah,[7] m. John Clemens, 1805.
563D. iv. Julia,[7] m. John Smith, 1807.
563E. v. Paulina,[7] m. Ichabod Hawks, of New Lebanon, N. Y., Dec. 3, 1811; he b. Hawley, 1792. Children: Dwight Whitney,[8] b. Nov. 27, 1812. Lucius Locke,[8] b. 1814. Henry N.,[8] b. 1817. Julia P.,[8] b. 1819. Henry N.,[8] b. 1822. Charles Knowlton,[8] b. 1824. Catharine M.,[8] b. 1826. Hiram Hamblin,[8] b. 1829. Samuel P.,[8] b, 1832.
563F. vi. Samuel,[7] m. Miriam Scott.
563G. vii. Aaron,[7] m. ——Hewlett.

313H

Joseph[6] Porter, of Rev. Nehemiah[5] Porter, born Jan. 7, 1760; married Leonora Graves, of Whately, April 30, 1784; he died in Ashfield, Mass., Mar. 15, 1825; she died in Scipio, N. Y., June 4, 1844. Children:

564. i. Nehemiah,[7] b. Oct. 10, 1785.
565. ii. Nathan,[7] b. Oct. 5, 1787.
566. iii. Joseph C.,[7] b. Aug. 30, 1789.
567. iv. Ebenezer,[7] b. Mar. 19, 1792.
568. v. Eunice,[7] b. Nov. 18, 1794.
569. vi. Wells,[7] b. Jan. 29, 1797.
569A. vii. Rebecca C.,[7] b. Jan. 26, 1790.
569B. viii. John,[7] b. Feb. 10, 1801.
569C. ix. Rev. Charles Shepherd,[7] b. Dec. 9, 1803.
569D. x. Leonard Graves,[7] b. Mar. 6, 1806.
569E. xi. Jemima,[7] b. June 27, 1808; m. Hiram Smith, 1836.

314A

Lydia[6] Porter, of Ebenezer[5] Porter, b. Dec. 14, 1759 ; m. Nathaniel Sawyer ; pub. in Ipswich, April 18, 1778 ; he born in Haverhill, Mass., May 12, 1757. Children:

- i. Nathaniel,[7] b. May 19, 1779.
- ii. Lydia,[7] b. Sept. 3, 1781 ; m. John Walker.
- iii. Sarah,[7] b. Feb. 10, 1783 ; m. Thomas Browning at Athens, Ohio.
- iv. John,[7] twin with above.
- v. Leonard,[7] b. May 5, 1785.
- vi. Porter,[7] b. June 29, 1788, Hannahstown, Westmoreland Co., Penn.
- vii. Francis,[7] b. June 2, 1790.
- viii. Harriet,[7] b. Oct. 26, 1792 ; m. Israel Hopkins.
- ix. John Leonard,[7] b. Feb. 17, 1795 ; died at Hockingport, Ohio, 1859.
- x. Benair (?) Clement,[7] b. Jan. 29, 1797, Belpre, Ohio.
- xi. Samuel Thompson,[7] b. Mar. 11, 1799.
- xii. Nathaniel,[7] b. Oct. 7, 1801.

314B

Solomon[6] Porter, of Ebenezer[5] Porter, b. May 30, 1762 ; m. Sarah Brown, in Penn. Children:

- i. John,[7] b. 1793 ; West Liberty, Washington Co., Penn. ; m. Harriet Hicks.
- ii. Margaret,[7] b. 1795 ; m. James Barnard, in Kentucky.
- iii. Polly,[7] b. 1798, in Kentucky ; m. Elliot Driggs.
- iv. David,[7] b. 181– ; m. Matilda Verote, Champaign Co., Ohio.
- v. Page.[7]
- vi. Edward.[7] died at Broken Sword, Crawford Co., Ohio.
- vii. Rebekah.[7]

314C

Sarah[6] Porter, of Ebenezer[5] Porter, b. Feb. 18, 1766 ; m. Joseph Cummings, at Braddock's Battle Ground, Alleghany Co., Penn., 1790 ; he son of Thomas and Lois (Boardman) Cummings, born at Topsfield, Mass., 1765. Children:

- i. Joseph,[7] b. Nov. 25, 1791, at Braddock's, Penn. ; m. Nancy Wells, at Goshen, Ohio.
- ii. Lois,[7] b. July 13, 1794, at Braddock's, Penn. ; m. David Beale, of Goshen, Ohio.

iii. Sophronia,[7] b. Oct. 2, 1796, at West Liberty, Ohio Co., Va.

iv. James B.,[7] b. Jan. 4, 1799, at West Liberty, Ohio Co., Va.; m. Rebecca Patrick, of Urbana, Ohio, 1828.

v. Eunice,[7] b. July 9, 1802, at Marietta, Ohio; m. Joseph Plummer, of Goshen, Ohio.

vi. Almira,[7] b. Feb. 26, 1805, at Marietta, Ohio; m. Thomas Humphries, at Salem, Ohio.

vii. James Boardman,[7] b. July 22, 1807, at Goshen, Ohio.

314E

Joseph[6] Porter, of Ebenezer[5] Porter, b. Mar. 18, 1770; m. Hannah, daughter of John Steele, at West Liberty, Washington Co., Va.; she born in same county. Children:

569F. i. Ebenezer,[7] b. W. Liberty, Va., Nov. 9, 1798; m. Mary P. McKaig, 1825.

ii. John Steele,[7] b. W. Liberty, Va., Feb. 9, 1800.

iii. Mary Wilmer,[7] b. Montgomery Co., Ohio, June 27, 1803; m. Daniel Edmanson, 1820.

iv. Lydia Cummings,[7] b. Montgomery Co., Ohio, Nov. 4, 1805; m. Samuel Matthews, New Carlisle, Ohio, 1835.

569G. v. Joseph,[7] b. in Goshen, Ohio, Jan. 5, 1808; m. Harriet J. Ahearn.

vi. Hannah,[7] b. in Goshen, Ohio, Aug. 3, 1839.

314F

Hannah[6] Porter, of Ebenezer[5] Porter, b. May 19, 1772; married Lewis Foster, at Ashfield, Jan. 1, 1792; he born at Tisbury, 1764; son of William Foster. Children, born in Ashfield except the last two, in Springfield:

Lydia Lewis,[7] b. Oct. 7, 1793. Susannah,[7] b. Oct. 27, 1795. Lewis,[7] b. Sept. 23, 1797. Almena,[7] (?) b. Sept. 14, 1799. William,[7] b. Nov. 6, 1801. Allen,[7] b. Mar. 10, 1804. Dexter,[7] b. May 27, 1806. Emily,[7] b. May 18, 1808. Joseph Cummings,[7] b. Feb. 12, 1810. John,[7] b. Oct. 31, 1812. Julia,[7] b. Mar. 18, 1815. John Milton,[7] b. Oct. 12, 1817.

William[7] Foster, of Lewis Foster, lived in Hampton, Conn., where he was born in 1801; married Eliza Ann Hall. Children, born in Springfield: William,[8] born July 24, 1824. Julia,[8] born Nov. 8, 1825. Maria,[8] born June 10, 1828. Lewis,[8] b. July 8, 1833. Allen P.,[8] b. Oct. 1, 1835.

Dexter[7] Foster, of Lewis Foster, married Euphrasia M. Allin, in Springfield, 1826; she born in Enfield, Conn. Children: Albert D.,[8] born Springfield, April 1, 1840. Emma M.,[8] born Springfield, Dec. 16, 1841. Wilbor,[8] born Springfield, April 13, 1834. Allen F.,[8] born in Springfield, Aug. 21, 1836. Francis E.,[8] born Springfield, Feb. 24, 1839. Edwin D.,[8] born Springfield, Feb. 25, 1841.

John M.[7] Foster, of Lewis Foster, married Minerva B. Brown, of Whately, 1839. Children: Emma E.,[8] born Springfield, April 1, 1840. Ellen,[8] born Springfield, Dec. 19, 1841. Frank D.,[8] born Springfield, Aug. 26, 1846. Charles A.,[8] born Springfield, Aug. 13, 1849. Elisabeth M.,[8] born Springfield, Oct. 12, 1851.

314G

John[6] Porter, of Ebenezer[5] Porter, born May 29, 1774; lived at the "Hamlet," Ipswich, Mass.; married at Ashfield, Dec. 12, 1793, Sarah, daughter of Solomon and Zipporah (Perkins) Fuller; he died at Springfield, Ohio, 1848. Children:

569H. i. Lucretia,[7] b. Sept. 13, 1794.
569I. ii. Zipporah,[7] b. Aug. 1, 1796.
569J. iii. Solomon Cummings,[7] b. Feb. 12, 1798.
iv. Lucy,[7] b. Sept. 1, 1801; d. in Marietta, Ohio.
569K. v. Russell Sumner,[7] b. Oct. 12, 1802.
vi. Elisabeth Newell,[7] b. Mar. 22, 1805; m. E. H. Plummer, at Alexander, Ohio, 1833.
vii. Pickering Putnam,[7] b. Aug. 6, 1808.
569L. viii. Marshall Sedgwick,[7] b. Oct 31, 1810.
569M. ix. Sarah Cutler,[7] b. Mar. 28, 1813.
x. Clarissa Putnam,[7] b. Mar. 27, 1816.
xi. John Dane,[7] b. Oct. 6, 1817.

314I

Cummings[6] Porter, of Ebenezer[5] Porter, born Sept. 27, 1778; m. Eleanor, daughter of Jonas and Sarah Johnson, March, 1815, at Philadelphia; she died at Little Hockhocking, Ohio, Feb. 26, 1861; he died same place, Feb. 17, 1861. Children, all born Little Hockhocking:

i. Lydia Ann,[7] b. Dec. 18, 1815; m. Isaac Barstow, of Hockhocking, Feb. 2, 1843.
569N. ii. Sarah Cutler,[7] b. Sept. 28, 1817.
569O. iii. Cummings,[7] b. Oct. 27, 1819.
iv. Rebecca White,[7] b. May 29, 1822.

569P. v. Cutler,[7] b. Mar. 25, 1825; m. Susan Rice, of Chester, Meigs Co., Ohio, Mar. 23, 1850.

vi. David Putnam,[7] b. June 27, 1827.

vii. Hannah Olive,[7] b. Feb. 8, 1830.

viii. Almira R,[7] b. May 6, 1838; m. Porter Forbes, of Jackson Point, Mo., 1851.

ix. Ellen Amelia,[7] b. Feb. 26, 1840.

314J

Priscilla[6] Porter, of Ebenezer[5] Porter, born April 19, 1780; married James Smith, at Little Hockhocking, Ohio, 1797; he born in Westchester Co., N. Y.; he died Dec. 19, 1800. She married 2d, Ebenezer Culver, at Little Hockhocking, April 1, 1801; he son of Benjamin Culver, born at Hillsdale, N. J., 1782. Children:

Olive,[7] b. Rome, Ohio, July 20, 1803. Benjamin,[7] b. Rome, Ohio, Mar. 25, 1805. Lewis,[7] b. Little Hockhocking, Feb. 10, 1807. Ozias,[7] b. Little Hockhocking, Jan. 7, 1809. Bedient,[7] b. Little Hockhocking, Dec. 9, 1810. Louisa,[7] b. Goshen, Champaign Co., Ohio, Sept. 15, 1812. Ebenezer,[7] b. Goshen, May 7, 1814. Asahel,[7] b. Goshen, Champaign Co., Ohio, June 19, 1816. Cummings,[7] b. Goshen, Champaign Co., Ohio, April 3, 1818. Franklin,[7] b. Goshen, Champaign Co., Ohio, Dec. 31, 1819. Priscilla Irene,[7] b. Goshen, Champaign Co., Ohio, July 23, 1825.

314K

Samuel[6] Porter, of Ebenezer[5] Porter, born Jan. 27, 1784; married Sarah, daughter of E. Barrows, at Rome, Ohio, 1810. Children, the first five born at Rome—the last two at Belpre, Ohio:

569R. i. Savannah Catharine,[7] b. 1811; m. Aaron Bickle, of Greene, Ohio, 1840.

ii. Barlow,[7] b. 1813.

iii. Adeline,[7] b. 1815.

569S. iv. Volumma,[7] b. 1817; m. E. C. Dustin, of Greene, O., 1845.

v. Alicia,[7] b. 1819.

vi. Hannah,[7] b. 1821.

569T. vii. Sarah M.,[7] b. 1824; m. Thos. B. Hubbard, of Belpre, O., 1848.

314L

Mary[6] Porter, of Ebenezer[5] Porter, b. Mar. 12, 1787; m. Amos Knowles. Children, b. at Newberry, Belpre, Ohio:

i. Addison Knowles,[7] b. June 5, 1812; died Oct. 23, 1824.

ii. Reuben C.,[7] b. Sept. 12, 1815.

iii. Welles Porter,[7] b. Sept. 11, 1817.
iv. William Wallace,[7] b. Dec. 3, 1819; died 1843.
v. Stephen W.,[7] b. Sept. 13, 1823.
vi. Addison M.,[7] b. Apr. 9, 1825.
vii. Harford,[7] b. Aug. 7, 1827. (?)
viii. Parletta Asenath.[7]

336

Thomas[6] Porter, of Thomas[5] Porter, b. June 29, 1776, (?) in Danvers; removed to Lynn; m. Eunice Feirn, of Lynn. Children:

570. i. Thomas,[7] m. Mary Ripley. Children: Mary.[8] Ben. Franklin.[8] John A. P.[8]
571. ii. James,[7] m. Elisabeth Cushing. Children: One[8] died. Francina E.[8] Emily M.[8] James C.,[8] b. about 1847; was a printer, at Lynn, and in the office of the Chicago Tribune; now a farmer, resides at Woburn. Benjamin C.,[8] resides Woburn. Ida E.[8]
572. iii. John,[7] m. Mrs. Mary Dow. Had Theopoilus H.,[8] and Martha E.[8]
573. iv. Samuel,[7] m. Eliza Ann Davis. Children: Eliza E.[8] Amelia.[8] Elmira.[8] Emma.[8] Elisabeth.[8] Samuel M.[8]
574. v. Abigail.[7]

342

Mary[6] Porter, of Thomas[5] Porter, born March 29, 1786; m. in Salem, May 23, 1807, Seth Low, second son of David and Hannah (Haskell) Low, born in west parish of Gloucester, Mar. 29, 1782. He was for many years a merchant in Salem; removed to Brooklyn, N. Y., in 1828, and was one of the founders of the Unitarian church there, of which the Rev. Alfred Porter Putnam, D. D.,* is now minister. During his twenty-five years residence in Brooklyn, he was identified with the educational, benevolent and religious interests of that city, and was distinguished for his purity and dignity of

*Mr. Putnam was born in Danvers, and is a descendant of John[1] Porter in several ways, and son of

1. Elias,[7] and Eunice (Ross) Putnam.
2. Israel,[6] and Anna (Endicott) Putnam.
3. Edmund,[5] and Anna (Andrews) Putnam.
4. John,[4] and Lydia (Porter) Putnam.
5. John,[3] and Hannah (Cutler) Putnam.
6. Nathaniel,[2] and Elis (Hutchinson) Putnam.
7. John,[1] and Priscilla Putnam.

character, his rare wisdom and unsullied honor, his unselfish, affectionate disposition, and his earnest Christian piety. He died June 19, 1853. Mrs. Low died in Brooklyn, July 17, 1872, greatly revered and beloved for her noble character and beautiful life. Children, all born in Salem:

584. i. Mary Ann,[7] b. Feb. 25, 1808; married.
585. ii. Harriet,[7] b. May 18, 1809; married.
586. iii. Abiel Abbot,[7] b. Feb. 7, 1811; the eminent New York merchant; m. Ellen A. Dow.
587. iv. Seth Haskell,[7] b. Oct. 30, 1812; married.
588. v. Edward Porter,[7] b. May 1, 1814; died Jan. 18, 1815.
589. vi. William Henry,[7] b. Feb. 1, 1816; married.
590. vii. Edward Allen,[7] b. Sept. 26, 1817; married.
591. viii. Francis,[7] b. Sept. 9, 1819; died May 5, 1836, on board ship Cabot, in China Sea.
592. ix. Josiah Orne,[7] b. Mar. 15, 1821; married.
593. x. Sarah Elisabeth,[7] b. Aug. 16, 1822; married.
594. xi. Charles Porter,[7] b. Sept. 19, 1824; married.
595. xii. Ellen Porter,[7] b. May 7, 1827; married.

345

Elijah[6] Porter, of Thomas[5] Porter, born Sept. 27, 1792; physician in Salem, and Brooklyn, N. Y.; m. in Salem, Nov. 28, or Dec. 6, 1816, Rebecca Abbott, dau. of Daniel and Rebecca (Allen) Abbott. Children:

610. i. Edward Elijah,[7] b. Jan. 8, 1820; married.
611. ii. Rebecca Abbott,[7] b. Aug. 9, 1821.
612. iii. Mary Allen,[7] b. May 15, 1823.
613. iv. Harriet Low,[7] b. June 8, 1825.
614. v. Daniel Abbott,[7] b. 1827; died in infancy.
615. vi. Henry Williams,[7] b. 1829; died in infancy.
616. vii. Ellen Maria,[7] b. Jan. 24, 1831; married.
617. viii. Caroline Elisabeth,[7] b. Sept. 20, 1833.
618. ix. William Henry,[7] b. Mar. 26, 1836; married.

374

Noah[6] Porter, of Noah[5] Porter, b. Wendell, Mass., Sept. 26, 1792; died in Illinois, while on a visit to his children, Oct. 8, 1855—his remains being brought to Wendell, for burial. He removed to New Salem, April 1, 1835. Married Nabby Comins, daughter of Reuben and Nabby Comins, of

Wendell, 1815; she born Mar. 17, 1795; died Jan. 24, 1868. (She having married 2d, Mr. Payne, of Montague.) Children:

700. i. Elijah F.,[7] b. Dec. 19, 1815; m. Sally Merriam, of New Salem; settled there, and has filled many prominent offices in the town. Children: Ellen.[8] Charles.[8]

701. ii. Reuben C.,[7] b. June 13, 1817; went to Pennsylvania, taught school there, thence to Kentucky; there m. Mary Stephens, daughter of James and Catharine Stephens; removed with his family in 1869 to Prairie City, Jasper Co., Iowa; merchant. Children: James N.,[8] b. 1843; now physician in Prairie City; m. Nettie Wyckoff, of Bushnell, Ill.; (has two children: Mamie.[9] Jessie.[9]) Mary,[8] b. 1845; m. John Neff, merchant, of Bushnell, Ill.; he is now county treasurer of McDonough Co.; (have three children: Porter.[9] Gertrude.[9] Blanche.[9]) Ella C.,[8] b. 1854; m. Jacob Mummert, merchant, of Prairie City, Iowa. Leoda,[8] b. 1856; m. Benjamin F. Roach, cashier of Citizens Bank, Prairie City; (one child: Walter,[9] b. 1877.) Marretta,[8] b. Iowa, 1859.

702. iii. Lyman,[7] b. June 1, 1819; resides Edgar, Nebraska.

703. iv. Joseph E.,[7] b. July 9, 1821; lived in Framingham and New Salem, from whence he removed to Adair, McDonough Co., Ill., in March, 1856, where he now lives; m. Sept. 14, 1842, Susan M., daughter of Jonathan Cogswell, of New Salem. Children: Lester W.,[8] b. Jan. 30, 1844, in Framingham; killed in battle at Memphis, Tenn., Aug. 21, 1864; a private in Co. I, 137 Reg't of Illinois volunteers. Ella Maria,[8] b. Aug. 18, 1845, in Framingham; m. Jan. 12, 1871, to William A. Wilson, of Adair, Ill, (they have two children: Clara.[9] Warner.[9]) George E.,[8] b. Dec. 3, 1850, in New Salem; m. Mary E. Ritter, Jan. 4, 1872. (Children; Albert,[9] b. Jan. 1, 1874. Royal,[9] b. Jan., 1877.) Arabella F.,[8] b. July 4, 1856; died Aug. 27, 1859. Josephine E.,[8] b. Sept. 28, 1860, at Adair. Eddie Eugene,[8] b. June 24, 1864, at Adair.

704. v. Ransom N.,[7] b. May 21, 1823; educated at New Salem and Williston Academy; in 1845 commenced study of profession of medicine, with Dr. A. Twitchell, of Keene, N. H.; attended medical lectures at Pittsfield, also at the University of Pennsylvania, Philadelphia; received degree of M. D., 1848; practiced his profession at Dublin, N. H., for four years; accepted an

offer from Dr. Calvin Cutter, to visit the principal educational centres of the west and introduce his text books; returning to New England, was married May 23, 1855, to Mrs. Fidelia P. Mason, widow of the late Thaddeus P. Mason, of Dublin, N. H., resuming the practice of his profession at Keene, N. H., and afterward, in 1856, removing to Deerfield, where he has since resided. Children: Nellie Brown,[8] b. Apr. 24, 1857. Gertrude G.,[8] b. Dec. 23, 1858. Ellery Rawson,[8] b. July 15, 1860. Susan Esther,[8] b. Sept. 8, 1862.

705. vi. Catharine A.,[7] b. May 19, 1825; died May 3, 1830.

706. vii. Royal H.,[7] b. Aug. 21, 1827; resides Keene, N. H.; cashier Cheshire National Bank.

707. viii. Anna J.,[7] b. July 14, 1829; m. 1st, John C. Gould, of Athol. Two children: Lewis.[8] Ida.[8] She m. 2d—

708. ix. Noah Dexter,[7] b. Nov. 27, 1831; died Dec 3, 1835.

709. x. John Dexter,[7] b. Aug. 11, 1835; m. and died.

710. xi. Warren W.,[7] b. July 27, 1839, in New Salem; resides Bridgeport, Conn.; commenced teaching at age of 15, in Hardwick; in 1855, in Illinois; in 1859, in Hill Co., Texas, on the Brazos; traveled the whole distance from Illinois to Texas and return, on horseback; returning before the war broke out; was 1st lieut. in 7th Illinois cavalry reg't, serving three years, going through with Grierson from Lagrange, Tenn., to Baton Rouge. Is now a successful teacher in one of the principal schools in Bridgeport; m. July 19, 1864, Mary E. Keith, of Enfield, Mass. Children: Herbert W.,[8] b. Sept. 15, 1865. Mabel Anna,[8] b. Dec. 25, 1867. Grace Inez,[8] b. Jan. 21, 1871. Edith May,[8] b. July 14, 1876.

390

William Lamb[6] Porter, of John[5] Porter, born in Charleston, S. C., 1786; lived and died there, 1860, aged 74; an eminent, enterprising, successful merchant; his father dying early, he was carried to Massachusetts while a child, and was brought up chiefly by his aunt, Phebe[5] Porter, at Malden and Medford; returned to Charleston, S. C., about 1804, when about eighteen years of age; he had very little education; but he improved himself greatly by reading standard authors; wrote for the press, both in poetry and prose, with good feeling and good taste; he was a perfect gentleman in manner and character, of the highest probity, and a model citizen; he sought no public station, but aimed to give his children the best possible education; he died June 26, 1860, with the universal esteem and regret of the community in which he lived; he left not an enemy behind him; it was happy for him that he died before the civil war began; it would have distressed him greatly, for he loved dearly and with equal fervor, the home of his childhood and the home of his birth and manhood. He married Annie Saylor, Jan. 17, 1810, in Charleston; died Mar. 15, 1833. Children:

720. i. William Dennison,[7] b. Charleston, S. C., Nov. 24, 1810.

721. ii. Normand McLeod,[7] b. Boston, June 11, 1813; went into business with his father, and succeeded him; his son James Gray[8] Porter, of Aiken, S. C., is a young man of remarkable promise,—an attorney at law.

722. iii. Ann Elisabeth,[7] b. Boston, Dec. 30, 1814; m. James W. Gray, of Charleston, S. C.; he was master in equity for over thirty years; one son, Alfred,[8] killed in Virginia during the late war,—and two daughters both living.

723. iv. Joseph Yates,[7] b. Boston, Feb. 24, 1817; went to Key West, Florida; m. Miss Randolph, of Virginia; had one son, Joseph,[8] now surgeon in U. S. Army.

724. v. Hannah Hayden,[7] b. Charleston, Oct. 28, 1818; died unmarried.

725. vi. John Woodbridge,[7] b. Charleston, Aug. 10, 1820; went to Key West, Florida; was mayor there; left two daughters living near Jacksonville, Fla.

726. vii. Mary Stephens,[7] b. Charleston, Aug. 12, 1822.

727. viii. Laura Saylor,[7] b. Charleston, Mar. 6, 1824; died unmarried.

728. ix. Frances Mary,[7] b. Charleston, April 1, 1826; married George W. King, and died without issue.

729. x. Margaret L.,[7] b. Charleston, April 15, 1828; m. Dr. Joseph Blackman, and has two sons living and married.

393

Samuel W.[6] Porter, of Samuel[5] Porter, b. Townshend, Vt., Nov. 4, 1792; received his education at Newfane, Brattleboro, and Chesterfield Academies; studied law with Wm. C. Bradley, of Westminster, Vt.; commenced practice of law at Putney, Vt., 1820; thence to Ludlow; and in 1822 removed to Springfield, Vt., where he now lives; he was representative in 1827 and 1828; county judge from 1828 to 1837; a member of the council of censors, and of the first senate in 1836 and 1837; he has been town clerk for the last thirty-one years, and now at the age of 86, performs all the duties of the office with perfect regularity; he is emphatically a gentleman of the old school, living in a fine old age,—venerable and respected. I am indebted to him, (through Rev. Dr. A. P. Putnam,) for the account of his father's family. He m. Fanny, dau. of Hon. Mark and Ann (Ruggles) Richards, of Westminster, Vt. Children, b. in Springfield, except the oldest:

730\. i. Helen Ann,[7] b. Westminster, Vt., Jan. 3, 1814; m. Dr. Henry F. Crane, of Springfield, Vt. Children: Helen A.[8] Ada Porter.[8] Mary Richards.[8] Mark Richards.[8] Noble.[8]

731\. ii. Mark Richards,[7] b. Dec. 10, 1821; died Aug. 11, 1848.

732\. iii. Frederick Wadsworth,[7] b. Oct. 27, 1823.

733\. iv. Frances Harriet,[7] b. Nov. 17, 1831; died in Springfield, Jan. 5, 1865; m. Royal B. Stearns, of Woodstock, Vt.; he died. Children: Margaret,[8] m. Halstead Burnett, now of St. Louis, Mo. Frederick,[8] resides in Santa Clara, Cal.; married.

394

Henry L.[6] Porter, of Samuel[5] Porter, b. Dec. 28, 1794; died May 17, 1862; m. 1st, Betsey Miller, of Dummerston, Vt. Married 2d, Mary Ann Miller. Children of Henry L. and Betsey M. Porter:

734\. i. Julia Ann,[7] b. Oct. 14, 1815; she m. 1st, Jesse Woodbury; and 2d, Thomas Barrett; died Nov. 12, 1844.

735\. ii. Abel Duncan,[7] b. Apr. 7, 1816; m. Electa Wells; resides in La Porte, Ind. Children: Henry Wells,[8] b. Aug. 30, 1845. William F.,[8] b. Nov. 4, 1848. Emma Louisa,[8] b. Aug. 9, 1850. Carrie A.,[8] b. Jan. 10, 1852. Charles Rawson.[8] Harvey.[8]

736\. iii. Henry Frederick,[7] b. June 17, 1823; m. 1st, Fidelia Dickerson; and 2d, Harriet F. Lyner; resides Waukegan, Ill. Children, by 1st wife: Frances E.,[8] b. Oct. 15, 1846; d. May 12, 1859. Carrie F.,[8] b. Dec. 22, 1852.

Frederick F.,[8] b. Apr. 7, 1856; died Mar. 1, 1859. By 2d wife: Hattie Frances,[8] b. Mar. 16, 1864.

737. iv. Charles Miller,[7] b. Sept. 21, 1827; died Nov. 3, 1828.

738. v. Elisabeth Sophia,[7] b. May 1, 1830; m. Calvin Wilson.

Children by 2d wife:

739. vi. Charles Miller,[7] b. Jan. 26, 1834; m. Julia Whitmore; resides Ottawa, Ill. Dau. Maggie,[8] b. July 1, 1861.

740. vii. Samuel Willis,[7] b. Jan. 8, 1837; resides Ottawa, Ill.

741. viii. George Randolph,[7] b. Mar. 22, 1843; resides Rock Island, Ill.

395

Frederick A.[6] Porter, of Samuel[5] Porter, b. Sept. 5, 1796; died in Springfield, Vt., Feb. 17, 1867. Married Hannah Thayer. Children:

742. i. Mary Elisabeth,[7] b. Aug. 16, 1829; m. Frederick Wilkinson, of New York city; deceased. Two sons: Byron,[8] b. July 17, 1857. Frederick.[8]

743. ii. Gratia Ann,[7] b. June 25, 1831; died Feb. 10, 1861.

397

George W.[6] Porter, of Samuel[5] Porter, b. July 28, 1800; resides Springfield, Vt.; m. Lucretia H. Bodurtha. (?) Children:

744. i. George C.,[7] b. May 24, 1830; resides Springfield, Vt.; m. 1st, Harriet Crane; she died Sept. 29, 1858. He m. 2d, Mary Milliken. Dau., Artie F..[8] b. Jan. 17, 1870.

745. ii. Maria Lucretia,[7] b. Oct. 18, 1832; died Sept. 1, 1833.

746. iii. Samuel Wadsworth,[7] b. Aug. 25, 1834; resides Springfield, Mass.; m. Sarah E. Daggett, in Springfield, Mass.; she died Aug. 10, 1864. He married 2d, Julia A. Pease. Children: Helen F.,[8] b. July 18, 1862. Sarah E.,[8] b. July 21, 1864.

747. iv. Helen Maria,[7] b. June 15, 1837; died Aug. 25, 1862.

748. v. Wm. Henry Harrison,[7] b. June 24, 1844; resides in Boston; merchant; married.

749. vi. Albert Gallatin,[7] b. June 5, 1849; of Springfield, Vt.

420

Rufus[6] Porter, of William[5] Porter, b. Mar. 27, 1775; died Apr. 25, 1825; lived in Medford; m. Abigail Grover, of Malden. Children:

770. i. Abigail,[7] b. Nov. 10, 1796; m. Wm. Gould, of Boston.

771. ii. Elisabeth,[7] b. Aug. 31, 1800; m. Samuel Taylor.
772. iii. Rufus.[7] b. Jan. 25, 1802; died 1824, unmarried.
773. iv. Mary,[7] b. April 9, 1806; m. Job Vinto, of Boston.
774. v. Horace,[7] b. Nov. 8, 1808; lost at sea; unmarried.
775. vi. James,[7] b. Mar. 29, 1812; m. Honora Callam, of Ireland.
776. vii. Sarah,[7] b. June 9, 1814; m. William Reed, of Weston.
777. viii. Matilda,[7] b. Nov. 15, 1816; m. David May, of Roxbury.
778. ix. Paulina,[7] b. Sept. 3, 1818; m. ——Stephens, of Princeton, New Jersey.

424

Josiah[6] Porter, of Dudley[5] Porter, of Yarmouth, N. S.; m. Edith Corning. Children:

780. i. Benjamin B.,[7] m. 1st, Zilpah Raymond. M. 2d, her sister, Rebecca Raymond.
781. ii. Daniel B.,[7] m. Susan Perry.
782. iii. Josiah,[7] m. Cynthia Cann.
783. iv. Ansley,[7] m. 1st, Sarah Perry; and 2d, Ann Perry.
784. v. William C.,[7] m. Sarah A. Goudy.
785. vi. Zephaniah,[7] m. Sarah A. Corning.
786. vii. Mary E.,[7] m. Eleazer Raymond.
787. viii. Isaac F.,[7] m. 1st, Harriet Raymond; and 2d, Lydia O. Moses.
788. ix. Edith A.,[7] m. Abijah Ellis.
789. x. Jacob J.,[7] m. Caroline Moses.
790. xi. Joseph C.,[7] m. Eliza J. Hoag.
791. xii. Eithuan W.,[7] b. Aug. 15, 1833; clergyman, of Lowell, Mass.; m. Susan A., daughter of Edward P. and Rebecca M. Prescott, of Concord, N. H., July 25, 1864; she born Mar. 26, 1842. Children: Edith R.,[8] b. Aug. 23, 1865. Stella May,[8] b. Dec. 13, 1868; died Sept. 9, 1870. Sadie Prescott,[8] b. Mar. 26, 1872. Ethie A.,[8] b. June 17, 1874.

435

Abijah[6] Porter, of Israel[5] Porter, (of Benj.,[3] of Israel,[2] of John,[1]) born Danvers, Aug. 2, 1776; died Oct. 15, 1854; married 1st, Sarah Dodge, of Wenham, Jan. 30, 1798; pub. Dec. 1, 1797. (Wenham records.) Other accounts say married July 31, 1800. Married 2d, Rebecca P.——. Children by Sarah:

800. i. Rebecca Cleaves,[7] b. Danville, Vt., Feb. 13, 1801; died there Jan. 13, 1817.

801 ii. Isaac,[7] b. Wheelock, Vt., Feb. 22, 1803; living 1853; m. 1st, Feb. 25, 1823, Sarah Hoyt, b. Wheelock, Vt., Feb. 4, 1804; died Corinth, N. H., Oct. 8, 1828. Married 2d, Sarah Kent, May 8, 1830; b. Newburyport, Nov. 2, 1792; died Lyme, N. H., Nov. 9, 1836. Married 3d, Eliza Josselyn, Aug. 20, 1837; b. Danvers, Feb. 4, 1798. His children: Luther Elliott,[8] b. Wheelock, Vt., Aug. 18, 1824. Allen Kimball,[8] b. Hartland, Vt., May 31, 1826. Sarah Rebecca,[8] b. Hartland, Vt., Feb. 10, 1828. Eliza Maria,[8] b. Corinth, N. H., Dec. 19, 1831. Adeline A.,[8] b. Danvers, Feb. 5, 1840; died April 8, 1842. Henrietta W.,[8] b. Aug. 3, 1841. Martha Ann,[8] b. Jan. 10, 1843.

iii. Israel,[7] b. Wheelock, Vt., Oct. 11, 1804; living 1853.

iv. Sarah,[7] b. Wheelock, Vt., May 5, 1805; died there June 11, 1805; child by Rebecca.

804. v. Rebecca,[7] b. Wheelock, Vt., 1824; m. Samuel C. Flint, July 22, 1839; he b. Danvers, Aug. 9, 1815; she died Aug. 6, 1850. Child: Horace Sprague,[8] b. April 3, 1840.

436

Benjamin[6] Porter, of Israel[5] Porter, b. Danvers, Sept. 7, 1786; died May 16, 1856; married 1st, Sept. 7, 1807, Rhoda Berry, b. Newburyport, Dec. 7, 1786; died Marblehead, June 26, 1821. Married 2d, Dec. 5, 1822, Harriet Berry, b. Newburyport, 1794; died Marblehead, Dec. 24, 1823, aged 29. Married 3d, Dec. 6, 1825, Nancy Kent, b. Danvers, Oct. 10, 1798; died Mar. 8, 1852. His children:

805. i. Benjamin F.,[7] b. 1808; died Marblehead, Sept. 4, 1827, aged 18.

806. ii. Sally Berry,[7] b. March 21, 1810; died Marblehead, Oct. 17, 1824.

807. iii. Mary Ann Abigail,[7] b. Jan. 25, 1812.

808. iv. Rhoda Berry,[7] b. April 17, 1814; m. ——Niles; resides Glendale, Hamilton Co., Ohio.

809. v. Israel,[7] b. Mar. 15, 1816; died April 22, 1816.

810. vi. Israel,[7] b. April 10, 1817; died Nov. 12, 1847.

811. vii. Huldah Smith,[7] b. Sept. 19, 1819; died Aug. 18, 1824.

812. viii. John Henry,[7] b. Marblehead, Dec. 7, 1826.

813. ix. Nancy Charlotte,[7] b. Marblehead, June 6, 1832.

814. x. Benjamin Franklin,[7] b. May 10, 1837; of Danversport, 1878.

442

Zacheus[6] Porter, of James[5] Porter, b. Oct. 25, 1780, in Peterboro, N. H. "His youth passed in Peterboro, N. H., where his father lived; removed to Belfast, Me., about 1813; lawyer; partner with Hon. John Wilson; died Nov. 9, 1824. Although the professional career of Mr. Porter was comparatively short, yet it was long enough to establish his character as a sound and successful lawyer. He was endowed with an active mind, a great share of good sense, was untiring in business, and faithfully devoted to the interests of his clients; scrupulously honest and exact in his dealings, he enjoyed an unusual share of the public confidence; but the laborious duties of his profession early broke down a constitution already impaired by disease when he came here. He died in the midst of business, highly esteemed for his many social, amiable and domestic virtues, and surrounded by every blessing but health to render life desirable." (Williamson's History of Belfast, Me.) Married Rachel, dau. of Samuel and Susan (Curtis) Cunningham, of Peterboro, N. H., Oct. 4, 1811; she born May 10, 1788; died June 16, 1861. Children:

815. i. Charles Curtis,[7] b. Peterboro, Mar. 20, 1813; grad. Bowdoin College, 1832; physician; died in Calais, Me., Dec. 14, 1875.

816. ii. Thos. Cunningham,[7] b. Mar. 15, 1815; died Feb. 17, 1820.

817. iii. Abigail Cunningham,[7] b. Mar. 15, 1815; resides in Belfast, Me.; married Hon. Albert Pillsbury, at Belfast, Mar. 23, 1836; he was son of Timothy (b. in Newbury, Apr. 12, 1789,) and Sarah Carpenter (Prince) Pillsbury, born Aug. 6, 1814; grad. Cambridge Law School; lawyer in Calais, Me.; clerk of courts for Washington Co., Me., 1841; appointed U. S. Consul to Halifax, N. S., 1855, where he died June 13, 1872. (His brother, Edward Pillsbury, is now mayor of New Orleans—a successful merchant there.) Children: Charles A.,[8] journalist, of Washington, D. C. Emily,[8] m. John George Bowrinot, in Halifax, N. S., Oct. 5, 1865; he is French and English clerk in the House of Commons, at Ottawa, Canada, and son of Hon. John Bowrinot, French consul at Cape Breton, and member of the Upper House of the Dominion Parliament.

818. iv. Rachel Caroline,[7] b. July 2, 1819; m. William H. Conner, of Belfast, Me.; an eminent merchant and ship builder; he died Nov., 1873; his widow died Sept. 13, 1875.

819. v. Thos. Cunningham,[7] b. Mar. 28, 1821; merchant in Boston.

vi. James Porter,[7] b. Dec. 15, 1822; died Feb. 9, 1823.

vii. Herman Abbott,[7] b. Jan. 14, 1824; died Aug. 23, 1825.

444

James[6] Porter, of James[5] Porter, born June 18, 1775; grad. Williams College, 1810; A. M. at Yale College, 1815; first preceptor of Belfast, Me., Academy, 1811–13; delivered the oration at dedication of academy building, May 18, 1811, for which the trustees passed a vote of thanks as "elegant and appropriate"; studied theology there with Rev. Alfred Johnson, of Belfast; ordained minister at Pomfret, Conn., Sept. 8, 1814; Rev. Elijah Dunbar, of Stoughton, Mass., preached the ordination sermon, (which was afterward printed, and a marginal note thereto says, "Mr. Porter was the fifth in descent from Col. Porter, (John[1]) of Danvers, the intimate friend of Gov. Endicott, and in the same grade collaterally from the Governor. Mr. Porter's maternal grandfather was the late Rev. Phillip Curtis, of Sharon, Mass.") In 1830, in consequence of ill health, he resigned, subsequently living in Ashford, South Woodstock, and Stafford, where he died June 6, 1856. He was a man of solid worth and fervent piety, heartily engaged in every good work, and much beloved wherever known." Married 1st, Eliza Nourse, his second cousin, of Merrimac, N. H., by whom he had three children. Married 2d, Lucinda Grant, of Ashford. Mr. Porter and all of his children sleep together in the ancient burying ground of Pomfret, Conn.

452

Lydia[7] Porter, of Isaac[6] Porter, b. Wenham, April 28, 1774; m. Capt. William Kimball, of Beverly, April 26, 1797; he was born March 3, 1772, (and was son of Paul Kimball and his wife, who was a daughter of Dr. Fairfield, and who with eight others were drowned June 17, 1773, by the sinking of a boat off Salem harbor;) this was his second marriage; his first wife was Polly Cole, by whom he had daughter Lydia,[8] b. Mar. 11, 1795; m. Perkins, and is now living in Wakefield. He died May 25, 1819; his widow died June 9, 1830. Children by 2d marriage:

820. i. William,[8] died young.
821. ii. Mary,[8] died.
822. iii. Mary Porter,[8] b. Oct. 23, 1809; m. Feb., 1828, Daniel Merrill, Jr.; he died June 15, 1851, aged 46; they had a large family of children—among them Harlan Page,[9] of Co. B., 40 regt. Mass. infantry, died in hospital, Brooklyn, N. Y., Oct. 15, 1863, aged 21. William K.,[9] two years in Co. I, 1st Mass. reg. heavy artillery.
823. iv. Nancy Woodbury,[8] b. Oct. 8, 1811; died Aug. 26, 1872; m. May 13, 1830, John Meldram, formerly of Shapleigh, Me.; large family of children.
824. v. Betsey,[8] b. July 18, 1814; m. Aug. 15, 1837, Samuel T. Plummer, formerly of Acton, Me.; (?) they had six children.
825. vi. Sarah,[8] b. Dec. 30, 1816; died unmarried.
826. vii. Lucy,[8] b. Dec. 17, 1818; m. Nov. 30, 1837, George W., son of Warren and Lydia (Dale) Peabody; they have two sons, married.

453

Col. Paul[7] Porter, of Isaac[6] Porter, born Wenham, April 21, 1776; lived there. He was a man of intelligence and character, and filled many positions of honor and trust. He commanded what was then known as the Ipswich regiment of militia, in the war of 1812. He represented the town in the Legislature in 1815, '16, '17, '18, '28, '29, and '30; town clerk from 1809 to 1818, inclusive; moderator and selectman many years, and also chorister in the sanctuary for many years. He married Nancy, daughter of Josiah and Rebecca (Tarbox) Moulton, Sept. 19, 1796. Children:

827. i. Isaac,[8] born March 18, 1797.
828. ii. Mary Ann,[8] born June 9, 1799.
829. iii. Lydia,[8] born Aug. 18, 1801.
830. iv. Angelina,[8] born Feb. 14, 1804; married Amos Gould, Nov. 2, 1835; boot manufacturer; no children; his second marriage. Has been selectman; representative to General Court, 1848.

831. v. Sophronia,[8] born July 17, 1806.
832. vi. William,[8] born Dec. 24, 1808.
833. vii. Samuel,[8] born April 29, 1811; died Jan. 22, 1813.
834. viii. Lucy,[8] born May 8, 1816.
835. ix. Samuel,[8] born May 8, 1816; resides Wenham; married Patience, daughter of Nicholas and Mary (Smith) Brown, of Strafford, N. H., Aug. 24, 1837; no children; deacon of Orthodox church; town treasurer; has been selectman, school committee, &c.

456

Capt. John[7] Porter, of Nathaniel[6] Porter, born July 10, 1786; lived in Beverly; widow living at age of 86, in 1878.

460D

Lemuel C.[8] Porter, of Lemuel[7] Porter, born Ellington, Conn., April 14, 1823; resides Winona, Minn.; banker; president First National Bank; m. Adele Horton, of Skeneateles, N. Y., March 3, 1852. Children:

i. Carrie H.,[9] b. Feb. 6, 1853; died Nov. 11, 1853.
ii. Clark Horton,[9] b. March 10, 1854.
iii. Adelbert,[9] b. April 21, 1861.
iv. Lillie Maud,[9] b. Aug. 28, 1864.

460E

Horace P.[8] Porter, of Philo[7] Porter, b. Feb. 6, 1839; resides Claremont, Minn.; physician; graduate Yale Medical School, 1861; sent as assistant surgeon in the late war, in 7th Conn. vols., and surgeon in 10th Conn. vols.; and acting assistant surgeon, U. S. A., in charge of 10th army corps hospital, in the army of the James river.

470

Aaron[7] Porter, of William[6] Porter, b. in Boxford, Mass., June 27, 1773; lived in Danville, Vermont; m. Rebecca, dau. of Capt. Peter and Sarah (Chandler) Blanchard, of Peacham, Vt., Nov. 2, 1807; she was the mother of all his children; died Oct. 11, 1847; he m. 2d, widow (Daley)

Ayres. M. 3d, widow (Porter) Lowler; he died; his widow died. Children:

870. i. Sarah Chandler,[8] b. Aug. 29, 1808; m. Dec. 13, 1826, to Maj. John Franklin Kelsey, of Chicago. Children: Sarah,[9] b. Sept. 3, 1827. John Franklin,[9] b. July 7, 1830; m. Martha Dana Seavey. Oliver Chandler,[9] b. Feb. 1, 1834; m. Julia Green. George Aaron,[9] b. Jan. 13, 1839; m. Jan. 1st, 1873, Emma Ellis. Susan Chandler,[9] b. Oct. 24, 1843; m. Oct. 29, 1862, Col. Wm. Augustus Ray, of Chicago, Ill. All b. in Danville, Vt. and now living in Chicago.

871. ii. Catharine Buel,[8] b. June 4, 1810; m. March 23, 1836, to Joseph Colton Fuller, of Danville, Vt.

872. iii. Rebecca Blanchard,[8] b. April 28, 1812; m. Dr. Samuel Livingston, Feb. 3, 1839; now resides Belmont, Ohio; Mrs. Livingston died Feb. 14, 1869.

873. iv. Mary Adams,[8] b. Jan. 1, 1815; died Sept. 21, 1875; m. Daniel Putnam Dana, Jan. 29, 1837; he died in Peoria, Ill., Aug. 13, 1837; no children. Widow married 2d, Giles Collins Dana, April 28, 1839; he died March 13, 1876. Children: Martha Porter,[9] m. Rev. Peter McVicker, of Topeka, Kan.; president of Washburn College. Alice Rebecca,[9] m. James Dexter Gilchrist, of Wyoming, Ill. Maria Castle,[9] died 1875; m. 1875, James D. Nichol, of Chicago, Ill. Mary Adams,[9] m. May, 1876, to Henry H. Markman, Esq., a leading lawyer in Milwaukie, Wis.

874. v. Martha Osgood,[8] b. Aug. 27, 1817; m. Sept. 18, 1839, Henry Mattocks, Esq., of Danville, Vt.; he was cashier of Caledonia Bank, and brother of ex-governor John Mattocks, of Vermont; he died April 16, 1844. Their only child was Charles Porter,[9] b. Oct. 11, 1840, who was a colonel in the late civil war, also brevet brigadier general; now a successful and rising lawyer in Portland, Me.; several years county attorney for Cumberland county; he married Ella Robinson, 187—. Mrs. Mattocks m. 2d, Hon. Isaac Dyer, of Baldwin, Me., Aug. 2, 1850, well known as largely interested in lands and lumbering. Their only child, Isaac Watson Dyer, b. Sept. 13, 1855.

875. vi. Charles William,[8] b. Jan. 14, 1821; resides in Plattsburg, Clinton Co., Missouri; one of the most prominent citizens there; president of the Plattsburg Bank; mayor; largely interested in farming and railroads; m.

Nov. 10, 1859, Mary E. Funkhouser. Children: Effie L.,[9] b. Dec. 18, 1860; died Aug. 16, 1862. Charles L.,[9] b. Dec. 31, 1863. Katie A.,[9] b. Dec. 13, 1868. Lena V.,[9] b. June 3, 1871. William A.,[9] b. Mar. 26, 1877.

876. vii. Luther Clark,[8] b. Feb. 18, 1824; resides in Neenah, Wis.; formerly an extensive manufacturer of flour; now an extensive land owner; married 1st, Genevieve Alexander, Sept. 11, 1856; she died Feb. 18, 1860. One child, May Genevieve, b. May 1, 1858. Married 2d, Martha Webster Porter, of Portland, Me., Aug. 18, 1868; she daughter of Deacon Eliphalet Webster.

493

Rufus King[7] Porter, of Dr. Aaron[6] Porter, born Sept. 3, 1794; died Dec. 11, 1856; graduated Bowdoin College, 1813; practised law at Machias, Me., nearly forty years; married at Machias, Oct. 2, 1820, Emma Elisabeth Cooper, daughter of General John and Elisabeth (Savage) Cooper; she died at Portland, 1827. Married second, at Wiscasset, Me., Sept. 6, 1829, Lucy Lee Hedge, of East Dennis, Mass.; she was the adopted daughter of Hon. Silas Lee, of Wiscasset, M. C.; she died 1862. Children, all born at Machias:

900. i. Emma Jane,[8] born Sept. 4, 1821; died at Chicago, Ill., July, 1866.

901. ii. Charles Wendell,[8] born May 1, 1823; graduated Bowdoin College, 1843; clerk of courts of Washington county, Me., from 1858 to 1864; removed to Batavia, Ill., where he married Susan Ellen Lockwood, Sept. 1, 1864; she daughter of Hon. Samuel D. Lockwood, of the Illinois supreme judicial court. Children: Mary King,[9] born June 8, 1865. Harriet Eddy,[9] born Oct. 27, 1867. Anna Lockwood.[9]

902. iii. John Cooper,[8] born Feb. 6, 1825; resides St. Louis, Mo.; banker; married Anna McKee, in St. Louis, June 9, 1852; she died 1867. Children: Elisabeth Savage,[9] born April 9, 1853; graduated Washington University, St. Louis, 1875. Charles Wendell,[9] born March 9, 1866. One son,[9] died in infancy.

903. iv. Caroline Elisabeth,[8] born Nov. 20, 1826; resides in Portland, Me.

904. v. Silas Lee,[8] born March 27, 1834; married at Perry, Me., March 26, 1857, Abby G., daughter of William D. Dana; he died in New York, August 8, 1871. No children.

905. vi. Henry Homes,[8] born Dec. 7, 1835; resides Chicago, Ill.; director in Chicago and North-Western Railway Co.; married Eliza French, Dec. 14, 1864; she born in Quincy, Mass. Children: Kittie Seymour,[9] born Sept., 1866. Henry Homes,[9] born January, 1876.

906. vii. George Thatcher,[8] born Sept. 23, 1837; studied medicine at New York City Medical College; physician at Calais, Me., where he died, January, 1876; married at Calais, 1863–4, Harriet L., daughter of Edward A. and Mary Ann (Sheperd) Barnard. Children, born in Calais: Frank Barnard,[9] born in 1865. Rufus King,[9] born in 1867. Edward A.,[9] born 1869. Lee,[9] born 1874.

907. viii. William Rufus,[8] born April 8, 1841; resides Batavia, Ill.

512

Stephen[7] Porter, of Benjamin[6] Porter, born Winthrop, Me.; farmer; lived in New Sharon, Me.; moved to Quincy, Ill., about 1854, and to Farmington, Minn., where he died, about 1860, aged 70; married Miriam Whittier. Children:

920. i. John C.[8] He was a fine scholar; professor of mathematics in New York Central College; died of consumption, at age of 35; married a Quaker lady.

921. ii. Martha,[8] married ——— Moore; died on Mississippi river, about 1855, of cholera, while moving to Minnesota.

922. iii. Artemas,[8] unmarried.

923. iv. Charles,[8] of Farmington, Minn.

924. v. George,[8] of Farmington, Minn.

513

Tyler[7] Porter, of Benjamin[6] Porter, farmer; of Newburgh, Me.; m. Mary Whittier; he died about forty years ago; his widow married John W. Hussey, and now lives in Chelsea. Children:

925. i. Jonathan,[8] born E. Dixmont, Me.; m. Sarah Folsom; one son, John Tyler.[9]

926. ii. Thomas W.,[8] lawyer, 63 Devonshire street, Boston; in late war col. 14th reg't Maine vols.; resides Revere; representative Mass. Legislature; married 1st, Almira Ewer. Married 2d, Almira Gardner. Five children.

927. iii. Byron,[8] physician; of Newport, Me.; mem. Maine legislature; grad. Brunswick Medical College; m. Almira Adams, of Brunswick. Has had four children.

928. iv. Pamela Barton,[8] m. William Gray, of Albion, Me.; resides Chelsea, Mass. Two children:

929. v. Dolly Ann,[8] married Ezekiel Weston, of St. Stephen, New Brunswick. Two children.

930. vi. Mary,[8] m. William Lewis, of South Newburgh, Me. One child, Caroline.[9]

514

Benjamin[7] Porter, of Benjamin[6] Porter, married 1st, Phebe Gould; married 2d, ———. Children by first wife:

931. i. Benjamin Franklin,[8] married, and lives at Mount Vernon, Me.; two children.

932. ii. Augusta,[8] married Rev. Mr. Byram, a Universalist clergyman.

933. iii. Russel,[8] married twice; and died about three years ago, aged about 40.

934. iv. Viola,[8] married ——— Taft, of North Oxford, Mass. Two children by second wife.

515

Dr. Byron[7] Porter, of Benjamin[6] Porter, born May 11, 1802; died Worcester, Mass., Feb., 1871; physician; grad. Medical School, Bowdoin College, 1827; had for many years a large practice in Dixmont, Me.; Hampden, Me.; Bangor, and Waterville, Me. Married Eliza J. Morse. Children:

935. i. Parker Cleveland,[8] b. June 15, 1833; grad. Maine Medical School, 1863; then went into a N. Y. City (three months) regiment as assistant surgeon; then in the army of Potomac, under Gen. Mead; then to Newberne, N. C., as assistant surgeon, 1863; then to Mt. Pleasant Hospital, Washington, June, 1864; then to Cony Hospital, Augusta, Me.; now resides at Chicago, Ill.; of firm of Porter & Welch. Married Fannie M. Brown, of Newport, Me., 1865. One son, Byron Cleveland,[9] born June 2, 1870.

936. ii. Octavia Frances,[8] m. Rev. Wm. C. Reed, of Hampden, Me.; a graduate of Yale and Andover; Orthodox clergyman; now minister at Milton, Mass.

937. iii. Emma Lavinia,[8] m. John H. Blaisdell, of Waterville, Me.; she died at Worcester, 1871.

938. iv. Mary Evelyn,[8] m. Joseph E. Brown, of Beverly, stationer and news dealer, of Boston.

939. v. Lizzie May,[8] lives with her mother, at Beverly.

517

James[7] Porter, of Benjamin[6] Porter, b. 1805; lived in Mt. Vernon, Me.; died there 1877; was deputy sheriff; held many official positions, and was much respected; m. Lucinda Gould. Children:

940. i. Horatio,[8] m. Anna E. Dearborn; lives Mt. Vernon, Me.

941. ii. Orestes Harlow,[8] died at New Orleans during the war; soldier in the army, age 23; m. Rachel Allen, of Mt. Vernon, Me.

942. iii. Victoria,[8] m. Geo. W. Davis, of Natick, Mass.; she died about the age of 20, leaving two children: James Porter,[9] and George W.[9]

525

Col. Warren[7] Porter, of Zerrubbabel[6] Porter, born in Danvers, Sept. 30, 1789; lived there; tanner and morocco dresser; was in the war of 1812; held commission of lieutenant, and after the war, of lieutenant colonel; he was a successful business man; also a gentleman remarkable for his love and attachment for books, and the knowledge acquired thereby; married Anna Welch, Oct. 9, 1823; she was daughter of Simeon and Susannah (Merrill) Welch, born at Plaistow, N. H., April 22, 1800, and is still living. He died July 20, 1861. Children:

960. i. Mary Endicott,[8] born Nov. 11, 1824; unmarried.

961. ii. Alfred,[8] born June 11, 1826; corporal Co. K, 8th regiment Massachusetts volunteers, in late war; died of disease contracted in the service, July 19, 1864.

962. iii. Warren,[8] born April 19, 1830; commander in U. S. navy, in late war; dentist, of Salem, Mass.; graduate of Boston Dental College; married, July 30, 1872, Sarah S. Holt, of North Reading, Mass., daughter of Charles and Sylvana (Batchelder) Holt.

963. iv. Matilda Welch,[8] born April 30, 1833; married Josiah Frank Bly, of Plaistow, N. H., son of Josiah Peabody and Fanny Bly; now resides North Andover, Mass.; lawyer; admitted to Essex bar, Oct. 10, 1872. Children: Frank Warren,[9] born Oct. 10, 1862. Jessie Endicott,[9] born May 10, 1870.

964. v. John W.,[8] born Sept. 27, 1835; resides in Danvers; lawyer in Salem; studied law with Phillips & Gillis, of Salem; admitted to Essex bar, January 14, 1864, and afterward to practice in United States courts; married, Feb. 6, 1864, Eliza Ann, daughter of Charles and Sylvana (Batchelder) Holt, born North Reading, Jan. 16, 1842. Children: Annie S.,[9] born Aug. 6, 1865. Catharine Welch,[9] born Feb. 23, 1867; died Aug. 26, 1867. Sarah Holt,[9] born May 9, 1868. Mary Endicott,[9] born March 11, 1870; died June 11, 1875. Helen Eliza,[9] born Sept. 16, 1874.

965. vi. Charles,[8] born May 30, 1838; resides Dover, N. H.; foreman of machine shop of the Cocheco mills; married Sarah Ellen Applebee, born in Milton, N. H., Aug. 7, 1844, daughter of Simeon and Joanna Applebe, now of Dover, N. H. One child, Alfred,[9] b. June 19, 1869.

526

Alfred[7] Porter, of Zerubbabel[6] Porter, born May 1, 1792; lived and died in Danvers, Sept. 3, 1826; m. Nov. 17, 1818, Clarissa Endicott, dau. of Elias and Nancy (Cressy) Endicott, born May 11, 1792; died Nov. 13, 1872. One child:

966. i. Elias Endicott,[8] b. Danvers, Aug. 22, 1819.

560

Ebenezer[7] Porter, of John[6] Porter, born 1780; married Ann Phillips. Children, born in Ashfield:

967. i. Phillip Phillips,[8] b. Feb. 1, 1804.
968. ii. Ebenezer,[8] b. Sept. 14, 1805.
969. iii. Mary A.,[8] b. Oct. 9, 1807.
970. iv. John,[8] b. Oct. 29, 1809.
971. v. Joshua,[8] b. Nov. 26, 1811.
972. vi. Levi,[8] b. Mar. 4, 1814.

561

Elisabeth Nowell[7] Porter, of John[6] Porter, born Mar. 18, 1783; married Elias Currier, (Carrier ?) at Ashfield, Mass., Sept. 18, 1808; he born Marlboro, Conn., 1780. Children, born at Conway except two last, at Hawley:

i. Rebecca,[8] b. Jan. 6, 1809; m. Robert Fife, 1833.

ii. David,[8] b. Oct. 4, 1810; m. Ann B. Tobey, 1833.
iii. Mary A., b. Oct. 29, 1812; m. Silas Dodge, 1833.
iv. Caroline,[8] b. Aug. 9, 1814; m. William Hedden, New Lebanon, N. Y., 1838.
v. Elias,[8] b. Aug. 30, 1816.
vi. Louisa,[8] b. Dec. 2, 1817; m. L. Phillips, of Greenfield, 1846.
vii. Joseph H.,[8] b. Mar. 18, 1825.

564

Nehemiah[7] Porter, of Joseph[6] Porter, b. Oct. 10, 1785; m. Rebecca, dau. of Daniel and Mary West, April 26, 1809, at Ashfield; she died Dover, Ohio, Jan. 16, 1841. He m. 2d, Harriet Loder, in Cleveland, Ohio; was divorced Mar. 3, 1852. M. 3d, Mrs. Catharine Phinney; she b. Schenectady, N. Y., Feb. 17, 1797. Children by first wife:

973. i. Nehemiah,[8] b. Ashfield, Dec. 19, 1811; died Richfield, Ohio, 1852.
974. ii. Dan West,[8] b. Ashfield, July 14, 1814.
975. iii. George,[8] b. Dover, Ohio, Feb. 9, 1817.
976. iv. Mary,[8] b. Dover, Ohio, April 6, 1819.
977. v. Leonard Graves,[8] b. June 16, 1821.
978. vi. Charles,[8] b. June 14, 1823.
979. vii. Lucy Ann,[8] b. Jan. 30, 1833.

565

Nathan[7] Porter, of Joseph[6] Porter, b. Oct. 5, 1787; m. at Buckland, Mass., April 21, 1814, Elisabeth, dau. of Jasper and Susannah Taylor. Children, born in Ashfield:

980. i. Doric,[8] b. Sept. 16, 1815.
981. ii. Dwight Wells,[8] b. June 17, 1817.
982. iii. William Pitt,[8] b. Aug. 25, 1819.
983. iv. Eliza,[8] b. Aug 15, 1821; m. Chas. S. Guilford, 1845.
984. v. Harriet Newell,[8] b. Feb. 11, 1828; died Aug. 5, 1844.

566

Joseph C.[7] Porter, of Joseph[6] Porter, b. Aug. 30, 1789; m. Sally Cranston, by Rev. Nehemiah Porter; she b. 1791; died Nov. 25, 1820. He m. 2d, Maria Lester; he died Scipio, N. Y., March 31, 1831; his widow died Nov. 29, 1835. Children:

985. i. Elisha Cranston,[8] b. Scipio, N. Y., Feb. 10, 1814; died New York, 1840.

986. ii. Leonard Groves,[8] b. Scipio, N. Y., Feb. 5, 1815; m. Hazlett.
987. iii. Hannah J.,[8] b. Scipio, N. Y., June 7, 1816.
988. iv. Sarah,[8] b. Scipio, N. Y., April 4, 1820.
989. v. Cynthia,[8] b. Scipio, N. Y., Apr. 20, 1822.
990. vi. Nathan Cranston,[8] b. Feb. 5, 1825.
991. vii. Caroline M.,[8] b. Oct. 24, 1826; d. New York, 1840.
992. viii. Emeline,[8] b. Jan. 8, 1829.
993. ix. Emily,[9] twin with Emeline, b. Jan. 8, 1829.

567

Ebenezer[7] Porter, of Joseph[6] Porter, b. Mar. 19, 1792; m. Aurilla, dau. of Joseph Crocker, at Dover, Ohio, April 19, 1819; she born at Lee, Mass., 1800. Children, born at Dover, Ohio:

994. i. Martha,[8] b. Oct. 31, 1820; m. Josiah Hurst, of Dover, Ohio.
994A. ii. Sarah Hall,[8] b. June 9, 1822; m. John Wilson, of Oberlin, Ohio.

568

Eunice[7] Porter, of Joseph[6] Porter, b. Nov. 18, 1794; m. Rufus Cook, of Ashfield, Mass. Married 2d, Levi Tallmadge, 1843. Children, by Cook:

i. Maria,[8] b. at York, N. Y., Jan. 15, 1814; m. Alex. Blakely, 1842.
ii. Joseph Graves,[8] b. Jan. 19, 1817.
iii. Charles H.,[8] b. Feb. 26, 1825.
iv. Emily,[8] b. Oct. 7, 1830.

569

Welles[7] Porter, of Joseph[6] Porter, b. Jan. 29, 1797; m. Philena, dau. of Jedediah Crocker, at Dover, Ohio, 1819; she died 1854. He married 2d, Hannah Davenport, 1854. Children:

995. i. Dwight Welles,[8] b. June, 1820.
995A ii. Edmund Waldo,[8] b. Sept., 1830.
995B iii. Louisa W.,[8] b. Sept., 1832.

569A

Rebecca Chipman[7] Porter, of Joseph[6] Porter, b. Jan. 26, 1799; m. Joseph Chipman Smith, at Ashfield, Nov. 7, 1820. Children, born at Ashfield:

i. Catharine M.,[8] b. Nov. 20, 1821; died young.
ii. Catharine E.,[8] b. April 18, 1832.
iii. Adeline Amelia,[8] b. April 19, 1834.
iv. Josephine Marie,[8] b. Feb. 27, 1836.
v. Ernestine Jemima,[8] b. Aug. 21, 1842.

569B

John[7] Porter, of Joseph[6] Porter, b. Feb. 10, 1801; m. Lydia, dau. of Nathan Bassett, Elyria, Ohio, Feb., 1836. Children, b. Dover, Ohio:

996. i. Nathan Bassett,[8] b. Dec. 2, 1837.
997. ii. Charles Fiske,[8] b. June 15, 1839.
998. iii. Harriet C.,[8] b. Nov. 21, 1842.
999. iv. Lucy Jane,[8] b. Dec. 30, 1844.

569D

Leonard G.[7] Porter, of Joseph[6] Porter, b. Mar. 6, 1806; married at Dover, Ohio, Catharine, dau. of Barzillai Hickok, Aug. 26, 1838; she b. March 22, 1822. One child:

i. Harriet Jemima,[8] b. Dover, Ohio, Oct. 22, 1840.

569F

Ebenezer[7] Porter, of Joseph[6] Porter, born at the Hamlet, Ipswich, Nov. 9, 1798; married Mary P. McKaig, in Greene Co., Ohio. Children, born in New Carlisle, Ohio:

i. Robert McKaig,[8] b. Aug. 7, 1826.
ii. Charles Anthony,[8] b. May 17, 1829.
iii. John Addison,[8] b. May 21, 1831.
iv. Martha H.,[8] b. Aug. 16, 1833.
v. Joseph Lee,[8] b. Aug. 3, 1835.
vi. Mary Jane,[8] b. Sept. 27, 1838.

569G

Rev. Joseph[7] Porter, of Joseph[6] Porter, born Jan. 5, 1808; missionary to India; married 1st, Harriet J. Ahearne, at Rising Sun, Indiana, 1835. Married 2d, Mary Rodney, born in Abington, Penn. Children, born in India:

i. Joseph Allen,[8] b. Nov. 5, 1837.

ii. John H.,[8] b. Nov. 26, 1839.
iii. William L.,[8] b. Feb. 9, 1842.
iv. Henry Martyn,[8] b. Sept. 14, 1851—by 2d wife.
v. Harriet Emily,[9] Aug. 29, 1852.

569H

Lucretia[7] Porter, of John[6] Porter, b. Sept. 13, 1794; m. Anaximander Warner, at Marietta, Ohio, Jan. 23, 1810; b. at Ashfield, Mass.; died at Lee, Ohio, 1845. Children:

Sarah Porter,[8] b. Marietta, Ohio, Oct. 1, 1811. Arthur W.,[8] b. Marietta, Ohio, Sept. 27, 1813. Jackson,[8] b. Marietta, Ohio, April 3, 1815. Putnam Porter,[8] b. Marietta, Ohio, Dec. 14, 1816. Ebenezer,[8] b. Marietta, Ohio, April 12, 1818. Thomas White,[8] b. Marietta, Ohio, Dec. 21, 1819. John Mayberry,[8] b. Marietta, Ohio, April 7, 1821. Lucretia,[8] b. Marietta, Ohio, Sept. 5, 1822. Mary Zipporah,[8] b. Marietta, Ohio, July 7, 1826. Robert Raikes,[8] b. Marietta, Ohio, Oct. 26, 1829. Olivia C.,[8] b. Portsmouth, Ohio, 1831. Dudley Woodbridge,[8] b. Alexander, Ohio, April 11, 1834. Lucretia M.,[8] b. Alexander, Ohio, April 9, 1836. Lyman Beecher,[8] b. Alexander, Ohio, June 28, 1838.

569I

Zipporah[7] Porter, of John[6] Porter, b. Aug. 1, 1796; m. Eliphaz Perkins, at Athens, Ohio, 1818; he born at Voluntown, Conn. Children, b. at Athens, Ohio:

Levi Perkins,[8] b. Jan. 8, 1819; died 1842. Lucretia Warner,[8] b. Jan. 14, 1821. Margaret R.,[8] b. May 27, 1822; married Abner M. Thornton, Athens, 1850. Henry Porter,[8] b. April 3, 1824. Eliphaz R.,[8] b. Jan. 4, 1827; died 1852. George,[8] b. July 17, 1829; married Eliza B. Beardsley. John Marshall,[8] b. Sept. 22, 1832. Julia C.,[8] b. Nov. 29, 1834. Louisa Z.,[8] b. Mar. 13, 1838.

569J

Solomon C.[7] Porter, of John[6] Porter, born Feb. 12, 1798; married 1st, Phebe Kimball, dau. of Jeremiah Burnham, at Athens, Ohio, May 12, 1820; she died Jan., 1828. He married 2d, at Marietta, Ohio, Elisabeth, daughter of Christopher Dodge, of Marietta, May 6, 1828; she died 1842. He married 3d, Mahala Glasbourne, born in Virginia, 1810. Children, the first ten born in Athens, Ohio:

i. Rufus Putnam,[8] b. May 22, 1821; m. Elisabeth Heaton.

ii. William Wilson,[8] b. Aug. 25, 1822; m. Mary J. Sanders, Newark, N. J.

iii. Almira Kimball,[8] b. Feb. 18, 1824; m. James Doughty, Springfield, O.

iv. Catherine E.,[8] b. April 24, 1825; m. E. P. Purdy, of Vergennes, Ill.

v. Phebe J.,[8] b. June 7, 1827; m. H. C. Tallman, of New London, Iowa.

vi. Elisabeth Putnam,[8] b. Apr. 29, 1829; m. W. A. Eachers, (?) 1854.

vii. Robert Russell,[8] b. April 15, 1831; m. Matilda Hamilton, 1853.

viii. Persis Pickering,[8] b. Aug. 7, 1833; m. Sam Clendennin, Liberty, Ill., 1854.

ix. Charles C.,[8] b. Aug. 8, 1835.

x. James Barnard,[8] b. June 4, 1837.

xi. Sarah L.,[8] b. Raccoon, Ohio, Mar. 1, 1844.

xii. Daniel,[8] b. Vergennes, Ill., Feb. 3, 1846.

xiii. Lucinda E., b. Vergennes, Dec. 19, 1849.

569K

Russell S.[7] Porter, of John[6] Porter, born Oct. 12, 1802; m. Dorothy, daughter of Jeremiah and Mehetable Burnham, at Marietta, Ohio, 1825. Children:

i. Benjamin F.,[8] b. Alexander, Ohio, Feb. 11, 1826; m. Elis T. Parish, at Jackson, Ill., Sept. 14, 1848. Children: Harlan Page,[9] b. Nov. 29, 1849. Edward[9] and Edmond,[9] b. Nov. 5, 1851. Henry S.,[9] b. Jan. 21, 1853.

ii. Eliphaz,[8] b. Alexander, Ohio, Sept. 4, 1827; m. Luanda (?) T. Parish, 1852.

iii. John Burnham,[8] b. Alexander, Ohio, Aug. 4, 1829.

iv. Solomon A.,[8] b. Alexander, Ohio, April 7, 1833.

v. Laura R.,[8] b. Alexander, Ohio, Dec. 11, 1834.

vi. Sarah J.,[8] b. Raccoon, O., Jan. 31, 1837.

vii. Phebe K.,[8] b. Raccoon, O., Jan. 19, 1839.

viii. Hiram House,[8] b. Raccoon, O., Mar. 19, 1843.

569L

Marshall S.[7] Porter, of John[6] Porter, b. Fearing, Ohio, Oct. 31, 1810; m. Celestia, dau. of Barnard and Mary Dewey (Burt) Case, of Lenox, Mass., at Wesleyville, Erie Co., Penn. Children:

i. John Barnard,[8] b. Hamburgh, (?) Ohio, July 12, 1835.

ii. Sarah C.,[8] twin, b. Aug. 3, 1837; m Wm. K. Lovejoy.
iii. Mary E.,[8] twin, b. Aug. 3, 1837.
iv. Luther Dane,[8] b. Aug. 15, 1839.
v. Solomon M.,[8] b. Chauncey, Ohio, Mar. 9, 1841.
vi. Levi A.,[8] b. Feb. 15, 1843.
vii. Chauncy Dewey,[8] b. Porter, Gallia Co., O., Mar. 25, 1846.
viii. George H.,[8] b. Porter, Gallia Co., O., Feb. 15, 1848.
ix. John L.,[8] b. Porter, Gallia Co., O., July 13, 1850.
x. Ellen L. W.,[8] b. Vergennes, Ill., June 16, 1854.

569M

Sarah C.[7] Porter, of John[6] Porter, b. Mar. 28, 1813; m. Cyrus D. Greene, at Alexander, O., July 20, 1825, (1835?) Children, b. at Gallipolis, Ohio:

i. James Barton,[8] b. Oct. 13, 1837.
ii. Mary F.,[8] b. Mar. 30, 1839.
iii. Cyrus D.,[8] b. May 4, 1840.
iv. Sarah L.,[8] b. June 1, 1842.
v. Ebenezer B.,[8] b. Oct. 12, 1844.
vi. Emily A.,[8] b. 1846.
vii. Mary G.,[8] b. Feb. 19, 1847.
viii. Henri Ernest,[8] b. April 24, 1849.
ix. Catharine L.,[8] b. Feb. 8, 1852.

569N

Sarah C.[7] Porter, of Cummings[6] Porter, b. Sept. 28, 1817; married Cyrus Ames, at Little Hockhocking, O., Aug. 18, 1844. Children, born at Belpre, Ohio:

i. Emma E.,[8] b. May 17, 1845.
ii. Edward L.,[8] b. April 6, 1847.
iii. Charles B.,[8] b. Oct. 20, 1849.
iv. Frank P.,[8] b. Nov. 3, 1852.

569O

Cummings[7] Porter, of Cummings[6] Porter, b. Sept. 28, 1817; married Frances, daughter of Reuben Skene, at Little Hockhocking, O., 1849; she born in Madison Co., Va. Children, born at Little Hockhocking:

i. Ella Frances,[8] b. 1849.
ii. De Witt Clinton,[8] b. Mar. 15, 1852.

569P

Cutler[7] Porter, of Cummings[6] Porter, born Mar. 1, 1825; married at Chester, Ohio, Mar. 20, 1850, Susan, daughter of Wm. Rice. Child:

i. Susan A.,[8] b. Indianola, Ind., Nov. 5, 1851.

569R

Savannah C.[7] Porter, of Samuel[6] Porter, born 1817; married Aaron Bickle, in Greene, Gallia county, Ohio, Nov. 5, 1840; he born Wythe county, Va., 1811. Children, all but last, born in Perry, Gallia county, Ohio:

i. Sarah D.,[8] born Aug. 24, 1841.
ii. Emarinda,[8] born March 1, 1844.
iii. Nancy Alla,[8] born July 31, 1846.
iv. Savannah F.,[8] born March 1, 1847.
v. Adeline L.,[8] born Sept. 5, 1848.
vi. Samuel A.,[8] born Hanging Rock, Ohio, Feb. 26, 1853.

569S

Volumnia[7] Porter, of Samuel[6] Porter, born 1815; married Edwin C. Dustin, at Greene, Gallia county, Ohio, April 4, 1845. Children:

i. Francis Marion,[8] born 1846.
ii. Morris Washington,[8] born 1848.
iii. Chastina Savannah,[8] born 1850.

569T

Sarah M.[7] Porter, of Samuel[6] Porter, born 1824; married Thomas Burt (Hubbard,) of Belpre, Ohio, Aug. 13, 1848. Child:

i. Edna Amelia,[8] b. April 1, 1851.

720

William D.[7] Porter, of William L.[6] Porter, b. Charleston, S. C., Nov. 24, 1810; resides there; a most worthy, honorable gentleman; distinguished as a lawyer and statesman; "grad. at the College of Charleston, in 1829; taught school and studied law; admitted to the bar in 1833, and commenced the practice of law in Charleston; in 1840, was elected to the house of representatives, of South Carolina, serving eight years; in 1844, elected corporation attorney, of Charleston, retaining that office for twenty years; elected to the state senate, and in 1857, elected president of that body, serving as such till the establishment of the provisional government, in 1866. After the war the state constitution was revised, giving the election of Governor and Lieut. Governor (which had always been in the legislature,) to the people. At the first popular election, Mr. Porter was elected Lieut. Governor without opposition, restoring him to his position of president of the senate, where he continued until the reconstruction measures officially decapitated him. In 1871, the grievances of misrule brought into being the tax payers convention, as it was called, in South Carolina. It was an assemblage of property holders and tax payers, embracing the best men in the state. Mr. Porter was elected president of the convention, which had two sessions, one in 1871, the other in 1874. The latter session sent a delegation of twenty-five to Washington, of which Mr. Porter was chairman, to seek an inquiry and investigation into the affairs in South Carolina, and bring the condition of things there before the country, and enlist the sympathy and moral support of all parties in favor of intelligence, education, property and culture. Mr. Porter was a presidential (Peirce) elector in 1852; chairman of South Carolina delegation to democratic convention which nominated Horace Greely, in 1872. He has recently been appointed by Gov. Wade Hampton, master in equity in the courts of South Carolina, an office embracing large legal and equitable jurisdiction. He married in 1839, Emma, second daughter of Capt. Nathaniel Haraden, of the U. S. Navy, by whom he has had seven children—two of his sons having served in the confederate army." Children:

i. William Henry,[8] b. Sept. 28, 1840; m. Lizzie Jennings, Jan. 24, 1867; they have one child, Jennings.[9]

ii. Emma Marion,[8] b. Sept. 17, 1843; m. William H. Brawley, Apr. 14, 1868. Two children: Hallie.[9] William Porter.[9]

iii. Joseph Howard,[8] b. Oct. 30, 1845.

iv. Nathaniel Haraden,[8] b. Sept. 14, 1849; died Jan. 18, 1878.

v. Normand McLeod,[8] b. Jan. 25, 1853.
vi. John Woodbridge,[8] b. Aug. 21, 1858.
vii. George Lise,[8] b. Jan. 2, 1862.

732

Frederick W.[7] Porter, of Samuel W.[6] Porter, born Oct. 27, 1823; resides Springfield, Vt.; jeweller; a gentleman much respected among his acquaintances; representative to legislature, 1878; married Caroline Silsby, of Charleston, N. H. Children:

i. Anna Silsby,[8] born June 22, 1851; married John W. Marsh; resides Chicago, Ill.
ii. William Bradley,[8] born Feb. 22, 1855; died Sept. 12, 1871.
iii. Frank Farrington,[8] born June 30, 1858.
iv. Elisabeth West,[8] born June 4, 1868.
v. Russell W.,[8] born Dec. 13, 1871.

827

Isaac[8] Porter, of Paul[7] Porter, born March 18, 1797; lived in Wenham; died of croup, Jan. 1, 1854; married Clarissa, daughter of Thomas and Huldah (Porter) Kimball, of Danvers, Feb. 13, 1820; (see 240;) she born Oct. 24, 1798. Children:

1000. i. Caroline,[9] born Nov. 21, 1820; mar. Benjamin Simonds; he died in Wenham, May 20, 1870, aged 50 years. Children: Charlotte P.,[10] mar. Allen Webster Dodge, of Hamilton, now of Wenham. Caroline A.,[10] married Ira F. Trask; she died in Ipswich, April 18, 1878, aged 32 years. Julia Ann,[10] married H. C. Norcross, Sept. 1, 1871. Ida May.[10]
1001. ii. Isaac,[9] born March 19, 1823.
1002. iii. Rebecca Dodge,[9] born March 12, 1826; married Oliver Burnham, of Essex—his fourth wife. Children: Alice Porter.[10] Oliver Perry.[10] Alden Chester.[10]
1003. iv. Clarissa Ann,[9] born Nov. 8, 1828; died March 7, 1830.
1004. v. Clarissa Ann,[9] born Aug. 1, 1833; married 1st. Benjamin Goodale, son of Ezekiel and Sarah Goodale; he died Dec. 16, 1852; no children. She married 2d, Henry Alley, of Newburyport, 1858. Children: Henry,[10] born September 19, 1858. Addie,[10] born April 30,

1860; died March 27, 1862. Annie Florence,[10] born June 25, 1865; died May 30, 1876, of hydrophobia. Lizzie,[10] born March 20, 1867.

1005. vi. William,[9] born Jan. 1, 1836; died Jan. 16, 1838.

828

Mary Ann[8] Porter, of Col. Paul[7] Porter, born June 9, 1799; married William S. Moulton, Aug. 13, 1819; he son of Capt. John and Sarah Moulton, teacher and cloth dresser; selectman, and of the school committee of Wenham several years. Children:

1006. i. William Porter,[9] b. Lynn, Oct. 9, 1820; died in Wenham, Dec. 25, 1825.

1007. ii. Charles Volney,[9] b. Lynn, Sept. 27, 1822.

1008. iii. Henry,[9] b. Westbrook, Me., Sept. 21, 1824; m. Lydia Spiller, of Newbury; resides in Boxford; retired master mariner.

1009. iv. Nathan Harris,[9] b. Westbrook, Me., Dec. 20, 1826; m. Abbie J. Davis, March 27, 1851; he died Dec. 28, 1854. Two children: Henry A.[10] Loretta.[10]

1010. v. Paul Porter,[9] b. Westbrook, Me., Nov. 24, 1828; died Wenham, June 26, 1832.

1011. vi. George Otis,[9] b. Lynn, Jan. 27, 1831; m. Cyntha Ricker; lives in Danvers.

1012. vii. Lucy C.,[9] b. Wenham. Aug. 9, 1835; died there Jan., 1864.

1013. viii. William Porter,[9] b. Wenham, Dec. 16, 1837; m. Rebecca Dudley, of Wenham; lives in Stewart, Iowa.

1014. ix. Albert,[9] b. June 19, 1840.

829

Lydia[8] Porter, of Col. Paul[7] Porter, born Aug. 18, 1801; married Amos C. White, 1819, of Wenham. Children:

1015. i. Nancy Porter,[9] born April 13, 18—; married Morris Webber, Sept. 17, 1837. Children: Lydia Ellen,[10] married Jacob Burton; one daughter, and died 1858. Aurelia M.,[10] married William S. Welch, of Topsfield, Apr. 25, 1870; five children. Joseph Abbott,[10] m. Jerusha Hatch, of N. Berwick, Me.; two children.

1016. ii. Amos Alden,[9] b. Feb. 25, 1821; died July 2, 1821-2.

1017. iii. Amos Alden,[9] b. Mar. 26, 1823; m. Harriet A. Perley, of Danvers, where he resides; she died. Children: Marion A.,[10] died aged 13. Alden Perley,[10] grad.

Amherst College, 1878, aged 22. Mr. White m. 2d, Adriadne Jewell, of Hampton, N. H.; have son Herbert Jewell,[10] b. Sept. 24, 1877.

1018. iv. Edward Francis,[9] b. Oct. 21, 1826; of Danvers; m. Sarah L., dau. of Benjamin Simonds. Child: Frances H.,[10] b. Oct. 7, 1856.

1019. v. Joseph Alfred,[9] b. Sept. 15, 1828; of Danvers; m. Elisabeth Curtis, of Peabody; they have five children, three sons and two daughters.

1020. vi. Henry Addison,[9] b. Nov. 24, 1830; of Danvers; m. 1st, Georgianna Putnam, by whom he had three daughters. Married 2d, Sarah Towne, by whom he has one son.

1021. vii. Paul Porter,[9] b. Nov. 30, 1832; died Oct. 24, 1834.

1022. viii. Mary Angeline,[9] b. Nov. 27, 1834; m. Warren Burpee, of Gloucester, Apr. 11, 1866; they have two children.

1023. ix. Harriet Mellissa,[9] b. Mar. 16, 1836.

1024. x. Caroline Sophronia,[9] b. Aug. 4, 1839; died Aug. 1, 1850.

1025. xi. Charles P.,[9] b. May 20, 1841; of Beverly; m. Sarah A. Woodbury, Oct. 10, 1865. Children, born Wenham: Everett L.,[10] b. April 4, 1866. Freddie C.,[10] b. Mar. 23, 1868.

831

Sophronia[8] Porter, of Col. Paul[7] Porter, b. July 17, 1806; married Dec. 22, 1826, Samuel Lummus, of N. Beverly; blacksmith. He died Nov. 22, 185—; she died Sept. 4, 1847, aged 40. Children, perhaps not in order:

1026. i. Emery Porter,[9] died June 18, 1853, aged 25.

1027. ii. Harriet,[9] died Feb. 27, 1830, aged 5 months and 20 days.

1028. iii. Elijah Elder,[9] b. Jan. 9, 1830; m. Dec. 15, 1853, Frances Ellen, daughter of Amos and Hannah (Hooker) Lord. Have six children: Nellie F.[10] Frank E.[10] Fred E.[10] Lizzie A.[10] Samuel P.[10] Carrie L.[10]

1029. iv. Samuel Austin,[9] died Jan. 9, 1830.

1030. v. David F.,[9] died Dec. 20, 1839, aged 5 years.

1031. vi. Ezra A.,[9] died July 5, 1845, aged 6 years.

1032. vii. Samuel F.,[9] died Feb. 24, 1844, aged 10 months.

1033. viii. Charles.[9]

1034. ix. Ellen Lord,[9] school teacher; died Sept. 13, 1875.

1035. x. Sarah Elisabeth,[9] m. Frank P. Clark, of Sudbury; she died Mar., 1877. Children: Fred S.,[10] b. Dec. 6, 1872. Charles E.,[10] born April 9, 1874. Ellen O.,[10] b. Aug., 1876.

832

Dea. William[8] Porter, of Col. Paul[7] Porter, b. in Wenham, Dec. 24; died there Aug. 13, 1878.

"Behold therefore, I will gather thee unto thy fathers, and thou shalt be gathered into thy grave in peace."

At an early hour Tuesday morning, Aug. 13th, after a long and painful illness, Dea. William Porter passed peacefully away, lacking but five months of having completed seventy years.

His funeral took place at his late residence, on Thursday last; the services at the house and at the grave being conducted by Rev. Will C. Wood, and Rev. A. D. Gorham. The several hymns selected were sung with taste and feeling, by a quartette composed of Mrs. Batchelder, Mrs. Clark, and Messrs. Burbank and Pool. His two sons and daughter who reside in town, and Rev. Isaac F. Porter, of Chicopee, Mass., were all present with their familes; a fourth son, who is in business at Kansas City, could not reach here in season. Besides the immediate family, many other relatives and friends were there to take a last look at one whose presence had been familiar to them from childhood. Flowers skilfully arranged by loving hands were placed upon the casket, and afterwards upon the grave.

The deceased was a native of this town, being a son of Col. Paul Porter, and has spent his days within its borders. Very early in life he interested himself in religious matters, and soon became a member of the Congregational Church, taking an active part in all measures pertaining to the welfare of the church and the advancement of the kingdom of God. During the pastorate of Rev. J. S. Sewall, he was chosen deacon, but was not ordained until the pastorate of Rev. W. C. Wood. This office he held at the time of his death. He never aspired to political honors, therefore contented himself with doing his duty as a citizen.

His loss will be severely felt in the family where he was a kind and loving father; the church which looked to him for counsel and example; and among those whose good fortune it has been to call him friend and neighbor. He has lived a sincere, consistent Christian life, dealing with scrupulous honesty with all men, and shows to us a life of purity and uprightness, well worthy of emulation.—[Salem paper.]

He married 1st, Caroline, daughter of Thomas and Sarah (Knowlton) Perkins, of Topsfield, April 21, 1831; she died May 5, 1833, aged 24. Married 2d, Sally, daughter of Warren and Lydia (Dale) Peabody, Sept. 28, or 25, 1835; she died Sept. 24, 1840, aged 33. Married 3d, Lucretia G.

Yeaton, of Epsom, N. H; she died July 19, 1873, aged 64 years 2 months 11 days. Children:

1036. i. William Edwin,[9] b. June 8, 1832; m. Lavinia E., daughter of William and Mary (Brown) Berry, of Strafford, N. H., Nov. 27, 1856. Children: George E.,[10] b. Nov. 13, 1857. Samuel Anderson,[10] b. June 22, 1861. Mary E.,[10] b. Apr. 24, 1863. Caribel,[10] b. Mar. 30, 1865. Fred F.,[10] b. Mar. 1, 1870. Edgar Nelson,[10] b. July 17, 1877.

1037. ii. Elbridge,[9] b. June 26, 1836; resides at Wenham; served in late war in U. S. Navy; was on board frigate Congress, in Hampton Roads, when the Cumberland was sunk by the confederate ram Merrimac; married Sarah E., daughter of Jona and Elisabeth (Cole) Wilson, of Cornish, Me., Oct. 14, 1871. Children: Harriet,[10] b. Oct. 11, 1872. Grace Frances,[10] b. Aug. 11, 1876.

1038. iii. Isaac Francis,[9] b. June 29, 1839; Unitarian clergyman, of Chicopee; served in late war in Co. A, 48th Mass. regiment; married Eliza W. Williams, Jan. 14, 1875.

1038. iv. Caroline Lucretia,[9] b. Mar. 18, 1844; m. Henry H. Demsey, Jan. 1, 1872. One child, Addie,[10] b. Dec. 30, 1873; died Jan. 1, 1874.

1039. v. John,[9] b. Nov. 17, 1846; resides in Kansas City, Mo.; m. Hester Theodosia Inskip, of Independence, Mo., Jan. 1, 1872. One child, William,[10] b. Jan. 3, 1878.

834

Lucy[8] Porter, of Col. Paul[7] Porter, born May 8, 1816; married Nathaniel Perkins, Jr., in Wenham, Nov. 3, 1836; he son of Nathaniel and Judith (Smith) Perkins, of Topsfield, born Wenham (while his parents resided there for a short time) Aug. 30, 1813; died in Topsfield, Jan. 22, 1846. Children:

1041. i. George Cowles,[9] b. Feb. 9, 1838, in Topsfield; died in Wenham, Dec. 28, 1858.

1042. ii. Nathaniel Porter,[9] b. in Topsfield, Nov. 7, 1840; m. Charlotte E., dau. of Henry and Elisabeth (Woodbury) Patch, May 23, 1872. One child: George Alden,[10] born Mar. 22, 1874; Mr. Perkins has held the offices of chairman of school committee, and selectman of Topsfield.

1043. iii. Albert Smith,[9] b. Wenham, June 8, 1845; died Topsfield, April 11, 1846.

1044

Anna Porter, born July 3, 1766; died at Newburyport, Aug. 31, 1795.

"Edmund Kimball, of Newburyport, and Mrs. Nancy Porter, of Wenham, entered their names with intention of marriage, Dec. 20, 1789, and were posted the next Sunday." (Wenham Records.) "Dec. 25, 1789, Mr. Edmund Kimball, of Newburyport, hath informed of his intention of marriage with Miss Nancy Porter, of Wenham." (Newburyport Records.) "Married by Rev. Joseph Swain, April 27, 1790, Capt. Edmund Kimball, of Newburyport, and Mrs. Nancy, or Anna Porter, of Wenham." (Wenham Records.) He was the son of Thomas and Mary Kimball, born in Wenham, Nov. 24, 1762; and died there Dec. 10, 1847. On the Kimball monument at Wenham, is the following inscription: "Anna, wife of Capt. Edmund Kimball, died (Aug. 31, 1795,) in her 29th year, at Newburyport, where rest her remains." In early life Capt. Kimball was a soldier in the service of his country; in early manhood a shipmaster; and afterward a successful ship owner and merchant of Newburyport. About 1822, having relinquished business, he returned to Wenham, where he lived honored and respected—kind, benevolent and just, without pretense or ostentation. Married 2d, Lucy Russell Balch, at Newburyport, Nov. 30, 1796, by Rev. Samuel Spring; she died in Wenham, Sept. 24, 1847, aged 69. Children:

i. Anne, b. June 14, 1791; m. Dr. Ebenezer[7] Alden, of Randolph, Apr. 14, 1818; he son of Dr. Ebenezer[6] and Sarah (Bass) Alden, of Randolph, born Mar. 17, 1788; grad. H. C., 1808; physician in his native town; now living in a venerable and respected old age. Mrs. Alden died April 14, 1871; her life was a benediction. Their children: Ebenezer,[8] b. Aug. 10, 1819; grad. Amherst College, 1839; minister at Marshfield. Mary Kimball,[8] b. April 27, 1822; died Aug. 18, 1860. Edmund Kimball,[8] b. April 11, 1825; grad. Amherst College, 1844; orthodox clergyman; now one of the secretaries of the American Board of Commissioners for Foreign Missions. Henry Augustus,[8] b. Aug. 8, 1826; died

June 9, 1852. Sarah Bass,[8] b. May 21, 1828. Anne Kimball,[8] b. Aug. 15, 1833; died Dec. 28, 1854.

ii. Edmund, b. Aug. 16, 1793; died Nov. 7, 1873; grad. Harvard College, 1814; distinguished as a lawyer; friend of Daniel Webster and other men of note. He changed the family name to Kemble. He and wife Mary, had children: Edward. Edmund. Arthur; physician, in Salem; m. Carrie Perkins. Mary B., m. Alden Robbins, now of Brooklyn, N. Y. Frank. Anne Alden. Walter. Elisabeth R., m. John Robinson, of Salem.

iii. Mary, b. Aug. 8, 1795; died in Reading, Aug. 4, 1812, much beloved and lamented.

JOHN PORTER, APPENDIX.

184

Jonathan[6] Porter, of Jonathan[5] Porter, born in Medford, Nov. 13, 1791; died there June 11, 1859, aged 67; he grad. at Harvard College, 1814, first in his class; studied law with Hon. Luther Lawrence, (H. C., 1801) of Groton, and Hon. Asahel Stearns, (H. C., 1797) of Chelmsford; was admitted to the bar in Middlesex county, 1817; he opened an office first in Medford, then in Boston; in 1822 he delivered the Phi Betta Kappa, at Cambridge.* He was an invalid for some years previous to his death. He married, July 22, 1823, Catharine, dau. of Samuel Gray, of Medford, and had three children: one, George Doane,[7] grad. Harvard College, 1851; died 1861.

312 (Page 262.)

Jonathan[6] Porter, of Tyler[5] Porter, born April 28, 1771; lived in Wenham; m. Martha, dau. of Dr. William Fairfield; pub. Oct. 14, 1792. Children:

- i. Harriet,[7] b. April 13, 1793.
- ii. John,[7] b. Oct. 27, 1799; dau. Elisabeth W., m. Tilton; and dau. Harriet S., m. Dodge.
- iii. Tyler,[7] b. Sept. 4, 1802.
- iv. William Fairfield,[7] b. April 18, 1806; died in Jacksonville, Florida, Nov. 20, 1878; he was a large owner in real estate there. Has a son William Henry,[8] residing in Wisconsin.

JOHN PORTER.

ALTERATIONS AND ADDITIONS.

Page 234, No. 24—Abel Gardner, born Sept. 1, 1678.

Page 234, No. 23—Joseph Putnam, will proved May 25, 1723.

Page 238, No. 13—Nath.[3] Porter, sold land to John Waters.

Page 245—Lieut. John Porter, born July 21, 1683. His wife died before he moved to Connecticut. His grave-stone now standing in the old burying-ground in Ellington, Conn.

Page 256, No. 90—Died June 10, 1794.

Page 258, No. 101—Changed location in Ellington, 1747, when he moved on to a farm, where he and his father both died.

Page 259—Moses[5] Porter, died Nov. 7, 1811.

Page 279, No. 251—Samuel Porter, lived in Hamilton.

Page 281, No. 254—Dudley Porter, Jr., of Gloucester, married Polly Austin, of Salem, April 6, 1793, by Rev. Mr. Barnard.

Page 282, No. 270—Horace Martin is not a physician.

Page 285—Sarah,[7] of Asa[6] Porter, mar. Hon. Mills Olcott, not Orcutt.

CHRISTIAN NAMES

OF

JOHN PORTER'S DESCENDANTS.

A

B

C

D

E

F

G

H

I

J

P

R

S

T

V

W

Z

SURNAMES OF PERSONS

WHO HAVE

INTERMARRIED WITH THE PORTERS (OF JOHN.)

A

B

C

D

E

F

G

H

I

J

K

L

M

N

O

P

R

S

T

U

V

W

Y

FINALLY,

The printing of this book having been unavoidably delayed, I have been able to add over one hundred pages more than I originally intended.

I shall be grateful to any one to whom it may come, for corrections and additions, that a possible new edition may be more correct. Considering the variety of hand-writing in the multitude of letters I have received, it may not be thought strange if there are many errors herein.

For assistance in the preparation of this book, I am much indebted to Mrs. Samuel Lunt, of Freeport, Me.; Miss Julia Henrietta Miller, of Middleborough; Perley Derby, Esquire, of Salem; Wellington Pool, Esquire, of Wenham; Rev. Alfred Porter Putnam, D. D., of Brooklyn, N. Y.; Henry Porter Andrews, of New York city, and many others. Few of the letters 1 have written for information remain unanswered. The town clerks of Danvers, Beverly and Ipswich could not be induced by any promises to give me any copies of records of those towns; they had a right not to be bored, and exércised it.

The price of this book will be three dollars per copy, postage included.

JOSEPH W. PORTER.

Burlington, Me., Dec. 25, 1878.

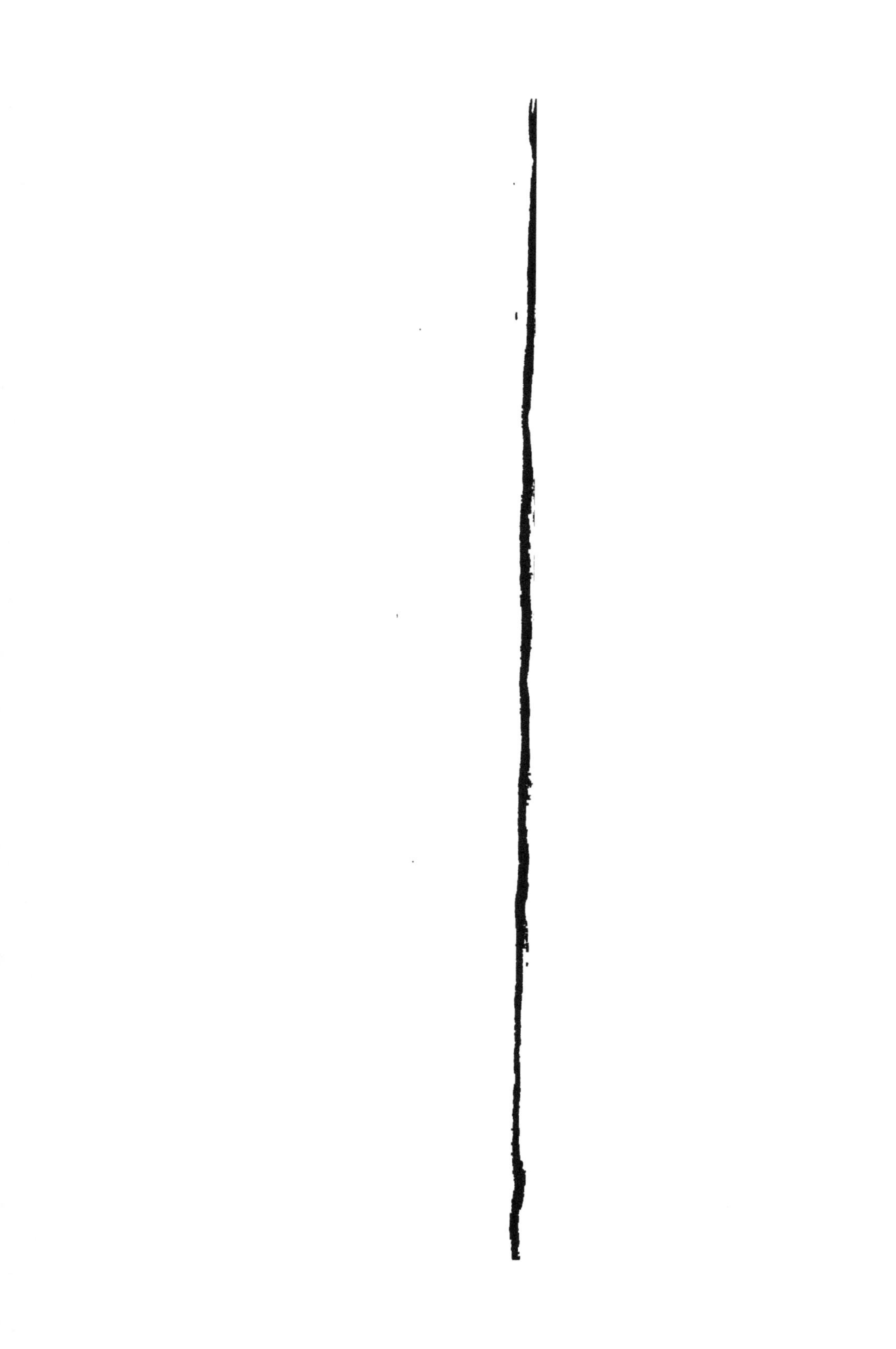